W9-AWA-945

MYTHS AND LEGENDS SERIES

CELTIC

T. W. ROLLESTON

Cuchulain and the Flaming Wheel

MYTHS AND LEGENDS SERIES

CELTIC

T. W. ROLLESTON

WITH ILLUSTRATIONS FROM DRAWINGS AND FAMOUS PAINTINGS

AVENEL BOOKS
NEW YORK

Celtic

Previously published by George G Harrap & Co

This edition published 1986 by Avenel Books
distributed by Crown Publishers Inc.,
225 Park Avenue South
New York, New York 10003

Copyright © BRACKEN BOOKS 1985

All rights reserved. No part of this publication may be reproduced, stored in a retrieval system, or transmitted, in any form or by any means, electronic, mechanical, photocopying, recording or otherwise, without the prior permission of the Copyright holder.

ISBN 0-517-60443-4

Printed and bound by
Grafoimpex, Yugoslavia

h g f e d c b

PREFACE

THE Past may be forgotten, but it never dies. The elements which in the most remote times have entered into a nation's composition endure through all its history, and help to mould that history, and to stamp the character and genius of the people.

The examination, therefore, of these elements, and the recognition, as far as possible, of the part they have actually contributed to the warp and weft of a nation's life, must be a matter of no small interest and importance to those who realise that the present is the child of the past, and the future of the present; who will not regard themselves, their kinsfolk, and their fellow-citizens as mere transitory phantoms, hurrying from darkness into darkness, but who know that, in them, a vast historic stream of national life is passing from its distant and mysterious origin towards a future which is largely conditioned by all the past wanderings of that human stream, but which is also, in no small degree, what they, by their courage, their patriotism, their knowledge, and their understanding, choose to make it.

The part played by the Celtic race as a formative influence in the history, the literature, and the art of the people inhabiting the British Islands—a people which from that centre has spread its dominions over so vast an area of the earth's surface—has been unduly obscured in popular thought. For this the current use of the term "Anglo-Saxon" applied to the British people as a designation of race is largely responsible. Historically the term is quite misleading. There is nothing to justify this singling out of two Low-German tribes when we wish to indicate the race-character of the British people. The use of it leads to such absurdities as that which the writer noticed not long ago, when the proposed elevation by the Pope of an Irish bishop to a cardinalate was described in an English newspaper as being prompted by the desire of the head of the Catholic Church to pay a compliment to "the Anglo-Saxon race."

The true term for the population of these islands, and for the typical and dominant part of the population of North America, is not Anglo-Saxon, but Anglo-Celtic. It is precisely in this blend of Germanic and Celtic elements that the British people are unique—it is precisely this blend which gives to this people the fire, the *élan*, and in literature and art the sense of style, colour, drama, which are not common growths of German soil, while at the same time it gives the deliberateness and depth, the reverence for ancient law and custom, and the passion for personal freedom, which are more or less strange to the Romance nations of the South of Europe. May they never become strange to the British Islands! Nor is the Celtic element in these islands to be regarded as contributed wholly, or even very predominantly, by the populations of the so-called "Celtic Fringe." It is now well known to ethnologists that the Saxons did not by any means exterminate the Celtic or Celticised populations whom they found in possession of Great Britain. Mr. E. W. B. Nicholson, librarian of the Bodleian, writes in his important work "Keltic Researches" (1904):

"Names which have not been purposely invented to describe race must never be taken as proof of race, but only as proof of community of language, or community of political organisation. We call a man who speaks English, lives in England, and bears an obviously English name (such as Freeman or Newton), an Englishman. Yet from the statistics of 'relative nigrescence' there is good reason to believe that Lancashire, West Yorkshire, Staffordshire, Worcestershire, Warwickshire, Leicestershire, Rutland, Cambridgeshire, Wiltshire, Somerset, and part of Sussex are as Keltic as Perthshire and North Munster; that Cheshire, Shropshire, Herefordshire, Monmouthshire, Gloucestershire, Devon, Dorset, Northamptonshire, Huntingdonshire, and Bedfordshire are more so—and equal to North Wales and Leinster; while Buckinghamshire and Hertfordshire exceed even this degree, and are on a level with South Wales and Ulster."[1]

It is, then, for an Anglo-Celtic, not an "Anglo-Saxon," people that this account of the early history, the religion, and the mythical and romantic literature of the Celtic race is written. It is hoped that that people will find in it things worthy to be remembered as contributions to the general stock of European culture, but worthy above all to be borne in mind by those who have inherited more than have any other living people of the blood, the instincts and the genius of the Celt.

[1] In reference to the name "Freeman," Mr. Nicholson adds: "No one was more intensely 'English' in his sympathies than the great historian of that name, and probably no one would have more strenuously resisted the suggestion that he might be of Welsh descent; yet I have met his close physical counterpart in a Welsh farmer (named Evans) living within a few minutes of Pwllheli."

CONTENTS

LIST OF ILLUSTRATIONS

LIST OF ILLUSTRATIONS

CHAPTER I: THE CELTS IN ANCIENT HISTORY

Earliest References

IN the chronicles of the classical nations for about five hundred years previous to the Christian era there are frequent references to a people associated with these nations, sometimes in peace, sometimes in war, and evidently occupying a position of great strength and influence in the Terra Incognita of Mid-Europe. This people is called by the Greeks the Hyperboreans or Celts, the latter term being first found in the geographer Hecatæus, about 500 B.C.[1]

Herodotus, about half a century later, speaks of the Celts as dwelling "beyond the pillars of Hercules"—*i.e.*, in Spain—and also of the Danube as rising in their country.

Aristotle knew that they dwelt "beyond Spain," that they had captured Rome, and that they set great store by warlike power. References other than geographical are occasionally met with even in early writers. Hellanicus of Lesbos, an historian of the fifth century B.C., describes the Celts as practising justice and righteousness. Ephorus, about 350 B.C., has three lines of verse about the Celts in which they are described as using "the same customs as the Greeks"—whatever that may mean—and being on the friendliest terms with that people, who established guest friendships among them. Plato, however, in the "Laws," classes the Celts among the races who are drunken and combative, and much barbarity is attributed to them on the occasion of their irruption into Greece and the

[1] He speaks of "Nyrax, a Celtic city," and "Massalia [Marseilles], a city of Liguria in the land of the Celts" ("Fragmenta Hist. Græc.").

sacking of Delphi in the year 273 B.C. Their attack on Rome and the sacking of that city by them about a century earlier is one of the landmarks of ancient history.

The history of this people during the time when they were the dominant power in Mid-Europe has to be divined or reconstructed from scattered references, and from accounts of episodes in their dealings with Greece and Rome, very much as the figure of a primæval monster is reconstructed by the zoologist from a few fossilised bones. No chronicles of their own have come down to us, no architectural remains have survived; a few coins, and a few ornaments and weapons in bronze decorated with enamel or with subtle and beautiful designs in chased or repoussé work—these, and the names which often cling in strangely altered forms to the places where they dwelt, from the Euxine to the British Islands, are well-nigh all the visible traces which this once mighty power has left us of its civilisation and dominion. Yet from these, and from the accounts of classical writers, much can be deduced with certainty, and much more can be conjectured with a very fair measure of probability. The great Celtic scholar whose loss we have recently had to deplore, M. d'Arbois de Jubainville, has, on the available data, drawn a convincing outline of Celtic history for the period prior to their emergence into full historical light with the conquests of Cæsar,[1] and it is this outline of which the main features are reproduced here.

The True Celtic Race

To begin with, we must dismiss the idea that Celtica was ever inhabited by a single pure and homogeneous race. The true Celts, if we accept on this point the carefully studied and elaborately argued conclusion of

[1] In his "Premiers Habitants de l'Europe," vol. ii.

Dr. T. Rice Holmes,[1] supported by the unanimous voice of antiquity, were a tall, fair race, warlike and masterful,[2] whose place of origin (as far as we can trace them) was somewhere about the sources of the Danube, and who spread their dominion both by conquest and by peaceful

[1] "Cæsar's Conquest of Gaul," pp. 251–327.

[2] The ancients were not very close observers of physical characteristics. They describe the Celts in almost exactly the same terms as those which they apply to the Germanic races. Dr. Rice Holmes is of opinion that the real difference, physically, lay in the fact that the fairness of the Germans was blond, and that of the Celts red. In an interesting passage of the work already quoted (p. 315) he observes that, "Making every allowance for the admixture of other blood, which must have considerably modified the type of the original Celtic or Gallic invaders of these islands, we are struck by the fact that among all our Celtic-speaking fellow subjects there are to be found numerous specimens of a type which also exists in those parts of Brittany which were colonised by British invaders, and in those parts of Gaul in which the Gallic invaders appear to have settled most thickly, as well as in Northern Italy, where the Celtic invaders were once dominant; and also by the fact that this type, *even among the more blond representatives of it, is strikingly different, to the casual as well as to the scientific observer, from that of the purest representatives of the ancient Germans.* The well-known picture of Sir David Wilkie, 'Reading of the Waterloo Gazette,' illustrates, as Daniel Wilson remarked, the difference between the two types. Put a Perthshire Highlander side by side with a Sussex farmer. Both will be fair; but the red hair and beard of the Scot will be in marked contrast with the fair hair of the Englishman, and their features will differ still more markedly. I remember seeing two gamekeepers in a railway carriage running from Inverness to Lairey. They were tall, athletic, fair men, evidently belonging to the Scandinavian type, which, as Dr. Beddoe says, is so common in the extreme north of Scotland; but both in colouring and in general aspect they were utterly different from the tall, fair Highlanders whom I had seen in Perthshire. There was not a trace of red in their hair, their long beards being absolutely yellow. The prevalence of red among the Celtic-speaking people is, it seems to me, a most striking characteristic. Not only do we find eleven men in every hundred whose hair is absolutely red, but underlying the blacks and the dark browns the same tint is to be discovered."

infiltration over Mid-Europe, Gaul, Spain, and the British Islands. They did not exterminate the original prehistoric inhabitants of these regions—palæolithic and neolithic races, dolmen-builders and workers in bronze—but they imposed on them their language, their arts, and their traditions, taking, no doubt, a good deal from them in return, especially, as we shall see, in the important matter of religion. Among these races the true Celts formed an aristocratic and ruling caste. In that capacity they stood, alike in Gaul, in Spain, in Britain, and in Ireland, in the forefront of armed opposition to foreign invasion. They bore the worst brunt of war, of confiscations, and of banishment. They never lacked valour, but they were not strong enough or united enough to prevail, and they perished in far greater proportion than the earlier populations whom they had themselves subjugated. But they disappeared also by mingling their blood with these inhabitants, whom they impregnated with many of their own noble and virile qualities. Hence it comes that the characteristics of the peoples called Celtic in the present day, and who carry on the Celtic tradition and language, are in some respects so different from those of the Celts of classical history and the Celts who produced the literature and art of ancient Ireland, and in others so strikingly similar. To take a physical characteristic alone, the more Celtic districts of the British Islands are at present marked by darkness of complexion, hair, &c. They are not very dark, but they are darker than the rest of the kingdom.[1] But the

[1] See the map of comparative nigrescence given in Ripley's "Races of Europe," p. 318. In France, however, the Bretons are not a dark race relatively to the rest of the population. They are composed partly of the ancient Gallic peoples and partly of settlers from Wales who were driven out by the Saxon invasion.

true Celts were certainly fair. Even the Irish Celts of the twelfth century are described by Giraldus Cambrensis as a fair race.

Golden Age of the Celts

But we are anticipating, and must return to the period of the origins of Celtic history. As astronomers have discerned the existence of an unknown planet by the perturbations which it has caused in the courses of those already under direct observation, so we can discern in the fifth and fourth centuries before Christ the presence of a great power and of mighty movements going on behind a veil which will never be lifted now. This was the Golden Age of Celtdom in Continental Europe. During this period the Celts waged three great and successful wars, which had no little influence on the course of South European history. About 500 B.C. they conquered Spain from the Carthaginians. A century later we find them engaged in the conquest of Northern Italy from the Etruscans. They settled in large numbers in the territory afterwards known as Cisalpine Gaul, where many names, such as *Mediolanum* (Milan), *Addua* (Adda), *Viro-dunum* (Verduno), and perhaps *Cremona* (*creamh*, garlic),[1] testify still to their occupation. They left a greater memorial in the chief of Latin poets, whose name, Vergil, appears to bear evidence of his Celtic ancestry.[2] Towards the end of the fourth

[1] See for these names Holder's "Altceltischer Sprachschatz."

[2] Vergil might possibly mean "the very-bright" or illustrious one, a natural form for a proper name. *Ver* in Gallic names (Vercingetorix, Vercassivellasimus, &c.) is often an intensive prefix, like the modern Irish *fior*. The name of the village where Vergil was born, Andes (now Pietola), is Celtic. His love of nature, his mysticism, and his strong feeling for a certain decorative quality

century they overran Pannonia, conquering the Illyrians.

Alliances with the Greeks

All these wars were undertaken in alliance with the Greeks, with whom the Celts were at this period on the friendliest terms. By the war with the Carthaginians the monopoly held by that people of the trade in tin with Britain and in silver with the miners of Spain was broken down, and the overland route across France to Britain, for the sake of which the Phocæans had in 600 B.C. created the port of Marseilles, was definitely secured to Greek trade. Greeks and Celts were at this period allied against Phœnicians and Persians. The defeat of Hamilcar by Gelon at Himera, in Sicily, took place in the same year as that of Xerxes at Salamis. The Carthaginian army in that expedition was made up of mercenaries from half a dozen different nations, but not a Celt is found in the Carthaginian ranks, and Celtic hostility must have counted for much in preventing the Carthaginians from lending help to the Persians for the overthrow of their common enemy. These facts show that Celtica played no small part in preserving the Greek type of civilisation from being overwhelmed by the despotisms of the East, and thus in keeping alive in Europe the priceless seed of freedom and humane culture.

Alexander the Great

When the counter-movement of Hellas against the East began under Alexander the Great we find the Celts again appearing as a factor of importance.

in language and rhythm are markedly Celtic qualities. Tennyson's phrases for him, "landscape-lover, lord of language," are suggestive in this connexion.

ALEXANDER THE GREAT

In the fourth century Macedon was attacked and almost obliterated by Thracian and Illyrian hordes. King Amyntas II. was defeated and driven into exile. His son Perdiccas II. was killed in battle. When Philip, a younger brother of Perdiccas, came to the obscure and tottering throne which he and his successors were to make the seat of a great empire he was powerfully aided in making head against the Illyrians by the conquests of the Celts in the valleys of the Danube and the Po. The alliance was continued, and rendered, perhaps, more formal in the days of Alexander. When about to undertake his conquest of Asia (334 B.C.) Alexander first made a compact with the Celts "who dwelt by the Ionian Gulf" in order to secure his Greek dominions from attack during his absence. The episode is related by Ptolemy Soter in his history of the wars of Alexander.[1] It has a vividness which stamps it as a bit of authentic history, and another singular testimony to the truth of the narrative has been brought to light by de Jubainville. As the Celtic envoys, who are described as men of haughty bearing and great stature, their mission concluded, were drinking with the king, he asked them, it is said, what was the thing they, the Celts, most feared. The envoys replied: "We fear no man: there is but one thing that we fear, namely, that the sky should fall on us; but we regard nothing so much as the friendship of a man such as thou." Alexander bade them farewell, and, turning to his nobles, whispered: "What a vainglorious people are these Celts!" Yet the answer, for all its Celtic bravura and flourish,

[1] Ptolemy, a friend, and probably, indeed, half-brother, of Alexander, was doubtless present when this incident took place. His work has not survived, but is quoted by Arrian and other historians.

was not without both dignity and courtesy. The reference to the falling of the sky seems to give a glimpse of some primitive belief or myth of which it is no longer possible to discover the meaning.[1] The national oath by which the Celts bound themselves to the observance of their covenant with Alexander is remarkable. "If we observe not this engagement," they said, "may the sky fall on us and crush us, may the earth gape and swallow us up, may the sea burst out and overwhelm us." De Jubainville draws attention most appositely to a passage from the "Táin Bo Cuailgne," in the Book of Leinster,[2] where the Ulster heroes declare to their king, who wished to leave them in battle in order to meet an attack in another part of the field: "Heaven is above us, and earth beneath us, and the sea is round about us. Unless the sky shall fall with its showers of stars on the ground where we are camped, or unless the earth shall be rent by an earthquake, or unless the waves of the blue sea come over the forests of the living world, we shall not give ground."[3] This survival of a peculiar oath-formula for more than a thousand years, and its reappearance, after being first heard of among the Celts of Mid-Europe, in a mythical romance of Ireland, is certainly most curious, and, with other facts which we shall note hereafter, speaks strongly for the community and persistence of Celtic culture.[4]

[1] One is reminded of the folk-tale about Henny Penny, who went to tell the king that the sky was falling.

[2] The Book of Leinster is a manuscript of the twelfth century. The version of the "Táin" given in it probably dates from the eighth. See de Jubainville, "Premiers Habitants," ii. 316.

[3] Dr. Douglas Hyde in his "Literary History of Ireland" (p. 7) gives a slightly different translation.

[4] It is also a testimony to the close accuracy of the narrative of Ptolemy.

The Sack of Rome

We have mentioned two of the great wars of the Continental Celts; we come now to the third, that with the Etruscans, which ultimately brought them into conflict with the greatest power of pagan Europe, and led to their proudest feat of arms, the sack of Rome. About the year 400 B.C. the Celtic Empire seems to have reached the height of its power. Under a king named by Livy Ambicatus, who was probably the head of a dominant tribe in a military confederacy, like the German Emperor in the present day, the Celts seem to have been welded into a considerable degree of political unity, and to have followed a consistent policy. Attracted by the rich land of Northern Italy, they poured down through the passes of the Alps, and after hard fighting with the Etruscan inhabitants they maintained their ground there. At this time the Romans were pressing on the Etruscans from below, and Roman and Celt were acting in definite concert and alliance. But the Romans, despising perhaps the Northern barbarian warriors, had the rashness to play them false at the siege of Clusium, 391 B.C., a place which the Romans regarded as one of the bulwarks of Latium against the North. The Celts recognised Romans who had come to them in the sacred character of ambassadors fighting in the ranks of the enemy. The events which followed are, as they have come down to us, much mingled with legend, but there are certain touches of dramatic vividness in which the true character of the Celts appears distinctly recognisable. They applied, we are told, to Rome for satisfaction for the treachery of the envoys, who were three sons of Fabius Ambustus, the chief pontiff. The Romans refused to listen to the claim, and elected the Fabii military tribunes for the ensuing year. Then the Celts abandoned the siege of Clusium and marched straight on Rome. The army showed perfect discipline. There was no indiscriminate plundering and devastation, no city or fortress was assailed. "We are bound for Rome" was their cry to the guards upon the walls of the provincial towns, who watched the host in wonder and fear as it rolled steadily to the south. At last they reached the river Allia, a few miles from Rome, where the whole available force of the city was ranged to meet them. The battle took place on July 18, 390, that ill-omened *dies Alliensis* which long perpetuated in the Roman calendar the memory of the deepest shame the republic had ever known. The Celts turned the flank of the Roman army, and annihilated it in one tremendous charge. Three days later they were in Rome, and for nearly a year they remained masters of the city, or of its ruins, till a great fine had been exacted and full vengeance taken for the perfidy at Clusium. For nearly a century after the treaty thus concluded there was peace between the Celts and the Romans, and the breaking of that peace when certain Celtic tribes allied themselves with their old enemy, the Etruscans, in the third Samnite war was coincident with the breaking up of the Celtic Empire.[1]

Two questions must now be considered before we can leave the historical part of this Introduction. First of all, what are the evidences for the widespread diffusion of Celtic power in Mid-Europe during this period? Secondly, where were the Germanic peoples, and what was their position in regard to the Celts?

[1] Roman history tells of various conflicts with the Celts during this period, but de Jubainville has shown that these narratives are almost entirely mythical. See "Premiers Habitants," ii. 318–323.

"We are bound for Rome"

Vercingetorix riding round the Roman Camp

Celtic Place-names in Europe

To answer these questions fully would take us (for the purposes of this volume) too deeply into philological discussions, which only the Celtic scholar can fully appreciate. The evidence will be found fully set forth in de Jubainville's work, already frequently referred to. The study of European place-names forms the basis of the argument. Take the Celtic name *Novio-magus*, composed of two Celtic words, the adjective meaning new, and *magos* (Irish *magh*) a field or plain.[1] There were nine places of this name known in antiquity. Six were in France, among them the places now called Noyon, in Oise, Nijon, in Vosges, Nyons, in Drôme. Three outside of France were Nimègue, in Belgium, Neumagen, in the Rhineland, and one at Speyer, in the Palatinate.

The word *dunum*, so often traceable in Gaelic place-names in the present day (Dundalk, Dunrobin, &c.), and meaning fortress or castle, is another typically Celtic element in European place-names. It occurred very frequently in France—*e.g.*, *Lug-dunum* (Lyons), *Viro-dunum* (Verdun). It is also found in Switzerland—*e.g.*, *Minno-dunum* (Moudon), *Eburo-dunum* (Yverdon)—and in the Netherlands, where the famous city of Leyden goes back to a Celtic *Lug-dunum*. In Great Britain the Celtic term was often changed by simple translation into *castra;* thus *Camulo-dunum* became Colchester, *Brano-dunum* Brancaster. In Spain and Portugal eight names terminating in *dunum* are mentioned by classical writers. In Germany the modern names Kempton, Karnberg, Liegnitz, go back respectively to the Celtic forms *Cambo-dunum*, *Carro-*

[1] *E.g.*, Moymell (*magh-meala*), the Plain of Honey, a Gaelic name for Fairyland, and many place-names.

aunum, *Lugi-dunum*, and we find a *Singi-dunum*, now Belgrade, in Servia, a *Novi-dunum*, now Isaktscha, in Roumania, a *Carro-dunum* in South Russia, near the Dniester, and another in Croatia, now Pitsmeza. *Sego-dunum*, now Rodez, in France, turns up also in Bavaria (Wurzburg), and in England (*Sege-dunum*, now Wall-send, in Northumberland), and the first term, *sego*, is traceable in Segorbe (*Sego-briga*), in Spain. *Briga* is a Celtic word, the origin of the German *burg*, and equivalent in meaning to *dunum*.

One more example: the word *magos*, a plain, which is very frequent as an element of Irish place-names, is found abundantly in France, and outside of France, in countries no longer Celtic, it appears in Switzerland (*Uro-magus*, now Promasens), in the Rhineland (*Broco-magus*, Brumath), in the Netherlands, as already noted (Nimègue), in Lombardy several times, and in Austria.

The examples given are by no means exhaustive, but they serve to indicate the wide diffusion of the Celts in Europe and their identity of language over their vast territory.[1]

Early Celtic Art

The relics of ancient Celtic art-work tell the same story. In the year 1846 a great pre-Roman necropolis was discovered at Hallstatt, near Salzburg, in Austria. It contains relics believed by Dr. Arthur Evans to date from about 750 to 400 B.C. These relics betoken in some cases a high standard of civilisation and considerable commerce. Amber from the Baltic is there, Phœnician glass, and gold-leaf of Oriental workmanship. Iron swords are found whose hilts and sheaths are richly decorated with gold, ivory, and amber.

[1] For these and many other examples see de Jubainville's "Premiers Habitants," ii. 255 *sqq*.

EARLY CELTIC ART

The Celtic culture illustrated by the remains at Hallstatt developed later into what is called the La Tène culture. La Tène was a settlement at the north-eastern end of the Lake of Neuchâtel, and many objects of great interest have been found there since the site was first explored in 1858. These antiquities represent, according to Dr. Evans, the culminating period of Gaulish civilisation, and date from round about the third century B.C. The type of art here found must be judged in the light of an observation recently made by Mr. Romilly Allen in his "Celtic Art" (p. 13):

"The great difficulty in understanding the evolution of Celtic art lies in the fact that although the Celts never seem to have invented any new ideas, they professed [*sic*; ? possessed] an extraordinary aptitude for picking up ideas from the different peoples with whom war or commerce brought them into contact. And once the Celt had borrowed an idea from his neighbours he was able to give it such a strong Celtic tinge that it soon became something so different from what it was originally as to be almost unrecognisable."

Now what the Celt borrowed in the art-culture which on the Continent culminated in the La Tène relics were certain originally naturalistic motives for Greek ornaments, notably the palmette and the meander motives. But it was characteristic of the Celt that he avoided in his art all imitation of, or even approximation to, the natural forms of the plant and animal world. He reduced everything to pure decoration. What he enjoyed in decoration was the alternation of long sweeping curves and undulations with the concentrated energy of close-set spirals or bosses, and with these simple elements and with the suggestion of a few motives derived from Greek art he elaborated a most beautiful, subtle, and varied system of decoration, applied to weapons, ornaments, and to toilet and household appliances of all kinds, in gold, bronze, wood, and stone, and possibly, if we had the means of judging, to textile fabrics also. One beautiful feature in the decoration of metal-work seems to have entirely originated in Celtica. Enamelling was unknown to the classical nations till they learned from the Celts. So late as the third century A.D. it was still strange to the classical world, as we learn from the reference of Philostratus :

"They say that the barbarians who live in the ocean [Britons] pour these colours upon heated brass, and that they adhere, become hard as stone, and preserve the designs that are made upon them."

Dr. J. Anderson writes in the "Proceedings of the Society of Antiquaries of Scotland" :

"The Gauls as well as the Britons—of the same Celtic stock—practised enamel-working before the Roman conquest. The enamel workshops of Bibracte, with their furnaces, crucibles, moulds, polishing-stones, and with the crude enamels in their various stages of preparation, have been recently excavated from the ruins of the city destroyed by Cæsar and his legions. But the Bibracte enamels are the work of mere dabblers in the art, compared with the British examples. The home of the art was Britain, and the style of the pattern, as well as the association in which the objects decorated with it were found, demonstrated with certainty that it had reached its highest stage of indigenous development before it came in contact with the Roman culture."[1]

The National Museum in Dublin contains many superb examples of Irish decorative art in gold, bronze,

[1] Quoted by Mr. Romilly Allen in "Celtic Art," p. 136.

and enamels, and the "strong Celtic tinge" of which Mr. Romilly Allen speaks is as clearly observable there as in the relics of Hallstatt or La Tène.

Everything, then, speaks of a community of culture, an identity of race-character, existing over the vast territory known to the ancient world as "Celtica."

Celts and Germans

But, as we have said before, this territory was by no means inhabited by the Celt alone. In particular we have to ask, who and where were the Germans, the Teuto-Gothic tribes, who eventually took the place of the Celts as the great Northern menace to classical civilisation?

They are mentioned by Pytheas, the eminent Greek traveller and geographer, about 300 B.C., but they play no part in history till, under the name of Cimbri and Teutones, they descended on Italy to be vanquished by Marius at the close of the second century. The ancient Greek geographers prior to Pytheas know nothing of them, and assign all the territories now known as Germanic to various Celtic tribes.

The explanation given by de Jubainville, and based by him on various philological considerations, is that the Germans were a subject people, comparable to those "un-free tribes" who existed in Gaul and in ancient Ireland. They lived under the Celtic dominion, and had no independent political existence. De Jubainville finds that all the words connected with law and government and war which are common both to the Celtic and Teutonic languages were borrowed by the latter from the former. Chief among them are the words represented by the modern German *Reich*, empire, *Amt*, office, and the Gothic *reiks*, a king, all of which are of unquestioned Celtic origin. De Jubainville also numbers among loan words from Celtic the words *Bann*, an order ; *Frei*, free ; *Geisel*, a hostage ; *Erbe*, an inheritance ; *Werth*, value ; *Weih*, sacred ; *Magus*, a slave (Gothic) ; *Wini*, a wife (Old High German) ; *Skalks*, *Schalk*, a slave (Gothic) ; *Hathu*, battle (Old German) ; *Helith*, *Held*, a hero, from the same root as the word Celt ; *Heer*, an army (Celtic *choris*) ; *Sieg*, victory ; *Beute*, booty ; *Burg*, a castle ; and many others.

The etymological history of some of these words is interesting. *Amt*, for instance, that word of so much significance in modern German administration, goes back to an ancient Celtic *ambhactos*, which is compounded of the words *ambi*, about, and *actos*, a past participle derived from the Celtic root *AG*, meaning to act. Now *ambi* descends from the primitive Indo-European *mbhi*, where the initial *m* is a kind of vowel, afterwards represented in Sanscrit by *a*. This *m* vowel became *n* in those Germanic words which derive directly from the primitive Indo-European tongue. But the word which is now represented by *amt* appears in its earliest Germanic form as *ambaht*, thus making plain its descent from the Celtic *ambhactos*.

Again, the word *frei* is found in its earliest Germanic form as *frijo-s*, which comes from the primitive Indo-European *prijo-s*. The word here does not, however, mean free ; it means beloved (Sanscrit *priya-s*). In the Celtic language, however, we find *prijos* dropping its initial *p*—a difficulty in pronouncing this letter was a marked feature in ancient Celtic ; it changed *j*, according to a regular rule, into *dd*, and appears in modern Welsh as *rhydd* = free. The Indo-European meaning persists in the Germanic languages in the name of the love-goddess, *Freia*, and in the word *Freund*, friend, *Friede*, peace. The sense borne by the word in the sphere of civil right is traceable to a Celtic origin, and in that sense appears to have been a loan from Celtic.

The German *Beute*, booty, plunder, has had an instructive history. There was a Gaulish word *bodi* found in compounds such as the place-name Segobodium (Seveux), and various personal and tribal names, including Boudicca, better known to us as the "British warrior queen," Boadicea. This word meant anciently "victory." But the fruits of victory are spoil, and in this material sense the word was adopted in German, in French (*butin*), in Norse (*byte*), and the Welsh (*budd*). On the other hand, the word preserved its elevated significance in Irish. In the Irish translation of Chronicles xxix. 11, where the Vulgate original has "Tua est, Domine, magnificentia et potentia et gloria et victoria," the word *victoria* is rendered by the Irish *búaidh*, and, as de Jubainville remarks, "ce n'est pas de butin qu'il s'agit." He goes on to say: "*Búaidh* has preserved in Irish, thanks to a vigorous and persistent literary culture, the high meaning which it bore in the tongue of the Gaulish aristocracy. The material sense of the word was alone perceived by the lower classes of the population, and it is the tradition of this lower class which has been preserved in the German, the French, and the Cymric languages."[1]

Two things, however, the Celts either could not or would not impose on the subjugated German tribes—their language and their religion. In these two great factors of race-unity and pride lay the seeds of the ultimate German uprising and overthrow of the Celtic supremacy. The names of the German are different from those of the Celtic deities, their funeral customs, with which are associated the deepest religious conceptions of primitive races, are different. The Celts, or

[1] "Premiers Habitants," ii. 355, 356.

at least the dominant section of them, buried their dead, regarding the use of fire as a humiliation, to be inflicted on criminals, or upon slaves or prisoners in those terrible human sacrifices which are the greatest stain on their native culture. The Germans, on the other hand, burned their illustrious dead on pyres, like the early Greeks—if a pyre could not be afforded for the whole body, the noblest parts, such as the head and arms, were burned and the rest buried.

Downfall of the Celtic Empire

What exactly took place at the time of the German revolt we shall never know; certain it is, however, that from about the year 300 B.C. onward the Celts appear to have lost whatever political cohesion and common purpose they had possessed. Rent asunder, as it were, by the upthrust of some mighty subterranean force, their tribes rolled down like lava-streams to the south, east, and west of their original home. Some found their way into Northern Greece, where they committed the outrage which so scandalised their former friends and allies in the sack of the shrine of Delphi (273 B.C.). Others renewed, with worse fortune, the old struggle with Rome, and perished in vast numbers at Sentinum (295 B.C.) and Lake Vadimo (283 B.C.). One detachment penetrated into Asia Minor, and founded the Celtic State of Galatia, where, as St. Jerome attests, a Celtic dialect was still spoken in the fourth century A.D. Others enlisted as mercenary troops with Carthage. A tumultuous war of Celts against scattered German tribes, or against other Celts who represented earlier waves of emigration and conquest, went on all over Mid-Europe, Gaul, and Britain. When this settled down Gaul and the British Islands remained practically the sole relics of the Celtic empire, the only countries still under Celtic law and leadership. By the commencement of the Christian era Gaul and Britain had fallen under the yoke of Rome, and their complete Romanisation was only a question of time.

Unique Historical Position of Ireland

Ireland alone was never even visited, much less subjugated, by the Roman legionaries, and maintained its independence against all comers nominally until the close of the twelfth century, but for all practical purposes a good three hundred years longer.

Ireland has therefore this unique feature of interest, that it carried an indigenous Celtic civilisation, Celtic institutions, art, and literature, and the oldest surviving form of the Celtic language,[1] right across the chasm which separates the antique from the modern world,

[1] Irish is probably an older form of Celtic speech than Welsh. This is shown by many philological peculiarities of the Irish language, of which one of the most interesting may here be briefly referred to. The Goidelic or Gaelic Celts, who, according to the usual theory, first colonised the British Islands, and who were forced by successive waves of invasion by their Continental kindred to the extreme west, had a peculiar dislike to the pronunciation of the letter *p*. Thus the Indo-European particle *pare*, represented by Greek παρά, beside or close to, becomes in early Celtic *are*, as in the name *Are-morici* (the Armoricans, those who dwell *ar muir*, by the sea); *Are-dunum* (Ardin, in France); *Are-cluta*, the place beside the Clota (Clyde), now Dumbarton; *Are-taunon*, in Germany (near the Taunus Mountains), &c. When this letter was not simply dropped it was usually changed into *c* (*k*, *g*). But about the sixth century B.C. a remarkable change passed over the language of the Continental Celts. They gained in some unexplained way the faculty for pronouncing *p*, and even substituted it for existing *c* sounds; thus the original *Cretanis* became *Pretanis*, Britain, the numeral *qetuares* (four) became *petuares*, and so forth. Celtic place-names in Spain show that this change must have taken place before the Celtic conquest of that country, 500 B.C. Now a comparison of many Irish and Welsh words shows

the pagan from the Christian world, and on into the full light of modern history and observation.

The Celtic Character

The moral no less than the physical characteristics attributed by classical writers to the Celtic peoples show a remarkable distinctness and consistency. Much of what is said about them might, as we should expect, be said of any primitive and unlettered people, but there remains so much to differentiate them among the races of mankind that if these ancient references to the Celts could be read aloud, without mentioning the name of the race to whom they referred, to any person acquainted with it through modern history alone, he would, I think, without hesitation, name the Celtic peoples as the subject of the description which he had heard.

Some of these references have already been quoted, and we need not repeat the evidence derived from Plato, Ephorus, or Arrian. But an observation of

distinctly this avoidance of *p* on the Irish side and lack of any objection to it on the Welsh. The following are a few illustrations:

Irish	*Welsh*	*English*
crann	prenn	tree
mac	map	son
cenn	pen	head
clumh (cluv)	pluv	feather
cúig	pimp	five

The conclusion that Irish must represent the older form of the language seems obvious. It is remarkable that even to a comparatively late date the Irish preserved their dislike to *p*. Thus they turned the Latin *Pascha* (Easter) to *Casg*; *purpur*, purple, to *corcair*, *pulsatio* (through French *pouls*) to *cuisle*. It must be noted, however, that Nicholson in his "Keltic Researches" endeavours to show that the so-called Indo-European *p*—that is, *p* standing alone and uncombined with another consonant—was pronounced by the Goidelic Celts at an early period. The subject can hardly be said to be cleared up yet.

M. Porcius Cato on the Gauls may be adduced. "There are two things," he says, "to which the Gauls are devoted—the art of war and subtlety of speech" ("rem militarem et argute loqui").

Cæsar's Account

Cæsar has given us a careful and critical account of them as he knew them in Gaul. They were, he says, eager for battle, but easily dashed by reverses. They were extremely superstitious, submitting to their Druids in all public and private affairs, and regarding it as the worst of punishments to be excommunicated and forbidden to approach the ceremonies of religion:

"They who are thus interdicted [for refusing to obey a Druidical sentence] are reckoned in the number of the vile and wicked; all persons avoid and fly their company and discourse, lest they should receive any infection by contagion; they are not permitted to commence a suit; neither is any post entrusted to them. . . . The Druids are generally freed from military service, nor do they pay taxes with the rest. . . . Encouraged by such rewards, many of their own accord come to their schools, and are sent by their friends and relations. They are said there to get by heart a great number of verses; some continue twenty years in their education; neither is it held lawful to commit these things [the Druidic doctrines] to writing, though in almost all public transactions and private accounts they use the Greek characters."

The Gauls were eager for news, besieging merchants and travellers for gossip,[1] easily influenced, sanguine,

[1] The Irish, says Edmund Spenser, in his "View of the Present State of Ireland," "use commonyle to send up and down to know newes, and yf any meet with another, his second woorde is, What newes?"

credulous, fond of change, and wavering in their counsels. They were at the same time remarkably acute and intelligent, very quick to seize upon and to imitate any contrivance they found useful. Their ingenuity in baffling the novel siege apparatus of the Roman armies is specially noticed by Cæsar. Of their courage he speaks with great respect, attributing their scorn of death, in some degree at least, to their firm faith in the immortality of the soul.[1] A people who in earlier days had again and again annihilated Roman armies, had sacked Rome, and who had more than once placed Cæsar himself in positions of the utmost anxiety and peril, were evidently no weaklings, whatever their religious beliefs or practices. Cæsar is not given to sentimental admiration of his foes, but one episode at the siege of Avaricum moves him to immortalise the valour of the defence. A wooden structure or *agger* had been raised by the Romans to overtop the walls, which had proved impregnable to the assaults of the battering-ram. The Gauls contrived to set this on fire. It was of the utmost moment to prevent the besiegers from extinguishing the flames, and a Gaul mounted a portion of the wall above the *agger*, throwing down upon it balls of tallow and pitch, which were handed up to him from within. He was soon struck down by a missile from a Roman catapult. Immediately another stepped over him as he lay, and continued his comrade's task. He too fell,

[1] Compare Spenser: "I have heard some greate warriors say, that in all the services which they had seen abroad in forrayne countreys, they never saw a more comely horseman than the Irish man, nor that cometh on more bravely in his charge . . . they are very valiante and hardye, for the most part great endurours of cold, labour, hunger and all hardiness, very active and stronge of hand, very swift of foote, very vigilaunte and circumspect in theyr enterprises, very present in perrils, very great scorners of death."

but a third instantly took his place, and a fourth; nor was this post ever deserted until the legionaries at last extinguished the flames and forced the defenders back into the town, which was finally captured on the following day.

Strabo on the Celts

The geographer and traveller Strabo, who died 24 A.D., and was therefore a little later than Cæsar, has much to tell us about the Celts. He notices that their country (in this case Gaul) is thickly inhabited and well tilled—there is no waste of natural resources. The women are prolific, and notably good mothers. He describes the men as warlike, passionate, disputatious, easily provoked, but generous and unsuspicious, and easily vanquished by stratagem. They showed themselves eager for culture, and Greek letters and science had spread rapidly among them from Massilia; public education was established in their towns. They fought better on horseback than on foot, and in Strabo's time formed the flower of the Roman cavalry. They dwelt in great houses made of arched timbers with walls of wickerwork—no doubt plastered with clay and lime, as in Ireland—and thickly thatched. Towns of much importance were found in Gaul, and Cæsar notes the strength of their walls, built of stone and timber. Both Cæsar and Strabo agree that there was a very sharp division between the nobles and priestly or educated class on the one hand and the common people on the other, the latter being kept in strict subjection. The social division corresponds roughly, no doubt, to the race distinction between the true Celts and the aboriginal populations subdued by them. While Cæsar tells us that the Druids taught the immortality of the soul, Strabo adds that they believed in the indestructibility, which implies in some sense the divinity, of the material universe.

The Celtic warrior loved display. Everything that gave brilliance and the sense of drama to life appealed to him. His weapons were richly ornamented, his horse-trappings were wrought in bronze and enamel, of design as exquisite as any relic of Mycenean or Cretan art, his raiment was embroidered with gold. The scene of the surrender of Vercingetorix, when his heroic struggle with Rome had come to an end on the fall of Alesia, is worth recording as a typically Celtic blend of chivalry and of what appeared to the sober-minded Romans childish ostentation.[1] When he saw that the cause was lost he summoned a tribal council, and told the assembled chiefs, whom he had led through a glorious though unsuccessful war, that he was ready to sacrifice himself for his still faithful followers—they might send his head to Cæsar if they liked, or he would voluntarily surrender himself for the sake of getting easier terms for his countrymen. The latter alternative was chosen. Vercingetorix then armed himself with his most splendid weapons, decked his horse with its richest trappings, and, after riding thrice round the Roman camp, went before Cæsar and laid at his feet the sword which was the sole remaining defence of Gallic independence. Cæsar sent him to Rome, where he lay in prison for six years, and was finally put to death when Cæsar celebrated his triumph.

But the Celtic love of splendour and of art were mixed with much barbarism. Strabo tells us how the warriors rode home from victory with the heads of

[1] The scene of the surrender of Vercingetorix is not recounted by Cæsar, and rests mainly on the authority of Plutarch and of the historian Florus, but it is accepted by scholars (Mommsen, Long, &c.) as historic.

fallen foemen dangling from their horses' necks, just as in the Irish saga the Ulster hero, Cuchulain, is represented as driving back to Emania from a foray into Connacht with the heads of his enemies hanging from his chariot-rim. Their domestic arrangements were rude; they lay on the ground to sleep, sat on couches of straw, and their women worked in the fields.

Polybius

A characteristic scene from the battle of Clastidium (222 B.C.) is recorded by Polybius. The Gæsati,[1] he tells us, who were in the forefront of the Celtic army, stripped naked for the fight, and the sight of these warriors, with their great stature and their fair skins, on which glittered the collars and bracelets of gold so loved as an adornment by all the Celts, filled the Roman legionaries with awe. Yet when the day was over those golden ornaments went in cartloads to deck the Capitol of Rome; and the final comment of Polybius on the character of the Celts is that they, "I say not usually, but always, in everything they attempt, are driven headlong by their passions, and never submit to the laws of reason." As might be expected, the chastity for which the Germans were noted was never, until recent times, a Celtic characteristic.

Diodorus

Diodorus Siculus, a contemporary of Julius Cæsar and Augustus, who had travelled in Gaul, confirms in the main the accounts of Cæsar and Strabo, but adds some

[1] These were a tribe who took their name from the *gæsum*, a kind of Celtic javelin, which was their principal weapon. The torque, or twisted collar of gold, is introduced as a typical ornament in the well-known statue of the dying Gaul, commonly called "The Dying Gladiator." Many examples are preserved in the National Museum of Dublin.

interesting details. He notes in particular the Gallic love of gold. Even cuirasses were made of it. This is also a very notable trait in Celtic Ireland, where an astonishing number of prehistoric gold relics have been found, while many more, now lost, are known to have existed. The temples and sacred places, say Posidonius and Diodorus, were full of unguarded offerings of gold, which no one ever touched. He mentions the great reverence paid to the bards, and, like Cato, notices something peculiar about the kind of speech which the educated Gauls cultivated: "they are not a talkative people, and are fond of expressing themselves in enigmas, so that the hearer has to divine the most part of what they would say." This exactly answers to the literary language of ancient Ireland, which is curt and allusive to a degree. The Druid was regarded as the prescribed intermediary between God and man—no one could perform a religious act without his assistance.

Ammianus Marcellinus

Ammianus Marcellinus, who wrote much later, in the latter half of the fourth century A.D., had also visited Gaul, which was then, of course, much Romanised. He tells us, however, like former writers, of the great stature, fairness, and arrogant bearing of the Gallic warrior. He adds that the people, especially in Aquitaine, were singularly clean and proper in their persons—no one was to be seen in rags. The Gallic woman he describes as very tall, blue-eyed, and singularly beautiful; but a certain amount of awe is mingled with his evident admiration, for he tells us that while it was dangerous enough to get into a fight with a Gallic man, your case was indeed desperate if his wife with her "huge snowy arms," which could strike like catapults, came to his assistance. One is irresistibly reminded of the gallery of vigorous, independent, fiery-hearted women, like Maeve, Grania, Findabair, Deirdre, and the historic Boadicea, who figure in the myths and in the history of the British Islands.

Rice Holmes on the Gauls

The following passage from Dr. Rice Holmes' "Cæsar's Conquest of Gaul" may be taken as an admirable summary of the social physiognomy of that part of Celtica a little before the time of the Christian era, and it corresponds closely to all that is known of the native Irish civilisation :

"The Gallic peoples had risen far above the condition of savages ; and the Celticans of the interior, many of whom had already fallen under Roman influence, had attained a certain degree of civilisation, and even of luxury. Their trousers, from which the province took its name of Gallia Bracata, and their many-coloured tartan skirts and cloaks excited the astonishment of their conquerors. The chiefs wore rings and bracelets and necklaces of gold ; and when these tall, fair-haired warriors rode forth to battle, with their helmets wrought in the shape of some fierce beast's head, and surmounted by nodding plumes, their chain armour, their long bucklers and their huge clanking swords, they made a splendid show. Walled towns or large villages, the strongholds of the various tribes, were conspicuous on numerous hills. The plains were dotted by scores of open hamlets. The houses, built of timber and wickerwork, were large and well thatched. The fields in summer were yellow with corn. Roads ran from town to town. Rude bridges spanned the rivers ; and barges laden with merchandise floated along them. Ships clumsy indeed but larger than any that were seen on the Mediterranean, braved the storms of the Bay of Biscay and carried cargoes between the ports of Brittany and the coast of Britain. Tolls were exacted on the goods which were transported on the great waterways; and it was from the farming of these dues that the nobles derived a large part of their wealth. Every tribe had its coinage; and the knowledge of writing in Greek and Roman characters was not confined to the priests. The Æduans were familiar with the plating of copper and of tin. The miners of Aquitaine, of Auvergne, and of the Berri were celebrated for their skill. Indeed, in all that belonged to outward prosperity the peoples of Gaul had made great strides since their kinsmen first came into contact with Rome."[1]

Weakness of the Celtic Policy

Yet this native Celtic civilisation, in many respects so attractive and so promising, had evidently some defect or disability which prevented the Celtic peoples from holding their own either against the ancient civilisation of the Græco-Roman world, or against the rude young vigour of the Teutonic races. Let us consider what this was.

[1] "Cæsar's Conquest of Gaul," pp. 10, 11. Let it be added that the aristocratic Celts were, like the Teutons, dolichocephalic—that is to say, they had heads long in proportion to their breadth. This is proved by remains found in the basin of the Marne, which was thickly populated by them. In one case the skeleton of the tall Gallic warrior was found with his war-car, iron helmet, and sword, now in the Musée de St.-Germain. The inhabitants of the British Islands are uniformly long-headed, the round-headed "Alpine" type occurring very rarely. Those of modern France are round-headed. The shape of the head, however, is now known to be by no means a constant racial character. It alters rapidly in a new environment, as is shown by measurements of the descendants of immigrants in America. See an article on this subject by Professor Haddon in "Nature," Nov. 3, 1910.

TEUTONIC LOYALTY

The Classical State

At the root of the success of classical nations lay the conception of the civic community, the πόλις, the *res publica*, as a kind of divine entity, the foundation of blessing to men, venerable for its age, yet renewed in youth with every generation; a power which a man might joyfully serve, knowing that even if not remembered in its records his faithful service would outlive his own petty life and go to exalt the life of his motherland or city for all future time. In this spirit Socrates, when urged to evade his death sentence by taking the means of escape from prison which his friends offered him, rebuked them for inciting him to an impious violation of his country's laws. For a man's country, he says, is more holy and venerable than father or mother, and he must quietly obey the laws, to which he has assented by living under them all his life, or incur the just wrath of their great Brethren, the Laws of the Underworld, before whom, in the end, he must answer for his conduct on earth. In a greater or less degree this exalted conception of the State formed the practical religion of every man among the classical nations of antiquity, and gave to the State its cohesive power, its capability of endurance and of progress.

Teutonic Loyalty

With the Teuton the cohesive force was supplied by another motive, one which was destined to mingle with the civic motive and to form, in union with it—and often in predominance over it—the main political factor in the development of the European nations. This was the sentiment of what the Germans called *Treue*, the personal fidelity to a chief, which in very early times extended itself to a royal dynasty, a sentiment rooted profoundly in the Teutonic nature, and one which has never been surpassed by any other human impulse as the source of heroic self-sacrifice.

Celtic Religion

No human influences are ever found pure and unmixed. The sentiment of personal fidelity was not unknown to the classical nations. The sentiment of civic patriotism, though of slow growth among the Teutonic races, did eventually establish itself there. Neither sentiment was unknown to the Celt, but there was another force which, in his case, overshadowed and dwarfed them, and supplied what it could of the political inspiration and unifying power which the classical nations got from patriotism and the Teutons from loyalty. This was Religion; or perhaps it would be more accurate to say Sacerdotalism—religion codified in dogma and administered by a priestly caste. The Druids, as we have seen from Cæsar, whose observations are entirely confirmed by Strabo and by references in Irish legends,[1] were the really sovran power in Celtica. All affairs, public and private, were subject to their authority, and the penalties which they could inflict for any assertion of lay independence, though resting for their efficacy, like the mediæval interdicts of the Catholic Church, on popular superstition

[1] In the "Táin Bo Cuailgne," for instance, the King of Ulster must not speak to a messenger until the Druid, Cathbad, has questioned him. One recalls the lines of Sir Samuel Ferguson in his Irish epic poem, "Congal":

"... For ever since the time
When Cathbad smothered Usnach's sons in that foul sea of slime
Raised by abominable spells at Creeveroe's bloody gate,
Do ruin and dishonour still on priest-led kings await."

alone, were enough to quell the proudest spirit. Here lay the real weakness of the Celtic polity. There is perhaps no law written more conspicuously in the teachings of history than that nations who are ruled by priests drawing their authority from supernatural sanctions are, just in the measure that they are so ruled, incapable of true national progress. The free, healthy current of secular life and thought is, in the very nature of things, incompatible with priestly rule. Be the creed what it may, Druidism, Islam, Judaism, Christianity, or fetichism, a priestly caste claiming authority in temporal affairs by virtue of extra-temporal sanctions is inevitably the enemy of that spirit of criticism, of that influx of new ideas, of that growth of secular thought, of human and rational authority, which are the elementary conditions of national development.

The Cursing of Tara

A singular and very cogent illustration of this truth can be drawn from the history of the early Celtic world. In the sixth century A.D., a little over a hundred years after the preaching of Christianity by St. Patrick, a king named Dermot MacKerval[1] ruled in Ireland. He was the Ard Righ, or High King, of that country, whose seat of government was at Tara, in Meath, and whose office, with its nominal and legal superiority to the five provincial kings, represented the impulse which was moving the Irish people towards a true national unity. The first condition of such a unity was evidently the establishment of an effective central authority. Such an authority, as we have said, the High King, in theory, represented. Now it happened that one of his officers was murdered in the discharge of his duty by a chief named Hugh Guairy. Guairy

[1] *Celtice,* Diarmuid mac Cearbhaill.

was the brother of a bishop who was related by fosterage to St. Ruadan of Lorrha, and when King Dermot sent to arrest the murderer these clergy found him a hiding-place. Dermot, however, caused a search to be made, haled him forth from under the roof of St. Ruadan, and brought him to Tara for trial. Immediately the ecclesiastics of Ireland made common cause against the lay ruler who had dared to execute justice on a criminal under clerical protection. They assembled at Tara, fasted against the king,[1] and laid their solemn malediction upon him and the seat of his government. Then the chronicler tells us that Dermot's wife had a prophetic dream:

"Upon Tara's green was a vast and wide-foliaged tree, and eleven slaves hewing at it; but every chip that they knocked from it would return into its place again and there adhere instantly, till at last there came one man that dealt the tree but a stroke, and with that single cut laid it low."[2]

The fair tree was the Irish monarchy, the twelve hewers were the twelve Saints or Apostles of Ireland, and the one who laid it low was St. Ruadan. The plea of the king for his country, whose fate he saw to be hanging in the balance, is recorded with moving force and insight by the Irish chronicler:[3]

[1] It was the practice, known in India also, for a person who was wronged by a superior, or thought himself so, to sit before the door-step of the denier of justice and fast until right was done him. In Ireland a magical power was attributed to the ceremony, the effect of which would be averted by the other person fasting as well.

[2] "Silva Gadelica," by S. H. O'Grady, p. 73.

[3] The authority here quoted is a narrative contained in a fifteenth-century vellum manuscript found in Lismore Castle in 1814, and translated by S. H. O'Grady in his "Silva Gadelica." The narrative is attributed to an officer of Dermot's court.

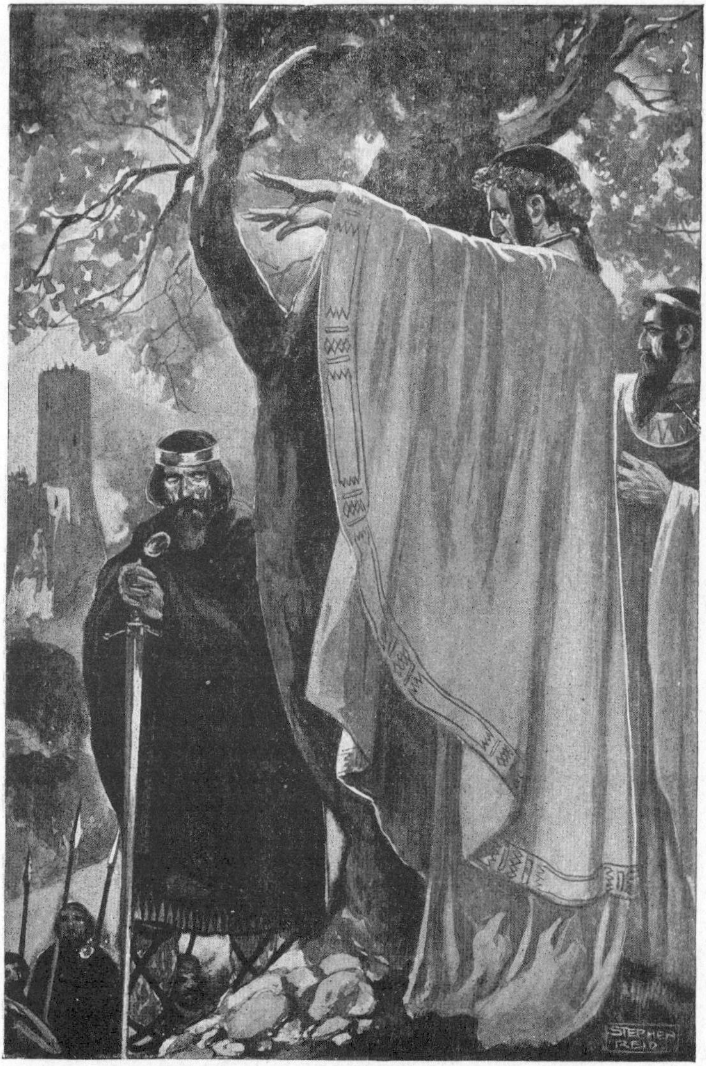

" Desolate be Tara for ever and ever ! "

Prehistoric Tumulus at New Grange

Photograph by R. Welch, Belfast

"'Alas,' he said, 'for the iniquitous contest that ye have waged against me; seeing that it is Ireland's good that I pursue, and to preserve her discipline and royal right; but 'tis Ireland's unpeace and murderousness that ye endeavour after.'"

But Ruadan said, "Desolate be Tara for ever and ever"; and the popular awe of the ecclesiastical malediction prevailed. The criminal was surrendered, Tara was abandoned, and, except for a brief space when a strong usurper, Brian Boru, fought his way to power, Ireland knew no effective secular government till it was imposed upon her by a conqueror. The last words of the historical tract from which we quote are Dermot's cry of despair:

"Woe to him that with the clergy of the churches battle joins."

This remarkable incident has been described at some length because it is typical of a factor whose profound influence in moulding the history of the Celtic peoples we can trace through a succession of critical events from the time of Julius Cæsar to the present day. How and whence it arose we shall consider later; here it is enough to call attention to it. It is a factor which forbade the national development of the Celts, in the sense in which we can speak of that of the classical or the Teutonic peoples.

What Europe Owes to the Celt

Yet to suppose that on this account the Celt was not a force of any real consequence in Europe would be altogether a mistake. His contribution to the culture of the Western world was a very notable one. For some four centuries—about A.D. 500 to 900—Ireland was the refuge of learning and the source of literary and philosophic culture for half Europe. The verse-forms of Celtic poetry have probably played the main part in determining the structure of all modern verse. The myths and legends of the Gaelic and Cymric peoples kindled the imagination of a host of Continental poets. True, the Celt did not himself create any great architectural work of literature, just as he did not create a stable or imposing national polity. His thinking and feeling were essentially lyrical and concrete. Each object or aspect of life impressed him vividly and stirred him profoundly; he was sensitive, impressionable to the last degree, but did not see things in their larger and more far-reaching relations. He had little gift for the establishment of institutions, for the service of principles; but he was, and is, an indispensable and never-failing assertor of humanity as against the tyranny of principles, the coldness and barrenness of institutions. The institutions of royalty and of civic patriotism are both very capable of being fossilised into barren formulæ, and thus of fettering instead of inspiring the soul. But the Celt has always been a rebel against anything that has not in it the breath of life, against any unspiritual and purely external form of domination. It is too true that he has been over-eager to enjoy the fine fruits of life without the long and patient preparation for the harvest, but he has done and will still do infinite service to the modern world in insisting that the true fruit of life is a spiritual reality, never without pain and loss to be obscured or forgotten amid the vast mechanism of a material civilisation.

CHAPTER II: THE RELIGION OF THE CELTS

Ireland and the Celtic Religion

WE have said that the Irish among the Celtic peoples possess the unique interest of having carried into the light of modern historical research many of the features of a native Celtic civilisation. There is, however, one thing which they did not carry across the gulf which divides us from the ancient world —and this was their religion.

It was not merely that they changed it; they left it behind them so entirely that all record of it is lost. St. Patrick, himself a Celt, who apostolised Ireland during the fifth century, has left us an autobiographical narrative of his mission, a document of intense interest, and the earliest extant record of British Christianity; but in it he tells us nothing of the doctrines he came to supplant. We learn far more of Celtic religious beliefs from Julius Cæsar, who approached them from quite another side. The copious legendary literature which took its present form in Ireland between the seventh and the twelfth centuries, though often manifestly going back to pre-Christian sources, shows us, beyond a belief in magic and a devotion to certain ceremonial or chivalric observances, practically nothing resembling a religious or even an ethical system. We know that certain chiefs and bards offered a long resistance to the new faith, and that this resistance came to the arbitrament of battle at Moyrath in the sixth century, but no echo of any intellectual controversy, no matching of one doctrine against another, such as we find, for instance, in the records of the controversy of Celsus with Origen, has reached us from this period of change and strife. The literature of ancient Ireland, as we shall see, embodied many ancient myths; and traces appear in it of beings who must, at one time, have been gods or elemental powers; but all has been emptied of religious significance and turned to romance and beauty. Yet not only was there, as Cæsar tells us, a very well-developed religious system among the Gauls, but we learn on the same authority that the British Islands were the authoritative centre of this system; they were, so to speak, the Rome of the Celtic religion.

What this religion was like we have now to consider, as an introduction to the myths and tales which more or less remotely sprang from it.

The Popular Religion of the Celts

But first we must point out that the Celtic religion was by no means a simple affair, and cannot be summed up as what we call "Druidism." Beside the official religion there was a body of popular superstitions and observances which came from a deeper and older source than Druidism, and was destined long to outlive it—indeed, it is far from dead even yet.

The Megalithic People

The religions of primitive peoples mostly centre on, or take their rise from, rites and practices connected with the burial of the dead. The earliest people inhabiting Celtic territory in the West of Europe of whom we have any distinct knowledge are a race without name or known history, but by their sepulchral monuments, of which so many still exist, we can learn a great deal about them. They were the so-called Megalithic People,[1] the builders of dolmens, cromlechs, and chambered tumuli, of which more than three

[1] From Greek *megas*, great, and *lithos*, a stone.

thousand have been counted in France alone. Dolmens are found from Scandinavia southwards, all down the western lands of Europe to the Straits of Gibraltar, and round by the Mediterranean coast of Spain. They occur in some of the western islands of the Mediterranean, and are found in Greece, where, in Mycenæ, an ancient dolmen yet stands beside the magnificent burial-chamber of the Atreidæ. Roughly, if we draw a line from the mouth of the Rhone northward to Varanger Fiord, one may say that, except for a few Mediterranean examples, all the dolmens in Europe lie to the west of that line. To the east none are found till we come into Asia. But they cross the Straits of Gibraltar, and are found all along the North African littoral, and thence eastwards through Arabia, India, and as far as Japan.

Dolmens, Cromlechs, and Tumuli

A dolmen, it may be here explained, is a kind of chamber composed of upright unhewn stones, and roofed generally with a single huge stone. They are usually wedge-shaped in plan, and traces of a porch or vestibule can often be noticed. The primary intention of the dolmen was to represent a house or dwelling-place for the dead. A cromlech (often confused in popular language with the dolmen) is properly a circular arrangement of standing stones, often with a dolmen in their midst. It is believed that most

Dolmen at Proleek, Ireland
(*After Borlase*)

if not all of the now exposed dolmens were originally covered with a great mound of earth or of smaller stones. Sometimes, as in the illustration we give from Carnac, in Brittany, great avenues or alignments are formed of single upright stones, and these, no doubt, had some purpose connected with the ritual of worship carried on in the locality. The later megalithic monuments, as at Stonehenge, may be of dressed stone, but in all cases their rudeness of construction, the absence of any sculpturing (except for patterns or symbols incised on the surface), the evident aim at creating a powerful impression by the brute strength of huge monolithic masses, as well as certain subsidiary features in their design which shall be described later on, give these megalithic monuments a curious family likeness and mark them out from the chambered tombs of the early Greeks, of the Egyptians, and of other more advanced races. The dolmens proper gave place in the end to great chambered mounds or tumuli, as at New Grange, which we also reckon as belonging to the Megalithic People. They are a natural development of the dolmen. The early dolmen-builders were in the neolithic stage of culture, their weapons were of polished stone. But in the tumuli not only stone, but also bronze, and even iron, instruments are found—at first evidently importations, but afterwards of local manufacture.

Origin of the Megalithic People

The language originally spoken by this people can only be conjectured by the traces of it left in that of their conquerors, the Celts.[1] But a map of the distribution of their monuments irresistibly suggests the idea that their builders were of North African origin; that they were not at first accustomed to traverse the

[1] See p. 78.

sea for any great distance; that they migrated westwards along North Africa, crossed into Europe where the Mediterranean at Gibraltar narrows to a strait of a few miles in width, and thence spread over the western regions of Europe, including the British Islands, while on the eastward they penetrated by Arabia into Asia. It must, however, be borne in mind that while originally, no doubt, a distinct race, the Megalithic People came in the end to represent, not a race, but a culture. The human remains found in these sepulchres, with their wide divergence in the shape of the skull, &c., clearly prove this.[1] These and other relics testify to the dolmen-builders in general as representing a superior and well-developed type, acquainted with agriculture, pasturage, and to some extent with seafaring. The monuments themselves, which are often of imposing size and imply much thought and organised effort in their construction, show unquestionably the existence, at this period, of a priesthood charged with the care of funeral rites and capable of controlling large bodies of men. Their dead were, as a rule, not burned, but buried whole—the greater monuments marking, no doubt, the sepulchres of important personages, while the common people were buried in tombs of which no traces now exist.

The Celts of the Plains

De Jubainville, in his account of the early history of the Celts, takes account of two main groups only—the Celts and the Megalithic People. But A. Bertrand, in his very valuable work "La Religion des Gaulois," distinguishes two elements among the Celts themselves. There are, besides the Megalithic People, the two groups

[1] See Borlase's "Dolmens of Ireland," pp. 605, 606, for a discussion of this question.

of lowland Celts and mountain Celts. The lowland Celts, according to his view, started from the Danube and entered Gaul probably about 1200 B.C. They were the founders of the lake-dwellings in Switzerland, in the Danube valley, and in Ireland. They knew the use of metals, and worked in gold, in tin, in bronze, and towards the end of their period in iron. Unlike the Megalithic People, they spoke a Celtic tongue,[1] though Bertrand seems to doubt their genuine racial affinity with the true Celts. They were perhaps Celticised rather than actually Celtic. They were not warlike; a quiet folk of herdsmen, tillers, and artificers. They did not bury, but burned their dead. At a great settlement of theirs, Golasecca, in Cisalpine Gaul, 6000 interments were found. In each case the body had been burned; there was not a single burial without previous burning.

This people entered Gaul not (according to Bertrand), for the most part, as conquerors, but by gradual infiltration, occupying vacant spaces wherever they found them along the valleys and plains. They came by the passes of the Alps, and their starting-point was the country of the Upper Danube, which Herodotus says "rises among the Celts." They blended peacefully with the Megalithic People among whom they settled, and did not evolve any of those advanced political institutions which are only nursed in war, but probably they contributed powerfully to the development of the Druidical system of religion and to the bardic poetry.

[1] Professor Ridgeway (see Report of the Brit. Assoc. for 1908) has contended that the Megalithic People spoke an Aryan language; otherwise he thinks more traces of its influence must have survived in the Celtic which supplanted it. The weight of authority, as well as such direct evidence as we possess, seems to be against his view.

The Celts of the Mountains

Finally, we have a third group, the true Celtic group, which followed closely on the track of the second. It was at the beginning of the sixth century that it first made its appearance on the left bank of the Rhine. While Bertrand calls the second group Celtic, these he styles Galatic, and identifies them with the Galatæ of the Greeks and the Galli and Belgæ of the Romans.

The second group, as we have said, were Celts of the plains. The third were Celts of the mountains. The earliest home in which we know them was the ranges of the Balkans and Carpathians. Their organisation was that of a military aristocracy—they lorded it over the subject populations on whom they lived by tribute or pillage. They are the warlike Celts of ancient history—the sackers of Rome and Delphi, the mercenary warriors who fought for pay and for the love of warfare in the ranks of Carthage and afterwards of Rome. Agriculture and industry were despised by them, their women tilled the ground, and under their rule the common population became reduced almost to servitude; "plebs pœne servorum habetur loco," as Cæsar tells us. Ireland alone escaped in some degree from the oppression of this military aristocracy, and from the sharp dividing line which it drew between the classes, yet even there a reflexion of the state of things in Gaul is found, even there we find free and unfree tribes and oppressive and dishonouring exactions on the part of the ruling order.

Yet, if this ruling race had some of the vices of untamed strength, they had also many noble and humane qualities. They were dauntlessly brave, fantastically chivalrous, keenly sensitive to the appeal of poetry, of music, and of speculative thought. Posidonius found the bardic institution flourishing among them about

100 B.C., and about two hundred years earlier Hecatæus of Abdera describes the elaborate musical services held by the Celts in a Western island—probably Great Britain—in honour of their god Apollo (Lugh).[1] Aryan of the Aryans, they had in them the making of a great and progressive nation; but the Druidic system—not on the side of its philosophy and science, but on that of its ecclesiastico-political organisation—was their bane, and their submission to it was their fatal weakness.

The culture of these mountain Celts differed markedly from that of the lowlanders. Their age was the age of iron, not of bronze; their dead were not burned (which they considered a disgrace), but buried.

The territories occupied by them in force were Switzerland, Burgundy, the Palatinate, and Northern France, parts of Britain to the west, and Illyria and Galatia to the east, but smaller groups of them must have penetrated far and wide through all Celtic territory, and taken up a ruling position wherever they went.

There were three peoples, said Cæsar, inhabiting Gaul when his conquest began; "they differ from each other in language, in customs, and in laws." These people he named respectively the Belgæ, the Celtæ, and the Aquitani. He locates them roughly, the Belgæ in the north and east, the Celtæ in the middle, and the Aquitani in the west and south. The Belgæ are the Galatæ of Bertrand, the Celtæ are the Celts, and the Aquitani are the Megalithic People. They had, of course, all been more or less brought under Celtic influences, and the differences of language which Cæsar noticed need not have been great; still it is noteworthy, and quite in accordance with Bertrand's views, that Strabo speaks of the Aquitani as differing markedly from the rest of the inhabitants, and as

[1] See Holder, "Altceltischer Sprachschatz," *sub voce* "Hyperboreoi."

Stone Alignments at Kermaris, Carnac

Arthur G. Bell

Modern Stone-worship at Locronan, Brittany

Arthur G. Bell

resembling the Iberians. The language of the other Gaulish peoples, he expressly adds, were merely dialects of the same tongue.

The Religion of Magic

This triple division is reflected more or less in all the Celtic countries, and must always be borne in mind when we speak of Celtic ideas and Celtic religion, and try to estimate the contribution of the Celtic peoples to European culture. The mythical literature and the art of the Celt have probably sprung mainly from the section represented by the Lowland Celts of Bertrand. But this literature of song and saga was produced by a bardic class for the pleasure and instruction of a proud, chivalrous, and warlike aristocracy, and would thus inevitably be moulded by the ideas of this aristocracy. But it would also have been coloured by the profound influence of the religious beliefs and observances entertained by the Megalithic People—beliefs which are only now fading slowly away in the spreading daylight of science. These beliefs may be summed up in the one term Magic. The nature of this religion of magic must now be briefly discussed, for it was a potent element in the formation of the body of myths and legends with which we have afterwards to deal. And, as Professor Bury remarked in his Inaugural Lecture at Cambridge, in 1903:

"For the purpose of prosecuting that most difficult of all inquiries, the ethnical problem, the part played by race in the development of peoples and the effects of race-blendings, it must be remembered that the Celtic world commands one of the chief portals of ingress into that mysterious pre-Aryan foreworld, from which it may well be that we modern Europeans have inherited far more than we dream."

The ultimate root of the word Magic is unknown, but proximately it is derived from the Magi, or priests of Chaldea and Media in pre-Aryan and pre-Semitic times, who were the great exponents of this system of thought, so strangely mingled of superstition, philosophy, and scientific observation. The fundamental conception of magic is that of the spiritual vitality of all nature. This spiritual vitality was not, as in polytheism, conceived as separated from nature in distinct divine personalities. It was implicit and immanent in nature; obscure, undefined, invested with all the awfulness of a power whose limits and nature are enveloped in impenetrable mystery. In its remote origin it was doubtless, as many facts appear to show, associated with the cult of the dead, for death was looked upon as the resumption into nature, and as the investment with vague and uncontrollable powers, of a spiritual force formerly embodied in the concrete, limited, manageable, and therefore less awful form of a living human personality. Yet these powers were not altogether uncontrollable. The desire for control, as well as the suggestion of the means for achieving it, probably arose from the first rude practices of the art of healing. Medicine of some sort was one of the earliest necessities of man. And the power of certain natural substances, mineral or vegetable, to produce bodily and mental effects often of a most startling character would naturally be taken as signal evidence of what we may call the "magical" conception of the universe.[1] The first magicians were those who attained a special knowledge of healing or poisonous herbs; but "virtue" of some sort being attributed to every natural object and pheno-

[1] Thus the Greek *pharmakon* = medicine, poison, or charm; and I am informed that the Central African word for magic or charm is *mankwala*, which also means medicine.

menon, a kind of magical science, partly the child of true research, partly of poetic imagination, partly of priestcraft, would in time spring up, would be codified into rites and formulas, attached to special places and objects, and represented by symbols. The whole subject has been treated by Pliny in a remarkable passage which deserves quotation at length:

Pliny on the Religion of Magic

"Magic is one of the few things which it is important to discuss at some length, were it only because, being the most delusive of all the arts, it has everywhere and at all times been most powerfully credited. Nor need it surprise us that it has obtained so vast an influence, for it has united in itself the three arts which have wielded the most powerful sway over the spirit of man. Springing in the first instance from Medicine—a fact which no one can doubt—and under cover of a solicitude for our health, it has glided into the mind, and taken the form of another medicine, more holy and more profound. In the second place, bearing the most seductive and flattering promises, it has enlisted the motive of Religion, the subject on which, even at this day, mankind is most in the dark. To crown all it has had recourse to the art of Astrology; and every man is eager to know the future and convinced that this knowledge is most certainly to be obtained from the heavens. Thus, holding the minds of men enchained in this triple bond, it has extended its sway over many nations, and the Kings of Kings obey it in the East.

"In the East, doubtless, it was invented—in Persia and by Zoroaster.[1] All the authorities agree in this.

[1] If Pliny meant that it was here first codified and organised he may be right, but the conceptions on which magic rest are practically universal, and of immemorial antiquity.

But has there not been more than one Zoroaster? . . . I have noticed that in ancient times, and indeed almost always, one finds men seeking in this science the climax of literary glory—at least Pythagoras, Empedocles, Democritus, and Plato crossed the seas, exiles, in truth, rather than travellers, to instruct themselves in this. Returning to their native land, they vaunted the claims of magic and maintained its secret doctrine. . . . In the Latin nations there are early traces of it, as, for instance, in our Laws of the Twelve Tables[1] and other monuments, as I have said in a former book. In fact, it was not until the year 657 after the foundation of Rome, under the consulate of Cornelius Lentulus Crassus, that it was forbidden by a *senatus consultum* to sacrifice human beings; a fact which proves that up to this date these horrible sacrifices were made. The Gauls have been captivated by it, and that even down to our own times, for it was the Emperor Tiberius who suppressed the Druids and all the herd of prophets and medicine-men. But what is the use of launching prohibitions against an art which has thus traversed the ocean and penetrated even to the confines of Nature?" (*Hist. Nat.* xxx.)

Pliny adds that the first person whom he can ascertain to have written on this subject was Osthanes, who accompanied Xerxes in his war against the Greeks, and who propagated the "germs of his monstrous art" wherever he went in Europe.

Magic was not—so Pliny believed—indigenous either in Greece or in Italy, but was so much at home in Britain and conducted with such elaborate ritual that

[1] Adopted 451 B.C. Livy entitles them "the fountain of all public and private right." They stood in the Forum till the third century A.D., but have now perished, except for fragments preserved in various commentaries.

Pliny says it would almost seem as if it was they who had taught it to the Persians, not the Persians to them.

Traces of Magic in Megalithic Monuments

The imposing relics of their cult which the Megalithic People have left us are full of indications of their religion. Take, for instance, the remarkable tumulus of Mané-er-H'oeck, in Brittany. This monument was explored in 1864 by M. René Galles, who describes it as absolutely intact—the surface of the earth unbroken, and everything as the builders left it.[1] At the entrance to the rectangular chamber was a sculptured slab, on which was graven a mysterious sign, perhaps the totem of a chief. Immediately on entering the chamber was found a beautiful pendant in green jasper about the size of an egg. On the floor in the centre of the chamber was a most singular arrangement, consisting of a large ring of jadite, slightly oval in shape, with a magnificent axe-head, also of jadite, its point resting on the ring. The axe was a well-known symbol of power or godhead, and is frequently found in rock-carvings of the Bronze Age, as well as in Egyptian hieroglyphs, Minoan carvings, &c. At a little distance from these there lay two large pendants of jasper, then an axe-head in white jade,[2] then another jasper pendant. All these objects were ranged with evident intention *en suite*, forming a straight line which coincided exactly with one of the diagonals of the chamber, running from north-west to south-east. In one of the corners of the chamber were found 101 axe-heads in jade, jadite, and

[1] See "Revue Archéologique," t. xii., 1865, "Fouilles de René Galles."

[2] Jade is not found in the native state in Europe, nor nearer than China.

fibrolite. There were no traces of bones or cinders, no funerary urn ; the structure was a cenotaph. "Are we not here," asks Bertrand, "in presence of some ceremony relating to the practices of magic ?"

Chiromancy at Gavr'inis

In connexion with the great sepulchral monument of Gavr'inis a very curious observation was made by

Stones from Brittany sculptured with Footprints, Axes, "Finger-markings," &c.
(*Sergi*)

M. Albert Maitre, an inspector of the Musée des Antiquités Nationales. There were found here—as commonly in other megalithic monuments in Ireland and Scotland—a number of stones sculptured with a singular and characteristic design in waving and concentric lines. Now if the curious lines traced upon the human hand at the roots and tips of the fingers be examined under a lens, it will be found that they bear an exact resemblance to these designs of megalithic sculpture. One seems almost like a cast of the other. These lines on the human hand are so distinct and peculiar that, as is well known, they have been adopted as a method of identification of criminals. Can this resemblance be the result of chance? Nothing like these peculiar assemblages of sculptured lines has ever been found except in connexion with these monuments. Have we not here a reference to chiromancy—a magical art much practised in ancient and even in modern times? The hand as a symbol of power was a well-known magical emblem, and has entered largely even into Christian symbolism—note, for instance, the great hand sculptured on the under side of one of the arms of the Cross of Muiredach at Monasterboice.

Holed Stones

Another singular and as yet unexplained feature which appears in many of these monuments, from Western Europe to India, is the presence of a small hole bored through one of the stones composing the chamber. Was it an aperture intended for the spirit of the dead? or for offerings to them? or the channel through which revelations from the spirit-world were supposed to come to a priest or magician? or did it partake of all these characters?

Dolmen at Trie, France
(*After Gailhabaud*)

Holed stones, not forming part of a dolmen, are, of course, among the commonest relics of the ancient cult, and are still venerated and used in practices connected

Dolmens in the Deccan, India
(*After Meadows-Taylor*)

with child-bearing, &c. Here we are doubtless to interpret the emblem as a symbol of sex.

Stone-Worship

Besides the heavenly bodies, we find that rivers, trees, mountains, and stones were all objects of veneration among this primitive people. Stone-worship was particularly common, and is not so easily explained as the worship directed toward objects possessing movement and vitality. Possibly an explanation of the veneration attaching to great and isolated masses of unhewn stone may be found in their resemblance to the artificial dolmens and cromlechs.[1] No superstition has proved more enduring. In A.D. 452 we find the Synod of Arles denouncing those who "venerate trees and wells and stones," and the denunciation was repeated by Charlemagne, and by numerous Synods and Councils down to recent times. Yet a drawing, here reproduced, which was lately made on the spot by Mr. Arthur Bell, shows this very act of worship still in full force in Brittany, and shows the symbols and the sacerdotal organisation of Christianity actually pressed into the service of this immemorial paganism. According to Mr. Bell, the clergy take part in these performances with much reluctance, but are compelled to do so by the force of local opinion. Holy wells, the water of which is supposed to cure diseases, are still very common in Ireland,

[1] Small stones, crystals, and gems were, however, also venerated. The celebrated Black Stone of Pergamos was the subject of an embassy from Rome to that city in the time of the Second Punic War, the Sibylline Books having predicted victory to its possessors. It was brought to Rome with great rejoicings in the year 205. It is stated to have been about the size of a man's fist, and was probably a meteorite. Compare the myth in Hesiod which relates how Kronos devoured a stone in the belief that it was his offspring, Zeus. It was then possible to mistake a stone for a god.

and the cult of the waters of Lourdes may, in spite of its adoption by the Church, be mentioned as a notable case in point on the Continent.

Cup-and-Ring Markings

Another singular emblem, upon the meaning of which no light has yet been thrown, occurs frequently in con-

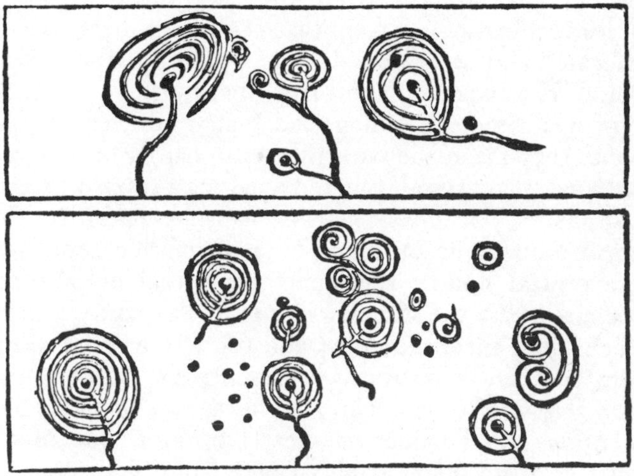

Cup-and-ring Markings from Scotland
(*After Sir J. Simpson*)

nexion with megalithic monuments. The accompanying illustrations show examples of it. Cup-shaped hollows are made in the surface of the stone, these are often surrounded with concentric rings, and from the cup one or more radial lines are drawn to a point outside the circumference of the rings. Occasionally a system of cups are joined by these lines, but more frequently they end a little way outside the widest of the rings. These strange markings are found in Great Britain and Ireland, in Brittany, and at various places in

India, where they are called *mahadéos*.[1] I have also found a curious example—for such it appears to be—in Dupaix' "Monuments of New Spain." It is reproduced in Lord Kingsborough's "Antiquities of Mexico," vol. iv. On the circular top of a cylindrical stone, known as the "Triumphal Stone," is carved a central cup, with nine concentric circles round it, and a duct or channel cut straight from the cup through all the circles to the rim. Except that the design here is richly decorated and accurately drawn, it closely resembles a typical European cup-and-ring marking. That these markings mean something, and that, wherever they are found, they mean the same thing, can hardly be doubted, but what that meaning is remains yet a puzzle to antiquarians. The guess may perhaps be hazarded that they are diagrams or plans of a megalithic sepulchre. The central hollow represents the actual burial-place. The circles are the standing stones, fosses, and ramparts which often surrounded it; and the line or duct drawn from the centre outwards represents the subterranean approach to the sepulchre. The apparent "avenue" intention of the duct is clearly brought out in the varieties given below, which I take from Simpson. As the sepulchre was also a holy place or shrine, the occurrence of a representation of it among other carvings of a sacred character is natural enough; it would seem symbolically to indicate that the place was holy ground. How far this suggestion might apply to the Mexican example I am unable to say.

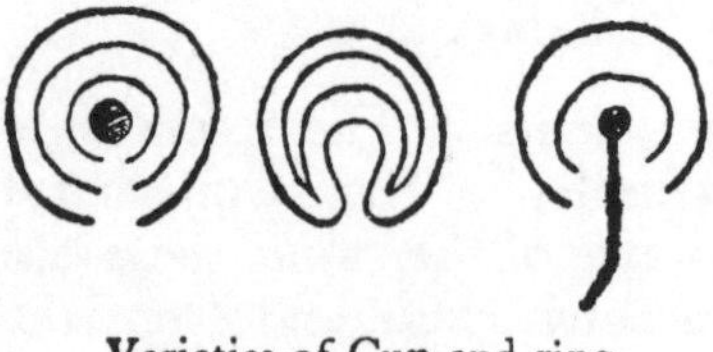

Varieties of Cup-and-ring Markings

[1] See Sir J. Simpson's "Archaic Sculpturings." 1867.

The Tumulus at New Grange

One of the most important and richly sculptured of European megalithic monuments is the great chambered tumulus of New Grange, on the northern bank of the Boyne, in Ireland. This tumulus, and the others which occur in its neighbourhood, appear in ancient Irish mythical literature in two different characters, the union of which is significant. They are regarded on the one hand as the dwelling-places of the *Sidhe* (pronounced Shee), or Fairy Folk, who represent, probably, the deities of the ancient Irish, and they are also, traditionally, the burial-places of the Celtic High Kings of pagan Ireland. The story of the burial of King Cormac, who was supposed to have heard of the Christian faith long before it was actually preached in Ireland by St. Patrick and who ordered that he should not be buried at the royal cemetery by the Boyne, on account of its pagan associations, points to the view that this place was the centre of a pagan cult involving more than merely the interment of royal personages in its precincts. Unfortunately these monuments are not intact; they were opened and plundered by the Danes in the ninth century,[1] but enough evidence remains to show that they were sepulchral in their origin, and were also associated with the cult of a primitive religion. The most important of them, the tumulus of New Grange, has been thoroughly explored and described by Mr. George Coffey, keeper of the collection of Celtic antiquities in the National Museum, Dublin.[2] It appears from the outside like a large mound, or knoll, now overgrown with bushes. It measures about 280 feet across,

[1] The fact is recorded in the "Annals of the Four Masters" under the date 861, and in the "Annals of Ulster" under 862.

[2] See "Transactions of the Royal Irish Academy," vol. xxx. pt. i., 1892, and "New Grange," by G. Coffey, 1912.

at its greatest diameter, and is about 44 feet in height. Outside it there runs a wide circle of standing stones originally, it would seem, thirty-five in number. Inside this circle is a ditch and rampart, and on top of this rampart was laid a circular curb of great stones 8 to 10 feet long, laid on edge, and confining what has proved to be a huge mound of loose stones, now overgrown, as we have said, with grass and bushes. It is in the interior of this mound that the interest of the monument lies. Towards the end of the seventeenth century some workmen who were getting road-material from the mound came across the entrance to a passage which led into the interior, and was marked by the fact that the boundary stone below it is richly carved with spirals and lozenges. This entrance faces exactly south-east. The passage is formed of upright slabs of unhewn stone roofed with similar slabs, and varies from nearly 5 feet to 7 feet 10 inches in height; it is about 3 feet wide, and runs for 62 feet straight into the heart of the mound. Here it ends in a cruciform chamber, 20 feet high, the roof, a kind of dome, being formed of large flat stones, overlapping inwards till they almost meet at the top, where a large flat stone covers all. In each of the three recesses of the cruciform chamber there stands a large stone basin, or rude sarcophagus, but no traces of any burial now remain.

Symbolic Carvings at New Grange

The stones are all raw and undressed, and were selected for their purpose from the river-bed and elsewhere close by. On their flat surfaces, obtained by splitting slabs from the original quarries, are found the carvings which form the unique interest of this strange monument. Except for the large stone with spiral carvings and one other at the entrance to the mound,

Entrance to Tumulus at New Grange

Photograph by R. Welch, Belfast

Human Sacrifices in Gaul

the intention of these sculptures does not appear to have been decorative, except in a very rude and primitive sense. There is no attempt to cover a given surface with a system of ornament appropriate to its size and shape. The designs are, as it were, scribbled upon the walls anyhow and anywhere.[1] Among them everywhere the spiral is prominent. The resemblance of some of these carvings to the supposed finger-markings of the stones at Gavr'inis is very remarkable. Triple and double spiral are also found, as well as lozenges and zigzags. A singular carving representing what looks like a palm-branch or fern-leaf is found in the west recess. The drawing of this object is naturalistic, and it is hard to interpret it, as Mr. Coffey is inclined to do, as merely a piece of so-called "herring-bone" pattern.[2] A similar palm-leaf design, but with the ribs arranged at right angles to the central axis, is found in the neighbouring tumulus of Dowth, at Loughcrew, and in combination with a solar emblem, the swastika, on a small altar in the Pyrenees, figured by Bertrand.

The Ship Symbol at New Grange

Another remarkable and, as far as Ireland goes, unusual figure is found sculptured in the west recess at New Grange. It has been interpreted by various critics as a mason's mark, a piece of Phœnician writing, a group of numerals, and finally (and no doubt correctly) by Mr. George Coffey as a rude representation of a ship with men on board and uplifted sail. It is noticeable that just above it is a small circle, forming, apparently, part of the design. Another example occurs at Dowth.

[1] It must be observed, however, that the decoration was, certainly in some, and perhaps in all cases, carried out before the stones were placed in position. This is also the case at Gavr'inis.

[2] He has modified this view in his latest work, "New Grange," 1912.

The significance of this marking, as we shall see, is possibly very great. It has been discovered that on certain stones in the tumulus of Locmariaker, in Brittany,[1] there occur a number of very similar figures, one of them showing the circle in much the same relative position as at New Grange. The axe, an Egyptian hieroglyph for godhead and a well-known magical emblem, is also represented on this stone.

Solar Ship (with Sail ?) from New Grange, Ireland

Again, in a brochure by Dr. Oscar Montelius on the rock-sculptures of Sweden[2] we find a reproduction (also given in Du Chaillu's "Viking Age") of a rude rock-carving showing a number of ships with men on board, and the circle quartered by a cross—unmistakably a solar emblem—just above one of them. That these ships (which, like the Irish example, are often so summarily represented as to be mere symbols which no one could identifiy as a ship were the clue not given by other and more elaborate representations) were drawn so frequently in conjunction with the solar disk merely for amusement or for a purely decorative object seems to me most

Solar Ship from Locmariaker, Brittany
(*After Ferguson*)

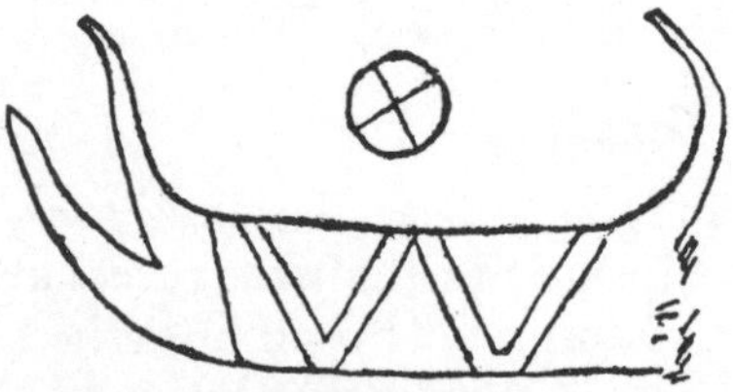

Solar Ship from Hallande, Sweden
(*After Montelius*)

[1] "Proc. Royal Irish Acad.," vol. viii. 1863, p. 400, and G. Coffey, *op. cit.* p. 30.

[2] "Les Sculptures de Rochers de la Suède," read at the Prehistoric Congress, Stockholm, 1874; and see G. Coffey, *op. cit.* p. 60.

improbable. In the days of the megalithic folk a sepulchral monument, the very focus of religious ideas, would hardly have been covered with idle and meaningless scrawls. " Man," as Sir J. Simpson has well said, " has ever conjoined together things sacred and things sepulchral." Nor do these scrawls, in the majority of instances, show any glimmering of a decorative intention. But if they had a symbolic intention, what is it that they symbolise ?

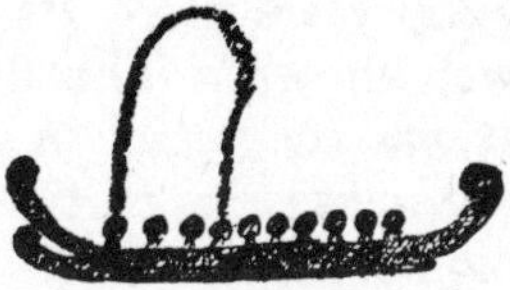

Ship (with Sail ?) from Ryxö
(*After Du Chaillu*)

We have here come, I believe, into a higher order of ideas than that of magic. The suggestion I have to make may seem a daring one; yet, as we shall see, it is quite in line with the results of certain other investigations as to the origin and character of the megalithic culture. If accepted, it will certainly give much greater definiteness to our views of the relations of the Megalithic People with North Africa, as well as of the true origin of Druidism and of the doctrines associated with that system. I think it may be taken as established that the frequent conjunction of the ship with the solar disk on rock-sculptures in Sweden, Ireland, and Brittany cannot be fortuitous. No one, for instance, looking at the example from Hallande given above, can doubt that the two objects are intentionally combined in one design.

Ship Carving (with Solar Emblem ?) from Scania, Sweden
(*After Du Chaillu*)

The Ship Symbol in Egypt

Now this symbol of the ship, with or without the actual portrayal of the solar emblem, is of very ancient and very common occurrence in the sepulchral art of Egypt. It is connected with the worship of Rā, which came in fully 4000 years B.C. Its meaning as an Egyptian symbol is well known. The ship was called the Boat of the Sun. It was the vessel in which the Sun-god performed his journeys; in particular, the journey which he made nightly to the shores of the Other-world, bearing with him in his bark the souls of the beatified dead. The

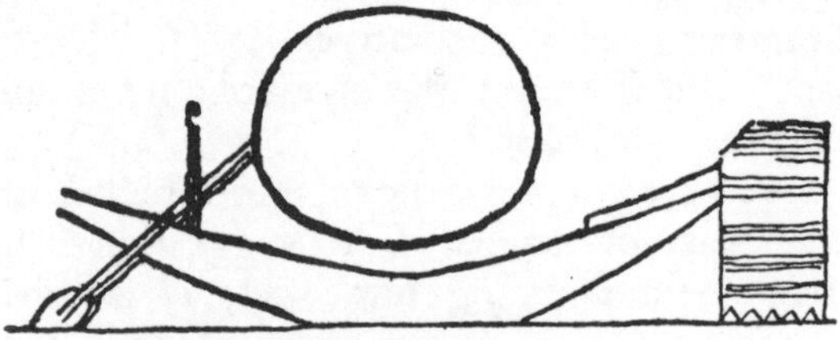

Egyptian Solar Bark, XXII Dynasty
(*British Museum*)

Sun-god, Rā, is sometimes represented by a disk, sometimes by other emblems, hovering above the vessel or contained within it. Any one who will look over the painted or sculptured sarcophagi in the British Museum will find a host of examples. Sometimes he will find representations of the life-giving rays of Rā pouring down upon the boat and its occupants. Now, in one of the Swedish rock-carvings of ships at Backa, Bohuslān, given by Montelius, a ship crowded with figures is shown beneath a disk with three descending rays, and again another ship with a two-rayed sun above it. It may be added that in the tumulus of Dowth, which is close to that of New Grange and is entirely of the same character and period, rayed figures and quartered circles, obviously solar emblems, occur abundantly, as also at Loughcrew and other places in Ireland, and one other ship figure has been identified at Dowth

THE SHIP SYMBOL IN EGYPT

In Egypt the solar boat is sometimes represented as containing the solar emblem alone, sometimes it contains the figure of a god with attendant deities, sometimes it contains a crowd of passengers representing human souls, and sometimes the figure of a single corpse on a bier. The megalithic carvings also sometimes show the solar emblem and sometimes not; the boats are sometimes filled with figures and are sometimes empty. When a symbol has once been accepted and understood, any conventional or summary representation of it is sufficient. I take it that the complete form of the megalithic symbol is that of a boat with figures in it and with the solar emblem overhead. These figures, assuming the foregoing interpretation of the design to be correct, must clearly be taken for representations of the dead on their way to the Other-world. They cannot be deities, for representations of the divine powers under human aspect were quite unknown to the Megalithic People, even after the coming of the Celts—they first occur in Gaul under Roman influence. But if these figures represent the dead, then we have clearly before us the origin of the so-called "Celtic" doctrine of immortality. The carvings in question are pre-Celtic. They are found where no Celts ever penetrated. Yet they point to the existence of just that Other-world doctrine which, from the time of Cæsar

Egyptian Solar Bark, with god Khnemu and attendant deities (*British Museum*)

Egyptian Bark, with figure of Rā holding an *Ankh*, enclosed in Solar Disk. XIX Dynasty (*British Museum*)

downwards, has been associated with Celtic Druidism, and this doctrine was distinctively Egyptian.

The "Navetas"

In connexion with this subject I may draw attention to the theory of Mr. W. C. Borlase that the typical design of an Irish dolmen was intended to represent a ship. In Minorca there are analogous structures, there popularly called *navetas* (ships), so distinct is the resemblance. But, he adds, "long before the caves and *navetas* of Minorca were known to me I had formed the opinion that what I have so frequently spoken of as the 'wedge-shape' observable so universally in the ground-plans of dolmens was due to an original conception of a ship. From sepulchral tumuli in Scandinavia we know actual vessels have on several occasions been disinterred. In cemeteries of the Iron Age, in the same country, as well as on the more southern Baltic coasts, the ship was a recognised form of sepulchral enclosure."[1] If Mr. Borlase's view is correct, we have here a very strong corroboration of the symbolic intention which I attribute to the solar ship-carvings of the Megalithic People.

The Ship Symbol in Babylonia

The ship symbol, it may be remarked, can be traced to about 4000 B.C. in Babylonia, where every deity had his own special ship (that of the god Sin was called the Ship of Light), his image being carried in procession on a litter formed like a ship. This is thought by Jastrow[2] to have originated at a time when the sacred cities of Babylonia were situated on the Persian Gulf, and when religious processions were often carried out by water.

[1] "Dolmens of Ireland," pp. 701–704.
[2] "The Religion of Babylonia and Assyria."

The Symbol of the Feet

Yet there is reason to think that some of these symbols were earlier than any known mythology, and were, so to say, mythologised differently by different peoples, who got hold of them from this now unknown source. A remarkable instance is that of the symbol of the Two Feet. In Egypt the Feet of Osiris formed one of the portions into which his body was cut up, in the well-known myth. They were a symbol of possession or of visitation. "I have come upon earth," says the "Book of the Dead" (ch. xvii.), "and with my two feet have taken possession. I am Tmu." Now this symbol of the feet or footprint is very widespread. It is found in India, as the print of the foot of Buddha,[1] it is found sculptured on dolmens in Brittany,[2] and it occurs in rock-carvings in Scandinavia.[3] In Ireland it passes for the footprints of St. Patrick or St. Columba. Strangest of all, it is found unmistakably in Mexico.[4] Tyler, in his "Primitive Culture" (ii. p. 197) refers to "the Aztec ceremony at the Second Festival of the Sun God, Tezcatlipoca, when they sprinkled maize flour before his sanctuary, and his high priest watched till he beheld the divine footprints, and then shouted to announce, 'Our Great God is come.'"

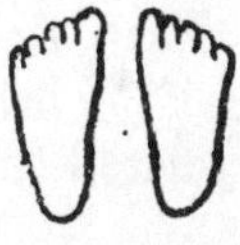

The Two Feet Symbol

The *Ankh* on Megalithic Carvings

There is very strong evidence of the connexion of the Megalithic People with North Africa. Thus, as

[1] A good example from Amaravati (after Fergusson) is given by Bertrand, "Rel. des G.," p. 389.

[2] Sergi, "The Mediterranean Race," p. 313.

[3] At Lökeberget, Bohuslän; see Montelius, *op. cit.*

[4] See Lord Kingsborough's "Antiquities of Mexico," *passim*, and the Humboldt fragment of Mexican painting (reproduced in Churchward's "Signs and Symbols of Primordial Man").

Sergi points out, many signs (probably numerical) found on ivory tablets in the cemetery at Naqada discovered by Flinders Petrie are to be met with on European dolmens. Several later Egyptian hieroglyphic signs, including the famous *Ankh*, or *crux ansata*, the symbol of vitality or resurrection, are also found in megalithic carvings.[1] From these correspondences Letourneau drew the conclusion "that the builders of our megalithic monuments came from the South, and were related to the races of North Africa."[2]

The *Ankh*

Evidence from Language

Approaching the subject from the linguistic side, Rhys and Brynmor Jones find that the African origin—at least proximately—of the primitive population of Great Britain and Ireland is strongly suggested. It is here shown that the Celtic languages preserve in their syntax the Hamitic, and especially the Egyptian type.[3]

Egyptian and "Celtic" Ideas of Immortality

The facts at present known do not, I think, justify us in framing any theory as to the actual historical relation of the dolmen-builders of Western Europe with the people who created the wonderful religion and civilisation of ancient Egypt. But when we consider all the lines of evidence that converge in this direction it seems clear that there was such a relation. Egypt was the classic land of religious symbolism. It gave to

[1] See Sergi, *op. cit.* p. 290, for the *Ankh* on a French dolmen.

[2] "Bulletin de la Soc. d'Anthropologie," Paris, April 1893.

[3] "The Welsh People," pp. 616–664, where the subject is fully discussed in an appendix by Professor J. Morris Jones. "The pre-Aryan idioms which still live in Welsh and Irish were derived from a language allied to Egyptian and the Berber tongues."

Europe the most beautiful and most popular of all its religious symbols, that of the divine mother and child.[1] I believe that it also gave to the primitive inhabitants of Western Europe the profound symbol of the voyaging spirits guided to the world of the dead by the God of Light.

The religion of Egypt, above that of any people whose ideas we know to have been developed in times so ancient, centred on the doctrine of a future life. The palatial and stupendous tombs, the elaborate ritual, the imposing mythology, the immense exaltation of the priestly caste, all these features of Egyptian culture were intimately connected with their doctrine of the immortality of the soul.

To the Egyptian the disembodied soul was no shadowy simulacrum, as the classical nations believed—the future life was a mere prolongation of the present; the just man, when he had won his place in it, found himself among his relatives, his friends, his workpeople, with tasks and enjoyments very much like those of earth. The doom of the wicked was annihilation; he fell a victim to the invisible monster called the Eater of the Dead.

Now when the classical nations first began to take an interest in the ideas of the Celts the thing that principally struck them was the Celtic belief in immortality, which the Gauls said was "handed down by the Druids." The classical nations believed in immortality; but what a picture does Homer, the Bible of the Greeks, give of the lost, degraded, dehumanised creatures which represented the departed souls of men! Take, as one example, the description of the spirits of the suitors slain by Odysseus as Hermes conducts them to the Underworld:

[1] Flinders Petrie, "Egypt and Israel," pp. 137, 899.

"Now were summoned the souls of the dead by Cyllenian Hermes. . . .
Touched by the wand they awoke, and obeyed him and followed him, squealing,
Even as bats in the dark, mysterious depths of a cavern
Squeal as they flutter around, should one from the cluster be fallen
Where from the rock suspended they hung, all clinging together;
So did the souls flock squealing behind him, as Hermes the Helper
Guided them down to the gloom through dank and mouldering pathways."[1]

The classical writers felt rightly that the Celtic idea of immortality was something altogether different from this. It was both loftier and more realistic; it implied a true persistence of the living man, as he was at present, in all his human relations. They noted with surprise that the Celt would lend money on a promissory note for repayment in the next world.[2] That is an absolutely Egyptian conception. And this very analogy occurred to Diodorus in writing of the Celtic idea of immortality—it was like nothing that he knew of out of Egypt.[3]

The Doctrine of Transmigration

Many ancient writers assert that the Celtic idea of immortality embodied the Oriental conception of the transmigration of souls, and to account for this the hypothesis was invented that they had learned the doctrine from Pythagoras, who represented it in classical antiquity. Thus Cæsar: "The principal point of their [the Druids'] teaching is that the soul does not perish, and that after death it passes from one body into another." And Diodorus: "Among them the doctrine of Pythagoras prevails, according to which the souls of men are immortal, and after a fixed term recommence

[1] I quote from Mr. H. B. Cotterill's beautiful hexameter version.

[2] Valerius Maximus (about A D 30) and other classical writers mention this practice.

[3] Book V.

to live, taking upon themselves a new body." Now traces of this doctrine certainly do appear in Irish legend. Thus the Irish chieftain, Mongan, who is an historical personage, and whose death is recorded about A.D. 625, is said to have made a wager as to the place of death of a king named Fothad, slain in a battle with the mythical hero Finn mac Cumhal in the third century. He proves his case by summoning to his aid a *revenant* from the Other-world, Keelta, who was the actual slayer of Fothad, and who describes correctly where the tomb is to be found and what were its contents. He begins his tale by saying to Mongan, "We were with thee," and then, turning to the assembly, he continues: "We were with Finn, coming from Alba. . . ." "Hush," says Mongan, "it is wrong of thee to reveal a secret." The secret is, of course, that Mongan was a reincarnation of Finn.[1] But the evidence on the whole shows that the Celts did not hold this doctrine at all in the same way as Pythagoras and the Orientals did. Transmigration was not, with them, part of the order of things. It *might* happen, but in general it did not; the new body assumed by the dead clothed them in another, not in this world, and so far as we can learn from any ancient authority, there does not appear to have been any idea of moral retribution connected with this form of the future life. It was not so much an article of faith as an idea which haunted the imagination, and which, as Mongan's caution indicates, ought not to be brought into clear light.

However it may have been conceived, it is certain that the belief in immortality was the basis of Celtic Druidism.[2] Cæsar affirms this distinctly, and declares

[1] De Jubainville, "Irish Mythological Cycle," p. 191 *sqq.*

[2] The etymology of the word "Druid" is no longer an unsolved problem. It had been suggested that the latter part of the word

the doctrine to have been fostered by the Druids rather for the promotion of courage than for purely religious reasons. An intense Other-world faith, such as that held by the Celts, is certainly one of the mightiest of agencies in the hands of a priesthood who hold the keys of that world. Now Druidism existed in the British Islands, in Gaul, and, in fact, so far as we know, wherever there was a Celtic race amid a population of dolmen-builders. There were Celts in Cisalpine Gaul, but there were no dolmens there, and there were no Druids.[1] What is quite clear is that when the Celts got to Western Europe they found there a people with a powerful priesthood, a ritual, and imposing religious monuments; a people steeped in magic and mysticism and the cult of the Underworld. The inferences, as I read the facts, seem to be that Druidism in its essential features was imposed upon the imaginative and sensitive nature of the Celt—the Celt with his "extraordinary aptitude" for picking up ideas—by the earlier population of Western Europe, the Megalithic People, while, as held by these, it stands in some historical relation, which I am not able to pursue in further detail, with the religious culture of ancient Egypt. Much obscurity still broods over the question, and perhaps will always do so, but if these

might be connected with the Aryan root VID, which appears in "wisdom," in the Latin *videre*, &c., Thurneysen has now shown that this root in combination with the intensive particle *dru* would yield the word *dru-vids*, represented in Gaelic by *draoi*, a Druid, just as another intensive, *su*, with *vids* yields the Gaelic *saoi*, a sage.

1 See Rice Holmes, "Cæsar's Conquest," p. 15, and pp. 532–536. Rhys, it may be observed, believes that Druidism was the religion of the aboriginal inhabitants of Western Europe "from the Baltic to Gibraltar" ("Celtic Britain," p. 73). But we only *know* of it where Celts and dolmen-builders combined. Cæsar remarks of the Germans that they had no Druids and cared little about sacrificial ceremonies.

suggestions have anything in them, then the Megalithic People have been brought a step or two out of the atmosphere of uncanny mystery which has surrounded them, and they are shown to have played a very important part in the religious development of Western Europe, and in preparing that part of the world for the rapid extension of the special type of Christianity which took place in it. Bertrand, in his most interesting chapter on "L'Irlande Celtique,"[1] points out that very soon after the conversion of Ireland to Christianity, we find the country covered with monasteries, whose complete organisation seems to indicate that they were really Druidic colleges transformed *en masse*. Cæsar has told us what these colleges were like in Gaul. They were very numerous. In spite of the severe study and discipline involved, crowds flocked into them for the sake of the power wielded by the Druidic order, and the civil immunities which its members of all grades enjoyed. Arts and sciences were studied there, and thousands of verses enshrining the teachings of Druidism were committed to memory. All this is very like what we know of Irish Druidism. Such an organisation would pass into Christianity of the type established in Ireland with very little difficulty. The belief in magical rites would survive—early Irish Christianity, as its copious hagiography plainly shows, was as steeped in magical ideas as ever was Druidic paganism. The belief in immortality would remain, as before, the cardinal doctrine of religion. Above all the supremacy of the sacerdotal order over the temporal power would remain unimpaired; it would still be true, as Dion Chrysostom said of the Druids, that "it is they who command, and kings on thrones of gold, dwelling in

[1] "Rel. des Gaulois," leçon xx.

splendid palaces, are but their ministers, and the servants of their thought." [1]

Cæsar on the Druidic Culture

The religious, philosophic, and scientific culture superintended by the Druids is spoken of by Cæsar with much respect. "They discuss and impart to the youth," he writes, "many things respecting the stars and their motions, respecting the extent of the universe and of our earth, respecting the nature of things, respecting the power and the majesty of the immortal gods" (bk. vi. 14). We would give much to know some particulars of the teaching here described. But the Druids, though well acquainted with letters, strictly forbade the committal of their doctrines to writing; an extremely sagacious provision, for not only did they thus surround their teaching with that atmosphere of mystery which exercises so potent a spell over the human mind, but they ensured that it could never be effectively controverted.

Human Sacrifices in Gaul

In strange discord, however, with the lofty words of Cæsar stands the abominable practice of human sacrifice whose prevalence he noted among the Celts. Prisoners and criminals, or if these failed even innocent victims, probably children, were encased, numbers at a time, in huge frames of wickerwork, and there burned alive to win the favour of the gods. The practice of human sacrifice is, of course, not specially Druidic—it is found in all parts both of the Old and of the New World at a certain stage of culture, and was doubtless a survival from the time of the Megalithic People. The fact that it should have continued in Celtic lands after an other-

[1] Quoted by Bertrand, *op. cit.* p. 279.

wise fairly high state of civilisation and religious culture had been attained can be paralleled from Mexico and Carthage, and in both cases is due, no doubt, to the uncontrolled dominance of a priestly caste.

Human Sacrifices in Ireland

Bertrand endeavours to dissociate the Druids from these practices, of which he says strangely there is "no trace" in Ireland, although there, as elsewhere in Celtica, Druidism was all-powerful. There is little doubt, however, that in Ireland also human sacrifices at one time prevailed. In a very ancient tract, the "Dinnsenchus," preserved in the "Book of Leinster," it is stated that on Moyslaught, "the Plain of Adoration," there stood a great gold idol, Crom Cruach (the Bloody Crescent). To it the Gaels used to sacrifice children when praying for fair weather and fertility—"it was milk and corn they asked from it in exchange for their children—how great was their horror and their moaning!"[1]

And in Egypt

In Egypt, where the national character was markedly easy-going, pleasure-loving, and little capable of fanatical exaltation, we find no record of any such cruel rites in the monumental inscriptions and paintings, copious as is the information which they give us on all features of the national life and religion.[2] Manetho, indeed, the

[1] "The Irish Mythological Cycle," by d'Arbois de Jubainville, p. 61. The "Dinnsenchus" in question is an early Christian document. No trace of a being like Crom Cruach has been found as yet in the pagan literature of Ireland, nor in the writings of St. Patrick, and I think it is quite probable that even in the time of St. Patrick human sacrifices had become only a memory.

[2] A representation of human sacrifice has, however, lately been discovered in a Temple of the Sun in the ancient Ethiopian capital, Meroë.

Egyptian historian who wrote in the third century B.C., tells us that human sacrifices were abolished by Amasis I. so late as the beginning of the XVIII Dynasty—about 1600 B.C. But the complete silence of the other records shows us that even if we are to believe Manetho, the practice must in historic times have been very rare, and must have been looked on with repugnance.

The Names of Celtic Deities

What were the names and the attributes of the Celtic deities? Here we are very much in the dark. The Megalithic People did not imagine their deities under concrete personal form. Stones, rivers, wells, trees, and other natural objects were to them the adequate symbols, or were half symbols, half actual embodiments, of the supernatural forces which they venerated. But the imaginative mind of the Aryan Celt was not content with this. The existence of personal gods with distinct titles and attributes is reported to us by Cæsar, who equates them with various figures in the Roman pantheon—Mercury, Apollo, Mars, and so forth. Lucan mentions a triad of deities, Æsus, Teutates, and Taranus;[1] and it is noteworthy that in these names we seem to be in presence of a true Celtic, *i.e.*, Aryan, tradition. Thus Æsus is derived by Belloguet from the Aryan root *as*, meaning "to be," which furnished the name of Asura-masda (*l'Esprit Sage*) to the Persians, Æsun to the Umbrians, Asa (Divine Being) to the Scandinavians. Teutates comes from a Celtic root meaning "valiant," "warlike," and indicates

[1] "You [Celts] who by cruel blood outpoured think to appease the pitiless Teutates, the horrid Æsus with his barbarous altars, and Taranus whose worship is no gentler than that of the Scythian Diana," to whom captives were offered up. (Lucan, "Pharsalia," i. 444.) An altar dedicated to Æsus has been discovered in Paris.

a deity equivalent to Mars. Taranus (? Thor), according to de Jubainville, is a god of the Lightning (*taran* in Welsh, Cornish, and Breton is the word for "thunderbolt"). Votive inscriptions to these gods have been found in Gaul and Britain. Other inscriptions and sculptures bear testimony to the existence in Gaul of a host of minor and local deities who are mostly mere names, or not even names, to us now. In the form in which we have them these conceptions bear clear traces of Roman influence. The sculptures are rude copies of the Roman style of religious art. But we meet among them figures of much wilder and stranger aspect—gods with triple faces, gods with branching antlers on their brows, ram-headed serpents, and other now unintelligible symbols of the older faith. Very notable is the frequent occurrence of the cross-legged "Buddha" attitude so prevalent in the religious art of the East and of Mexico, and also the tendency, so well known in Egypt, to group the gods in triads.

Cæsar on the Celtic Deities

Cæsar, who tries to fit the Gallic religion into the framework of Roman mythology—which was exactly what the Gauls themselves did after the conquest—says they held Mercury to be the chief of the gods, and looked upon him as the inventor of all the arts, as the presiding deity of commerce, and as the guardian of roads and guide of travellers. One may conjecture that he was particularly, to the Gauls as to the Romans, the guide of the dead, of travellers to the Other-world, Many bronze statues to Mercury, of Gaulish origin. still remain, the name being adopted by the Gauls, as many place-names still testify.[1] Apollo was regarded

[1] Mont Mercure, Mercœur, Mercoirey, Montmartre (*Mons Mercurii*), &c.

as the deity of medicine and healing, Minerva was the initiator of arts and crafts, Jupiter governed the sky, and Mars presided over war. Cæsar is here, no doubt, classifying under five types and by Roman names a large number of Gallic divinities.

The God of the Underworld

According to Cæsar, a most notable deity of the Gauls was (in Roman nomenclature) Dis, or Pluto, the god of the Underworld inhabited by the dead. From him all the Gauls claimed to be descended, and on this account, says Cæsar, they began their reckoning of the twenty-four hours of the day with the oncoming of night.[1] The name of this deity is not given. D'Arbois de Jubainville considers that, together with Æsus, Teutates, Taranus, and, in Irish mythology, Balor and the Fomorians, he represents the powers of darkness, death, and evil, and Celtic mythology is thus interpreted as a variant of the universal solar myth, embodying the conception of the eternal conflict between Day and Night.

The God of Light

The God of Light appears in Gaul and in Ireland as Lugh, or Lugus, who has left his traces in many place-names such as *Lug-dunum* (Leyden), Lyons, &c. Lugh appears in Irish legend with distinctly solar attributes. When he meets his army before the great conflict with the Fomorians, they feel, says the saga, as if they beheld the rising of the sun. Yet he is also, as we shall see, a god of the Underworld, belonging on the side of his mother Ethlinn, daughter of Balor, to the Powers of Darkness.

[1] To this day in many parts of France the peasantry use terms like *annuit*, *o'né*, *anneue*, &c., all meaning "to-night," for *aujourd'hui* (Bertrand, "Rel. des G.," p. 356).

FACTORS IN ANCIENT CELTIC CULTURE

The Celtic Conception of Death

The fact is that the Celtic conception of the realm of death differed altogether from that of the Greeks and Romans, and, as I have already pointed out, resembled that of Egyptian religion. The Other-world was not a place of gloom and suffering, but of light and liberation. The Sun was as much the god of that world as he was or this. Evil, pain, and gloom there were, no doubt, and no doubt these principles were embodied by the Irish Celts in their myths of Balor and the Fomorians, of which we shall hear anon; but that they were particularly associated with the idea of death is, I think, a false supposition founded on misleading analogies drawn from the ideas of the classical nations. Here the Celts followed North African or Asiatic conceptions rather than those of the Aryans of Europe. It is only by realising that the Celts as we know them in history, from the break-up of the Mid-European Celtic empire onwards, formed a singular blend of Aryan with non-Aryan characteristics, that we shall arrive at a true understanding of their contribution to European history and their influence in European culture.

The Five Factors in Ancient Celtic Culture

To sum up the conclusions indicated: we can, I think, distinguish five distinct factors in the religious and intellectual culture of Celtic lands as we find them prior to the influx of classical or of Christian influences. First, we have before us a mass of popular superstitions and of magical observances, including human sacrifice. These varied more or less from place to place, centring as they did largely on local features which were regarded as embodiments or vehicles of divine or of diabolic power. Secondly, there was certainly in existence a thoughtful and philosophic creed, having as its central object of worship the Sun, as an emblem of divine power and constancy, and as its central doctrine the immortality of the soul. Thirdly, there was a worship of personified deities, Æsus, Teutates, Lugh, and others, conceived as representing natural forces, or as guardians of social laws. Fourthly, the Romans were deeply impressed with the existence among the Druids of a body of teaching of a quasi-scientific nature about natural phenomena and the constitution of the universe, of the details of which we unfortunately know practically nothing. Lastly, we have to note the prevalence of a sacerdotal organisation, which administered the whole system of religious and of secular learning and literature,[1] which carefully confined this learning to a privileged caste, and which, by virtue of its intellectual supremacy and of the atmosphere of religious awe with which it was surrounded, became the sovran power, social, political, and religious, in every Celtic country. I have spoken of these elements as distinct, and we can, indeed, distinguish them in thought, but in practice they were inextricably intertwined, and the Druidic organisation pervaded and ordered all. Can we now, it may be asked, distinguish among them what is of Celtic and what of pre-Celtic and probably non-Aryan origin? This is a more difficult task; yet, looking at all the analogies and probabilities, I think we shall not be far wrong in assigning to the Megalithic People the special doctrines, the ritual, and the sacerdotal organisation of Druidism, and to the Celtic element the personified deities, with the zest for learning and for speculation; while the popular superstitions were merely the local form assumed by conceptions as widespread as the human race.

[1] The *fili*, or professional poets, it must be remembered, were a branch of the Druidic order.

The Celts of To-day

In view of the undeniably mixed character of the populations called "Celtic" at the present day, it is often urged that this designation has no real relation to any ethnological fact. The Celts who fought with Cæsar in Gaul and with the English in Ireland are, it is said, no more—they have perished on a thousand battlefields from Alesia to the Boyne, and an older racial stratum has come to the surface in their place. The true Celts, according to this view, are only to be found in the tall, ruddy Highlanders of Perthshire and North-west Scotland, and in a few families of the old ruling race still surviving in Ireland and in Wales. In all this I think it must be admitted that there is a large measure of truth. Yet it must not be forgotten that the descendants of the Megalithic People at the present day are, on the physical side, deeply impregnated with Celtic blood, and on the spiritual with Celtic traditions and ideals. Nor, again, in discussing these questions of race-character and its origin, must it ever be assumed that the character of a people can be analysed as one analyses a chemical compound, fixing once for all its constituent parts and determining its future behaviour and destiny. Race-character, potent and enduring though it be, is not a dead thing, cast in an iron mould, and thereafter incapable of change and growth. It is part of the living forces of the world; it is plastic and vital; it has hidden potencies which a variety of causes, such as a felicitous cross with a different, but not too different, stock, or—in another sphere—the adoption of a new religious or social ideal, may at any time unlock and bring into action.

Of one thing I personally feel convinced—that the problem of the ethical, social, and intellectual development of the people constituting what is called the

"Celtic Fringe" in Europe ought to be worked for on Celtic lines; by the maintenance of the Celtic tradition, Celtic literature, Celtic speech—the encouragement, in short, of all those Celtic affinities of which this mixed race is now the sole conscious inheritor and guardian. To these it will respond, by these it can be deeply moved; nor has the harvest ever failed those who with courage and faith have driven their plough into this rich field. On the other hand, if this work is to be done with success it must be done in no pedantic, narrow, intolerant spirit; there must be no clinging to the outward forms of the past simply because the Celtic spirit once found utterance in them. Let it be remembered that in the early Middle Ages Celts from Ireland were the most notable explorers, the most notable pioneers of religion, science, and speculative thought in Europe.[1] Modern investigators have traced their footprints of light over half the heathen continent, and the schools of Ireland were thronged with foreign pupils who could get learning nowhere else. The Celtic spirit was then playing its true part in the world-drama, and a greater it has never played. The legacy of these men should be cherished indeed, but not as a museum curiosity; nothing could be more opposed to their free, bold, adventurous spirit than to let that legacy petrify in the hands of those who claim the heirship of their name and fame.

The Mythical Literature

After the sketch contained in this and the foregoing chapter of the early history of the Celts, and of the forces

[1] For instance, Pelagius in the fifth century; Columba, Columbanus, and St. Gall in the sixth; Fridolin, named *Viator*, "the Traveller," and Fursa in the seventh; Virgilius (Feargal) of Salzburg, who had to answer at Rome for teaching the sphericity of the earth, in the eighth; Dicuil, "the Geographer," and Johannes Scotus Erigena—the master mind of his epoch—in the ninth.

which have moulded it, we shall now turn to give an account of the mythical and legendary literature in which their spirit most truly lives and shines. We shall not here concern ourselves with any literature which is not Celtic. With all that other peoples have made—as in the Arthurian legends—of myths and tales originally Celtic, we have here nothing to do. No one can now tell how much is Celtic in them and how much is not. And in matters of this kind it is generally the final recasting that is of real importance and value. Whatever we give, then, we give without addition or reshaping. Stories, of course, have often to be summarised, but there shall be nothing in them that did not come direct from the Celtic mind, and that does not exist to-day in some variety, Gaelic or Cymric, of the Celtic tongue.

CHAPTER III: THE IRISH INVASION MYTHS

The Celtic Cosmogony

AMONG those secret doctrines about the "nature of things" which, as Cæsar tells us, the Druids never would commit to writing, was there anything in the nature of a cosmogony, any account of the origin of the world and of man? There surely was. It would be strange indeed if, alone among the races of the world, the Celts had no world-myth. The spectacle of the universe with all its vast and mysterious phenomena in heaven and on earth has aroused, first the imagination, afterwards the speculative reason, in every people which is capable of either. The Celts had both in abundance, yet, except for that one phrase about the "indestructibility" of the world handed down to us by Strabo, we know nothing of their early imaginings or their reasonings on this subject. Ireland possesses a copious legendary literature. All of this, no doubt, assumed its present form in Christian times; yet so much essential paganism has been allowed to remain in it that it would be strange if Christian influences had led to the excision of everything in these ancient texts that pointed to a non-Christian conception of the origin of things—if Christian editors and transmitters had never given us even the least glimmer of the existence of such a conception. Yet the fact is that they do not give it; there is nothing in the most ancient legendary literature of the Irish Gaels, which is the oldest Celtic literature in existence, corresponding to the Babylonian conquest of Chaos, or the wild Norse myth of the making of Midgard out of the corpse of Ymir, or the Egyptian creation of the universe out of the primeval Water by Thoth, the Word of God, or even to the primitive folk-lore conceptions found in almost every savage tribe. That the Druids had some doctrine on this subject it is impossible to doubt. But, by resolutely confining it to the initiated and forbidding all lay speculation on the subject, they seem to have completely stifled the myth-making instinct in regard to questions of cosmogony among the people at large, and ensured that when their own order perished, their teaching, whatever it was, should die with them.

In the early Irish accounts, therefore, of the beginnings of things, we find that it is not with the World that the narrators make their start—it is simply with their own country, with Ireland. It was the practice, indeed, to prefix to these narratives of early invasions and colonisations the Scriptural account of the making of the world and man, and this shows that something of the kind was felt to be required; but what took the place of the Biblical narrative in pre-Christian days we do not know, and, unfortunately, are now never likely to know.

The Cycles of Irish Legend

Irish mythical and legendary literature, as we have it in the most ancient form, may be said to fall into four main divisions, and to these we shall adhere in our presentation of it in this volume. They are, in chronological order, the Mythological Cycle, or Cycle of the Invasions, the Ultonian or Conorian Cycle, the Ossianic or Fenian Cycle, and a multitude of miscellaneous tales and legends which it is hard to fit into any historical framework.

The Mythological Cycle

The Mythological Cycle comprises the following sections:

1. The coming of Partholan into Ireland.
2. The coming of Nemed into Ireland.
3. The coming of the Firbolgs into Ireland.
4. The invasion of the *Tuatha De Danann*, or People of the god Dana.
5. The invasion of the Milesians (Sons of Miled) from Spain, and their conquest of the People of Dana.

With the Milesians we begin to come into something resembling history—they represent, in Irish legend, the Celtic race; and from them the ruling families of Ireland are supposed to be descended. The People of Dana are evidently gods. The pre-Danaan settlers or invaders are huge phantom-like figures, which loom vaguely through the mists of tradition, and have little definite characterisation. The accounts which are given of them are many and conflicting, and out of these we can only give here the more ancient narratives.

The Coming of Partholan

The Celts, as we have learned from Cæsar, believed themselves to be descended from the God of the Underworld, the God of the Dead. Partholan is said to have come into Ireland from the West, where beyond the vast, unsailed Atlantic Ocean the Irish Fairyland, the Land of the Living—*i.e.*, the land of the Happy Dead—was placed. His father's name was Sera (? the West). He came with his queen Dalny[1] and a number of companions of both sexes. Ireland—and this is an imaginative touch intended to suggest extreme antiquity—was then a different country, physically, from what it is now. There were then but three lakes in Ireland, nine rivers, and only one plain. Others were added gradually

[1] Dealgnaid. I have been obliged here, as occasionally elsewhere, to modify the Irish names so as to make them pronounceable by English readers.

St. Finnen and the Pagan Chief

Tuan watches Nemed

during the reign of the Partholanians. One, Lake Rury, was said to have burst out as a grave was being dug for Rury, son of Partholan.

The Fomorians

The Partholanians, it is said, had to do battle with a strange race, called the Fomorians, of whom we shall hear much in later sections of this book. They were a huge, misshapen, violent and cruel people, representing, we may believe, the powers of evil. One of these was surnamed *Cenchos*, which means The Footless, and thus appears to be related to Vitra, the God of Evil in Vedantic mythology, who had neither feet nor hands. With a host of these demons Partholan fought for the lordship of Ireland, and drove them out to the northern seas, whence they occasionally harried the country under its later rulers.

The end of the race of Partholan was that they were afflicted by pestilence, and having gathered together on the Old Plain (Senmag) for convenience of burying their dead, they all perished there; and Ireland once more lay empty for reoccupation.

The Legend of Tuan mac Carell

Who, then, told the tale? This brings us to the mention of a very curious and interesting legend—one of the numerous legendary narratives in which these tales of the Mythical Period have come down to us. It is found in the so-called "Book of the Dun Cow," a manuscript of about the year A.D. 1100, and is entitled "The Legend of Tuan mac Carell."

St. Finnen, an Irish abbot of the sixth century, is said to have gone to seek hospitality from a chief named Tuan mac Carell, who dwelt not far from Finnen's monastery at Moville, Co. Donegal. Tuan refused him admittance. The saint sat down on the doorstep of the chief and fasted for a whole Sunday,[1] upon which the surly pagan warrior opened the door to him. Good relations were established between them, and the saint returned to his monks.

"Tuan is an excellent man," said he to them; "he will come to you and comfort you, and tell you the old stories of Ireland."[2]

This humane interest in the old myths and legends of the country is, it may here be observed, a feature as constant as it is pleasant in the literature of early Irish Christianity.

Tuan came shortly afterwards to return the visit of the saint, and invited him and his disciples to his fortress. They asked him of his name and lineage, and he gave an astounding reply. "I am a man of Ulster," he said. "My name is Tuan son of Carell. But once I was called Tuan son of Starn, son of Sera, and my father, Starn, was the brother of Partholan."

"Tell us the history of Ireland," then said Finnen, and Tuan began. Partholan, he said, was the first of men to settle in Ireland. After the great pestilence already narrated he alone survived, "for there is never a slaughter that one man does not come out of it to tell the tale." Tuan was alone in the land, and he wandered about from one vacant fortress to another, from rock to rock, seeking shelter from the wolves. For twenty-two years he lived thus alone, dwelling in waste places, till at last he fell into extreme decrepitude and old age.

"Then Nemed son of Agnoman took possession of Ireland. He [Agnoman] was my father's brother. I

[1] See p. 48, *note* 1.

[2] I follow in this narrative R. I. Best's translation of the "Irish Mythological Cycle" of d'Arbois de Jubainville.

saw him from the cliffs, and kept avoiding him. I was long-haired, clawed, decrepit, grey, naked, wretched, miserable. Then one evening I fell asleep, and when I woke again on the morrow I was changed into a stag. I was young again and glad of heart. Then I sang of the coming of Nemed and of his race, and of my own transformation. . . . 'I have put on a new form, a skin rough and grey. Victory and joy are easy to me; a little while ago I was weak and defenceless.'"

Tuan is then king of all the deer of Ireland, and so remained all the days of Nemed and his race.

He tells how the Nemedians sailed for Ireland in a fleet of thirty-two barks, in each bark thirty persons. They went astray on the seas for a year and a half, and most of them perished of hunger and thirst or of shipwreck. Nine only escaped—Nemed himself, with four men and four women. These landed in Ireland, and increased their numbers in the course of time till they were 8060 men and women. Then all of them mysteriously died.

Again old age and decrepitude fell upon Tuan, but another transformation awaited him. "Once I was standing at the mouth of my cave—I still remember it —and I knew that my body changed into another form. I was a wild boar. And I sang this song about it:

> "'To-day I am a boar. . . . Time was when I sat in the assembly that gave the judgments of Partholan. It was sung, and all praised the melody. How pleasant was the strain of my brilliant judgment! How pleasant to the comely young women! My chariot went along in majesty and beauty. My voice was grave and sweet. My step was swift and firm in battle. My face was full of charm. To-day, lo! I am changed into a black boar.'

"That is what I said. Yea, of a surety I was a wild boar. Then I became young again, and I was glad. I was king of the boar-herds in Ireland; and, faithful to any custom, I went the rounds of my abode when I returned into the lands of Ulster, at the times old age and wretchedness came upon me. For it was always there that my transformations took place, and that is why I went back thither to await the renewal of my body."

Tuan then goes on to tell how Semion son of Stariat settled in Ireland, from whom descended the Firbolgs and two other tribes who persisted into historic times. Again old age comes on, his strength fails him, and he undergoes another transformation; he becomes "a great eagle of the sea," and once more rejoices in renewed youth and vigour. He then tells how the People of Dana came in, "gods and false gods from whom every one knows the Irish men of learning are sprung." After these came the Sons of Miled, who conquered the People of Dana. All this time Tuan kept the shape of the sea-eagle, till one day, finding himself about to undergo another transformation, he fasted nine days; "then sleep fell upon me, and I was changed into a salmon." He rejoices in his new life, escaping for many years the snares of the fishermen, till at last he is captured by one of them and brought to the wife of Carell, chief of the country. "The woman desired me and ate me by herself, whole, so that I passed into her womb." He is born again, and passes for Tuan son of Carell; but the memory of his pre-existence and all his transformations and all the history of Ireland that he witnessed since the days of Partholan still abides with him, and he teaches all these things to the Christian monks, who carefully preserve them.

This wild tale, with its atmosphere of grey antiquity and of childlike wonder, reminds us of the transformations of the Welsh Taliessin, who also became an eagle, and points to that doctrine of the transmigration of the soul which, as we have seen, haunted the imagination of the Celt.

We have now to add some details to the sketch of the successive colonisations of Ireland outlined by Tuan mac Carell.

The Nemedians

The Nemedians, as we have seen, were akin to the Partholanians. Both of them came from the mysterious regions of the dead, though later Irish accounts, which endeavoured to reconcile this mythical matter with Christianity, invented for them a descent from Scriptural patriarchs and an origin in earthly lands such as Spain or Scythia. Both of them had to do constant battle with the Fomorians, whom the later legends make out to be pirates from oversea, but who are doubtless divinities representing the powers of darkness and evil. There is no legend of the Fomorians coming into Ireland, nor were they regarded as at any time a regular portion of the population. They were coeval with the world itself. Nemed fought victoriously against them in four great battles, but shortly afterwards died of a plague which carried off 2000 of his people with him. The Fomorians were then enabled to establish their tyranny over Ireland. They had at this period two kings, Morc and Conann. The stronghold of the Formorian power was on Tory Island, which uplifts its wild cliffs and precipices in the Atlantic off the coast of Donegal—a fit home for this race of mystery and horror. They extracted a crushing tribute from the people of Ireland, two-thirds of all the milk and two-thirds of the children of the land. At last the Nemedians rise in revolt. Led by three chiefs, they land on Tory Island, capture Conann's Tower, and Conann himself falls by the hand of the Nemedian chief, Fergus. But Morc at this moment comes into the battle with a fresh host, and utterly routs the Nemedians, who are all slain but thirty:

> "The men of Erin were all at the battle,
> After the Fomorians came;
> All of them the sea engulphed,
> Save only three times ten."
>
> *Poem by Eochy O'Flann, circ.* A.D. 960.

The thirty survivors leave Ireland in despair. According to the most ancient belief they perished utterly, leaving no descendants, but later accounts, which endeavour to make sober history out of all these myths, represent one family, that of the chief Britan, as settling in Great Britain and giving their name to that country, while two others returned to Ireland, after many wanderings, as the Firbolgs and People of Dana.

The Coming of the Firbolgs

Who were the Firbolgs, and what did they represent in Irish legend? The name appears to mean "Men of the Bags," and a legend was in later times invented to account for it. It was said that after settling in Greece they were oppressed by the people of that country, who set them to carry earth from the fertile valleys up to the rocky hills, so as to make arable ground of the latter. They did their task by means of leathern bags; but at last, growing weary of the oppression, they made boats or coracles out of their bags, and set sail in them for Ireland. Nennius, however, says they came from Spain, for according to him all the various races that inhabited Ireland came originally from Spain; and "Spain" with him is a rationalistic rendering of the Celtic words designating the Land of the Dead.[1] They came in three

[1] De Jubainville, "Irish Mythological Cycle," p. 75.

groups, the Fir-Bolg, the Fir-Domnan, and the Galioin, who are all generally designated as Firbolgs. They play no great part in Irish mythical history, and a certain character of servility and inferiority appears to attach to them throughout.

One of their kings, Eochy[1] mac Erc, took in marriage Taltiu, or Telta, daughter of the King of the "Great Plain" (the Land of the Dead). Telta had a palace at the place now called after her, Telltown (properly Teltin). There she died, and there, even in mediæval Ireland, a great annual assembly or fair was held in her honour.

The Coming of the People of Dana

We now come to by far the most interesting and important of the mythical invaders and colonisers of Ireland, the People of Dana. The name, *Tuatha De Danann*, means literally "the folk of the god whose mother is Dana." Dana also sometimes bears another name, that of Brigit, a goddess held in much honour by pagan Ireland, whose attributes are in a great measure transferred in legend to the Christian St. Brigit of the sixth century. Her name is also found in Gaulish inscriptions as "Brigindo," and occurs in several British inscriptions as "Brigantia." She was the daughter of the supreme head of the People of Dana, the god Dagda, "The Good." She had three sons, who are said to have had in common one only son, named Ecne—that is to say, "Knowledge," or "Poetry."[2] Ecne, then, may be said to be the god whose mother was Dana, and the race to whom she gave her name are the clearest representatives we have in Irish myths of

[1] Pronounced "Yeo'hee." See Glossary for this and other words.

[2] The science of the Druids, as we have seen, was conveyed in verse, and the professional poets were a branch of the Druidic Order.

the powers of Light and Knowledge. It will be remembered that alone among all these mythical races Tuan mac Carell gave to the People of Dana the name of "gods." Yet it is not as gods that they appear in the form in which Irish legends about them have now come down to us. Christian influences reduced them to the rank of fairies or identified them with the fallen angels. They were conquered by the Milesians, who are conceived as an entirely human race, and who had all sorts of relations of love and war with them until quite recent times. Yet even in the later legends a certain splendour and exaltation appears to invest the People of Dana, recalling the high estate from which they had been dethroned.

The Popular and the Bardic Conceptions

Nor must it be overlooked that the popular conception of the Danaan deities was probably at all times something different from the bardic and Druidic, or in other words the scholarly, conception. The latter, as we shall see, represents them as the presiding deities of science and poetry. This is not a popular idea; it is the product of the Celtic, the Aryan imagination, inspired by a strictly intellectual conception. The common people, who represented mainly the Megalithic element in the population, appear to have conceived their deities as earth-powers—*dei terreni*, as they are explicitly called in the eighth-century "Book of Armagh"[1]—presiding, not over science and poetry, but rather agriculture, controlling the fecundity of the earth and water, and dwelling in hills, rivers, and lakes. In the bardic literature the Aryan idea is prominent; the other is to be found in innumerable folk-tales and popular observances; but of course in each case a considerable amount

[1] Meyer and Nutt, "Voyage of Bran," ii. 197.

of interpenetration of the two conceptions is to be met with—no sharp dividing line was drawn between them in ancient times, and none can be drawn now.

The Treasures of the Danaans

Tuan mac Carell says they came to Ireland "out of heaven." This is embroidered in later tradition into a narrative telling how they sprang from four great cities, whose very names breathe of fairydom and romance—Falias, Gorias, Finias, and Murias. Here they learned science and craftsmanship from great sages one of whom was enthroned in each city, and from each they brought with them a magical treasure. From Falias came the stone called the *Lia Fail*, or Stone of Destiny, on which the High-Kings of Ireland stood when they were crowned, and which was supposed to confirm the election of a rightful monarch by roaring under him as he took his place on it. The actual stone which was so used at the inauguration of a reign did from immemorial times exist at Tara, and was sent thence to Scotland early in the sixth century for the crowning of Fergus the Great, son of Erc, who begged his brother Murtagh mac Erc, King of Ireland, for the loan of it. An ancient prophecy told that wherever this stone was, a king of the Scotic (*i.e.*, Irish-Milesian) race should reign. This is the famous Stone of Scone, which never came back to Ireland, but was removed to England by Edward I. in 1297, and is now the Coronation Stone in Westminster Abbey. Nor has the old prophecy been falsified, since through the Stuarts and Fergus mac Erc the descent of the British royal family can be traced from the historic kings of Milesian Ireland.

The second treasure of the Danaans was the invincible sword of Lugh of the Long Arm, of whom we shall hear later, and this sword came from the city of

Gorias. From Finias came a magic spear, and from Murias the Cauldron of the Dagda, a vessel which had the property that it could feed a host of men without ever being emptied.

With these possessions, according to the version given in the "Book of Invasions," the People of Dana came into Ireland.

The Danaans and the Firbolgs

They were wafted into the land in a magic cloud, making their first appearance in Western Connacht. When the cloud cleared away, the Firbolgs discovered them in a camp which they had already fortified at Moyrein.

The Firbolgs now sent out one of their warriors, named Sreng, to interview the mysterious new-comers; and the People of Dana, on their side, sent a warrior named Bres to represent them. The two ambassadors examined each other's weapons with great interest. The spears of the Danaans, we are told, were light and sharp-pointed; those of the Firbolgs were heavy and blunt. To contrast the power of science with that of brute force is here the evident intention of the legend, and we are reminded of the Greek myth of the struggle of the Olympian deities with the Titans.

Bres proposed to the Firbolg that the two races should divide Ireland equally between them, and join to defend it against all comers for the future. They then exchanged weapons and returned each to his own camp.

The First Battle of Moytura

The Firbolgs, however, were not impressed with the superiority of the Danaans, and decided to refuse their offer. The battle was joined on the Plain of Moytura,[1]

[1] "Moytura" means "The Plain of the Towers"—*i.e.*, sepulchral monuments.

The Two Ambassadors

" Sawan gave the cow's halter to the boy "

in the south of Co. Mayo, near the spot now called Cong. The Firbolgs were led by their king, mac Erc, and the Danaans by Nuada of the Silver Hand, who got his name from an incident in this battle. His hand, it is said, was cut off in the fight, and one of the skilful artificers who abounded in the ranks of the Danaans made him a new one of silver. By their magical and healing arts the Danaans gained the victory, and the Firbolg king was slain. But a reasonable agreement followed: the Firbolgs were allotted the province of Connacht for their territory, while the Danaans took the rest of Ireland. So late as the seventeenth century the annalist Mac Firbis discovered that many of the inhabitants of Connacht traced their descent to these same Firbolgs. Probably they were a veritable historic race, and the conflict between them and the People of Dana may be a piece of actual history invested with some of the features of a myth.

The Expulsion of King Bres

Nuada of the Silver Hand should now have been ruler of the Danaans, but his mutilation forbade it, for no blemished man might be a king in Ireland. The Danaans therefore chose Bres, who was the son of a Danaan woman named Eri, but whose father was unknown, to reign over them instead. This was another Bres, not the envoy who had treated with the Firbolgs and who was slain in the battle of Moytura. Now Bres, although strong and beautiful to look on, had no gift of kingship, for he not only allowed the enemy of Ireland, the Fomorians, to renew their oppression and taxation in the land, but he himself taxed his subjects heavily too; and was so niggardly that he gave no hospitality to chiefs and nobles and harpers. Lack of generosity and hospitality was always reckoned the worst of vices in an Irish prince. One day it is said that there came to his court the poet Corpry, who found himself housed in a small, dark chamber without fire or furniture, where, after long delay, he was served with three dry cakes and no ale. In revenge he composed a satirical quatrain on his churlish host:

> "Without food quickly served,
> Without a cow's milk, whereon a calf can grow,
> Without a dwelling fit for a man under the gloomy night,
> Without means to entertain a bardic company,—
> Let such be the condition of Bres."

Poetic satire in Ireland was supposed to have a kind of magical power. Kings dreaded it; even rats could be exterminated by it.[1] This quatrain of Corpry's was repeated with delight among the people, and Bres had to lay down his sovranty. This was said to be the first satire ever made in Ireland. Meantime, because Nuada had got his silver hand through the art of his physician Diancecht, or because, as some versions of the legend say, a still greater healer, the son of Diancecht, had made the veritable hand grow again to the stump, he was chosen to be king in place of Bres.

The latter now betook himself in wrath and resentment to his mother Eri, and begged her to give him counsel and to tell him of his lineage. Eri then declared to him that his father was Elatha, a king of the Fomorians, who had come to her secretly from over sea, and when he departed had given her a ring, bidding her never bestow it on any man save him whose finger it would fit. She now brought forth the ring, and it fitted the finger of Bres, who went

[1] Shakespeare alludes to this in "As You Like It." "I never was so be-rhymed," says Rosalind, "since Pythagoras' time, that I was an Irish rat—which I can hardly remember."

down with her to the strand where the Fomorian lover had landed, and they sailed together for his father's home.

The Tyranny of the Fomorians

Elatha recognised the ring, and gave his son an army wherewith to reconquer Ireland, and also sent him to seek further aid from the greatest of the Fomorian kings, Balor. Now Balor was surnamed "of the Evil Eye," because the gaze of his one eye could slay like a thunderbolt those on whom he looked in anger. He was now, however, so old and feeble that the vast eyelid drooped over the death-dealing eye, and had to be lifted up by his men with ropes and pulleys when the time came to turn it on his foes. Nuada could make no more head against him than Bres had done when king; and the country still groaned under the oppression of the Fomorians and longed for a champion and redeemer.

The Coming of Lugh

A new figure now comes into the myth, no other than Lugh son of Kian, the Sun-god *par excellence* of all Celtica, whose name we can still identify in many historic sites on the Continent.[1] To explain his appearance we must desert for a moment the ancient manuscript authorities, which are here incomplete, and have to be supplemented by a folk-tale which was fortunately discovered and taken down orally so late as the nineteenth century by the great Irish antiquary, O'Donovan.[2]

[1] Lyons, Leyden, Laon were all in ancient times known as *Lug-dunum*, the Fortress of Lugh. *Luguvallum* was the name of a town near Hadrian's Wall in Roman Britain.

[2] It is given by him in a note to the "Four Masters," vol. i. p. 18, and is also reproduced by de Jubainville.

In this folk-tale the names of Balor and his daughter Ethlinn (the latter in the form "Ethnea") are preserved, as well as those of some other mythical personages, but that of the father of Lugh is faintly echoed in MacKineely; Lugh's own name is forgotten, and the death of Balor is given in a manner inconsistent with the ancient myth. In the story as I give it here the antique names and mythical outline are preserved, but are supplemented where required from the folk-tale, omitting from the latter those modern features which are not reconcilable with the myth.

The story, then, goes that Balor, the Fomorian king, heard in a Druidic prophecy that he would be slain by his grandson. His only child was an infant daughter named Ethlinn. To avert the doom he, like Acrisios, father of Danae, in the Greek myth, had her imprisoned in a high tower which he caused to be built on a precipitous headland, the Tor Mŏr, in Tory Island. He placed the girl in charge of twelve matrons, who were strictly charged to prevent her from ever seeing the face of man, or even learning that there were any beings of a different sex from her own. In this seclusion Ethlinn grew up—as all sequestered princesses do—into a maiden of surpassing beauty.

Now it happened that there were on the mainland three brothers, namely, Kian, Sawan, and Goban the Smith, the great armourer and artificer of Irish myth, who corresponds to Wayland Smith in Germanic legend. Kian had a magical cow, whose milk was so abundant that every one longed to possess her, and he had to keep her strictly under protection.

Balor determined to possess himself of this cow. One day Kian and Sawan had come to the forge to have some weapons made for them, bringing fine steel for that purpose. Kian went into the forge, leaving

Sawan in charge of the cow. Balor now appeared on the scene, taking on himself the form of a little red-headed boy, and told Sawan that he had overheard the brothers inside the forge concocting a plan for using all the fine steel for their own swords, leaving but common metal for that of Sawan. The latter, in a great rage, gave the cow's halter to the boy and rushed into the forge to put a stop to this nefarious scheme. Balor immediately carried off the cow, and dragged her across the sea to Tory Island.

Kian now determined to avenge himself on Balor, and to this end sought the advice of a Druidess named Birōg. Dressing himself in woman's garb, he was wafted by magical spells across the sea, where Birōg, who accompanied him, represented to Ethlinn's guardians that they were two noble ladies cast upon the shore in escaping from an abductor, and begged for shelter. They were admitted; Kian found means to have access to the Princess Ethlinn while the matrons were laid by Birōg under the spell of an enchanted slumber, and when they awoke Kian and the Druidess had vanished as they came. But Ethlinn had given Kian her love, and soon her guardians found that she was with child. Fearing Balor's wrath, the matrons persuaded her that the whole transaction was but a dream, and said nothing about it; but in due time Ethlinn was delivered of three sons at a birth.

News of this event came to Balor, and in anger and fear he commanded the three infants to be drowned in a whirlpool off the Irish coast. The messenger who was charged with this command rolled up the children in a sheet, but in carrying them to the appointed place the pin of the sheet came loose, and one of the children dropped out and fell into a little bay, called to this day *Port na Delig*, or the Haven of the Pin. The other two were duly drowned, and the servant reported his mission accomplished.

But the child who had fallen into the bay was guarded by the Druidess, who wafted it to the home of its father, Kian, and Kian gave it in fosterage to his brother the smith, who taught the child his own trade and made it skilled in every manner of craft and handiwork. This child was Lugh. When he was grown to a youth the Danaans placed him in charge of Duach, "The Dark," king of the Great Plain (Fairyland, or the "Land of the Living," which is also the Land of the Dead), and here he dwelt till he reached manhood.

Lugh was, of course, the appointed redeemer of the Danaan people from their servitude. His coming is narrated in a story which brings out the solar attributes of universal power, and shows him, like Apollo, as the presiding deity of all human knowledge and of all artistic and medicinal skill. He came, it is told, to take service with Nuada of the Silver Hand, and when the doorkeeper at the royal palace of Tara asked him what he could do, he answered that he was a carpenter.

"We are in no need of a carpenter," said the doorkeeper; "we have an excellent one in Luchta son of Luchad." "I am a smith too," said Lugh. "We have a master-smith," said the doorkeeper, "already." "Then I am a warrior," said Lugh. "We do not need one," said the doorkeeper, "while we have Ogma." Lugh goes on to name all the occupations and arts he can think of—he is a poet, a harper, a man of science, a physician, a spencer, and so forth, always receiving the answer that a man of supreme accomplishment in that art is already installed at the court of Nuada. "Then ask the King," said Lugh, "if he has in his service any one man who is accomplished in every one of these arts, and if he have, I shall stay here no longer, nor seek to enter his palace." Upon this Lugh is received, and the surname Ildánach is conferred upon him, meaning "The All-Craftsman," Prince of all the Sciences; while another name that he commonly bore was Lugh Lamfada, or Lugh of the Long Arm. We are reminded here, as de Jubainville points out, of the Gaulish god whom Cæsar identifies with Mercury, "inventor of all the arts," and to whom the Gauls put up many statues. The Irish myth supplements this information and tells us the Celtic name of this deity.

When Lugh came from the Land of the Living he brought with him many magical gifts. There was the Boat of Mananan, son of Lir the Sea God, which knew a man's thoughts and would travel whithersoever he would, and the Horse of Mananan, that could go alike over land and sea, and a terrible sword named *Fragarach* ("The Answerer"), that could cut through any mail. So equipped, he appeared one day before an assembly of the Danaan chiefs who were met to pay their tribute to the envoys of the Fomorian oppressors; and when the Danaans saw him, they felt, it is said, as if they beheld the rising of the sun on a dry summer's day. Instead of paying the tribute, they, under Lugh's leadership, attacked the Fomorians, all of whom were slain but nine men, and these were sent back to tell Balor that the Danaans defied him and would pay no tribute henceforward. Balor then made him ready for battle, and bade his captains, when they had subdued the Danaans, make fast the island by cables to their ships and tow it far northward to the Fomorian regions of ice and gloom, where it would trouble them no longer.

The Quest of the Sons of Turenn

Lugh, on his side, also prepared for the final combat; but to ensure victory certain magical instruments were still needed for him, and these had now to be obtained. The story of the quest of these objects, which incidentally tells us also of the end of Lugh's father, Kian, is one of the most valuable and curious in Irish legend, and formed one of a triad of mythical tales which were reckoned as the flower of Irish romance.[1]

Kian, the story goes, was sent northward by Lugh to summon the fighting men of the Danaans in Ulster to the hosting against the Fomorians. On his way, as he crosses the Plain of Murthemney, near Dundalk, he meets with three brothers, Brian, Iuchar, and Iucharba, sons of Turenn, between whose house and that of Kian there was a blood-feud. He seeks to avoid them by changing into the form of a pig and joining a herd which is rooting in the plain, but the brothers detect him and Brian wounds him with a cast from a spear. Kian, knowing that his end is come, begs to be allowed to change back into human form before he is slain. "I had liefer kill a man than a pig," says Brian, who takes throughout the leading part in all the brothers' adventures. Kian then stands before them as a man, with the blood from Brian's spear trickling from his breast. "I have outwitted ye," he cries, "for if ye had slain a pig ye would have paid but the eric [blood-fine] of a pig, but now ye shall pay the eric of a man; never was greater eric than that which ye shall pay; and the weapons ye slay me with shall tell the tale to the avenger of blood."

"Then you shall be slain with no weapons at all,"

[1] The other two were "The Fate of the Children of Lir" and "The Fate of the Sons of Usna." The stories of the Quest of the Sons of Turenn and that of the Children of Lir have been told in full by the author in his "High Deeds of Finn and other Bardic Romances," and that of the "Sons of Usna" (the Deirdre Legend) by Miss Eleanor Hull in her "Cuchulain," both published by Harrap and Co

The Boat of Mananan

At the Revels of the Fairy Folk

says Brian, and he and the brothers stone him to death and bury him in the ground as deep as the height of a man.

But when Lugh shortly afterwards passes that way the stones on the plain cry out and tell him of his father's murder at the hands of the sons of Turenn. He uncovers the body, and, vowing vengeance, returns to Tara. Here he accuses the sons of Turenn before the High King, and is permitted to have them executed, or to name the eric he will accept in remission of that sentence. Lugh chooses to have the eric, and he names it as follows, concealing things of vast price, and involving unheard-of toils, under the names of common objects: Three apples, the skin of a pig, a spear, a chariot with two horses, seven swine, a hound, a cooking-spit, and, finally, to give three shouts on a hill. The brothers bind themselves to pay the fine, and Lugh then declares the meaning of it. The three apples are those which grow in the Garden of the Sun; the pig-skin is a magical skin which heals every wound and sickness if it can be laid on the sufferer, and it is a possession of the King of Greece; the spear is a magical weapon owned by the King of Persia (these names, of course, are mere fanciful appellations for places in the mysterious world of Faëry); the seven swine belong to King Asal of the Golden Pillars, and may be killed and eaten every night and yet be found whole next day; the spit belongs to the sea-nymphs of the sunken Island of Finchory; and the three shouts are to be given on the hill of a fierce warrior, Mochaen, who, with his sons, are under vows to prevent any man from raising his voice on that hill. To fulfil any one of these enterprises would be an all but impossible task, and the brothers must accomplish them all before they can clear themselves of the guilt and penalty of Kian's death.

The story then goes on to tell how with infinite daring and resource the sons of Turenn accomplish one by one all their tasks, but when all are done save the capture of the cooking-spit and the three shouts on the Hill of Mochaen, Lugh, by magical arts, causes forgetfulness to fall upon them, and they return to Ireland with their treasures. These, especially the spear and the pig-skin, are just what Lugh needs to help him against the Fomorians; but his vengeance is not complete, and after receiving the treasures he reminds the brothers of what is yet to be won. They, in deep dejection, now begin to understand how they are played with, and go forth sadly to win, if they can, the rest of the eric. After long wandering they discover that the Island of Finchory is not above, but under the sea. Brian in a magical "water-dress" goes down to it, sees the thrice fifty nymphs in their palace, and seizes the golden spit from their hearth. The ordeal of the Hill of Mochaen is the last to be attempted. After a desperate combat which ends in the slaying of Mochaen and his sons, the brothers, mortally wounded, uplift their voices in three faint cries, and so the eric is fulfilled. The life is still in them, however, when they return to Ireland, and their aged father, Turenn, implores Lugh for the loan of the magic pig-skin to heal them; but the implacable Lugh refuses, and the brothers and their father die together. So ends the tale.

The Second Battle of Moytura

The Second Battle of Moytura took place on a plain in the north of Co. Sligo, which is remarkable for the number of sepulchral monuments still scattered over it. The first battle, of course, was that which the Danaans had waged with the Firbolgs, and the Moytura there referred to was much further south, in Co. Mayo.

THE DEATH OF BALOR

The battle with the Fomorians is related with an astounding wealth of marvellous incident. The craftsmen of the Danaans, Goban the smith, Credné the artificer (or goldsmith), and Luchta the carpenter, keep repairing the broken weapons of the Danaans with magical speed—three blows of Goban's hammer make a spear or sword, Luchta flings a handle at it and it sticks on at once, and Credné jerks the rivets at it with his tongs as fast as he makes them and they fly into their places. The wounded are healed by the magical pig-skin. The plain resounds with the clamour of battle:

"Fearful indeed was the thunder which rolled over the battlefield; the shouts of the warriors, the breaking of the shields, the flashing and clashing of the swords, of the straight, ivory-hilted swords, the music and harmony of the 'belly-darts' and the sighing and winging of the spears and lances."[1]

The Death of Balor

The Fomorians bring on their champion, Balor, before the glance of whose terrible eye Nuada of the Silver Hand and others of the Danaans go down. But Lugh, seizing an opportunity when the eyelid drooped through weariness, approached close to Balor, and as it began to lift once more he hurled into the eye a great stone which sank into the brain, and Balor lay dead, as the prophecy had foretold, at the hand of his grandson. The Fomorians were then totally routed, and it is not recorded that they ever again gained any authority or committed any extensive depredations in Ireland. Lugh, the Ildánach, was then enthroned in place of Nuada, and the myth of the victory of the solar

[1] O'Curry's translation from the bardic tale, "The Battle of Moytura."

hero over the powers of darkness and brute force is complete.

The Harp of the Dagda

A curious little incident bearing on the power which the Danaans could exercise by the spell of music may here be inserted. The flying Fomorians, it is told, had made prisoner the harper of the Dagda and carried him off with them. Lugh, the Dagda, and the warrior Ogma followed them, and came unknown into the banqueting-hall of the Fomorian camp. There they saw the harp hanging on the wall. The Dagda called to it, and immediately it flew into his hands, killing nine men of the Fomorians on its way. The Dagda's invocation of the harp is very singular, and not a little puzzling:

"Come, apple-sweet murmurer," he cries, "come, four-angled frame of harmony, come, Summer, come, Winter, from the mouths of harps and bags and pipes."[1]

The allusion to summer and winter suggests the practice in Indian music of allotting certain musical modes to the different seasons of the year (and even to different times of day), and also an Egyptian legend referred to in Burney's "History of Music," where the three strings of the lyre were supposed to answer respectively to the three seasons, spring, summer, and winter.[2]

When the Dagda got possession of the harp, the tale goes on, he played on it the "three noble strains"

[1] O'Curry, "Manners and Customs," iii. 214.

[2] The ancient Irish division of the year contained only these three seasons, including autumn in summer (O'Curry, "Manners and Customs," iii. 217).

which every great master of the harp should command, namely, the Strain of Lament, which caused the hearers to weep, the Strain of Laughter, which made them merry, and the Strain of Slumber, or Lullaby, which plunged them all in a profound sleep. And under cover of that sleep the Danaan champion stole out and escaped. It may be observed that throughout the whole of the legendary literature of Ireland skill in music, the art whose influence most resembles that of a mysterious spell or gift of Faëry, is the prerogative of the People of Dana and their descendants. Thus in the "Colloquy of the Ancients," a collection of tales made about the thirteenth or fourteenth century, St. Patrick is introduced to a minstrel, Cascorach, "a handsome, curly-headed, dark-browed youth," who plays so sweet a strain that the saint and his retinue all fall asleep. Cascorach, we are told, was son of a minstrel of the Danaan folk. St. Patrick's scribe, Brogan, remarks, "A good cast of thine art is that thou gavest us." "Good indeed it were," said Patrick, "but for a twang of the fairy spell that infests it; barring which nothing could more nearly resemble heaven's harmony."[1] Some of the most beautiful of the antique Irish folk-melodies,—*e.g.*, the *Coulin*—are traditionally supposed to have been overheard by mortal harpers at the revels of the Fairy Folk.

Names and Characteristics of the Danaan Deities

I may conclude this narrative of the Danaan conquest with some account of the principal Danaan gods and their attributes, which will be useful to readers of the subsequent pages. The best with which I am acquainted is to be found in Mr. Standish O'Grady's "Critical

[1] S. H. O'Grady, "Silva Gadelica," p. 191.

History of Ireland."[1] This work is no less remarkable for its critical insight—it was published in 1881, when scientific study of the Celtic mythology was little heard of—than for the true bardic imagination, kindred to that of the ancient myth-makers themselves, which recreates the dead forms of the past and dilates them with the breath of life. The broad outlines in which Mr. O'Grady has laid down the typical characteristics of the chief personages in the Danaan cycle hardly need any correction at this day, and have been of much use to me in the following summary of the subject.

The Dagda

The Dagda Mōr was the father and chief of the People of Dana. A certain conception of vastness attaches to him and to his doings. In the Second Battle of Moytura his blows sweep down whole ranks of the enemy, and his spear, when he trails it on the march, draws a furrow in the ground like the fosse which marks the mearing of a province. An element of grotesque humour is present in some of the records about this deity. When the Fomorians give him food on his visit to their camp, the porridge and milk are poured into a great pit in the ground, and he eats it with a spoon big enough, it was said, for a man and a woman to lie together in it. With this spoon he scrapes the pit, when the porridge is done, and shovels earth and gravel unconcernedly down his throat. We have already seen that, like all the Danaans, he is a master of music, as well as of other magical endowments, and owns a harp which comes flying through the air at his call. "The tendency to attribute life to inanimate things is apparent in the Homeric literature, but exercises a very great influence in the mythology

[1] Pp. 104 *sqq.*, and *passim.*

of this country. The living, fiery spear of Lugh; the magic ship of Mananan; the sword of Conary Mōr, which sang; Cuchulain's sword, which spoke; the Lia Fail, Stone of Destiny, which roared for joy beneath the feet of rightful kings; the waves of the ocean, roaring with rage and sorrow when such kings are in jeopardy; the waters of the Avon Dia, holding back for fear at the mighty duel between Cuchulain and Ferdia, are but a few out of many examples."[1] A legend of later times tells how once, at the death of a great scholar, all the books in Ireland fell from their shelves upon the floor.

Angus Ōg

Angus Ōg (Angus the Young), son of the Dagda, by Boanna (the river Boyne), was the Irish god of love. His palace was supposed to be at New Grange, on the Boyne. Four bright birds that ever hovered about his head were supposed to be his kisses taking shape in this lovely form, and at their singing love came springing up in the hearts of youths and maidens. Once he fell sick of love for a maiden whom he had seen in a dream. He told the cause of his sickness to his mother Boanna, who searched all Ireland for the girl, but could not find her. Then the Dagda was called in, but he too was at a loss, till he called to his aid Bōv the Red, king of the Danaans of Munster—the same whom we have met with in the tale of the Children of Lir, and who was skilled in all mysteries and enchantments. Bōv undertook the search, and after a year had gone by declared that he had found the visionary maiden at a lake called the Lake of the Dragon's Mouth.

[1] O'Grady, *loc. cit.*

Angus goes to Bōv, and, after being entertained by him three days, is brought to the lake shore, where he sees thrice fifty maidens walking in couples, each couple linked by a chain of gold, but one of them is taller than the rest by a head and shoulders. "That is she!" cries Angus. "Tell us by what name she is known." Bōv answers that her name is Caer, daughter of Ethal Anubal, a prince of the Danaans of Connacht. Angus laments that he is not strong enough to carry her off from her companions, but, on Bōv's advice, betakes himself to Ailell and Maev, the mortal King and Queen of Connacht, for assistance. The Dagda and Angus then both repair to the palace of Ailell, who feasts them for a week, and then asks the cause of their coming. When it is declared he answers, "We have no authority over Ethal Anubal." They send a message to him, however, asking for the hand of Caer for Angus, but Ethal refuses to give her up. In the end he is besieged by the combined forces of Ailell and the Dagda, and taken prisoner. When Caer is again demanded of him he declares that he cannot comply, "for she is more powerful than I." He explains that she lives alternately in the form of a maiden and of a swan year and year about, "and on the first of November next," he says, "you will see her with a hundred and fifty other swans at the Lake of the Dragon's Mouth."

Angus goes there at the appointed time, and cries to her, "Oh, come and speak to me!" "Who calls me?" asks Caer. Angus explains who he is, and then finds himself transformed into a swan. This is an indication of consent, and he plunges in to join his love in the lake. After that they fly together to the palace on the Boyne, uttering as they go a music so divine that all hearers are lulled to sleep for three days and nights.

Angus is the special deity and friend of beautiful

youths and maidens. Dermot of the Love-spot, a follower of Finn mac Cumhal, and lover of Grania, of whom we shall hear later, was bred up with Angus in the palace on the Boyne. He was the typical lover of Irish legend. When he was slain by the wild boar of Ben Bulben, Angus revives him and carries him off to share his immortality in his fairy palace.

Len of Killarney

Of Bōv the Red, brother of the Dagda, we have already heard. He had, it is said, a goldsmith named Len, who "gave their ancient name to the Lakes of Killarney, once known as Locha Lein, the Lakes of Len of the Many Hammers. Here by the lake he wrought, surrounded by rainbows and showers of fiery dew."[1]

Lugh

Lugh has already been described.[2] He has more distinctly solar attributes than any other Celtic deity; and, as we know, his worship was spread widely over Continental Celtica. In the tale of the Quest of the Sons of Turenn we are told that Lugh approached the Fomorians from the west. Then Bres, son of Balor, arose and said: "I wonder that the sun is rising in the west to-day, and in the east every other day." "Would it were so," said his Druids. "Why, what else but the sun is it?" said Bres. "It is the radiance of the face of Lugh of the Long Arm," they replied.

Lugh was the father, by the Milesian maiden Dectera, of Cuchulain, the most heroic figure in Irish legend, in whose story there is evidently a strong element of the solar myth.[3]

[1] O'Grady, *loc. cit.*

[2] See p. 112.

[3] Miss Hull has discussed this subject fully in the introduction to her invaluable work, "The Cuchullin Saga."

Midir the Proud

Midir the Proud is a son of the Dagda. His fairy palace is at *Bri Leith*, or Slieve Callary, in Co. Longford. He frequently appears in legends dealing partly with human, partly with Danaan personages, and is always represented as a type of splendour in his apparel and in personal beauty. When he appears to King Eochy on the Hill of Tara he is thus described :[1]

"It chanced that Eochaid Airemm, the King of Tara, arose upon a certain fair day in the time of summer; and he ascended the high ground of Tara[2] to behold the plain of Breg; beautiful was the colour of that plain, and there was upon it excellent blossom glowing with all hues that are known. And as the aforesaid Eochy looked about and around him, he saw a young strange warrior upon the high ground at his side. The tunic that the warrior wore was purple in colour, his hair was of a golden yellow, and of such length that it reached to the edge of his shoulders. The eyes of the young warrior were lustrous and grey; in the one hand he held a fine pointed spear, in the other a shield with a white central boss, and with gems of gold upon it. And Eochaid held his peace, for he knew that none such had been in Tara on the night before, and the gate that led into the *Liss* had not at that time been thrown open."[3]

[1] See the tale of "Etain and Midir," in Chap. IV.

[2] The name Tara is derived from an oblique case of the nominative *Teamhair*, meaning "the place of the wide prospect." It is now a broad grassy hill, in Co. Meath, covered with earthworks representing the sites of the ancient royal buildings, which can all be clearly located from ancient descriptions.

[3] A. H. Leahy, "Heroic Romances," i. 27.

Lir and Mananan

Lir, as Mr. O'Grady remarks, "appears in two distinct forms. In the first he is a vast, impersonal presence commensurate with the sea; in fact, the Greek Oceanus. In the second, he is a separate person dwelling invisibly on Slieve Fuad," in Co. Armagh. We hear little of him in Irish legend, where the attributes of the sea-god are mostly conferred on his son, Mananan.

This deity is one of the most popular in Irish mythology. He was lord of the sea, beyond or under which the Land of Youth or Islands of the Dead were supposed to lie; he therefore was the guide of man to this country. He was master of tricks and illusions, and owned all kinds of magical possessions—the boat named Ocean-sweeper, which obeyed the thought of those who sailed in it and went without oar or sail, the steed Aonbarr, which could travel alike on sea or land, and the sword named The Answerer, which no armour could resist. White-crested waves were called the Horses of Mananan, and it was forbidden (*tabu*) for the solar hero, Cuchulain, to perceive them—this indicated the daily death of the sun at his setting in the western waves. Mananan wore a great cloak which was capable of taking on every kind of colour, like the widespread field of the sea as looked on from a height; and as the protector of the island of Erin it was said that when any hostile force invaded it they heard his thunderous tramp and the flapping of his mighty cloak as he marched angrily round and round their camp at night. The Isle of Man, seen dimly from the Irish coast, was supposed to be the throne of Mananan, and to take its name from this deity.

The Goddess Dana

The greatest of the Danaan goddesses was Dana, "mother of the Irish gods," as she is called in an early text. She was daughter of the Dagda, and, like him, associated with ideas of fertility and blessing. According to d'Arbois de Jubainville, she was identical with the goddess Brigit, who was so widely worshipped in Celtica. Brian, Iuchar, and Iucharba are said to have been her sons—these really represent but one person, in the usual Irish fashion of conceiving the divine power in triads. The name of Brian, who takes the lead in all the exploits of the brethren,[1] is a derivation from a more ancient form, Brenos, and under this form was the god to whom the Celts attributed their victories at the Allia and at Delphi, mistaken by Roman and Greek chroniclers for an earthly leader.

The Morrigan

There was also an extraordinary goddess named the Morrigan,[2] who appears to embody all that is perverse and horrible among supernatural powers. She delighted in setting men at war, and fought among them herself, changing into many frightful shapes and often hovering above fighting armies in the aspect of a crow. She met Cuchulain once and proffered him her love in the guise of a human maid. He refused it, and she persecuted him thenceforward for the most of his life. Warring with him once in the middle of the stream, she turned herself into a water-serpent, and then into a mass of water-weeds, seeking to entangle and drown him. But he conquered and wounded her, and she afterwards

[1] See p. 114.

[2] I cannot agree with Mr. O'Grady's identification of this goddess with Dana, though the name appears to mean "The Great Queen."

became his friend. Before his last battle she passed through Emain Macha at night, and broke the pole of his chariot as a warning.

Cleena's Wave

One of the most notable landmarks of Ireland was the *Tonn Cliodhna*, or "Wave of Cleena," on the seashore at Glandore Bay, in Co. Cork. The story about Cleena exists in several versions, which do not agree with each other except in so far as she seems to have been a Danaan maiden once living in Mananan's country, the Land of Youth beyond the sea. Escaping thence with a mortal lover, as one of the versions tells, she landed on the southern coast of Ireland, and her lover, Keevan of the Curling Locks, went off to hunt in the woods. Cleena, who remained on the beach, was lulled to sleep by fairy music played by a minstrel of Mananan, when a great wave of the sea swept up and carried her back to Fairyland, leaving her lover desolate. Hence the place was called the Strand of Cleena's Wave.

The Goddess Ainé

Another topical goddess was Ainé, the patroness of Munster, who is still venerated by the people of that county. She was the daughter of the Danaan Owel, a foster-son of Mananan and a Druid. She is in some sort a love-goddess, continually inspiring mortals with passion. She was ravished, it was said, by Ailill Olum, King of Munster, who was slain in consequence by her magic arts, and the story is repeated in far later times about another mortal lover, who was not, however, slain, a Fitzgerald, to whom she bore the famous wizard Earl.[1] Many of the aristocratic

[1] Gerald, the fourth Earl of Desmond. He disappeared, it is said, in 1398, and the legend goes that he still lives beneath the waters of

families of Munster claimed descent from this union. Her name still clings to the "Hill of Ainé" (Knockainey), near Loch Gur, in Munster. All the Danaan deities in the popular imagination were earth-gods, *dei terreni*, associated with ideas of fertility and increase. Ainé is not heard much of in the bardic literature, but she is very prominent in the folk-lore of the neighbourhood. At the bidding of her son, Earl Gerald, she planted all Knockainey with pease in a single night. She was, and perhaps still is, worshipped on Midsummer Eve by the peasantry, who carried torches of hay and straw, tied on poles and lighted, round her hill at night. Afterwards they dispersed themselves among their cultivated fields and pastures, waving the torches over the crops and the cattle to bring luck and increase for the following year. On one night, as told by Mr. D. Fitzgerald,[1] who has collected the local traditions about her, the ceremony was omitted owing to the death of one of the neighbours. Yet the peasantry at night saw the torches in greater number than ever circling the hill, and Ainé herself in front, directing and ordering the procession.

"On another St. John's Night a number of girls had stayed late on the Hill watching the *cliars* (torches) and joining in the games. Suddenly Ainé appeared among them, thanked them for the honour they had done her, but said she now wished them to go home, as *they wanted the hill to themselves*. She let them understand whom she

Loch Gur, and may be seen riding round its banks on his white steed once every seven years. He was surnamed "Gerald the Poet" from the "witty and ingenious" verses he composed in Gaelic. Wizardry, poetry, and science were all united in one conception in the mind of the ancient Irish.

[1] "Popular Tales of Ireland," by D. Fitzgerald, in "Revue Celtique," vol. iv.

Sinend and Connla's Well

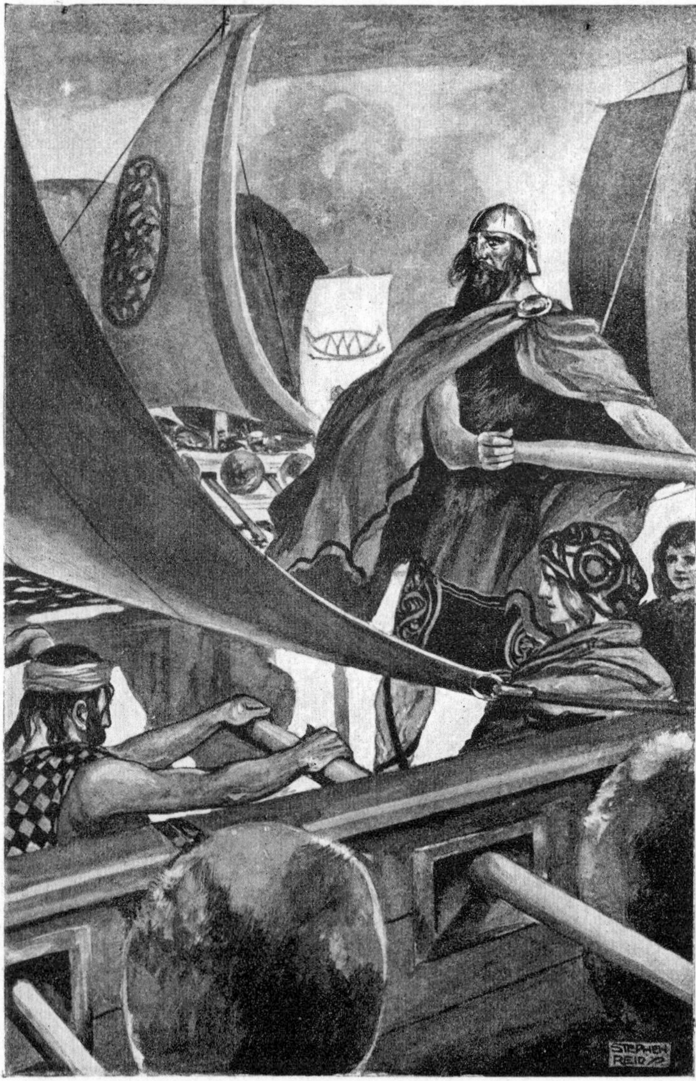

The Coming of the Sons of Miled

meant by *they*, for calling some of the girls she made them look through a ring, when behold, the hill appeared crowded with people before invisible."

"Here," observed Mr. Alfred Nutt, "we have the antique ritual carried out on a spot hallowed to one of the antique powers, watched over and shared in by those powers themselves. Nowhere save in Gaeldom could be found such a pregnant illustration of the identity of the fairy class with the venerable powers to ensure whose goodwill rites and sacrifices, originally fierce and bloody, now a mere simulacrum of their pristine form, have been performed for countless ages."[1]

Sinend and the Well of Knowledge

There is a singular myth which, while intended to account for the name of the river Shannon, expresses the Celtic veneration for poetry and science, combined with the warning that they may not be approached without danger. The goddess Sinend, it was said, daughter of Lodan son of Lir, went to a certain well named Connla's Well, which is under the sea—*i.e.*, in the Land of Youth in Fairyland. "That is a well," says the bardic narrative, "at which are the hazels of wisdom and inspirations, that is, the hazels of the science of poetry, and in the same hour their fruit and their blossom and their foliage break forth, and then fall upon the well in the same shower, which raises upon the water a royal surge of purple." When Sinend came to the well we are not told what rites or preparation she had omitted, but the angry waters broke forth and overwhelmed her, and washed her up on the Shannon shore, where she died, giving to the river its name.[2] This myth of the hazels of inspiration and

[1] "The Voyage of Bran," vol. ii. p. 219.

[2] In Irish, *Sionnain*.

knowledge and their association with springing water runs through all Irish legend, and has been finely treated by a living Irish poet, Mr. G. W. Russell, in the following verses :

"A cabin on the mountain-side hid in a grassy nook,
With door and window open wide, where friendly stars may look :
The rabbit shy may patter in, the winds may enter free
Who roam around the mountain throne in living ecstasy.

"And when the sun sets dimmed in eve, and purple fills the air,
I think the sacred hazel-tree is dropping berries there,
From starry fruitage, waved aloft where Connla's Well o'erflows ;
For sure, the immortal waters run through every wind that blows.

"I think when Night towers up aloft and shakes the trembling dew,
How every high and lonely thought that thrills my spirit through
Is but a shining berry dropped down through the purple air,
And from the magic tree of life the fruit falls everywhere."

The Coming of the Milesians

After the Second Battle of Moytura the Danaans held rule in Ireland until the coming of the Milesians, the sons of Miled. These are conceived in Irish legend as an entirely human race, yet in their origin they, like the other invaders of Ireland, go back to a divine and mythical ancestry. Miled, whose name occurs as a god in a Celtic inscription from Hungary, is represented as a son of Bilé. Bilé, like Balor, is one of the names of the god of Death, *i.e.*, of the Underworld. They come from "Spain"—the usual term employed by the later rationalising historians for the Land of the Dead.

The manner of their coming into Ireland was as follows : Ith, the grandfather of Miled, dwelt in a great tower which his father, Bregon, had built in "Spain." One clear winter's day, when looking out westwards from this lofty tower, he saw the coast of Ireland in the distance, and resolved to sail to the unknown land.

He embarked with ninety warriors, and took land at Corcadyna, in the south-west. In connexion with this episode I may quote a passage of great beauty and interest from de Jubainville's "Irish Mythological Cycle":[1]

"According to an unknown writer cited by Plutarch, who died about the year 120 of the present era, and also by Procopius, who wrote in the sixth century A.D., 'the Land of the Dead' is the western extremity of Great Britain, separated from the eastern by an impassable wall. On the northern coast of Gaul, says the legend, is a populace of mariners whose business is to carry the dead across from the continent to their last abode in the island of Britain. The mariners, awakened in the night by the whisperings of some mysterious voice, arise and go down to the shore, where they find ships awaiting them which are not their own,[2] and, in these, invisible beings, under whose weight the vessels sink almost to the gunwales. They go on board, and with a single stroke of the oar, says one text, in one hour, says another, they arrive at their destination, though with their own vessels, aided by sails, it would have taken them at least a day and a night to reach the coast of Britain. When they come to the other shore the invisible passengers land, and at the same time the unloaded ships are seen to rise above the waves, and a voice is heard announcing the names of the new arrivals, who have just been added to the inhabitants of the Land of the Dead.

"One stroke of the oar, one hour's voyage at most, suffices for the midnight journey which transfers the

[1] Translation by R. I. Best.

[2] The solar vessels found in dolmen carvings. See Chap. II. p. 71 *sqq*. Note that the Celtic spirits, though invisible, are material and have weight; not so those in Vergil and Dante.

Dead from the Gaulish continent to their final abode. Some mysterious law, indeed, brings together in the night the great spaces which divide the domain of the living from that of the dead in daytime. It was the same law which enabled Ith one fine winter evening to perceive from the Tower of Bregon, in the Land of the Dead, the shores of Ireland, or the land of the living. The phenomenon took place in winter ; for winter is a sort of night ; winter, like night, lowers the barriers between the regions of Death and those of Life ; like night, winter gives to life the semblance of death, and suppresses, as it were, the dread abyss that lies between the two."

At this time, it is said, Ireland was ruled by three Danaan kings, grandsons of the Dagda. Their names were MacCuill, MacCecht, and MacGrené, and their wives were named respectively Banba, Fohla, and Eriu. The Celtic habit of conceiving divine persons in triads is here illustrated. These triads represent one person each, and the mythical character of that personage is evident from the name of one of them, MacGrené, Son of the Sun. The names of the three goddesses have each at different times been applied to Ireland, but that of the third, Eriu, has alone persisted, and in the dative form, Erinn, is a poetic name for the country to this day. That Eriu is the wife of MacGrené means, as de Jubainville observes, that the Sun-god, the god of Day, Life, and Science, has wedded the land and is reigning over it.

Ith, on landing, finds that the Danaan king, Neit, has just been slain in a battle with the Fomorians, and the three sons, MacCuill and the others, are at the fortress of Aileach, in Co. Donegal, arranging for a division of the land among themselves. At first they welcome Ith, and ask him to settle their inheritance. Ith gives his judgment, but, in concluding, his admiration for the newly discovered country breaks out: "Act," he says, "according to the laws of justice, for the country you dwell in is a good one, it is rich in fruit and honey, in wheat and in fish; and in heat and cold it is temperate." From this panegyric the Danaans conclude that Ith has designs upon their land, and they seize him and put him to death. His companions, however, recover his body and bear it back with them in their ships to "Spain"; when the children of Miled resolve to take vengeance for the outrage and prepare to invade Ireland.

They were commanded by thirty-six chiefs, each having his own ship with his family and his followers. Two of the company are said to have perished on the way. One of the sons of Miled, having climbed to the masthead of his vessel to look out for the coast of Ireland, fell into the sea and was drowned. The other was Skena, wife of the poet Amergin, son of Miled, who died on the way. The Milesians buried her when they landed, and called the place "Inverskena" after her; this was the ancient name of the Kenmare River in Co. Kerry.

"It was on a Thursday, the first of May, and the seventeenth day of the moon, that the sons of Miled arrived in Ireland. Partholan also landed in Ireland on the first of May, but on a different day of the week and of the moon; and it was on the first day of May, too, that the pestilence came which in the space of one week destroyed utterly his race. The first of May was sacred to Beltené, one of the names of the god of Death, the god who gives life to men and takes it away from them again. Thus it was on the feast day of this god that the sons of Miled began their conquest of Ireland."[1]

The Poet Amergin

When the poet Amergin set foot upon the soil of Ireland it is said that he chanted a strange and mystical lay:

"I am the Wind that blows over the sea,
I am the Wave of the Ocean;
I am the Murmur of the billows;
I am the Ox of the Seven Combats;
I am the Vulture upon the rock;
I am a Ray of the Sun;
I am the fairest of Plants;
I am a Wild Boar in valour;
I am a Salmon in the Water;
I am a Lake in the plain;
I am the Craft of the artificer;
I am a Word of Science;
I am the Spear-point that gives battle;
I am the god that creates in the head of man the fire of thought.
Who is it that enlightens the assembly upon the mountain, if not I?
Who telleth the ages of the moon, if not I?
Who showeth the place where the sun goes to rest, if not I?"

De Jubainville, whose translation I have in the main followed, observes upon this strange utterance:

"There is a lack of order in this composition, the ideas, fundamental and subordinate, are jumbled together without method; but there is no doubt as to the meaning: the *filé* [poet] is the Word of Science, he is the god who gives to man the fire of thought; and as science is not distinct from its object, as God and Nature are but one, the being of the *filé* is mingled with the

[1] De Jubainville, "Irish Mythological Cycle," p. 136. Beltené is the modern Irish name for the month of May, and is derived from an ancient root preserved in the Old Irish compound *epelta*, "dead."

winds and the waves, with the wild animals and the warrior's arms."[1]

Two other poems are attributed to Amergin, in which he invokes the land and physical features of Ireland to aid him :

> "I invoke the land of Ireland,
> Shining, shining sea;
> Fertile, fertile Mountain ;
> Gladed, gladed wood !
> Abundant river, abundant in water !
> Fish-abounding lake ! "[2]

The Judgment of Amergin

The Milesian host, after landing, advance to Tara, where they find the three kings of the Danaans awaiting them, and summon them to deliver up the island. The Danaans ask for three days' time to consider whether they shall quit Ireland, or submit, or give battle ; and they propose to leave the decision, upon their request, to Amergin. Amergin pronounces judgment—"the first judgment which was delivered in Ireland." He agrees that the Milesians must not take their foes by surprise—they are to withdraw the length of nine waves from the shore, and then return ; if they then conquer the Danaans the land is to be fairly theirs by right of battle.

The Milesians submit to this decision and embark on their ships. But no sooner have they drawn off for this mystical distance of the nine waves than a mist and storm are raised by the sorceries of the Danaans—the coast of Ireland is hidden from their sight, and they wander dispersed upon the ocean. To ascertain if it is

[1] "Irish Mythological Cycle," p. 138.

[2] I follow again de Jubainville's translation ; but in connexion with this and the previous poems see also Ossianic Society's "Transactions," vol. v.

a natural or a Druidic tempest which afflicts them, a man named Aranan is sent up to the masthead to see if the wind is blowing there also or not. He is flung from the swaying mast, but as he falls to his death he cries his message to his shipmates: "There is no storm aloft." Amergin, who as poet—that is to say, Druid—takes the lead in all critical situations, thereupon chants his incantation to the land of Erin. The wind falls, and they turn their prows, rejoicing, towards the shore. But one of the Milesian lords, Eber Donn, exults in brutal rage at the prospect of putting all the dwellers in Ireland to the sword; the tempest immediately springs up again, and many of the Milesian ships founder, Eber Donn's being among them. At last a remnant of the Milesians find their way to shore, and land in the estuary of the Boyne.

The Defeat of the Danaans

A great battle with the Danaans at Telltown[1] then follows. The three kings and three queens of the Danaans, with many of their people, are slain, and the children of Miled—the last of the mythical invaders of Ireland—enter upon the sovranty of Ireland. But the People of Dana do not withdraw. By their magic art they cast over themselves a veil of invisibility, which they can put on or off as they choose. There are two Irelands henceforward, the spiritual and the earthly. The Danaans dwell in the spiritual Ireland, which is portioned out among them by their great overlord, the Dagda. Where the human eye can see but green mounds and ramparts, the relics of ruined fortresses or sepulchres, there rise the fairy palaces of the defeated divinities; there they hold their revels in eternal sunshine, nourished by the magic meat and ale that give

[1] Teltin; so named after the goddess Telta. See p. 103.

them undying youth and beauty; and thence they come forth at times to mingle with mortal men in love or in war. The ancient mythical literature conceives them as heroic and splendid in strength and beauty. In later times, and as Christian influences grew stronger, they dwindle into fairies, the People of the Sidhe;[1] but they have never wholly perished; to this day the Land of Youth and its inhabitants live in the imagination of the Irish peasant.

The Meaning of the Danaan Myth

All myths constructed by a primitive people are symbols, and if we can discover what it is that they symbolise we have a valuable clue to the spiritual character, and sometimes even to the history, of the people from whom they sprang. Now the meaning of the Danaan myth as it appears in the bardic literature, though it has undergone much distortion before it reached us, is perfectly clear. The Danaans represent the Celtic reverence for science, poetry, and artistic skill, blended, of course, with the earlier conception of the divinity of the powers of Light. In their combat with the Firbolgs the victory of the intellect over dulness and ignorance is plainly portrayed—the comparison of the heavy, blunt weapon of the Firbolgs with the light and penetrating spears of the People of Dana is an indication which it is impossible to mistake. Again, in their struggle with a far more powerful and dangerous enemy, the Fomorians, we are evidently to see the combat of the powers of Light with evil of a more positive kind than that represented by the Firbolgs. The Fomorians stand not for mere dulness or

[1] Pronounced "Shee." It means literally the People of the [Fairy] Mounds.

stupidity, but for the forces of tyranny, cruelty, and greed—for moral rather than for intellectual darkness.

The Meaning of the Milesian Myth

But the myth of the struggle of the Danaans with the sons of Miled is more difficult to interpret. How does it come that the lords of light and beauty, wielding all the powers of thought (represented by magic and sorcery), succumbed to a human race, and were dispossessed by them of their hard-won inheritance? What is the meaning of this shrinking of their powers which at once took place when the Milesians came on the scene? The Milesians were not on the side of the powers of darkness. They were guided by Amergin, a clear embodiment of the idea of poetry and thought. They were regarded with the utmost veneration, and the dominant families of Ireland all traced their descent to them. Was the Kingdom of Light, then, divided against itself? Or, if not, to what conception in the Irish mind are we to trace the myth of the Milesian invasion and victory?

The only answer I can see to this puzzling question is to suppose that the Milesian myth originated at a much later time than the others, and was, in its main features, the product of Christian influences. The People of Dana were in possession of the country, but they were pagan divinities—they could not stand for the progenitors of a Christian Ireland. They had somehow or other to be got rid of, and a race of less embarrassing antecedents substituted for them. So the Milesians were fetched from "Spain" and endowed with the main characteristics, only more humanised, of the People of Dana. But the latter, in contradistinction to the usual attitude of early Christianity, are treated very tenderly in the story of their overthrow.

One of them has the honour of giving her name to the island, the brutality of one of the conquerors towards them is punished with death, and while dispossessed of the lordship of the soil they still enjoy life in the fair world which by their magic art they have made invisible to mortals. They are no longer gods, but they are more than human, and frequent instances occur in which they are shown as coming forth from their fairy world, being embraced in the Christian fold, and entering into heavenly bliss. With two cases of this redemption of the Danaans we shall close this chapter on the Invasion Myths of Ireland.

The first is the strange and beautiful tale of the Transformation of the Children of Lir.

The Children of Lir

Lir was a Danaan divinity, the father of the sea-god Mananan who continually occurs in magical tales of the Milesian cycle. He had married in succession two sisters, the second of whom was named Aoife.[1] She was childless, but the former wife of Lir had left him four children, a girl named Fionuala[2] and three boys. The intense love of Lir for the children made the step-mother jealous, and she ultimately resolved on their destruction. It will be observed, by the way, that the People of Dana, though conceived as unaffected by time, and naturally immortal, are nevertheless subject to violent death either at the hands of each other or even of mortals.

With her guilty object in view, Aoife goes on a journey to a neighbouring Danaan king, Bōv the Red, taking the four children with her. Arriving at a lonely place by Lake Derryvaragh, in Westmeath, she

[1] Pronounced "Eefa."

[2] This name means "The Maid of the Fair Shoulder."

orders her attendants to slay the children. They refuse, and rebuke her. Then she resolves to do it herself; but, says the legend, "her womanhood overcame her," and instead of killing the children she transforms them by spells of sorcery into four white swans, and lays on them the following doom: three hundred years they are to spend on the waters of Lake Derryvaragh, three hundred on the Straits of Moyle (between Ireland and Scotland), and three hundred on the Atlantic by Erris and Inishglory. After that, "when the woman of the South is mated with the man of the North," the enchantment is to have an end.

When the children fail to arrive with Aoife at the palace of Bōv her guilt is discovered, and Bōv changes her into "a demon of the air." She flies forth shrieking, and is heard of no more in the tale. But Lir and Bōv seek out the swan-children, and find that they have not only human speech, but have preserved the characteristic Danaan gift of making wonderful music. From all parts of the island companies of the Danaan folk resort to Lake Derryvaragh to hear this wondrous music and to converse with the swans, and during that time a great peace and gentleness seemed to pervade the land.

But at last the day came for them to leave the fellowship of their kind and take up their life by the wild cliffs and ever angry sea of the northern coast. Here they knew the worst of loneliness, cold, and storm. Forbidden to land, their feathers froze to the rocks in the winter nights, and they were often buffeted and driven apart by storms. As Fionuala sings:

"Cruel to us was Aoife
Who played her magic upon us,
And drove us out on the water—
Four wonderful snow-white swans.

The Danaan Folk listen to the Music of the Swans

Ethné hears Voices

"Our bath is the frothing brine,
In bays by red rocks guarded;
For mead at our father's table
We drink of the salt, blue sea.

"Three sons and a single daughter,
In clefts of the cold rocks dwelling,
The hard rocks, cruel to mortals—
We are full of keening to-night."

Fionuala, the eldest of the four, takes the lead in ali their doings, and mothers the younger children most tenderly, wrapping her plumage round them on nights of frost. At last the time comes to enter on the third and last period of their doom, and they take flight for the western shores of Mayo. Here too they suffer much hardship; but the Milesians have now come into the land, and a young farmer named Evric, dwelling on the shores of Erris Bay, finds out who and what the swans are, and befriends them. To him they tell their story, and through him it is supposed to have been preserved and handed down. When the final period of their suffering is close at hand they resolve to fly towards the palace of their father Lir, who dwells, we are told, at the Hill of the White Field, in Armagh, to see how things have fared with him. They do so; but not knowing what has happened on the coming of the Milesians, they are shocked and bewildered to find nothing but green mounds and whin-bushes and nettles where once stood—and still stands, only that they cannot see it—the palace of their father. Their eyes are holden, we are to understand, because a higher destiny was in store for them than to return to the Land of Youth.

On Erris Bay they hear for the first time the sound of a Christian bell. It comes from the chapel of a hermit who has established himself there. The swans are at first startled and terrified by the "thin, dreadful sound," but afterwards approach and make themselves known to the hermit, who instructs them in the faith, and they join him in singing the offices of the Church.

Now it happens that a princess of Munster, Deoca, (the "woman of the South") became betrothed to a Connacht chief named Lairgnen, and begged him as a wedding gift to procure for her the four wonderful singing swans whose fame had come to her. He asks them of the hermit, who refuses to give them up, whereupon the "man of the North" seizes them violently by the silver chains with which the hermit had coupled them, and drags them off to Deoca. This is their last trial. Arrived in her presence, an awful transformation befalls them. The swan plumage falls off, and reveals, not, indeed, the radiant forms of the Danaan divinities, but four withered, snowy-haired, and miserable human beings, shrunken in the decrepitude of their vast old age. Lairgnen flies from the place in horror, but the hermit prepares to administer baptism at once, as death is rapidly approaching them. "Lay us in one grave," says Fionuala, "and place Conn at my right hand and Fiachra at my left, and Hugh before my face, for there they were wont to be when I sheltered them many a winter night upon the seas of Moyle." And so it was done, and they went to heaven; but the hermit, it is said, sorrowed for them to the end of his earthly days.[1]

In all Celtic legend there is no more tender and beautiful tale than this of the Children of Lir.

The Tale of Ethné

But the imagination of the Celtic bard always played with delight on the subjects of these transition tales,

[1] The story here summarised is given in full in the writer's "High Deeds of Finn" (Harrap and Co.).

where the reconciling of the pagan order with the Christian was the theme. The same conception is embodied in the tale of Ethné, which we have now to tell.

It is said that Mananan mac Lir had a daughter who was given in fosterage to the Danaan prince Angus, whose fairy palace was at Brugh na Boyna. This is the great sepulchral tumulus now called New Grange, on the Boyne. At the same time the steward of Angus had a daughter born to him whose name was Ethné, and who was allotted to the young princess as her handmaiden.

Ethné grew up into a lovely and gentle maiden, but it was discovered one day that she took no nourishment of any kind, although the rest of the household fed as usual on the magic swine of Mananan, which might be eaten to-day and were alive again for the feast to-morrow. Mananan was called in to penetrate the mystery, and the following curious story came to light. One of the chieftains of the Danaans who had been on a visit with Angus, smitten by the girl's beauty, had endeavoured to possess her by force. This woke in Ethné's pure spirit the moral nature which is proper to man, and which the Danaan divinities know not. As the tale says, her "guardian demon" left her, and an angel of the true God took its place. After that event she abstained altogether from the food of Faëry, and was miraculously nourished by the will of God. After a time, however, Mananan and Angus, who had been on a voyage to the East, brought back thence two cows whose milk never ran dry, and as they were supposed to have come from a sacred land Ethné lived on their milk thenceforward.

All this is supposed to have happened during the reign of Eremon, the first Milesian king of all Ireland, who was contemporary with King David. At the time of the coming of St. Patrick, therefore, Ethné would have been about fifteen hundred years of age. The Danaan folk grow up from childhood to maturity, but then they abide unaffected by the lapse of time.

Now it happened one summer day that the Danaan princess whose handmaid Ethné was went down with all her maidens to bathe in the river Boyne. When arraying themselves afterwards Ethné discovered, to her dismay—and this incident was, of course, an instance of divine interest in her destiny—that she had lost the Veil of Invisibility, conceived here as a magic charm worn on the person, which gave her the entrance to the Danaan fairyland and hid her from mortal eyes. She could not find her way back to the palace of Angus, and wandered up and down the banks of the river seeking in vain for her companions and her home. At last she came to a walled garden, and, looking through the gate, saw inside a stone house of strange appearance and a man in a long brown robe. The man was a Christian monk, and the house was a little church or oratory. He beckoned her in, and when she had told her story to him he brought her to St. Patrick, who completed her adoption into the human family by giving her the rite of baptism.

Now comes in a strangely pathetic episode which reveals the tenderness, almost the regret, with which early Irish Christianity looked back on the lost world of paganism. As Ethné was one day praying in the little church by the Boyne she heard suddenly a rushing sound in the air, and innumerable voices, as it seemed from a great distance, lamenting and calling her name. It was her Danaan kindred, who were still seeking for her in vain. She sprang up to reply, but was so overcome with emotion that she fell in a swoon on the floor. She recovered her senses after a while, but from that day she was struck with a mortal sickness, and in no long time she died, with her head upon the breast of St. Patrick, who administered to her the last rites, and ordained that the church should be named after her, Kill Ethné—a name doubtless borne, at the time the story was composed, by some real church on the banks of Boyne.[1]

Christianity and Paganism in Ireland

These, taken together with numerous other legendary incidents which might be quoted, illustrate well the attitude of the early Celtic Christians, in Ireland at least, towards the divinities of the older faith. They seem to preclude the idea that at the time of the conversion of Ireland the pagan religion was associated with cruel and barbarous practices, on which the national memory would look back with horror and detestation.

[1] It may be mentioned that the syllable "Kill," which enters into so many Irish place-names (Kilkenny, Killiney, Kilcooley, &c.), usually represents the Latin *cella*, a monastic cell, shrine, or church.

CHAPTER IV : THE EARLY MILESIAN KINGS

The Danaans after the Milesian Conquest

THE kings and heroes of the Milesian race now fill the foreground of the stage in Irish legendary history. But, as we have indicated, the Danaan divinities are by no means forgotten. The fairyland in which they dwell is ordinarily inaccessible to mortals, yet it is ever near at hand ; the invisible barriers may be, and often are, crossed by mortal men, and the Danaans themselves frequently come forth from them ; mortals may win brides of Faëry who mysteriously leave them after a while, and women bear glorious children of supernatural fatherhood. Yet whatever the Danaans may have been in the original pre-Christian conceptions of the Celtic Irish, it would be a mistake to suppose that they figure in the legends, as these have now come down to us, in the light of gods as we understand this term. They are for the most part radiantly beautiful, they are immortal (with limitations), and they wield mysterious powers of sorcery and enchantment. But no sort of moral governance of the world is ever for a moment ascribed to them, nor (in the bardic literature) is any act of worship paid to them. They do not die naturally, but they can be slain both by each other and by mortals, and on the whole the mortal race is the stronger. Their strength when they come into conflict (as frequently happens) with men lies in stratagem and illusion ; when the issue can be fairly knit between the rival powers it is the human that conquers. The early kings and heroes of the Milesian race are, indeed, often represented as so mightily endowed with supernatural power that it is impossible to draw a clear distinction between them and the People of Dana in this respect.

DANAANS AFTER THE MILESIAN CONQUEST

The Danaans are much nobler and more exalted beings, as they figure in the bardic literature, than the fairies into which they ultimately degenerated in the popular imagination; they may be said to hold a position intermediate between these and the Greek deities as portrayed in Homer. But the true worship of the Celts, in Ireland as elsewhere, seems to have been paid, not to these poetical personifications of their ideals of power and beauty, but rather to elemental forces represented by actual natural phenomena—rocks, rivers, the sun, the wind, the sea. The most binding of oaths was to swear by the Wind and Sun, or to invoke some other power of nature; no name of any Danaan divinity occurs in an Irish oath formula. When, however, in the later stages of the bardic literature, and still more in the popular conceptions, the Danaan deities had begun to sink into fairies, we find rising into prominence a character probably older than that ascribed to them in the literature, and, in a way, more august. In the literature it is evident that they were originally representatives of science and poetry—the intellectual powers of man. But in the popular mind they represented, probably at all times and certainly in later Christian times, not intellectual powers, but those associated with the fecundity of earth. They were, as a passage in the Book of Armagh names them, *dei terreni*, earth-gods, and were, and are still, invoked by the peasantry to yield increase and fertility. The literary conception of them is plainly Druidic in origin, the other popular; and the popular and doubtless older conception has proved the more enduring.

But these features of Irish mythology will appear better in the actual tales than in any critical discussion of them; and to the tales let us now return.

The Milesian Settlement of Ireland

The Milesians had three leaders when they set out for the conquest of Ireland—Eber Donn (Brown Eber), Eber Finn (Fair Eber), and Eremon. Of these the first-named, as we have seen, was not allowed to enter the land—he perished as a punishment for his brutality. When the victory over the Danaans was secure the two remaining brothers turned to the Druid Amergin for a judgment as to their respective titles to the sovranty. Eremon was the elder of the two, but Eber refused to submit to him. Thus Irish history begins, alas! with dissension and jealousy. Amergin decided that the land should belong to Eremon for his life, and pass to Eber after his death. But Eber refused to submit to the award, and demanded an immediate partition of the new-won territory. This was agreed to, and Eber took the southern half of Ireland, "from the Boyne to the Wave of Cleena,"[1] while Eremon occupied the north. But even so the brethren could not be at peace, and after a short while war broke out between them. Eber was slain, and Eremon became sole King of Ireland, which he ruled from Tara, the traditional seat of that central authority which was always a dream of the Irish mind, but never a reality of Irish history.

Tiernmas and Crom Cruach

Of the kings who succeeded Eremon, and the battles they fought and the forests they cleared away and the rivers and lakes that broke out in their reign, there is little of note to record till we come to the reign of Tiernmas, fifth in succession from Eremon. He is said

[1] Cleena (*Cliodhna*) was a Danaan princess about whom a legend is told connected with the Bay of Glandore in Co. Cork. See p. 127.

to have introduced into Ireland the worship of Crom Cruach, on Moyslaught (The Plain of Adoration[1]), and to have perished himself with three-fourths of his people while worshipping this idol on November Eve, the period when the reign of winter was inaugurated. Crom Cruach was no doubt a solar deity, but no figure at all resembling him can be identified among the Danaan divinities. Tiernmas also, it is said, found the first gold-mine in Ireland, and introduced variegated colours into the clothing of the people. A slave might wear but one colour, a peasant two, a soldier three, a wealthy landowner four, a provincial chief five, and an Ollav, or royal person, six. Ollav was a term applied to a certain Druidic rank; it meant much the same as "doctor," in the sense of a learned man—a master of science. It is a characteristic trait that the Ollav is endowed with a distinction equal to that of a king.

Ollav Fōla

The most distinguished Ollav of Ireland was also a king, the celebrated Ollav Fōla, who is supposed to have been eighteenth from Eremon and to have reigned about 1000 B.C. He was the Lycurgus or Solon of Ireland, giving to the country a code of legislature, and also subdividing it, under the High King at Tara, among the provincial chiefs, to each of whom his proper rights and obligations were allotted. To Ollav Fōla is also attributed the foundation of an institution which, whatever its origin, became of great importance in Ireland—the great triennial Fair or Festival at Tara, where the sub-kings and chiefs, bards, historians, and musicians from all parts of Ireland assembled to make up the genealogical records of the clan chieftainships, to enact laws, hear disputed cases, settle succession, and so

[1] See p. 85.

forth; all these political and legislative labours being lightened by song and feast. It was a stringent law that at this season all enmities must be laid aside; no man might lift his hand against another, or even institute a legal process, while the Assembly at Tara was in progress. Of all political and national institutions of this kind Ollav Fōla was regarded as the traditional founder, just as Goban the Smith was the founder of artistry and handicraft, and Amergin of poetry. But whether the Milesian king had any more objective reality than the other more obviously mythical figures it is hard to say. He is supposed to have been buried in the great tumulus at Loughcrew, in Westmeath.

Kimbay and the Founding of Emain Macha

With Kimbay (*Cimbaoth*), about 300 B.C., we come to a landmark in history. "All the historical records of the Irish, prior to Kimbay, were dubious"—so, with remarkable critical acumen for his age, wrote the eleventh-century historian Tierna of Clonmacnois.[1] There is much that is dubious in those that follow, but we are certainly on firmer historical ground. With the reign of Kimbay one great fact emerges into light: we have the foundation of the kingdom of Ulster at its centre, Emain Macha, a name redolent to the Irish student of legendary splendour and heroism. Emain Macha is now represented by the grassy ramparts of a great hill-fortress close to Ard Macha (Armagh). According to one of the derivations offered in Keating's "History of Ireland," *Emain* is derived from *eo*, a bodkin, and *muin*, the neck, the word being thus equivalent to

[1] "Omnia monumenta Scotorum ante Cimbaoth incerta erant." Tierna, who died in 1088, was Abbot of Clonmacnois, a great monastic and educational centre in mediæval Ireland.

"brooch," and Emain Macha means the Brooch of Macha. An Irish brooch was a large circular wheel of gold or bronze, crossed by a long pin, and the great circular rampart surrounding a Celtic fortress might well be imaginatively likened to the brooch of a giantess guarding her cloak, or territory.[1] The legend of Macha tells that she was the daughter of Red Hugh, an Ulster prince who had two brothers, Dithorba and Kimbay. They agreed to enjoy, each in turn, the sovranty of Ireland. Red Hugh came first, but on his death Macha refused to give up the realm and fought Dithorba for it, whom she conquered and slew. She then, in equally masterful manner, compelled Kimbay to wed her, and ruled all Ireland as queen. I give the rest of the tale in the words of Standish O'Grady:

"The five sons of Dithorba, having been expelled out of Ulster, fled across the Shannon, and in the west of the kingdom plotted against Macha. Then the Queen went down alone into Connacht and found the brothers in the forest, where, wearied with the chase, they were cooking a wild boar which they had slain, and were carousing before a fire which they had kindled. She appeared in her grimmest aspect, as the war-goddess, red all over, terrible and hideous as war itself but with bright and flashing eyes. One by one the brothers were inflamed by her sinister beauty, and one by one she overpowered and bound them. Then she lifted her burthen of champions upon her back and returned with them into the north. With the spear of her brooch she marked out on the plain the circuit of the city of Emain Macha, whose ramparts and trenches

[1] Compare the fine poem of a modern Celtic writer (Sir Samuel Ferguson), "The Widow's Cloak"—*i.e.*, the British Empire in the days of Queen Victoria.

were constructed by the captive princes, labouring like slaves under her command."

"The underlying idea of all this class of legend," remarks Mr. O'Grady, "is that if men cannot master war, war will master them; and that those who aspired to the Ard-Rieship [High-Kingship] of all Erin must have the war-gods on their side."[1]

Macha is an instance of the intermingling of the attributes of the Danaan with the human race of which I have already spoken.

Laery and Covac

The next king who comes into legendary prominence is Ugainy the Great, who is said to have ruled not only all Ireland, but a great part of Western Europe, and to have wedded a Gaulish princess named Kesair. He had two sons, Laery and Covac. The former inherited the kingdom, but Covac, consumed and sick with envy, sought to slay him, and asked the advice of a Druid as to how this could be managed, since Laery, justly suspicious, never would visit him without an armed escort. The Druid bade him feign death, and have word sent to his brother that he was on his bier ready for burial. This Covac did, and when Laery arrived and bent over the supposed corpse Covac stabbed him to the heart, and slew also one of his sons, Ailill,[2] who attended him. Then Covac ascended the throne, and straightway his illness left him.

Legends of Maon, Son of Ailill

He did a brutal deed, however, upon a son of Ailill's named Maon, about whom a number of legends

[1] "Critical History of Ireland," p. 180.

[2] Pronounced "El'yill."

cluster. Maon, as a child, was brought into Covac's presence, and was there compelled, says Keating, to swallow a portion of his father's and grandfather's hearts, and also a mouse with her young. From the disgust he felt, the child lost his speech, and seeing him dumb, and therefore innocuous, Covac let him go. The boy was then taken into Munster, to the kingdom of Feramorc, of which Scoriath was king, and remained with him some time, but afterwards went to Gaul, his great-grandmother Kesair's country, where his guards told the king that he was heir to the throne of Ireland, and he was treated with great honour and grew up into a noble youth. But he left behind him in the heart of Moriath, daughter of the King of Feramorc, a passion that could not be stilled, and she resolved to bring him back to Ireland. She accordingly equipped her father's harper, Craftiny, with many rich gifts, and wrote for him a love-lay, in which her passion for Maon was set forth, and to which Craftiny composed an enchanting melody. Arrived in France, Craftiny made his way to the king's court, and found occasion to pour out his lay to Maon. So deeply stirred was he by the beauty and passion of the song that his speech returned to him and he broke out into praises of it, and was thenceforth dumb no more. The King of Gaul then equipped him with an armed force and sent him to Ireland to regain his kingdom. Learning that Covac was at a place near at hand named Dinrigh, Maon and his body of Gauls made a sudden attack upon him and slew him there and then, with all his nobles and guards. After the slaughter a Druid of Covac's company asked one of the Gauls who their leader was. "The Mariner" (*Loingseach*), replied the Gaul, meaning the captain of the fleet—*i.e.*, Maon. "Can he speak?" inquired the Druid, who had begun to suspect the truth. "He does speak" (*Labraidh*), said the man; and henceforth the name "Labra the Mariner" clung to Maon son of Ailill, nor was he known by any other. He then sought out Moriath, wedded her, and reigned over Ireland ten years.

From this invasion of the Gauls the name of the province of Leinster is traditionally derived. They were armed with spears having broad blue-green iron heads called *laighne* (pronounced "lyna"), and as they were allotted lands in Leinster and settled there, the province was called in Irish *Laighin* ("Ly-in") after them—the Province of the Spearmen.[1]

Of Labra the Mariner, after his accession, a curious tale is told. He was accustomed, it is said, to have his hair cropped but once a year, and the man to do this was chosen by lot, and was immediately afterwards put to death. The reason of this was that, like King Midas in the similar Greek myth, he had long ears like those of a horse, and he would not have this deformity known. Once it fell, however, that the person chosen to crop his hair was the only son of a poor widow, by whose tears and entreaties the king was prevailed upon to let him live, on condition that he swore by the Wind and Sun to tell no man what he might see. The oath was taken, and the young man returned to his mother. But by-and-by the secret so preyed on his mind that he fell into a sore sickness, and was near to death, when a wise Druid was called in to heal him. "It is the secret that

[1] The ending *ster* in three of the names of the Irish provinces is of Norse origin, and is a relic of the Viking conquests in Ireland. Connacht, where the Vikings did not penetrate, alone preserves its Irish name unmodified. Ulster (in Irish *Ulaidh*) is supposed to derive its name from Ollav Fōla, Munster (*Mumhan*) from King Eocho Mumho, tenth in succession from Eremon, and Connacht was "the land of the children of Conn"—he who was called Conn of the Hundred Battles, and who died A.D. 157.

" The first tree was a willow "

Midir and Etain

is killing him," said the Druid, "and he will never be well till he reveals it. Let him therefore go along the high-road till he come to a place where four roads meet. Let him there turn to the right, and the first tree he shall meet on the road, let him tell his secret to that, and he shall be rid of it, and recover." So the youth did ; and the first tree was a willow. He laid his lips close to the bark, whispered his secret to it, and went home, light-hearted as of old. But it chanced that shortly after this the harper Craftiny broke his harp and needed a new one, and as luck would have it the first suitable tree he came to was the willow that had the king's secret. He cut it down, made his harp from it, and performed that night as usual in the king's hall ; when, to the amazement of all, as soon as the harper touched the strings the assembled guests heard them chime the words, "Two horse's ears hath Labra the Mariner." The king then, seeing that the secret was out, plucked off his hood and showed himself plainly ; nor was any man put to death again on account of this mystery. We have seen that the compelling power of Craftiny's music had formerly cured Labra's dumbness. The sense of something magical in music, as though supernatural powers spoke through it, is of constant recurrence in Irish legend.

Legend-Cycle of Conary Mōr

We now come to a cycle of legends centering on, or rather closing with, the wonderful figure of the High King Conary Mōr—a cycle so charged with splendour, mystery, and romance that to do it justice would require far more space than can be given to it within the limits of this work.[1]

[1] The reader may, however, be referred to the tale of Etain and Midir as given in full by A. H. Leahy ("Heroic Romances of

Etain in Fairyland

The preliminary events of the cycle are transacted in the "Land of Youth," the mystic country of the People of Dana after their dispossession by the Children of Miled. Midir the Proud son of the Dagda, a Danaan prince dwelling on Slieve Callary, had a wife named Fuamnach. After a while he took to himself another bride, Etain, whose beauty and grace were beyond compare, so that "as fair as Etain" became a proverbial comparison for any beauty that exceeded all other standards. Fuamnach therefore became jealous of her rival, and having by magic art changed her into a butterfly, she raised a tempest that drove her forth from the palace, and kept her for seven years buffeted hither and thither throughout the length and breadth of Erin. At last, however, a chance gust of wind blew her through a window of the fairy palace of Angus on the Boyne. The immortals cannot be hidden from each other, and Angus knew what she was. Unable to release her altogether from the spell of Fuamnach, he made a sunny bower for her, and planted round it all manner of choice and honey-laden flowers, on which she lived as long as she was with him, while in the secrecy of the night he restored her to her own form and enjoyed her love. In time, however, her refuge was discovered by Fuamnach; again the magic tempest descended upon her and drove her forth; and this time a singular fate was hers. Blown into the palace of an Ulster chieftain named Etar, she fell into the drinking-cup of Etar's wife just as the latter was about to drink. She was swallowed in the draught, and in due time, having

Ireland"), and by the writer in his "High Deeds of Finn," and to the tale of Conary rendered by Sir S. Ferguson ("Poems," 1886), in what Dr. Whitley Stokes has described as the noblest poem ever written by an Irishman.

passed into the womb of Etar's wife, she was born as an apparently mortal child, and grew up to maidenhood knowing nothing of her real nature and ancestry.

Eochy and Etain

About this time it happened that the High King of Ireland, Eochy,[1] being wifeless and urged by the nobles of his land to take a queen—"for without thou do so," they said, "we will not bring our wives to the Assembly at Tara"—sent forth to inquire for a fair and noble maiden to share his throne. The messengers report that Etain, daughter of Etar, is the fairest maiden in Ireland, and the king journeys forth to visit her. A piece of description here follows which is one of the most highly wrought and splendid in Celtic or perhaps in any literature. Eochy finds Etain with her maidens by a spring of water, whither she had gone forth to wash her hair:

"A clear comb of silver was held in her hand, the comb was adorned with gold; and near her, as for washing, was a bason of silver whereon four birds had been chased, and there were little bright gems of carbuncles on the rims of the bason. A bright purple mantle waved round her; and beneath it was another mantle ornamented with silver fringes: the outer mantle was clasped over her bosom with a golden brooch. A tunic she wore with a long hood that might cover her head attached to it; it was stiff and glossy with green silk beneath red embroidery of gold, and was clasped over her breasts with marvellously wrought clasps of silver and gold; so that men saw the bright gold and the green silk flashing against the sun. On her head were two tresses of golden hair,

[1] Pronounced "Yeo'hee."

and each tress had been plaited into four strands; at the end of each strand was a little ball of gold. And there was that maiden undoing her hair that she might wash it, her two arms out through the armholes of her smock. Each of her two arms was as white as the snow of a single night, and each of her cheeks was as rosy as the foxglove. Even and small were the teeth in her head, and they shone like pearls. Her eyes were as blue as a hyacinth, her lips delicate and crimson; very high, soft and white were her shoulders. Tender, polished and white were her wrists; her fingers long and of great whiteness; her nails were beautiful and pink. White as snow, or the foam of a wave, was her neck; long was it, slender, and as soft as silk. Smooth and white were her thighs; her knees were round and firm and white; her ankles were as straight as the rule of a carpenter. Her feet were slim and as white as the ocean's foam; evenly set were her eyes; her eyebrows were of a bluish black, such as you see upon the shell of a beetle. Never a maid fairer than she, or more worthy of love, was till then seen by the eyes of men; and it seemed to them that she must be one of those that have come from the fairy mounds."[1]

The king wooed her and made her his wife, and brought her back to Tara.

The Love-Story of Ailill

It happened that the king had a brother named Ailill, who, on seeing Etain, was so smitten with her beauty that he fell sick of the intensity of his passion and wasted almost to death. While he was in this condition Eochy had to make a royal progress

[1] I quote Mr. A. H. Leahy's translation from a fifteenth-century Egerton manuscript ("Heroic Romances of Ireland," vol. i. p. 12). The story is, however, found in much more ancient authorities.

through Ireland. He left his brother—the cause of whose malady none suspected—in Etain's care, bidding her do what she could for him, and, if he died, to bury him with due ceremonies and erect an Ogham stone above his grave.[1] Etain goes to visit the brother; she inquires the cause of his illness; he speaks to her in enigmas, but at last, moved beyond control by her tenderness, he breaks out in an avowal of his passion. His description of the yearning of hopeless love is a lyric of extraordinary intensity. "It is closer than the skin," he cries, "it is like a battle with a spectre, it overwhelms like a flood, it is a weapon under the sea, it is a passion for an echo." By "a weapon under the sea" the poet means that love is like one of the secret treasures of the fairy-folk in the kingdom of Mananan—as wonderful and as unattainable.

Etain is now in some perplexity; but she decides, with a kind of naïve good-nature, that although she is not in the least in love with Ailill, she cannot see a man die of longing for her, and she promises to be his. Possibly we are to understand here that she was prompted by the fairy nature, ignorant of good and evil, and alive only to pleasure and to suffering. It must be said, however, that in the Irish myths in general this, as we may call it, "fairy" view of morality is the one generally prevalent both among Danaans and mortals—both alike strike one as morally irresponsible.

Etain now arranges a tryst with Ailill in a house outside of Tara—for she will not do what she calls her "glorious crime" in the king's palace. But Ailill on the eve of the appointed day falls into a profound

[1] Ogham letters, which were composed of straight lines arranged in a certain order about the axis formed by the edge of a squared pillar-stone, were used for sepulchral inscription and writing generally before the introduction of the Roman alphabet in Ireland.

slumber and misses his appointment. A being in his shape does, however, come to Etain, but merely to speak coldly and sorrowfully of his malady, and departs again. When the two meet once more the situation is altogether changed. In Ailill's enchanted sleep his unholy passion for the queen has passed entirely away. Etain, on the other hand, becomes aware that behind the visible events there are mysteries which she does not understand.

Midir the Proud

The explanation soon follows. The being who came to her in the shape of Ailill was her Danaan husband, Midir the Proud. He now comes to woo her in his true shape, beautiful and nobly apparelled, and entreats her to fly with him to the Land of Youth, where she can be safe henceforward, since her persecutor, Fuamnach, is dead. He it was who shed upon Ailill's eyes the magic slumber. His description of the fairyland to which he invites her is given in verses of great beauty:

The Land of Youth

"O fair-haired woman, will you come with me to the marvellous land, full of music, where the hair is primrose-yellow and the body white as snow?
There none speaks of 'mine' or 'thine'—white are the teeth and black the brows; eyes flash with many-coloured lights, and the hue of the foxglove is on every cheek.
Pleasant to the eye are the plains of Erin, but they are a desert to the Great Plain.
Heady is the ale of Erin, but the ale of the Great Plain is headier.
It is one of the wonders of that land that youth does not change into age.
Smooth and sweet are the streams that flow through it; mead and wine abound of every kind; there men are

all fair, without blemish ; there women conceive without sin.

We see around us on every side, yet no man seeth us ; the cloud of the sin of Adam hides us from their observation.

O lady, if thou wilt come to my strong people, the purest of gold shall be on thy head—thy meat shall be swine's flesh unsalted,[1] new milk and mead shalt thou drink with me there, O fair-haired woman.'"

I have given this remarkable lyric at length because, though Christian and ascetic ideas are obviously discernible in it, it represents on the whole the pagan and mythical conception of the Land of Youth, the country of the Dead.

Etain, however, is by no means ready to go away with a stranger and to desert the High King for a man "without name or lineage." Midir tells her who he is, and all her own history of which, in her present incarnation, she knows nothing; and he adds that it was one thousand and twelve years from Etain's birth in the Land of Youth till she was born a mortal child to the wife of Etar. Ultimately Etain agrees to return with Midir to her ancient home, but only on condition that the king will agree to their severance, and with this Midir has to be content for the time.

A Game of Chess

Shortly afterwards he appears to King Eochy, as already related,[2] on the Hill of Tara. He tells the king that he has come to play a game of chess with him, and produces a chessboard of silver with pieces of gold studded with jewels. To be a skilful chess-player was a necessary accomplishment of kings and nobles in

[1] The reference is to the magic swine of Mananan, which were killed and eaten afresh every day, and whose meat preserved the eternal youth of the People of Dana.

[2] See p. 124.

Ireland, and Eochy enters into the game with zest. Midir allows him to win game after game, and in payment for his losses he performs by magic all kinds of tasks for Eochy, reclaiming land, clearing forests, and building causeways across bogs—here we have a touch of the popular conception of the Danaans as earth deities associated with agriculture and fertility. At last, having excited Eochy's cupidity and made him believe himself the better player, he proposes a final game, the stakes to be at the pleasure of the victor after the game is over. Eochy is now defeated.

"My stake is forfeit to thee," said Eochy.

"Had I wished it, it had been forfeit long ago," said Midir.

"What is it that thou desirest me to grant?" said Eochy.

"That I may hold Etain in my arms and obtain a kiss from her," said Midir.

The king was silent for a while; then he said: "One month from to-day thou shalt come, and the thing thou desirest shall be granted thee."

Midir and Etain

Eochy's mind foreboded evil, and when the appointed day came he caused the palace of Tara to be surrounded by a great host of armed men to keep Midir out. All was in vain, however; as the king sat at the feast, while Etain handed round the wine, Midir, more glorious than ever, suddenly stood in their midst. Holding his spears in his left hand, he threw his right around Etain, and the couple rose lightly in the air and disappeared through a roof-window in the palace. Angry and bewildered, the king and his warriors rushed out of doors, but all they could see was two white swans that circled in the air above the palace, and then departed in long, steady flight towards the fairy mountain of Slievenamon. And thus Queen Etain rejoined her kindred.

War with Fairyland

Eochy, however, would not accept defeat, and now ensues what I think is the earliest recorded war with Fairyland since the first dispossession of the Danaans. After searching Ireland for his wife in vain, he summoned to his aid the Druid Dalan. Dalan tried for a year by every means in his power to find out where she was. At last he made what seems to have been an operation of wizardry of special strength—"he made three wands of yew, and upon the wands he wrote an ogham; and by the keys of wisdom that he had, and by the ogham, it was revealed to him that Etain was in the fairy mound of Bri-Leith, and that Midir had borne her thither."

Eochy then assembled his forces to storm and destroy the fairy mound in which was the palace of Midir. It is said that he was nine years digging up one mound after another, while Midir and his folk repaired the devastation as fast as it was made. At last Midir, driven to the last stronghold, attempted a stratagem—he offered to give up Etain, and sent her with fifty handmaids to the king, but made them all so much alike that Eochy could not distinguish the true Etain from her images. She herself, it is said, gave him a sign by which to know her. The motive of the tale, including the choice of the mortal rather than the god, reminds one of the beautiful Hindu legend of Damayanti and Nala. Eochy regained his queen, who lived with him till his death, ten years afterwards, and bore him one daughter, who was named Etain, like herself.

The Tale of Conary Mōr

From this Etain ultimately sprang the great king Conary Mōr, who shines in Irish legend as the supreme type of royal splendour, power, and beneficence, and whose overthrow and death were compassed by the Danaans in vengeance for the devastation of their sacred dwellings by Eochy. The tale in which the death of Conary is related is one of the most antique and barbaric in conception of all Irish legends, but it has a magnificence of imagination which no other can rival. To this great story the tale of Etain and Midir may be regarded as what the Irish called a *priomscel*, "introductory tale," showing the more remote origin of the events related. The genealogy of Conary Mōr will help the reader to understand the connexion of events.

Eochy=Etain.
|
Cormac, King of Ulster.=Etain Oig (Etain the younger).
|
Eterskel, King of Erin.=Messbuachalla (the cowherd's fosterling).
|
Conary Mōr.

The Law of the Geis

The tale of Conary introduces us for the first time to the law or institution of the *geis*, which plays henceforward a very important part in Irish legend, the violation or observance of a *geis* being frequently the turning-point in a tragic narrative. We must therefore delay a moment to explain to the reader exactly what this peculiar institution was.

Dineen's "Irish Dictionary" explains the word *geis*

(pronounced "gaysh"—plural, "gaysha") as meaning "a bond, a spell, a prohibition, a taboo, a magical injunction, the violation of which led to misfortune and death."[1] Every Irish chieftain or personage of note had certain *geise* peculiar to himself which he must not transgress. These *geise* had sometimes reference to a code of chivalry—thus Dermot of the Love-spot, when appealed to by Grania to take her away from Finn, is under *geise* not to refuse protection to a woman. Or they may be merely superstitious or fantastic—thus Conary, as one of his *geise*, is forbidden to follow three red horsemen on a road, nor must he kill birds (this is because, as we shall see, his totem was a bird). It is a *geis* to the Ulster champion, Fergus mac Roy, that he must not refuse an invitation to a feast; on this turns the Tragedy of the Sons of Usnach. It is not at all clear who imposed these *geise* or how any one found out what his personal *geise* were—all that was doubtless an affair of the Druids. But they were regarded as sacred obligations, and the worst misfortunes were to be apprehended from breaking them. Originally, no doubt, they were regarded as a means of keeping oneself in proper relations with the other world—the world of Faëry—and were akin to the well-known Polynesian practice of the "tabu." I prefer, however, to retain the Irish word as the only fitting one for the Irish practice.

The Cowherd's Fosterling

We now return to follow the fortunes of Etain's great-grandson, Conary. Her daughter, Etain Oig, as we have seen from the genealogical table, married Cormac, King of Ulster. She bore her husband no children save one daughter only. Embittered by her

[1] The meaning quoted will be found in the Dictionary under the alternative form *geas*

barrenness and his want of an heir, the king put away Etain, and ordered her infant to be abandoned and thrown into a pit. "Then his two thralls take her to a pit, and she smiles a laughing smile at them as they were putting her into it."[1] After that they cannot leave her to die, and they carry her to a cowherd of Eterskel, King of Tara, by whom she is fostered and taught "till she became a good embroidress and there was not in Ireland a king's daughter dearer than she." Hence the name she bore, Messbuachalla ("Messboo'hala"), which means "the cowherd's foster-child."

For fear of her being discovered, the cowherds keep the maiden in a house of wickerwork having only a roof-opening. But one of King Eterskel's folk has the curiosity to climb up and look in, and sees there the fairest maiden in Ireland. He bears word to the king, who orders an opening to be made in the wall and the maiden fetched forth, for the king was childless, and it had been prophesied to him by his Druid that a woman of unknown race would bear him a son. Then said the king: "This is the woman that has been prophesied to me."

Parentage and Birth of Conary

Before her release, however, she is visited by a denizen from the Land of Youth. A great bird comes down through her roof-window. On the floor of the hut his bird-plumage falls from him and reveals a glorious youth. Like Danaë, like Leda, like Ethlinn daughter of Balor, she gives her love to the god. Ere they part he tells her that she will be taken to the king, but that she will bear to her Danaan lover a son

[1] I quote from Whitley Stokes' translation, *Revue Celtique*, January 1901, and succeeding numbers.

"On the floor of the hut his bird-plumage falls from him"

The Curse of Macha

whose name shall be Conary, and that it shall be forbidden to him to go a-hunting after birds.

So Conary was born, and grew up into a wise and noble youth, and he was fostered with a lord named Desa, whose three great-grandsons grew up with him from childhood. Their names were Ferlee and Fergar and Ferrogan; and Conary, it is said, loved them well and taught them his wisdom.

Conary the High King

Then King Eterskel died, and a successor had to be appointed. In Ireland the eldest son did not succeed to the throne or chieftaincy as a matter of right, but the ablest and best of the family at the time was supposed to be selected by the clan. In this tale we have a curious account of this selection by means of divination. A "bull-feast" was held—*i.e.*, a bull was slain, and the diviner would "eat his fill and drink its broth"; then he went to bed, where a truth-compelling spell was chanted over him. Whoever he saw in his dream would be king. So at Ægira, in Achæa, as Whitley Stokes points out, the priestess of Earth drank the fresh blood of a bull before descending into the cave to prophesy. The dreamer cried in his sleep that he saw a naked man going towards Tara with a stone in his sling.

The bull-feast was held at Tara, but Conary was then with his three foster-brothers playing a game on the Plains of Liffey. They separated, Conary going towards Dublin, where he saw before him a flock of great birds, wonderful in colour and beauty. He drove after them in his chariot, but the birds would go a spear-cast in front and light, and fly on again, never letting him come up with them till they reached the sea-shore. Then he lighted down from his chariot and took out his sling to cast at them, whereupon they changed into armed men and turned on him with spears and swords. One of them, however, protected him, and said: "I am Nemglan, king of thy father's birds; and thou hast been forbidden to cast at birds, for here there is no one but is thy kin." "Till to-day," said Conary, "I knew not this."

"Go to Tara to-night," said Nemglan; "the bull-feast is there, and through it thou shalt be made king. A man stark naked, who shall go at the end of the night along one of the roads to Tara, having a stone and a sling—'tis he that shall be king."

So Conary stripped off his raiment and went naked through the night to Tara, where all the roads were being watched by chiefs having changes of royal raiment with them to clothe the man who should come according to the prophecy. When Conary meets them they clothe him and bring him in, and he is proclaimed King of Erin.

Conary's Geise

A long list of his *geise* is here given, which are said to have been declared to him by Nemglan. "The bird-reign shall be noble," said he, "and these shall be thy *geise*:

> "Thou shalt not go right-handwise round Tara, nor left-handwise round Bregia,[1]
> Thou shalt not hunt the evil-beasts of Cerna,
> Thou shalt not go out every ninth night beyond Tara.
> Thou shalt not sleep in a house from which firelight shows after sunset, or in which light can be seen from without.
> No three Reds shall go before thee to the house of Red.
> No rapine shall be wrought in thy reign.

[1] Bregia was the great plain lying eastwards of Tara between Boyne and Liffey

After sunset, no one woman alone or man alone shall enter the house in which thou art.
Thou shalt not interfere in a quarrel between two of thy thralls."

Conary then entered upon his reign, which was marked by the fair seasons and bounteous harvests always associated in the Irish mind with the reign of a good king. Foreign ships came to the ports. Oak-mast for the swine was up to the knees every autumn; the rivers swarmed with fish. "No one slew another in Erin during his reign, and to every one in Erin his fellow's voice seemed as sweet as the strings of lutes. From mid-spring to mid-autumn no wind disturbed a cow's tail."

Beginning of the Vengeance

Disturbance, however, came from another source. Conary had put down all raiding and rapine, and his three foster-brothers, who were born reavers, took it ill. They pursued their evil ways in pride and wilfulness, and were at last captured red-handed. Conary would not condemn them to death, as the people begged him to do, but spared them for the sake of his kinship in fosterage. They were, however, banished from Erin and bidden to go raiding overseas, if raid they must. On the seas they met another exiled chief, Ingcel the One-Eyed, son of the King of Britain, and joining forces with him they attacked the fortress in which Ingcel's father, mother, and brothers were guests at the time, and all were destroyed in a single night. It was then the turn of Ingcel to ask their help in raiding the land of Erin, and gathering a host of other outlawed men, including the seven Manés, sons of Ailell and Maev of Connacht, besides Ferlee, Fergar, and Ferrogan, they made a descent upon Ireland, taking land on the Dublin coast near Howth.

Meantime Conary had been lured by the machinations of the Danaans into breaking one after another of his *geise*. He settles a quarrel between two of his serfs in Munster, and travelling back to Tara they see the country around it lit with the glare of fires and wrapped in clouds of smoke. A host from the North, they think, must be raiding the country, and to escape it Conary's company have to turn right-handwise round Tara and then left-handwise round the Plain of Bregia. But the smoke and flames were an illusion made by the Fairy Folk, who are now drawing the toils closer round the doomed king. On his way past Bregia he chases "the evil beasts of Cerna"—whatever they were—"but he saw it not till the chase was ended."

Da Derga's Hostel and the Three Reds

Conary had now to find a resting-place for the night, and he recollects that he is not far from the Hostel of the Leinster lord, Da Derga, which gives its name to this bardic tale.[1] Conary had been generous to him when Da Derga came visiting to Tara, and he determined to seek his hospitality for the night. Da Derga dwelt in a vast hall with seven doors near to the present town of Dublin, probably at Donnybrook, on the high-road to the south. As the cavalcade are journeying thither an ominous incident occurs—Conary marks in front of them on the road three horsemen clad all in red and riding on red horses. He remembers his *geis* about the "three Reds," and sends a messenger forward to bid them fall behind. But however the messenger lashes his horse he fails to get nearer than the length of a spear-cast to the three Red Riders. He shouts to them to turn back and follow the king, but one of them, looking over his shoulder, bids him ironically look out for "great

[1] "The Destruction of Da Derga's Hostel."

news from a Hostel." Again and again the messenger is sent to them with promises of great reward if they will fall behind instead of preceding Conary. At last one of them chants a mystic and terrible strain. "Lo, my son, great the news. Weary are the steeds we ride —the steeds from the fairy mounds. Though we are living, we are dead. Great are the signs: destruction of life; sating of ravens; feeding of crows; strife of slaughter; wetting of sword-edge; shields with broken bosses after sundown. Lo, my son!" Then they ride forward, and, alighting from their red steeds, fasten them at the portal of Da Derga's Hostel and sit down inside. "Derga," it may be explained, means "red." Conary had therefore been preceded by three red horsemen to the House of Red. "All my *geise*," he remarks forebodingly, "have seized me to-night."

Gathering of the Hosts

From this point the story of Conary Mōr takes on a character of supernatural vastness and mystery, the imagination of the bardic narrator dilating, as it were, with the approach of the crisis. Night has fallen, and the pirate host of Ingcel is encamped on the shores of Dublin Bay. They hear the noise of the royal cavalcade, and a long-sighted messenger is sent out to discover what it is. He brings back word of the glittering and multitudinous host which has followed Conary to the Hostel. A crashing noise is heard—Ingcel asks of Ferrogan what it may be—it is the giant warrior mac Cecht striking flint on steel to kindle fire for the king's feast. "God send that Conary be not there to-night," cry the sons of Desa; "woe that he should be under the hurt of his foes." But Ingcel reminds them of their compact—he had given them the plundering of his own father and brethren; they cannot refuse to stand by him in the attack he meditates on Conary in the Hostel. A glare of the fire lit by mac Cecht is now perceived by the pirate host, shining through the wheels of the chariots which are drawn up around the open doors of the Hostel. Another of the *geise* of Conary has been broken.

Ingcel and his host now proceed to build a great cairn of stones, each man contributing one stone, so that there may be a memorial of the fight, and also a record of the number slain when each survivor removes his stone again.

The Morrigan

The scene now shifts to the Hostel, where the king's party has arrived and is preparing for the night. A solitary woman comes to the door and seeks admission. "As long as a weaver's beam were each of her two shins, and they were as dark as the back of a stag-beetle. A greyish, woolly mantle she wore. Her hair reached to her knee. Her mouth was twisted to one side of her head." It was the Morrigan, the Danaan goddess of Death and Destruction. She leant against the doorpost of the house and looked evilly on the king and his company. "Well, O woman," said Conary, "if thou art a witch, what seest thou for us?" "Truly I see for thee," she answered, "that neither fell nor flesh of thine shall escape from the place into which thou hast come, save what birds will bear away in their claws." She asks admission. Conary declares that his *geis* forbids him to receive a solitary man or woman after sunset. "If in sooth," she says, "it has befallen the king not to have room in his house for the meal and bed of a solitary woman, they will be gotten apart from him from some one possessing generosity." "Let her in, then," says Conary, "though it is a *geis* of mine."

Conary and his Retinue

A lengthy and brilliant passage now follows describing how Ingcel goes to spy out the state of affairs in the Hostel. Peeping through the chariot-wheels, he takes note of all he sees, and describes to the sons of Desa the appearance and equipment of each prince and mighty man in Conary's retinue, while Ferrogan and his brother declare who he is and what destruction he will work in the coming fight. There is Cormac, son of Conor, King of Ulster, the fair and good; there are three huge, black and black-robed warriors of the Picts; there is Conary's steward, with bristling hair, who settles every dispute—a needle would be heard falling when he raises his voice to speak, and he bears a staff of office the size of a mill-shaft; there is the warrior mac Cecht, who lies supine with his knees drawn up—they resemble two bare hills, his eyes are like lakes, his nose a mountain-peak, his sword shines like a river in the sun. Conary's three sons are there, golden-haired, silk-robed, beloved of all the household, with "manners of ripe maidens, and hearts of brothers, and valour of bears." When Ferrogan hears of them he weeps and cannot proceed till hours of the night have passed. Three Fomorian hostages of horrible aspect are there also; and Conall of the Victories with his blood-red shield; and Duftach of Ulster with his magic spear, which, when there is a premonition of battle, must be kept in a brew of soporific herbs, or it will flame on its haft and fly forth raging for massacre; and three giants from the Isle of Man with horses' manes reaching to their heels. A strange and unearthly touch is introduced by a description of three naked and bleeding forms hanging by ropes from the roof—they are the daughters of the Bav, another name for the Morrigan, or war-goddess, "three of awful boding," says the tale enigmatically, "those are the three that are slaughtered at every time." We are probably to regard them as visionary beings, portending war and death, visible only to Ingcel. The hall with its separate chambers is full of warriors, cup-bearers, musicians playing, and jugglers doing wonderful feats; and Da Derga with his attendants dispensing food and drink. Conary himself is described as a youth; "the ardour and energy of a king has he and the counsel of a sage; the mantle I saw round him is even as the mist of May-day—lovelier in each hue of it than the other." His golden-hilted sword lies beside him —a forearm's length of it has escaped from the scabbard, shining like a beam of light. "He is the mildest and gentlest and most perfect king that has come into the world, even Conary son of Eterskel . . . great is the tenderness of the sleepy, simple man till he has chanced on a deed of valour. But if his fury and his courage are awakened when the champions of Erin and Alba are at him in the house, the Destruction will not be wrought so long as he is therein . . . sad were the quenching of that reign."

Champions at the House

Ingcel and the sons of Desa then march to the attack and surround the Hostel:

"Silence a while!" says Conary, "what is this?"

"Champions at the house," says Conall of the Victories.

"There are warriors for them here," answers Conary.

"They will be needed to-night," Conall rejoins.

One of Desa's sons rushes first into the Hostel. His head is struck off and cast out of it again. Then the great struggle begins. The Hostel is set on fire, but the fire is quenched with wine or any liquids that are in it. Conary and his people sally forth—hundreds are slain, and the reavers, for the moment, are routed. But Conary, who has done prodigies of fighting, is athirst and can do no more till he gets water. The reavers by advice of their wizards have cut off the river Dodder, which flowed through the Hostel, and all the liquids in the house had been spilt on the fires.

Death of Conary

The king, who is perishing of thirst, asks mac Cecht to procure him a drink, and mac Cecht turns to Conall and asks him whether he will get the drink for the king or stay to protect him while mac Cecht does it. "Leave the defence of the king to us," says Conall, "and go thou to seek the drink, for of thee it is demanded." Mac Cecht then, taking Conary's golden cup, rushes forth, bursting through the surrounding host, and goes to seek for water. Then Conall, and Cormac of Ulster, and the other champions, issue forth in turn, slaying multitudes of the enemy; some return wounded and weary to the little band in the Hostel, while others cut their way through the ring of foes. Conall, Sencha, and Duftach stand by Conary till the end; but mac Cecht is long in returning, Conary perishes of thirst, and the three heroes then fight their way out and escape, "wounded, broken, and maimed."

Meantime mac Cecht has rushed over Ireland in frantic search for the water. But the Fairy Folk, who are here manifestly elemental powers controlling the forces of nature, have sealed all the sources against him. He tries the Well of Kesair in Wicklow in vain; he goes to the great rivers, Shannon and Slayney, Bann and Barrow—they all hide away at his approach; the lakes deny him also; at last he finds a lake, Loch Gara Roscommon, which failed to hide itself in time, an thereat he fills his cup. In the morning he returne to the Hostel with the precious and hard-won draugh but found the defenders all dead or fled, and two the reavers in the act of striking off the head of Conar Mac Cecht struck off the head of one of them, an hurled a huge pillar stone after the other, who wa escaping with Conary's head. The reaver fell dead o the spot, and mac Cecht, taking up his master's hea poured the water into its mouth. Thereupon the hea spoke, and praised and thanked him for the deed.

Mac Cecht's Wound

A woman then came by and saw mac Cecht lyin exhausted and wounded on the field.

"Come hither, O woman," says mac Cecht.

"I dare not go there," says the woman, "for horro and fear of thee."

But he persuades her to come, and says: "I kno not whether it is a fly or gnat or an ant that nips m in the wound."

The woman looked and saw a hairy wolf buried a far as the two shoulders in the wound. She seized by the tail and dragged it forth, and it took "the fu of its jaws out of him."

"Truly," says the woman, "this is an ant of th Ancient Land."

And mac Cecht took it by the throat and smote it o the forehead, so that it died.

"Is thy Lord Alive?"

The tale ends in a truly heroic strain. Conall of th Victories, as we have seen, had cut his way out afte the king's death, and made his way to Teltin, where h found his father, Amorgin, in the garth before his dūn. Conall's shield-arm had been wounded by thrice fifty spears, and he reached Teltin now with half a shield, and his sword, and the fragments of his two spears.

"Swift are the wolves that have hunted thee, my son," said his father.

"'Tis this that has wounded us, old hero, an evil conflict with warriors," Conall replied.

"Is thy lord alive?" asked Amorgin.

"He is *not* alive," says Conall.

"I swear to God what the great tribes of Ulster swear: he is a coward who goes out of a fight alive having left his lord with his foes in death."

"My wounds are not white, old hero," says Conall. He showed him his shield-arm, whereon were thrice fifty spear-wounds. The sword-arm, which the shield had not guarded, was mangled and maimed and wounded and pierced, save that the sinews kept it to the body without separation.

"That arm fought to-night, my son," says Amorgin.

"True is that, old hero," says Conall of the Victories. "Many are they to whom it gave drinks of death to-night in front of the Hostel."

So ends the story of Etain, and of the overthrow of Fairyland and the fairy vengeance wrought on the great-grandson of Eochy the High King.

CHAPTER V: TALES OF THE ULTONIAN CYCLE

The Curse of Macha

THE centre of interest in Irish legend now shifts from Tara to Ulster, and a multitude of heroic tales gather round the Ulster king Conor mac Nessa, round Cuchulain,[1] his great vassal, and the Red Branch Order of chivalry, which had its seat in Emain Macha.

The legend of the foundation of Emain Macha has already been told.[2] But Macha, who was no mere woman, but a supernatural being, appears again in connexion with the history of Ulster in a very curious tale which was supposed to account for the strange debility or helplessness that at critical moments sometimes fell, it was believed, upon the warriors of the province.

The legend tells that a wealthy Ulster farmer named Crundchu, son of Agnoman, dwelling in a solitary place among the hills, found one day in his dūn a young woman of great beauty and in splendid array, whom he had never seen before. Crundchu, we are told, was a widower, his wife having died after bearing him four sons. The strange woman, without a word, set herself to do the houshold tasks, prepared dinner, milked the cow, and took on herself all the duties of the mistress of the household. At night she lay down at Crundchu's side, and thereafter dwelt with him as his wife; and they loved each other dearly. Her name was Macha.

One day Crundchu prepared himself to go to a great fair or assembly of the Ultonians, where there would be feasting and horse-racing, tournaments and music, and merrymaking of all kinds. Macha begged her husband

[1] Pronounced "Koohoo'lin." [2] See p. 150.

not to go. He persisted. "Then," she said, "at least do not speak of me in the assembly, for I may dwell with you only so long as I am not spoken of."

It has been observed that we have here the earliest appearance in post-classical European literature of the well-known motive of the fairy bride who can stay with her mortal lover only so long as certain conditions are observed, such as that he shall not spy upon her, ill-treat her, or ask of her origin.

Crundchu promised to obey the injunction, and went to the festival. Here the two horses of the king carried off prize after prize in the racing, and the people cried: "There is not in Ireland a swifter than the King's pair of horses."

"I have a wife at home," said Crundchu, in a moment of forgetfulness, "who can run quicker than these horses."

"Seize that man," said the angry king, "and hold him till his wife be brought to the contest."

So messengers went for Macha, and she was brought before the assembly; and she was with child. The king bade her prepare for the race. She pleaded her condition. "I am close upon my hour," she said. "Then hew her man in pieces," said the king to his guards. Macha turned to the bystanders. "Help me," she cried, "for a mother hath borne each of you! Give me but a short delay till I am delivered." But the king and all the crowd in their savage lust for sport would hear of no delay. "Then bring up the horses," said Macha, "and because you have no pity a heavier infamy shall fall upon you." So she raced against the horses, and outran them, but as she came to the goal she gave a great cry, and her travail seized her, and she gave birth to twin children. As she uttered that cry, however, all the spectators felt themselves seized with pangs like her own and had no more strength than a woman in her travail. And Macha prophesied: "From this hour the shame you have wrought on me will fall upon each man of Ulster. In the hours of your greatest need ye shall be weak and helpless as women in childbirth, and this shall endure for five days and four nights—to the ninth generation the curse shall be upon you." And so it came to pass; and this is the cause of the Debility of the Ultonians that was wont to afflict the warriors of the province.

Conor mac Nessa

The chief occasion on which this Debility was manifested was when Maev, Queen of Connacht, made the famous Cattle-raid of Quelgny (*Tain Bo Cuailgnê*), which forms the subject of the greatest tale in Irish literature. We have now to relate the preliminary history leading up to this epic tale and introducing its chief characters.

Fachtna the Giant, King of Ulster, had to wife Nessa, daughter of Echid Yellow-heel, and she bore him a son named Conor. But when Fachtna died Fergus son of Roy, his half-brother, succeeded him, Conor being then but a youth. Now Fergus loved Nessa, and would have wedded her, but she made conditions. "Let my son Conor reign one year," she said, "so that his posterity may be the descendants of a king, and I consent." Fergus agreed, and young Conor took the throne. But so wise and prosperous was his rule and so sagacious his judgments that, at the year's end, the people, as Nessa foresaw, would have him remain king; and Fergus, who loved the feast and the chase better than the toils of kingship, was content to have it so, and remained at Conor's court for a time, great, honoured, and happy, but king no longer.

THE RED BRANCH

The Red Branch

In his time was the glory of the "Red Branch" in Ulster, who were the offspring of Ross the Red, King of Ulster, with collateral relatives and allies, forming ultimately a kind of warlike Order. Most of the Red Branch heroes appear in the Ultonian Cycle of legend, so that a statement of their names and relationships may be usefully placed here before we proceed to speak of their doings. It is noticeable that they have a partly supernatural ancestry. Ross the Red, it is said, wedded a Danaan woman, Maga, daughter of Angus Ōg.[1] As a second wife he wedded a maiden named Roy. His descendants are as follows:

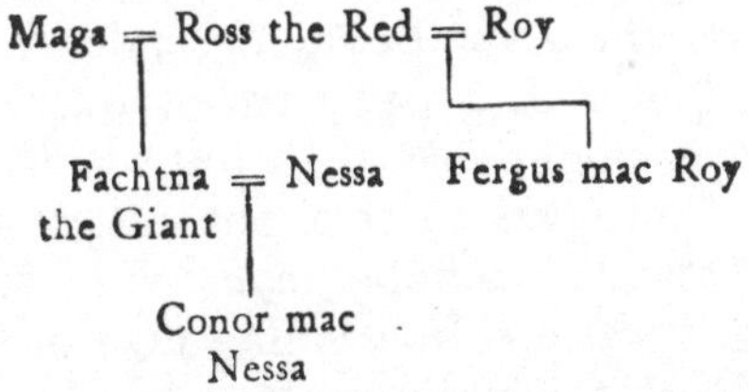

But Maga was also wedded to the Druid Cathbad, and by him had three daughters, whose descendants played a notable part in the Ultonian legendary cycle.

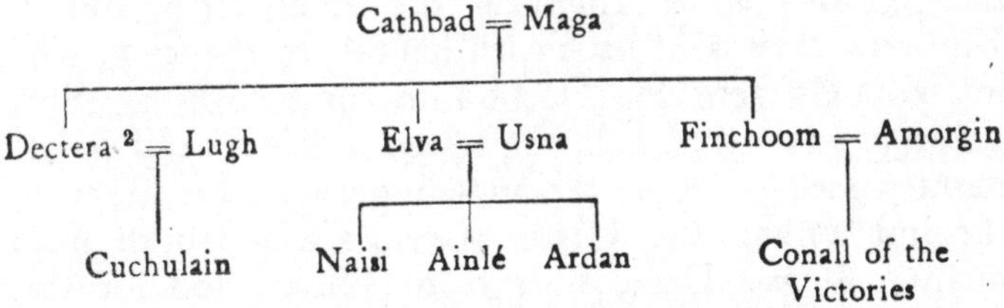

[1] See pp. 121–123 for an account of this deity.

[2] Dectera also had a mortal husband, Sualtam, who passed as Cuchulain's father.

Birth of Cuchulain

It was during the reign of Conor mac Nessa that the birth of the mightiest hero of the Celtic race, Cuchulain came about, and this was the manner of it. The maiden Dectera, daughter of Cathbad, with fifty young girls her companions at the court of Conor, one day disappeared, and for three years no searching availed to discover their dwelling-place or their fate. At last one summer day a flock of birds descended on the fields about Emain Macha and began to destroy the crops and fruit. The king, with Fergus and others of his nobles, went out against them with slings, but the birds flew only a little way off, luring the party on and on till at last they found themselves near the Fairy Mound of Angus on the river Boyne. Night fell, and the king sent Fergus with a party to discover some habitation where they might sleep. A hut was found, where they betook themselves to rest, but one of them, exploring further, came to a noble mansion by the river, and on entering it was met by a young man of splendid appearance. With the stranger was a lovely woman, his wife, and fifty maidens, who saluted the Ulster warrior with joy. And he recognised in them Dectera and her maidens, whom they had missed for three years, and in the glorious youth Lugh of the Long Arm, son of Ethlinn. He went back with his tale to the king, who immediately sent for Dectera to come to him. She, alleging that she was ill, requested a delay; and so the night passed; but in the morning there was found in the hut among the Ulster warriors a new-born male infant. It was Dectera's gift to Ulster, and for this purpose she had lured them to the fairy palace by the Boyne. The child was taken home by the warriors and was given to Dectera's sister, Finchoom, who was then

The Boy Setanta follows King Connor

The Hound of Cullan

nursing her own child, Conall, and the boy's name was called Setanta. And the part of Ulster from Dundalk southward to Usna in Meath, which is called the Plain of Murthemney, was allotted for his inheritance, and in later days his fortress and dwelling-place was in Dundalk.

It is said that the Druid Morann prophesied over the infant: "His praise will be in the mouths of all men; charioteers and warriors, kings and sages will recount his deeds; he will win the love of many. This child will avenge all your wrongs; he will give combat at your fords, he will decide all your quarrels."

The Hound of Cullan

When he was old enough the boy Setanta went to the court of Conor to be brought up and instructed along with the other sons of princes and chieftains. It was now that the event occurred from which he got the name of Cuchulain, by which he was hereafter to be known.

One afternoon King Conor and his nobles were going to a feast to which they were bidden at the dūn of a wealthy smith named Cullan, in Quelgny, where they also meant to spend the night. Setanta was to accompany them, but as the cavalcade set off he was in the midst of a game of hurley with his companions and bade the king go forward, saying he would follow later when his play was done. The royal company arrived at their destination as night began to fall. Cullan received them hospitably, and in the great hall they made merry over meat and wine while the lord of the house barred the gates of his fortress and let loose outside a huge and ferocious dog which every night guarded the lonely mansion, and under whose protection, it was said, Cullan feared nothing less than the onset of an army.

But they had forgotten Setanta! In the middle of the laughter and music of the feast a terrible sound was heard which brought every man to his feet in an instant. It was the tremendous baying of the hound of Cullan, giving tongue as it saw a stranger approach. Soon the noise changed to the howls of a fierce combat, but, on rushing to the gates, they saw in the glare of the lanterns a young boy and the hound lying dead at his feet. When it flew at him he had seized it by the throat and dashed its life out against the side-posts of the gate. The warriors bore in the lad with rejoicing and wonder, but soon the triumph ceased, for there stood their host, silent and sorrowful over the body of his faithful friend, who had died for the safety of his house and would never guard it more.

"Give me," then said the lad Setanta, "a whelp of that hound, O Cullan, and I will train him to be all to you that his sire was. And until then give me shield and spear and I will myself guard your house; never hound guarded it better than I will."

And all the company shouted applause at the generous pledge, and on the spot, as a commemoration of his first deed of valour, they named the lad Cuchulain,[1] the Hound of Cullan, and by that name he was known until he died.

Cuchulain Assumes Arms

When he was older, and near the time when he might assume the weapons of manhood, it chanced one day that he passed close by where Cathbad the Druid

[1] It is noticeable that among the characters figuring in the Ultonian legendary cycle many names occur of which the word *Cu* (hound) forms a part. Thus we have Curoi, Cucorb, Beälcu, &c. The reference is no doubt to the Irish wolf-hound, a fine type of valour and beauty.

was teaching to certain of his pupils the art of divination and augury. One of them asked of Cathbad for what kind of enterprise that same day might be favourable; and Cathbad, having worked a spell of divination, said: "The youth who should take up arms on this day would become of all men in Erin most famous for great deeds, yet will his life be short and fleeting." Cuchulain passed on as though he marked it not, and he came before the king. "What wilt thou?" asked Conor. "To take the arms of manhood," said Cuchulain. "So be it," said the king, and he gave the lad two great spears. But Cuchulain shook them in his hand, and the staves splintered and broke. And so he did with many others; and the chariots in which they set him to drive he broke to pieces with stamping of his foot, until at last the king's own chariot of war and his two spears and sword were brought to the lad, and these he could not break, do what he would; so this equipment he retained.

His Courtship of Emer

The young Cuchulain was by this grown so fair and noble a youth that every maid or matron on whom he looked was bewitched by him, and the men of Ulster bade him take a wife of his own. But none were pleasing to him, till at last he saw the lovely maiden Emer, daughter of Forgall, the lord of Lusca,[1] and he resolved to woo her for his bride. So he bade harness his chariot, and with Laeg, his friend and charioteer, he journeyed to Dūn Forgall.

As he drew near, the maiden was with her companions, daughters of the vassals of Forgall, and she was teaching them embroidery, for in that art she excelled all women. She had "the six gifts of

[1] Now Lusk, a village on the coast a few miles north of Dublin.

womanhood—the gift of beauty, the gift of voice, the gift of sweet speech, the gift of needlework, the gift of wisdom, and the gift of chastity."

Hearing the thunder of horse-hoofs and the clangour of the chariot from afar, she bade one of the maidens go to the rampart of the Dūn and tell her what she saw. "A chariot is coming on," said the maiden, "drawn by two steeds with tossing heads, fierce and powerful; one is grey, the other black. They breathe fire from their jaws, and the clods of turf they throw up behind them as they race are like a flock of birds that follow in their track. In the chariot is a dark, sad man, comeliest of the men of Erin. He is clad in a crimson cloak, with a brooch of gold, and on his back is a crimson shield with a silver rim wrought with figures of beasts. With him as his charioteer is a tall, slender, freckled man with curling red hair held by a fillet of bronze, with plates of gold at either side of his face. With a goad of red gold he urges the horses."

When the chariot drew up Emer went to meet Cuchulain and saluted him. But when he urged his love upon her she told him of the might and the wiliness of her father Forgall, and of the strength of the champions that guarded her lest she should wed against his will. And when he pressed her more she said: "I may not marry before my sister Fial, who is older than I. She is with me here—she is excellent in handiwork." "It is not Fial whom I love," said Cuchulain. Then as they were conversing he saw the breast of the maiden over the bosom of her smock, and said to her: "Fair is this plain, the plain of the noble yoke." "None comes to this plain," said she, "who has not slain his hundreds, and thy deeds are still to do."

So Cuchulain then left her, and drove back to Emain Macha.

Cuchulain in the Land of Skatha

Next day Cuchulain bethought himself how he could prepare himself for war and for the deeds of heroism which Emer had demanded of him. Now he had heard of a mighty woman-warrior named Skatha, who dwelt in the Land of Shadows,[1] and who could teach to young heroes who came to her wonderful feats of arms. So Cuchulain went overseas to find her, and many dangers he had to meet, black forests and desert plains to traverse, before he could get tidings of Skatha and her land. At last he came to the Plain of Ill-luck, where he could not cross without being mired in its bottomless bogs or sticky clay, and while he was debating what he should do he saw coming towards him a young man with a face that shone like the sun,[2] and whose very look put cheerfulness and hope into his heart. The young man gave him a wheel and told him to roll it before him on the plain, and to follow it whithersoever it went. So Cuchulain set the wheel rolling, and as it went it blazed with light that shot like rays from its rim, and the heat of it made a firm path across the quagmire, where Cuchulain followed safely.

When he had passed the Plain of Ill-luck, and escaped the beasts of the Perilous Glen, he came to the Bridge of the Leaps, beyond which was the country of Skatha. Here he found on the hither side many sons of the princes of Ireland who were come to learn feats of war from Skatha, and they were playing at hurley on the green. And among them was his friend Ferdia, son of the Firbolg, Daman ; and they all asked him of

[1] Owing to the similarity of the name the supernatural country of Skatha, "the Shadowy," was early identified with the islands of Skye, where the Cuchulain Peaks still bear witness to the legend.

[2] This, of course, was Cuchulain's father, Lugh.

the news from Ireland. When he had told them all he asked Ferdia how he should pass to the dūn of Skatha. Now the Bridge of Leaps was very narrow and very high, and it crossed a gorge where far below swung the tides of a boiling sea, in which ravenous monsters could be seen swimming.

"Not one of us has crossed that bridge," said Ferdia, "for there are two feats that Skatha teaches last, and one is the leap across the bridge, and the other the thrust of the Gae Bolg.[1] For if a man step upon one end of that bridge, the middle straightway rises up and flings him back, and if he leap upon it he may chance to miss his footing and fall into the gulf, where the sea-monsters are waiting for him."

But Cuchulain waited till evening, when he had recovered his strength from his long journey, and then essayed the crossing of the bridge. Three times he ran towards it from a distance, gathering all his powers together, and strove to leap upon the middle, but three times it rose against him and flung him back, while his companions jeered at him because he would not wait for the help of Skatha. But at the fourth leap he lit fairly on the centre of the bridge, and with one leap more he was across it, and stood before the strong fortress of Skatha; and she wondered at his courage and vigour, and admitted him to be her pupil.

For a year and a day Cuchulain abode with Skatha, and all the feats she had to teach he learned easily, and last of all she taught him the use of the Gae Bolg, and gave him that dreadful weapon, which she had deemed no champion before him good enough to have. And the manner of using the Gae Bolg was that it was thrown with the foot, and if it entered an enemy's

[1] This means probably "the belly spear." With this terrible weapon Cuchulain was fated in the end to slay his friend Ferdia.

body it filled every limb and crevice of him with its barbs. While Cuchulain dwelt with Skatha his friend above all friends and his rival in skill and valour was Ferdia, and ere they parted they vowed to love and help one another as long as they should live.

Cuchulain and Aifa

Now whilst Cuchulain was in the Land of the Shadows it chanced that Skatha made war on the people of the Princess Aifa, who was the fiercest and strongest of the woman-warriors of the world, so that even Skatha feared to meet her in arms. On going forth to the war, therefore, Skatha mixed with Cuchulain's drink a sleepy herb so that he should not wake for four-and-twenty hours, by which time the host would be far on its way, for she feared lest evil should come to him ere he had got his full strength. But the potion that would have served another man for a day and a night only held Cuchulain for one hour; and when he waked up he seized his arms and followed the host by its chariot-tracks till he came up with them. Then it is said that Skatha uttered a sigh, for she knew that he would not be restrained from the war.

When the armies met, Cuchulain and the two sons of Skatha wrought great deeds on the foe, and slew six of the mightiest of Aifa's warriors. Then Aifa sent word to Skatha and challenged her to single combat. But Cuchulain declared that he would meet the fair Fury in place of Skatha, and he asked first of all what were the things she most valued. "What Aifa loves most," said Skatha, "are her two horses, her chariot and her charioteer." Then the pair met in single combat, and every champion's feat which they knew they tried on each other in vain, till at last a blow of Aifa's shattered the sword of Cuchulain to the hilt.

At this Cuchulain cried out: "Ah me! behold the chariot and horses of Aifa, fallen into the glen!" Aifa glanced round, and Cuchulain, rushing in, seized her round the waist and slung her over his shoulder and bore her back to the camp of Skatha. There he flung her on the ground and put his knife to her throat. She begged for her life, and Cuchulain granted it on condition that she made a lasting peace with Skatha, and gave hostages for her fulfilment of the pledge. To this she agreed, and Cuchulain and she became not only friends but lovers.

The Tragedy of Cuchulain and Connla

Before Cuchulain left the Land of Shadows he gave Aifa a golden ring, saying that if she should bear him a son he was to be sent to seek his father in Erin so soon as he should have grown so that his finger would fit the ring. And Cuchulain said, "Charge him under *geise* that he shall not make himself known, that he never turn out of the way for any man, nor ever refuse a combat. And be his name called Connla."

In later years it is narrated that one day when King Conor of Ulster and the lords of Ulster were at a festal gathering on the Strand of the Footprints they saw coming towards them across the sea a little boat of bronze, and in it a young lad with gilded oars in his hands. In the boat was a heap of stones, and ever and anon the lad would put one of these stones into a sling and cast it at a flying sea-bird in such fashion that it would bring down the bird alive to his feet. And many other wonderful feats of skill he did. Then Conor said, as the boat drew nearer: "If the grown men of that lad's country came here they would surely grind us to powder. Woe to the land into which that boy shall come!"

When the boy came to land, a messenger, Condery, was sent to bid him be off. "I will not turn back for thee," said the lad, and Condery repeated what he had said to the king. Then Conall of the Victories was sent against him, but the lad slung a great stone at him, and the whizz and wind of it knocked him down, and the lad sprang upon him, and bound his arms with the strap of his shield. And so man after man was served; some were bound, and some were slain, but the lad defied the whole power of Ulster to turn him back, nor would he tell his name or lineage.

"Send for Cuchulain," then said King Conor. And they sent a messenger to Dundalk, where Cuchulain was with Emer his wife, and bade him come to do battle against a stranger boy whom Conall of the Victories could not overcome. Emer threw her arm round Cuchulain's neck. "Do not go," she entreated. "Surely this is the son of Aifa. Slay not thine only son." But Cuchulain said: "Forbear, woman! Were it Connla himself I would slay him for the honour of Ulster," and he bade yoke his chariot and went to the Strand. Here he found the boy tossing up his weapons and doing marvellous feats with them. "Delightful is thy play, boy," said Cuchulain; "who art thou and whence dost thou come?" "I may not reveal that," said the lad. "Then thou shalt die," said Cuchulain. "So be it," said the lad, and then they fought with swords for a while, till the lad delicately shore off a lock of Cuchulain's hair. "Enough of trifling," said Cuchulain, and they closed with each other, but the lad planted himself on a rock and stood so firm that Cuchulain could not move him, and in the stubborn wrestling they had the lad's two feet sank deep into the stone and made the footprints whence the Strand of the Footprints has its name. At last they both fell into the sea, and Cuchulain was near being drowned, till he bethought himself of the Gae Bolg, and he drove that weapon against the lad and it ripped up his belly. "That is what Skatha never taught me," cried the lad. "Woe is me, for I am hurt." Cuchulain looked at him and saw the ring on his finger. "It is true," he said; and he took up the boy and bore him on shore and laid him down before Conor and the lords of Ulster. "Here is my son for you, men of Ulster," he said. And the boy said: "It is true. And if I had five years to grow among you, you would conquer the world on every side of you and rule as far as Rome. But since it is as it is, point out to me the famous warriors that are here, that I may know them and take leave of them before I die." Then one after another they were brought to him, and he kissed them and took leave of his father, and he died; and the men of Ulster made his grave and set up his pillar-stone with great mourning. This was the only son Cuchulain ever had, and this son he slew.

This tale, as I have given it here, dates from the ninth century, and is found in the "Yellow Book of Lecan." There are many other Gaelic versions of it in poetry and prose. It is one of the earliest extant appearances in literature of the since well-known theme of the slaying of a heroic son by his father. The Persian rendering of it in the tale of Sohrab and Rustum has been made familiar by Matthew Arnold's fine poem. In the Irish version it will be noted that the father is not without a suspicion of the identity of his antagonist, but he does battle with him under the stimulus of that passionate sense of loyalty to his prince and province which was Cuchulain's most signal characteristic.

To complete the story of Aifa and her son we have anticipated events, and now turn back to take up the thread again.

CUCHULAIN'S FIRST FORAY

Cuchulain's First Foray

After a year and a day of training in warfare under Skatha, Cuchulain returned to Erin, eager to test his prowess and to win Emer for his wife. So he bade harness his chariot and drove out to make a foray upon the fords and marches of Connacht, for between Connacht and Ulster there was always an angry surf of fighting along the borders.

And first he drove to the White Cairn, which is on the highest of the Mountains of Mourne, and surveyed the land of Ulster spread out smiling in the sunshine far below and bade his charioteer tell him the name of every hill and plain and dūn that he saw. Then turning southwards he looked over the plains of Bregia, and the charioteer pointed out to him Tara and Teltin, and Brugh na Boyna and the great dūn of the sons of Nechtan. "Are they," asked Cuchulain, "those sons of Nechtan of whom it is said that more of the men of Ulster have fallen by their hands than are yet living on the earth?" "The same," said the charioteer. "Then let us drive thither," said Cuchulain. So, much unwilling, the charioteer drove to the fortress of the sons of Nechtan, and there on the green before it they found a pillar-stone, and round it a collar of bronze having on it writing in Ogham. This Cuchulain read, and it declared that any man of age to bear arms who should come to that green should hold it *geis* for him to depart without having challenged one of the dwellers in the dūn to single combat. Then Cuchulain flung his arms round the stone, and, swaying it backwards and forwards, heaved it at last out of the earth and flung it, collar and all, into the river that ran hard by. "Surely," said the charioteer, "thou art seeking for a violent death, and now thou wilt find it without delay."

Then Foill son of Nechtan came forth from the dūn, and seeing Cuchulain, whom he deemed but a lad, he was annoyed. But Cuchulain bade him fetch his arms, "for I slay not drivers nor messengers nor unarmed men," and Foill went back into the dūn. "Thou canst not slay him," then said the charioteer, "for he is invulnerable by magic power to the point or edge of any blade." But Cuchulain put in his sling a ball of tempered iron, and when Foill appeared he slung at him so that it struck his forehead, and went clean through brain and skull; and Cuchulain took his head and bound it to his chariot-rim. And other sons of Nechtan, issuing forth, he fought with and slew by sword or spear; and then he fired the dūn and left it in a blaze and drove on exultant. And on the way he saw a flock of wild swans, and sixteen of them he brought down alive with his sling, and tied them to the chariot; and seeing a herd of wild deer which his horses could not overtake he lighted down and chased them on foot till he caught two great stags, and with thongs and ropes he made them fast to the chariot.

But at Emain Macha a scout of King Conor came running in to give him news. "Behold, a solitary chariot is approaching swiftly over the plain; wild white birds flutter round it and wild stags are tethered to it; it is decked all round with the bleeding heads of enemies." And Conor looked to see who was approaching, and he saw that Cuchulain was in his battle-fury, and would deal death around him whomsoever he met; so he hastily gave order that a troop of the women of Emania should go forth to meet him, and, having stripped off their clothing, should stand naked in the way. This they did, and when the lad saw them, smitten with shame, he bowed his head upon the chariot-rim. Then Conor's men instantly seized him and plunged him into a vat of cold water which had been made ready, but the water boiled around him and the staves and hoops of the vat were burst asunder. This they did again and yet again, and at last his fury left him, and his natural form and aspect were restored. Then they clad him in fresh raiment and bade him in to the feast in the king's banqueting-hall.

The Winning of Emer

Next day he went to the dūn of Forgall the Wily, father of Emer, and he leaped "the hero's salmon leap," that he had learned of Skatha, over the high ramparts of the dūn. Then the mighty men of Forgall set on him, and he dealt but three blows, and each blow slew eight men, and Forgall himself fell lifeless in leaping from the rampart of the dūn to escape Cuchulain. So he carried off Emer and her foster-sister and two loads of gold and silver. But outside the dūn the sister of Forgall raised a host against him, and his battle-fury came on him, and furious were the blows he dealt, so that the ford of Glondath ran blood and the turf on Crofot was trampled into bloody mire. A hundred he slew at every ford from Olbiny to the Boyne; and so was Emer won as she desired, and he brought her to Emain Macha and made her his wife, and they were not parted again until he died.

Cuchulain Champion of Erin

A lord of Ulster named Briccriu of the Poisoned Tongue once made a feast to which he bade King Conor and all the heroes of the Red Branch, and because it was always his delight to stir up strife among men or women he set the heroes contending among themselves as to who was the champion of the land of Erin. At last it was agreed that the championship must lie among three of them, namely, Cuchulain, and Conall of the Victories and Laery the Triumphant. To decide between these three a demon named The Terrible was summoned from a lake in the depth of which he dwelt. He proposed to the heroes a test of courage. Any one of them, he said, might cut off his head to-day provided that he, the claimant of the championship, would lay down his own head for the axe to-morrow. Conall and Laery shrank from the test, but Cuchulain accepted it, and after reciting a charm over his sword, he cut off the head of the demon, who immediately rose, and taking the bleeding head in one hand and his axe in the other, plunged into the lake.

Next day he reappeared, whole and sound, to claim the fulfilment of the bargain. Cuchulain, quailing but resolute, laid his head on the block. "Stretch out your neck, wretch," cried the demon; "'tis too short for me to strike at." Cuchulain does as he is bidden. The demon swings his axe thrice over his victim, brings down the butt with a crash on the block, and then bids Cuchulain rise unhurt, Champion of Ireland and her boldest man.

Deirdre and the Sons of Usna

We have now to turn to a story in which Cuchulain takes no part. It is the chief of the preliminary tales to the Cattle-spoil of Quelgny.

There was among the lords of Ulster, it is said, one named Felim son of Dall, who on a certain day made a great feast for the king. And the king came with his Druid Cathbad, and Fergus mac Roy, and many heroes of the Red Branch, and while they were making merry over the roasted flesh and wheaten cakes and Greek wine a messenger from the women's apartments came to tell Felim that his wife had just borne him a daughter. So all the lords and warriors drank health to the new-born infant, and the king bade Cathbade perform divination in the manner of the Druids and foretell what the future would have in store for Felim's babe. Cathbad gazed upon the stars and drew the horoscope of the child, and he was much troubled; and at length he said: "The infant shall be fairest among the women of Erin, and shall wed a king, but because of her shall death and ruin come upon the Province of Ulster." Then the warriors would have put her to death upon the spot, but Conor forbade them. "I will avert the doom," he said, "for she shall wed no foreign king, but she shall be my own mate when she is of age." So he took away the child, and committed it to his nurse Levarcam, and the name they gave it was Deirdre. And Conor charged Levarcam that the child should be brought up in a strong dūn in the solitude of a great wood, and that no young man should see her or she him until she was of marriageable age for the king to wed. And there she dwelt, seeing none but her nurse and Cathbad, and sometimes the king, now growing an aged man, who would visit the dūn from time to time to see that all was well with the folk there, and that his commands were observed.

One day, when the time for the marriage of Deirdre and Conor was drawing near, Deirdre and Levarcam looked over the rampart of their dūn. It was winter, a heavy snow had fallen in the night, and in the still, frosty air the trees stood up as if wrought in silver, and the green before the dūn was a sheet of unbroken white, save that in one place a scullion had killed a calf for their dinner, and the blood of the calf lay on the snow. And as Deirdre looked, a raven lit down from a tree hard by and began to sip the blood. "O nurse," cried Deirdre suddenly, "such, and not like Conor, would be the man that I would love—his hair like the raven's wing, and in his cheek the hue of blood, and his skin as white as snow." "Thou hast pictured a man of Conor's household," said the nurse. "Who is he?" asked Deirdre. "He is Naisi, son of Usna,[1] a champion of the Red Branch," said the nurse. Thereupon Deirdre entreated Levarcam to bring her to speak with Naisi; and because the old woman loved the girl and would not have her wedded to the aged king, she at last agreed. Deirdre implored Naisi to save her from Conor, but he would not, till at last her entreaties and her beauty won him, and he vowed to be hers. Then secretly one night he came with his two brethren, Ardan and Ainlé, and bore away Deirdre with Levarcam, and they escaped the king's pursuit and took ship for Scotland, where Naisi took service with the King of the Picts. Yet here they could not rest, for the king got sight of Deirdre, and would have taken her from Naisi, but Naisi with his brothers escaped, and in the solitude of Glen Etive they made their dwelling by the lake, and there lived in the wild wood by hunting and fishing, seeing no man but themselves and their servants.

And the years went by and Conor made no sign, but he did not forget, and his spies told him of all that befell Naisi and Deirdre. At last, judging that Naisi and his brothers would have tired of solitude, he sent the bosom friend of Naisi, Fergus son of Roy, to bid them return, and to promise them that all would be forgiven. Fergus went joyfully, and joyfully did Naisi and his brothers hear the message, but Deirdre foresaw evil, and would fain have sent Fergus home alone.

[1] See genealogical table, p. 181.

ut Naisi blamed her for her doubt and suspicion, and ade her mark that they were under the protection of ergus, whose safeguard no king in Ireland would are to violate; and they at last made ready to go.

On landing in Ireland they were met by Baruch, a rd of the Red Branch, who had his dūn close by, nd he bade Fergus to a feast he had prepared for him hat night. "I may not stay," said Fergus, "for I ust first convey Deirdre and the sons of Usna safely Emain Macha." "Nevertheless," said Baruch, thou must stay with me to-night, for it is a *geis* for hee to refuse a feast." Deirdre implored him not leave them, but Fergus was tempted by the feast, nd feared to break his *geis*, and he bade his two sons llan the Fair and Buino the Red take charge of the arty in his place, and he himself abode with Baruch.

And so the party came to Emain Macha, and they vere lodged in the House of the Red Branch, but onor did not receive them. After the evening meal, s he sat, drinking heavily and silently, he sent a nessenger to bid Levarcam come before him. "How s it with the sons of Usna?" he said to her. "It is vell," she said. "Thou hast got the three most valorous hampions in Ulster in thy court. Truly the king who as those three need fear no enemy." "Is it well with eirdre?" he asked. "She is well," said the nurse, "but she has lived many years in the wildwood, and oil and care have changed her—little of her beauty of ld now remains to her, O King." Then the king lismissed her, and sat drinking again. But after a vhile he called to him a servant named Trendorn, and ade him go to the Red Branch House and mark who vas there and what they did. But when Trendorn ame the place was bolted and barred for the night, nd he could not get an entrance, and at last he mounted on a ladder and looked in at a high windov And there he saw the brothers of Naisi and the sons c Fergus, as they talked or cleaned their arms, or mad them ready for slumber, and there sat Naisi with chess-board before him, and playing chess with hir was the fairest of women that he had ever seen. Bu as he looked in wonder at the noble pair, suddenly on caught sight of him and rose with a cry, pointing t the face at the window. And Naisi looked up an saw it, and seizing a chessman from the board h hurled it at the face of the spy, and it struck out hi eye. Then Trendorn hastily descended, and went bac with his bloody face to the king. "I have seen them, he cried, "I have seen the fairest woman of the worl and but that Naisi had struck my eye out I had bee looking on her still."

Then Conor arose and called for his guards and bad them bring the sons of Usna before him for maimin his messenger. And the guards went; but first Buin son of Fergus, with his retinue, met them, and at th sword's point drove them back; but Naisi and Deirdr continued quietly to play chess, "For," said Naisi, " is not seemly that we should seek to defend ourselve while we are under the protection of the sons of Fergus. But Conor went to Buino, and with a great gift of land he bought him over to desert his charge. Then Illa took up the defence of the Red Branch Hostel, but th two sons of Conor slew him. And then at last Nais and his brothers seized their weapons and rushed ami the foe, and many were they who fell before the onset Then Conor entreated Cathbad the Druid to cast spell upon them lest they should get away and become th enemies of the province, and he vowed to do them n hurt if they were taken alive. So Cathbad conjure up, as it were, a lake of slime that seemed to be abou ıe feet of the sons of Usna, and they could not tear ıeir feet from it, and Naisi caught up Deirdre and put er on his shoulder, for they seemed to be sinking in ıe slime. Then the guards and servants of Conor eized and bound them and brought them before the ing. And the king called upon man after man to ome forward and slay the sons of Usna, but none vould obey him, till at last Owen son of Duracht and 'rince of Ferney came and took the sword of Naisi, nd with one sweep he shore off the heads of all three, nd so they died.

Then Conor took Deirdre perforce, and for a year he abode with him in the palace in Emain Macha, but luring all that time she never smiled. At length Conor said: "What is it that you hate most of all on arth, Deirdre?" And she said: "Thou thyself and Owen son of Duracht," and Owen was standing by. "Then thou shalt go to Owen for a year," said Conor. But when Deirdre mounted the chariot behind Owen he kept her eyes on the ground, for she would not ook on those who thus tormented her; and Conor aid, taunting her: "Deirdre, the glance of thee between ne and Owen is the glance of a ewe between two ams." Then Deirdre started up, and, flinging herself ıead foremost from the chariot, she dashed her head gainst a rock and fell dead.

And when they buried her it is said there grew from ıer grave and from Naisi's two yew-trees, whose tops, vhen they were full-grown, met each other over the 'oof of the great church of Armagh, and intertwined ogether, and none could part them.

The Rebellion of Fergus

When Fergus mac Roy came home to Emain Macha fter the feast to which Baruch bade him and found the sons of Usna slain and one of his own sons dea and the other a traitor, he broke out against Conor i a storm of wrath and cursing, and vowed to be avenge on him with fire and sword. And he went o straightway to Connacht to take service of arms wit Ailell and Maev, who were king and queen of tha country.

Queen Maev

But though Ailell was king, Maev was the ruler i truth, and ordered all things as she wished, and too what husbands she wished, and dismissed them a pleasure; for she was as fierce and strong as a goddes of war, and knew no law but her own wild will. Sh was tall, it is said, with a long, pale face and masses c hair yellow as ripe corn. When Fergus came to he in her palace at Rathcroghan in Roscommon she gav him her love, as she had given it to many before, an they plotted together how to attack and devastate th Province of Ulster.

The Brown Bull of Quelgny

Now it happened that Maev possessed a famous re bull with white front and horns named Finnbenach and one day when she and Ailell were counting u their respective possessions and matching them agains each other he taunted her because the Finnbenac would not stay in the hands of a woman, but ha attached himself to Ailell's herd. So Maev in vexatio went to her steward, mac Roth, and asked of him i there were anywhere in Erin a bull as fine as th Finnbenach. "Truly," said the steward, "there is— for the Brown Bull of Quelgny, that belongs to Dar son of Fachtna, is the mightiest beast that is in Ireland." And after that Maev felt as if she had no flocks an herds that were worth anything at all unless she possessed the Brown Bull of Quelgny. But this was in Ulster, and the Ulstermen knew the treasure they possessed, and Maev knew that they would not give up the bull without fighting for it. So she and Fergus and Ailell agreed to make a foray against Ulster for the Brown Bull, and thus to enter into war with the province, for Fergus longed for vengeance, and Maev for fighting, for glory, and for the bull, and Ailell to satisfy Maev.

Here let us note that this contest for the bull, which is the ostensible theme of the greatest of Celtic legendary tales, the "Tain Bo Cuailgné," has a deeper meaning than appears on the surface. An ancient piece of Aryan mythology is embedded in it. The Brown Bull is the Celtic counterpart of the Hindu sky-deity, Indra, represented in Hindu myth as a mighty bull, whose roaring is the thunder and who lets loose the rains "like cows streaming forth to pasture." The advance of the Western (Connacht) host for the capture of this bull is emblematic of the onset of Night. The bull is defended by the solar hero Cuchulain, who, however, is ultimately overthrown and the bull is captured for a season. The two animals in the Celtic legend probably typify the sky in different aspects. They are described with a pomp and circumstance which shows that they are no common beasts. Once, we are told, they were swineherds of the people of Dana. "They had been successively transformed into two ravens, two sea-monsters, two warriors, two demons, two worms or animalculæ, and finally into two kine."[1] The Brown Bull is described as having a back broad enough for fifty children to play on; when he is angry with his keeper he stamps the

[1] Miss Hull, "The Cuchullin Saga," p. lxxii, where the solar theory of the Brown Bull is dealt with at length.

man thirty feet into the ground; he is likened to a sea wave, to a bear, to a dragon, a lion, the writer heaping up images of strength and savagery. We are therefore concerned with no ordinary cattle-raid, but with a myth, the features of which are discernible under the dressing given it by the fervid imagination of the unknown Celtic bard who composed the "Tain," although the exact meaning of every detail may be difficult to ascertain.

The first attempt of Maev to get possession of the bull was to send an embassy to Dara to ask for the loan of him for a year, the recompense offered being fifty heifers, besides the bull himself back, and if Dara chose to settle in Connacht he should have as much land there as he now possessed in Ulster, and a chariot worth thrice seven *cumals*,[1] with the patronage and friendship of Maev.

Dara was at first delighted with the prospect, but tales were borne to him of the chatter of Maev's messengers, and how they said that if the bull was not yielded willingly it would be taken by force; and he sent back a message of refusal and defiance. "'Twas known," said Maev, "the bull will not be yielded by fair means; he shall now be won by foul." And so she sent messengers around on every side to summon her hosts for the Raid.

The Hosting of Queen Maev

And there came all the mighty men of Connacht—first the seven Mainés, sons of Ailell and Maev, each with his retinue; and Ket and Anluan, sons of Maga, with thirty hundreds of armed men; and yellow-haired Ferdia, with his company of Firbolgs, boisterous giants

[1] A *cumal* was the unit of value in Celtic Ireland. It is mentioned as such by St. Patrick. It meant the price of a woman-slave.

Queen Maev and the Druid

Cuchulain in Battle

who delighted in war and in strong ale. And there came also the allies of Maev—a host of the men of Leinster, who so excelled the rest in warlike skill that they were broken up and distributed among the companies of Connacht, lest they should prove a danger to the host; and Cormac son of Conor, with Fergus mac Roy and other exiles from Ulster, who had revolted against Conor for his treachery to the sons of Usna.

Ulster under the Curse

But before the host set forth towards Ulster Maev sent her spies into the land to tell her of the preparations there being made. And the spies brought back a wondrous tale, and one that rejoiced the heart of Maev, for they said that the Debility of the Ultonians[1] had descended on the province. Conor the king lay in pangs at Emain Macha, and his son Cuscrid in his island-fortress, and Owen Prince of Ferney was helpless as a child; Celtchar, the huge grey warrior, son of Uthecar Hornskin, and even Conall of the Victories, lay moaning and writhing on their beds, and there was no hand in Ulster that could lift a spear.

Prophetic Voices

Nevertheless Maev went to her chief Druid, and demanded of him what her own lot in the war should be. And the Druid said only: "Whoever comes back in safety, or comes not, thou thyself shalt come." But on her journey back she saw suddenly standing before her chariot-pole a young maiden with tresses of yellow hair that fell below her knees, and clad in a mantle of green; and with a shuttle of gold she wove a fabric upon a loom. "Who art thou, girl?" said Maev,

[1] The curse laid on them by Macha. See p. 180.

"and what dost thou?" "I am the prophetess, Fedelma, from the Fairy Mound of Croghan," said the maid, "and I weave the four provinces of Ireland together for the foray into Ulster." "How seest thou our host?" asked Maev. "I see them all be-crimsoned, red," replied the prophetess. "Yet the Ulster heroes are all in their pangs—there is none that can lift a spear against us," said Maev. "I see the host all be-crimsoned," said Fedelma. "I see a man of small stature, but the hero's light is on his brow—a stripling young and modest, but in battle a dragon; he is like unto Cuchulain of Murthemney; he doth wondrous feats with his weapons; by him your slain shall lie thickly."[1]

At this the vision of the weaving maiden vanished, and Maev drove homewards to Rathcroghan wondering at what she had seen and heard.

Cuchulain Puts the Host under Geise

On the morrow the host set forth, Fergus mac Roy leading them, and as they neared the confines of Ulster he bade them keep sharp watch lest Cuchulain of Murthemney, who guarded the passes of Ulster to the south, should fall upon them unawares. Now Cuchulain and his father Sualtam[2] were on the borders of the province, and Cuchulain, from a warning Fergus had sent him, suspected the approach of a great host, and bade Sualtam go northwards to Emania and warn the men of Ulster. But Cuchulain himself would not stay there, for he said he had a tryst to keep with a handmaid of the wife of Laery the *bodach* (farmer), so he went into the forest, and there, standing on one leg,

[1] Cuchulain, as the son of the god Lugh, was not subject to the curse of Macha which afflicted the other Ultonians.

[2] His reputed father, the mortal husband of Dectera

and using only one hand and one eye, he cut an oak sapling and twisted it into a circular withe. On this he cut in Ogham characters how the withe was made, and he put the host of Maev under *geise* not to pass by that place till one of them had, under similar conditions, made a similar withe; "and I except my friend Fergus mac Roy," he added, and wrote his name at the end. Then he placed the withe round the pillar-stone of Ardcullin, and went his way to keep his tryst with the handmaid.[1]

When the host of Maev came to Ardcullin, the withe upon the pillar-stone was found and brought to Fergus to decipher it. There was none amongst the host who could emulate the feat of Cuchulain, and so they went into the wood and encamped for the night. A heavy snowfall took place, and they were all in much distress, but next day the sun rose gloriously, and over the white plain they marched away into Ulster, counting the prohibition as extending only for one night.

The Ford of the Forked Pole

Cuchulain now followed hard on their track, and as he went he estimated by the tracks they had left the number of the host at eighteen *triucha cét* (54,000 men). Circling round the host, he now met them in front, and soon came upon two chariots containing scouts sent ahead by Maev. These he slew, each man with his driver, and having with one sweep of his sword cut a forked pole of four prongs from the wood, he drove the pole deep into a river-ford at the place called Athgowla,[2] and impaled on each prong a bloody head. When the host came up they wondered and feared at

[1] In the Irish bardic literature, as in the Homeric epics, chastity formed no part of the masculine ideal either for gods or men.

[2] "The Ford of the Forked Pole."

the sight, and Fergus declared that they were under *geise* not to pass that ford till one of them had plucked out the pole even as it was driven in, with the finger-tips of one hand. So Fergus drove into the water to essay the feat, and seventeen chariots were broken under him as he tugged at the pole, but at last he tore it out; and as it was now late the host encamped upon the spot. These devices of Cuchulain were intended to delay the invaders until the Ulster men had recovered from their debility.

In the epic, as given in the Book of Leinster, and other ancient sources, a long interlude now takes place in which Fergus explains to Maev who it is—viz., "my little pupil Setanta"—who is thus harrying the host, and his boyish deeds, some of which have been already told in this narrative, are recounted.

The Charioteer of Orlam

The host proceeded on its way next day, and the next encounter with Cuchulain shows the hero in a kindlier mood. He hears a noise of timber being cut, and going into a wood he finds there a charioteer belonging to a son of Ailell and Maev cutting down chariot-poles of holly. "For," says he, "we have damaged our chariots sadly in chasing that famous deer, Cuchulain." Cuchulain—who, it must be remembered, was at ordinary times a slight and unimposing figure, though in battle he dilated in size and underwent a fearful distortion, symbolic of Berserker fury—helps the driver in his work. "Shall I," he asks, "cut the poles or trim them for thee?" "Do thou the trimming," says the driver. Cuchulain takes the poles by the tops and draws them against the set of the branches through his toes, and then runs his fingers down them the same way, and gives them over as smooth and polished as if they were planed by a carpenter. The driver stares at him. "I doubt this work I set thee to is not thy proper work," he says. "Who art thou then at all?" "I am that Cuchulain of whom thou spakest but now." "Surely I am but a dead man," says the driver. "Nay," replies Cuchulain, "I slay not drivers nor messengers nor men unarmed. But run, tell thy master Orlam that Cuchulain is about to visit him." The driver runs off, but Cuchulain outstrips him, meets Orlam first, and strikes off his head. For a moment the host of Maev see him as he shakes this bloody trophy before them; then he disappears from sight—it is the first glimpse they have caught of their persecutor.

The Battle-Frenzy of Cuchulain

A number of scattered episodes now follow. The host of Maev spreads out and devastates the territories of Bregia and of Murthemney, but they cannot advance further into Ulster. Cuchulain hovers about them continually, slaying them by twos and threes, and no man knows where he will swoop next. Maev herself is awed when, by the bullets of an unseen slinger, a squirrel and a pet bird are killed as they sit upon her shoulders. Afterwards, as Cuchulain's wrath grows fiercer, he descends with supernatural might upon whole companies of the Connacht host, and hundreds fall at his onset. The characteristic distortion or *riastradh* which seized him in his battle-frenzy is then described. He became a fearsome and multiform creature such as never was known before. Every particle of him quivered like a bulrush in a running stream. His calves and heels and hams shifted to the front, and his feet and knees to the back, and the muscles of his neck stood out like the head of a young child. One eye was engulfed deep in his head, the other protruded, his mouth met his ears, foam poured from his jaws like the fleece of a three-year-old wether. The beats of his heart sounded like the roars of a lion as he rushes on his prey. A light blazed above his head, and "his hair became tangled about as it had been the branches of a red thorn-bush stuffed into the gap of a fence. . . . Taller, thicker, more rigid, longer than the mast of a great ship was the perpendicular jet of dusky blood which out of his scalp's very central point shot upwards and was there scattered to the four cardinal points, whereby was formed a magic mist of gloom resembling the smoky pall that drapes a regal dwelling, what time a king at nightfall of a winter's day draws near to it."[1]

Such was the imagery by which Gaelic writers conveyed the idea of superhuman frenzy. At the sight of Cuchulain in his paroxysm it is said that once a hundred of Maev's warriors fell dead from horror.

The Compact of the Ford

Maev now tried to tempt him by great largesse to desert the cause of Ulster, and had a colloquy with him, the two standing on opposite sides of a glen across which they talked. She scanned him closely, and was struck by his slight and boyish appearance. She failed to move him from his loyalty to Ulster, and death descends more thickly than ever upon the Connacht host; the men are afraid to move out for plunder save in twenties and thirties, and at night the stones from Cuchulain's sling whistle continually through the camp, braining or maiming. At last, through the mediation of Fergus, an agreement was come to. Cuchulain undertook not to harry the host provided they would

[1] I quote from Standish Hayes O'Grady's translation, in Miss Hull's "Cuchullin Saga."

only send against him one champion at a time, whom Cuchulain would meet in battle at the ford of the River Dee, which is now called the Ford of Ferdia.[1] While each fight was in progress the host might move on, but when it was ended they must encamp till the morrow morning. "Better to lose one man a day than a hundred," said Maev, and the pact was made.

Fergus and Cuchulain

Several single combats are then narrated, in which Cuchulain is always a victor. Maev even persuades Fergus to go against him, but Fergus and Cuchulain will on no account fight each other, and Cuchulain, by agreement with Fergus, pretends to fly before him, on Fergus's promise that he will do the same for Cuchulain when required. How this pledge was kept we shall see later.

Capture of the Brown Bull

During one of Cuchulain's duels with a famous champion, Natchrantal, Maev, with a third of her army, makes a sudden foray into Ulster and penetrates as far as Dunseverick, on the northern coast, plundering and ravaging as they go. The Brown Bull, who was originally at Quelgny (Co. Down), has been warned at an earlier stage by the Morrigan[2] to withdraw himself, and he has taken refuge, with his herd of cows, in a glen of Slievegallion, Co. Armagh. The raiders of Maev find him there, and drive him off with the herd in triumph, passing Cuchulain as they return. Cuchulain slays the leader of the escort—Buic son of Banblai—but cannot

[1] *Ath Fherdia*, which is pronounced and now spelt "Ardee." It is in Co. Louth, at the southern border of the Plain of Murthemney, which was Cuchulain's territory.

[2] See p. 126.

rescue the Bull, and "this," it is said, "was the greatest affront put on Cuchulain during the course of the raid."

The Morrigan

The raid ought now to have ceased, for its object has been attained, but by this time the hostings of the four southern provinces[1] had gathered together under Maev for the plunder of Ulster, and Cuchulain remained still the solitary warder of the marches. Nor did Maev keep her agreement, for bands of twenty warriors at a time were loosed against him and he had much ado to defend himself. The curious episode of the fight with the Morrigan now occurs. A young woman clad in a mantle of many colours appears to Cuchulain, telling him that she is a king's daughter, attracted by the tales of his great exploits, and she has come to offer him her love. Cuchulain tells her rudely that he is worn and harassed with war and has no mind to concern himself with women. "It shall go hard with thee," then said the maid, "when thou hast to do with men, and I shall be about thy feet as an eel in the bottom of the Ford." Then she and her chariot vanished from his sight and he saw but a crow sitting on a branch of a tree, and he knew that he had spoken with the Morrigan.

The Fight with Loch

The next champion sent against him by Maev was Loch son of Mofebis. To meet this hero it is said that Cuchulain had to stain his chin with blackberry juice so as to simulate a beard, lest Loch should disdain to do combat with a boy. So they fought in the Ford, and the

[1] In ancient Ireland there were five provinces, Munster being counted as two, or, as some ancient authorities explain it, the High King's territory in Meath and Westmeath being reckoned a separate province.

Morrigan came against him in the guise of a white heifer with red ears, but Cuchulain fractured her eye with a cast of his spear. Then she came swimming up the river like a black eel and twisted herself about his legs, and ere he could rid himself of her Loch wounded him. Then she attacked him as a grey wolf, and again, before he could subdue her, he was wounded by Loch. At this his battle-fury took hold of him and he drove the Gae Bolg against Loch, splitting his heart in two. "Suffer me to rise," said Loch, "that I may fall on my face on thy side of the ford, and not backward toward the men of Erin." "It is a warrior's boon thou askest," said Cuchulain, "and it is granted." So Loch died; and a great despondency, it is said, now fell upon Cuchulain, for he was outwearied with continued fighting, and sorely wounded, and he had never slept since the beginning of the raid, save leaning upon his spear; and he sent his charioteer, Laeg, to see if he could rouse the men of Ulster to come to his aid at last.

Lugh the Protector

But as he lay at evening by the grave-mound of Lerga in gloom and dejection, watching the camp-fires of the vast army encamped over against him and the glitter of their innumerable spears, he saw coming through the host a tall and comely warrior who strode impetuously forward, and none of the companies through which he passed turned his head to look at him or seemed to see him. He wore a tunic of silk embroidered with gold, and a green mantle fastened with a silver brooch; in one hand was a black shield bordered with silver and two spears in the other. The stranger came to Cuchulain and spoke gently and sweetly to him of his long toil and waking, and his sore wounds, and said in the end: "Sleep now, Cuchulain, by the grave in Lerga; sleep and slumber deeply for three days, and for that time I will take thy place and defend the Ford against the host of Maev." Then Cuchulain sank into a profound slumber and trance, and the stranger laid healing balms of magical power to his wounds so that he awoke whole and refreshed, and for the time that Cuchulain slept the stranger held the Ford against the host. And Cuchulain knew that this was Lugh his father, who had come from among the People of Dana to help his son through his hour of gloom and despair.

The Sacrifice of the Boy Corps

But still the men of Ulster lay helpless. Now there was at Emain Macha a band of thrice fifty boys, the sons of all the chieftains of the provinces, who were there being bred up in arms and in noble ways, and these suffered not from the curse of Macha, for it fell only on grown men. But when they heard of the sore straits in which Cuchulain, their playmate not long ago, was lying they put on their light armour and took their weapons and went forth for the honour of Ulster, under Conor's young son, Follaman, to aid him. And Follaman vowed that he would never return to Emania without the diadem of Ailell as a trophy. Three times they drove against the host of Maev, and thrice their own number fell before them, but in the end they were overwhelmed and slain, not one escaping alive.

The Carnage of Murthemney

This was done as Cuchulain lay in his trance, and when he awoke, refreshed and well, and heard what had been done, his frenzy came upon him and he leaped into his war-chariot and drove furiously round and round the host of Maev. And the chariot ploughed the earth till the ruts were like the ramparts of a fortress, and the scythes upon its wheels caught and mangled the bodies of the crowded host till they were piled like a wall around the camp, and as Cuchulain shouted in his wrath the demons and goblins and wild things in Erin yelled in answer, so that with the terror and the uproar the host of men heaved and surged hither and thither, and many perished from each other's weapons, and many from horror and fear. And this was the great carnage, called the Carnage of Murthemney, that Cuchulain did to avenge the boy-corps of Emania; six score and ten princes were then slain of the host of Maev, besides horses and women and wolf-dogs and common folk without number. It is said that Lugh mac Ethlinn fought there by his son.

The Clan Calatin

Next the men of Erin resolved to send against Cuchulain, in single combat, the Clan Calatin.[1] Now Calatin was a wizard, and he and his seven-and-twenty sons formed, as it were, but one being, the sons being organs of their father, and what any one of them did they all did alike. They were all poisonous, so that any weapon which one of them used would kill in nine days the man who was but grazed by it. When this multiform creature met Cuchulain each hand of it hurled a spear at once, but Cuchulain caught the twenty-eight spears on his shield and not one of them drew blood. Then he drew his sword to lop off the spears that bristled from his shield, but as he did so the Clan Calatin rushed upon him and flung him down, thrusting his face into the gravel. At this Cuchulain gave a great cry of distress at the unequal combat, and one of

[1] "Clan" in Gaelic means children or offspring. Clan Calatin = the sons of Calatin.

the Ulster exiles, Fiacha son of Firaba, who was with the host of Maev, and was looking on at the fight, could not endure to see the plight of the champion, and he drew his sword and with one stroke he lopped off the eight-and-twenty hands that were grinding the face of Cuchulain into the gravel of the Ford. Then Cuchulain arose and hacked the Clan Calatin into fragments, so that none survived to tell Maev what Fiacha had done, else had he and his thirty hundred followers of Clan Rury been given by Maev to the edge of the sword.

Ferdia to the Fray

Cuchulain had now overcome all the mightiest of Maev's men, save only the mightiest of them all after Fergus, Ferdia son of Daman. And because Ferdia was the old friend and fellow pupil of Cuchulain he had never gone out against him; but now Maev begged him to go, and he would not. Then she offered him her daughter, Findabair of the Fair Eyebrows, to wife, if he would face Cuchulain at the Ford, but he would not. At last she bade him go, lest the poets and satirists of Erin should make verses on him and put him to open shame, and then in wrath and sorrow he consented to go, and bade his charioteer make ready for to-morrow's fray. Then was gloom among all his people when they heard of that, for they knew that if Cuchulain and their master met, one of them would return alive no more.

Very early in the morning Ferdia drove to the Ford, and lay down there on the cushions and skins of the chariot and slept till Cuchulain should come. Not till it was full daylight did Ferdia's charioteer hear the thunder of Cuchulain's war-car approaching, and then he woke his master, and the two friends faced each other across the Ford. And when they had greeted each other Cuchulain said: "It is not thou, O Ferdia, who shouldst have come to do battle with me. When we were with Skatha did we not go side by side in every battle, through every wood and wilderness? were we not heart-companions, comrades, in the feast and the assembly? did we not share one bed and one deep slumber?" But Ferdia replied: "O Cuchulain, thou of the wondrous feats, though we have studied poetry and science together, and though I have heard thee recite our deeds of friendship, yet it is my hand that shall wound thee. I bid thee remember not our comradeship, O Hound of Ulster; it shall not avail thee, it shall not avail thee."

They then debated with what weapons they should begin the fight, and Ferdia reminded Cuchulain of the art of casting small javelins that they had learned from Skatha, and they agreed to begin with these. Backwards and forwards, then, across the Ford, hummed the light javelins like bees on a summer's day, but when noonday had come not one weapon had pierced the defence of either champion. Then they took to the heavy missile spears, and now at last blood began to flow, for each champion wounded the other time and again. At last the day came to its close. "Let us cease now," said Ferdia, and Cuchulain agreed. Each then threw his arms to his charioteer, and the friends embraced and kissed each other three times, and went to their rest. Their horses were in the same paddock, their drivers warmed themselves over the same fire, and the heroes sent each other food and drink and healing herbs for their wounds.

Next day they betook themselves again to the Ford, and this time, because Ferdia had the choice of weapons the day before, he bade Cuchulain take it now.[1] Cuchulain chose then the heavy, broad-bladed spears for close fighting, and with them they fought from the chariots till the sun went down, and drivers and horses were weary, and the body of each hero was torn with wounds. Then at last they gave over, and threw away their weapons. And they kissed each other as before, and as before they shared all things at night, and slept peacefully till the morning.

When the third day of the combat came Ferdia wore an evil and lowering look, and Cuchulain reproached him for coming out in battle against his comrade for the bribe of a fair maiden, even Findabair, whom Maev had offered to every champion and to Cuchulain himself if the Ford might be won thereby; but Ferdia said: "Noble Hound, had I not faced thee when summoned, my troth would be broken, and there would be shame on me in Rathcroghan." It is now the turn of Ferdia to choose the weapons, and they betake themselves to their "heavy, hard-smiting swords," and though they hew from each other's thighs and shoulders great cantles of flesh, neither can prevail over the other, and at last night ends the combat. This time they parted from each other in heaviness and gloom, and there was no interchange of friendly acts, and their drivers and horses slept apart. The passions of the warriors had now risen to a grim sternness.

[1] Together with much that is wild and barbaric in this Irish epic of the "Tain" the reader will be struck by the ideals of courtesy and gentleness which not infrequently come to light in it. It must be remembered that, as Mr. A. H. Leahy points out in his "Heroic Romances of Ireland," the legend of the Raid of Quelgny is, at the very latest, a century earlier than all other known romances of chivalry, Welsh or Continental. It is found in the "Book of Leinster," a manuscript of the twelfth century, as well as in other sources, and was doubtless considerably older than the date of its transcription there. "The whole thing," says Mr. Leahy, "stands at the very beginning of the literature of modern Europe."

"Cuchulain seized Ferdia as he fell"

" The head still went on crying and exhorting "

Death of Ferdia

On the fourth day Ferdia knew the contest would be decided, and he armed himself with especial care. Next his skin was a tunic of striped silk bordered with golden spangles, and over that hung an apron of brown leather. Upon his belly he laid a flat stone, large as a millstone, and over that a strong, deep apron of iron, for he dreaded that Cuchulain would use the Gae Bolg that day. And he put on his head his crested helmet studded with carbuncle and inlaid with enamels, and girt on his golden-hilted sword, and on his left arm hung his broad shield with its fifty bosses of bronze. Thus he stood by the Ford, and as he waited he tossed up his weapons and caught them again and did many wonderful feats, playing with his mighty weapons as a juggler plays with apples; and Cuchulain, watching him, said to Laeg, his driver: "If I give ground to-day, do thou reproach and mock me and spur me on to valour, and praise and hearten me if I do well, for I shall have need of all my courage."

"O Ferdia," said Cuchulain when they met, "what shall be our weapons to-day?" "It is thy choice to-day," said Ferdia. "Then let it be all or any," said Cuchulain, and Ferdia was cast down at hearing this, but he said, "So be it," and thereupon the fight began. Till midday they fought with spears, and none could gain any advantage over the other. Then Cuchulain drew his sword and sought to smite Ferdia over the rim of his shield; but the giant Firbolg flung him off. Thrice Cuchulain leaped high into the air, seeking to strike Ferdia over his shield, but each time as he descended Ferdia caught him upon the shield and flung him off like a little child into the Ford. And Laeg mocked him, crying: "He casts thee off as a river flings its foam, he grinds thee as a millstone grinds a corn of wheat; thou elf, never call thyself a warrior."

Then at last Cuchulain's frenzy came upon him, and he dilated giant-like, till he overtopped Ferdia, and the hero-light blazed about his head. In close contact the two were interlocked, whirling and trampling, while the demons and goblins and unearthly things of the glens screamed from the edges of their swords, and the waters of the Ford recoiled in terror from them, so that for a while they fought on dry land in the midst of the river-bed. And now Ferdia found Cuchulain a moment off his guard, and smote him with the edge of the sword, and it sank deep into his flesh, and all the river ran red with his blood. And he pressed Cuchulain sorely after that, hewing and thrusting so that Cuchulain could endure it no longer, and he shouted to Laeg to fling him the Gae Bolg. When Ferdia heard that he lowered his shield to guard himself from below, and Cuchulain drove his spear over the rim of the shield and through his breastplate into his chest. And Ferdia raised his shield again, but in that moment Cuchulain seized the Gae Bolg in his toes and drove it upward against Ferdia, and it pierced through the iron apron and burst in three the millstone that guarded him, and deep into his body it passed, so that every crevice and cranny of him was filled with its barbs. "'Tis enough," cried Ferdia; "I have my death of that. It is an ill deed that I fall by thy hand, O Cuchulain." Cuchulain seized him as he fell, and carried him northward across the Ford, that he might die on the further side of it, and not on the side of the men of Erin. Then he laid him down, and a faintness seized Cuchulain, and he was falling, when Laeg cried: "Rise up, Cuchulain, for the host of Erin will be upon us. No single combat will they give after Ferdia has fallen." But Cuchulain said: "Why should

I rise again, O my servant, now he that lieth here has fallen by my hand?" and he fell in a swoon like death. And the host of Maev with tumult and rejoicing, with tossing of spears and shouting of war-songs, poured across the border into Ulster.

But before they left the Ford they took the body of Ferdia and laid it in a grave, and built a mound over him and set up a pillar-stone with his name and lineage in Ogham. And from Ulster came certain of the friends of Cuchulain, and they bore him away into Murthemney, where they washed him and bathed his wounds in the streams, and his kin among the Danaan folk cast magical herbs into the rivers for his healing. But he lay there in weakness and in stupor for many days.

The Rousing of Ulster

Now Sualtam, the father of Cuchulain, had taken his son's horse, the Grey of Macha, and ridden off again to see if by any means he might rouse the men of Ulster to defend the province. And he went crying abroad: "The men of Ulster are being slain, the women carried captive, the kine driven!" Yet they stared on him stupidly, as though they knew not of what he spake. At last he came to Emania, and there were Cathbad the Druid and Conor the King, and all their nobles and lords, and Sualtam cried aloud to them: "The men of Ulster are being slain, the women carried captive, the kine driven; and Cuchulain alone holds the gap of Ulster against the four provinces of Erin. Arise and defend yourselves!" But Cathbad only said: "Death were the due of him who thus disturbs the King"; and Conor said: "Yet it is true what the man says"; and the lords of Ulster wagged their heads and murmured: "True indeed it is."

Then Sualtam wheeled round his horse in anger and

was about to depart when, with a start which the Grey made, his neck fell against the sharp rim of the shield upon his back, and it shore off his head, and the head fell on the ground. Yet still it cried its message as it lay, and at last Conor bade put it on a pillar that it might be at rest. But it still went on crying and exhorting, and at length into the clouded mind of the king the truth began to penetrate, and the glazed eyes of the warriors began to glow, and slowly the spell of Macha's curse was lifted from their minds and bodies. Then Conor arose and swore a mighty oath, saying: "The heavens are above us and the earth beneath us, and the sea is round about us; and surely, unless the heavens fall on us and the earth gape to swallow us up, and the sea overwhelm the earth, I will restore every woman to her hearth, and every cow to its byre."[1] His Druid proclaimed that the hour was propitious, and the king bade his messengers go forth on every side and summon Ulster to arms, and he named to them warriors long dead as well as the living, for the cloud of the curse still lingered in his brain.

With the curse now departed from them the men of Ulster flocked joyfully to the summons, and on every hand there was grinding of spears and swords, and buckling on of armour and harnessing of war-chariots for the rising-out of the province.[2] One host came under Conor the King and Keltchar, son of Uthecar Hornskin, from Emania southwards, and another from the west along the very track of the host of Maev. And Conor's host fell upon eight score of

[1] Another instance of the survival of the oath formula recited by the Celtic envoys to Alexander the Great. See p. 23.

[2] "Rising-out" is the vivid expression used by Irish writers for a clan or territory going on the war-path. "Hosting" is also used in a similar sense.

the men of Erin in Meath, who were carrying away a great booty of women-captives, and they slew every man of the eight score and rescued the women. Maev and her host then fell back toward Connacht, but when they reached Slemon Midi, the Hill of Slane, in Meath, the Ulster bands joined each other there and prepared to give battle. Maev sent her messenger mac Roth to view the Ulster host on the Plain of Garach and report upon it. Mac Roth came back with an awe-striking description of what he beheld. When he first looked he saw the plain covered with deer and other wild beasts. These, explains Fergus, had been driven out of the forests by the advancing host of the Ulster men. The second time mac Roth looked he saw a mist that filled the valleys, the hill-tops standing above it like islands. Out of the mist there came thunder and flashes of light, and a wind that nearly threw him off his feet. "What is this?" asks Maev, and Fergus tells her that the mist is the deep breathing of the warriors as they march, and the light is the flashing of their eyes, and the thunder is the clangour of their war-cars and the clash of their weapons as they go to the fight: "They think they will never reach it," says Fergus. "We have warriors to meet them," says Maev. "You will need that," says Fergus, "for in all Ireland, nay, in all the Western world, to Greece and Scythia and the Tower of Bregon[1] and the Island of Gades, there live not who can face the men of Ulster in their wrath."

A long passage then follows describing the appearance and equipment of each of the Ulster chiefs.

The Battle of Garach

The battle was joined on the Plain of Garach, in Meath. Fergus, wielding a two-handed sword, the

[1] See p. 130.

sword which, it was said, when swung in battle made circles like the arch of a rainbow, swept down whole ranks of the Ulster men at each blow,[1] and the fierce Maev charged thrice into the heart of the enemy.

Fergus met Conor the King, and smote him on his golden-bordered shield, but Cormac, the king's son, begged for his father's life. Fergus then turned on Conall of the Victories.

"Too hot art thou," said Conall, "against thy people and thy race for a wanton."[2] Fergus then turned from slaying the Ulstermen, but in his battle-fury he smote among the hills with his rainbow-sword, and struck off the tops of the three *Maela* of Meath, so that they are flat-topped (*mael*) to this day.

Cuchulain in his stupor heard the crash of Fergus's blows, and coming slowly to himself he asked of Laeg what it meant. "It is the sword-play of Fergus," said Laeg. Then he sprang up, and his body dilated so that the wrappings and swathings that had been bound on him flew off, and he armed himself and rushed into the battle. Here he met Fergus. "Turn hither, Fergus," he shouted; "I will wash thee as foam in a pool, I will go over thee as the tail goes over a cat, I will smite thee as a mother smites her infant." "Who speaks thus to me?" cried Fergus. "Cuchulain mac Sualtam; and now do thou avoid me as thou art pledged."[3]

"I have promised even that," said Fergus, and then went out of the battle, and with him the men of Leinster and the men of Munster, leaving Maev with her seven sons and the hosting of Connacht alone.

[1] The sword of Fergus was a fairy weapon called the *Caladcholg* (hard dinter), a name of which Arthur's more famous "Excalibur" is a Latinised corruption.

[2] The reference is to Deirdre.

[3] See p. 211.

Cuchulain and the Fairy Maidens

Emer hears of the Tryst

It was midday when Cuchulain came into the fight; when the evening sun was shining through the leaves of the trees his war-chariot was but two wheels and a handful of shattered ribs, and the host of Connacht was in full flight towards the border. Cuchulain overtook Maev, who crouched under her chariot and entreated grace. "I am not wont to slay women," said Cuchulain, and he protected her till she had crossed the Shannon at Athlone.

The Fight of the Bulls

But the Brown Bull of Quelgny, that Maev had sent into Connacht by a circuitous way, met the white-horned Bull of Ailell on the Plain of Aei, and the two beasts fought; but the Brown Bull quickly slew the other, and tossed his fragments about the land so that pieces of him were strewn from Rathcroghan to Tara; and then careered madly about till he fell dead, bellowing and vomiting black gore, at the Ridge of the Bull, between Ulster and Iveagh. Ailell and Maev made peace with Ulster for seven years, and the Ulster men returned home to Emain Macha with great glory.

Thus ends the "Tain Bo Cuailgnè," or Cattle Raid of Quelgny; and it was written out in the "Book of Leinster" in the year 1150 by the hand of Finn mac Gorman, Bishop of Kildare, and at the end is written: "A blessing on all such as faithfully shall recite the "Tain" as it stands here, and shall not give it in any other form."

Cuchulain in Fairyland

One of the strangest tales in Celtic legend tells how Cuchulain, as he lay asleep after hunting, against a pillar-stone, had a vision of two Danaan women who came to him armed with rods and alternately beat him till he was all but dead, and he could not lift a hand to defend himself. Next day, and for a year thereafter, he lay in sore sickness, and none could heal him.

Then a man whom none knew came and told him to go to the pillar-stone where he had seen the vision, and he would learn what was to be done for his recovery. There he found a Danaan woman in a green mantle, one of those who had chastised him, and she told him that Fand, the Pearl of Beauty, wife of Mananan the Sea-god, had set her love on him; and she was at enmity with her husband Mananan; and her realm was besieged by three demon kings, against whom Cuchulain's help was sought, and the price of his help would be the love of Fand. Laeg, the charioteer, was then sent by Cuchulain to report upon Fand and her message. He entered Fairyland, which lies beyond a lake across which he passed in a magic boat of bronze, and came home with a report of Fand's surpassing beauty and the wonders of the kingdom; and Cuchulain then betook himself thither. Here he had a battle in a dense mist with the demons, who are described as resembling sea-waves—no doubt we are to understand that they are the folk of the angry husband, Mananan. Then he abode with Fand, enjoying all the delights of Fairyland for a month, after which he bade her farewell, and appointed a trysting-place on earth, the Strand of the Yew Tree, where she was to meet him.

Fand, Emer, and Cuchulain

But Emer heard of the tryst; and though not commonly disturbed at Cuchulain's numerous infidelities, she came on this occasion with fifty of her maidens armed with sharp knives to slay Fand. Cuchulain and Fand perceive their chariots from afar, and the armed angry women with golden clasps shining on their breasts, and he prepares to protect his mistress. He addresses Emer in a curious poem, describing the beauty and skill and magical powers of Fand—"There is nothing the spirit can wish for that she has not got." Emer replies: "In good sooth, the lady to whom thou dost cling seems in no way better than I am, but the new is ever sweet and the well-known is sour; thou hast all the wisdom of the time, Cuchulain! Once we dwelled in honour together, and still might dwell if I could find favour in thy sight." "By my word thou dost," said Cuchulain, "and shalt find it so long as I live."

"Give me up," then said Fand. But Emer said: "Nay, it is more fitting that I be the deserted one." "Not so," said Fand; "it is I who must go." "And an eagerness for lamentation seized upon Fand, and her soul was great within her, for it was shame for her to be deserted and straightway to return to her home; moreover, the mighty love that she bore to Cuchulain was tumultuous in her."[1]

But Mananan, the Son of the Sea, knew of her sorrow and her shame, and he came to her aid, none seeing him but she alone, and she welcomed him in a mystic song. "Wilt thou return to me?" said Mananan, "or abide with Cuchulain?" "In truth," said Fand, "neither of ye is better or nobler than the other, but I will go with thee, Mananan, for thou hast no other mate worthy of thee, but that Cuchulain has in Emer."

So she went to Mananan, and Cuchulain, who did not see the god, asked Laeg what was happening. "Fand," he replied, "is going away with the Son of the Sea, since she hath not been pleasing in thy sight."

[1] A. H. Leahy's translation, "Heroic Romances of Ireland," vol. i.

Then Cuchulain bounded into the air and fled from the place, and lay a long time refusing meat and drink, until at last the Druids gave him a draught of forgetfulness; and Mananan, it is said, shook his cloak between Cuchulain and Fand, so that they might meet no more throughout eternity.[1]

The Vengeance of Maev

Though Maev made peace with Ulster after the battle of Garech she vowed the death of Cuchulain for all the shame and loss he had brought upon her and on her province, and she sought how she might take her vengeance upon him.

Now the wife of the wizard Calatin, whom Cuchulain slew at the Ford, brought forth, after her husband's death, six children at a birth, namely, three sons and three daughters. Misshapen, hideous, poisonous, born for evil were they; and Maev, hearing of these, sent them to learn the arts of magic, not in Ireland only, but in Alba; and even as far as Babylon they went to seek for hidden knowledge, and they came back mighty in their craft, and she loosed them against Cuchulain.

Cuchulain and Blanid

Besides the Clan Calatin, Cuchulain had also other foes, namely Erc, the King of Ireland, son to Cairpre, whom Cuchulain had slain in battle, and Lewy son of Curoi, King of Munster.[2] For Curoi's wife, Blanid, had set her love on Cuchulain, and she bade him come and take her from Curoi's dūn, and watch his time to

[1] The cloak of Mananan (see p. 125) typifies the sea—here, in its dividing and estranging power.

[2] This Curoi appears in various tales of the Ultonian Cycle with attributes which show that he was no mortal king, but a local deity.

attack the dūn, when he would see the stream that flowed from it turn white. So Cuchulain and his men waited in a wood hard by till Blanid judged that the time was fit, and she then poured into the stream the milk of three cows. Then Cuchulain attacked the dūn, and took it by surprise, and slew Curoi, and bore away the woman. But Fercartna, the bard of Curoi, went with them and showed no sign, till, finding himself near Blanid as she stood near the cliff-edge of Beara, he flung his arms round her, and leaped with her over the cliff, and so they perished, and Curoi was avenged upon his wife.

All these now did Maev by secret messages and by taunts and exhortations arouse against Cuchulain, and they waited till they heard that the curse of Macha was again heavy on the men of Ulster, and then they assembled a host and marched to the Plain of Murthemney.

The Madness of Cuchulain

And first the Children of Calatin caused a horror and a despondency to fall upon the mind of Cuchulain, and out of the hooded thistles and puff-balls and fluttering leaves of the forest they made the semblance of armed battalions marching against Murthemney, and Cuchulain seemed to see on every side the smoke of burning dwellings going up. And for two days he did battle with the phantoms till he was sick and wearied out. Then Cathbad and the men of Ulster persuaded him to retire to a solitary glen, where fifty of the princesses of Ulster, and among them Niam, wife of his faithful friend Conall of the Victories, tended him, and Niam made him vow that he would not leave the dūn where he was until she gave him leave.

But still the Children of Calatin filled the land with apparitions of war, and smoke and flames went up, and wild cries and wailings with chattering, goblin laughter and the braying of trumpets and horns were borne upon the winds. And Bave, Calatin's daughter, went into the glen, and, taking the form of a handmaid of Niam, she beckoned her away and led her to a distance among the woods and put a spell of straying on her so that she was lost and could find her way home no more. Bave then went in the form of Niam to Cuchulain and bade him up and rescue Ulster from the hosts that were harrying it, and the Morrigan came in the form of a great crow where Cuchulain sat with the women, and croaked of war and slaughter. Then Cuchulain sprang up and called Laeg to harness his chariot. But when Laeg sought for the Grey of Macha to harness him, the horse fled from him, and resisted, and only with great difficulty could Laeg yoke him in the chariot, while large tears of dark blood trickled down his face.

Then Cuchulain, having armed himself, drove forth; and on every side shapes and sounds of dread assailed him and clouded his mind, and then it appeared to him that he saw a great smoke, lit with bursts of red flame, over the ramparts of Emain Macha, and he thought he saw the corpse of Emer tossed out over the ramparts. But when he came to his dūn at Murthemney, there was Emer living, and she entreated him to leave the phantoms alone, but he would not listen to her, and he bade her farewell. Then he bade farewell to his mother Dectera, and she gave him a goblet of wine to drink, but ere he could drink it the wine turned to blood, and he flung it away, saying, "My life's end is near; this time I shall not return alive from the battle." And Dectera and Cathbad besought him to await the coming of Conall of the Victories, who was away on a journey, but he would not.

The Washer at the Ford

When he came to the ford upon the plain of Emania he saw there kneeling by the stream as it were a young maiden, weeping and wailing, and she washed a heap of bloody raiment and warlike arms in the stream, and when she raised a dripping vest or corselet from the water Cuchulain saw that they were his own. And as they crossed the ford she vanished from their sight.[1]

Clan Calatin Again

Then, having taken his leave of Conor and of the womenfolk in Emania, he turned again towards Murhemney and the foe. But on his way he saw by the roadside three old crones, each blind of one eye, hideous and wretched, and they had made a little fire of sticks, and over it they were roasting a dead dog on spits of rowan wood. As Cuchulain passed they called to him to alight and stay with them and share their food. "That will I not, in sooth," said he. "Had we a great feast," they said, "thou wouldst soon have stayed; it doth not become the great to despise the small." Then Cuchulain, because he would not be thought discourteous to the wretched, lighted down, and he took a piece of the roast and ate it, and the hand with which he took it was stricken up to the shoulder so that its former strength was gone. For it was *geis* to Cuchulain to approach a cooking hearth and take food from it, and it was *geis* to him to eat of his namesake.

[1] This apparition of the Washer of the Ford is of frequent occurrence in Irish legend.

[2] See p. 164 for the reference to *geis*. "His namesake" refers, of course, to the story of the Hound of Cullan, pp. 183, 184.

Death of Cuchulain

Near to Slieve Fuad, south of Armagh, Cuchulain found the host of his enemies, and drove furiously against them, plying the champion's "thunder-feat" upon them until the plain was strewn with their dead. Then a satirist, urged on by Lewy, came near him and demanded his spear.[1] "Have it, then," said Cuchulain, and flung it at him with such force that it went clear through him and killed nine men beyond. "A king will fall by that spear," said the Children of Calatin to Lewy, and Lewy seized it and flung it at Cuchulain, but it smote Laeg, the king of charioteers, so that his bowels fell out on the cushions of the chariot, and he bade farewell to his master and he died.

Then another satirist demanded the spear, and Cuchulain said: "I am not bound to grant more than one request on one day." But the satirist said: "Then I will revile Ulster for thy default," and Cuchulain flung him the spear as before, and Erc now got it, and this time in flying back it struck the Grey of Macha with a mortal wound. Cuchulain drew out the spear from the horse's side, and they bade each other farewell, and the Grey galloped away with half the yoke hanging to its neck.

And a third time Cuchulain flung the spear to a satirist, and Lewy took it again and flung it back, and it struck Cuchulain, and his bowels fell out in the chariot, and the remaining horse, Black Sainglend, broke away and left him.

"I would fain go as far as to that loch-side to drink," said Cuchulain, knowing the end was come, and they suffered him to go when he had promised to return to them again. So he gathered up his bowels into his

[1] It was a point of honour to refuse nothing to a bard; one king is said to have given his eye when it was demanded of him.

The Death of Cuchulain

Forbay and Queen Maev

breast and went to the loch-side, and drank, and bathed himself, and came forth again to die. Now there was close by a tall pillar-stone that stood westwards of the loch, and he went up to it and slung his girdle over it and round his breast, so that he might die in his standing and not in his lying down; and his blood ran down in a little stream into the loch, and an otter came out of the loch and lapped it. And the host gathered round, but feared to approach him while the life was still in him, and the hero-light shone above his brow. Then came the Grey of Macha to protect him, scattering his foes with biting and kicking.

And then came a crow and settled on his shoulder.

Lewy, when he saw this, drew near and pulled the hair of Cuchulain to one side over his shoulder, and with his sword he smote off his head; and the sword fell from Cuchulain's hand, and smote off the hand of Lewy as it fell. They took the hand of Cuchulain in revenge for this, and bore the head and hand south to Tara, and there buried them, and over them they raised a mound. But Conall of the Victories, hastening to Cuchulain's side on the news of the war, met the Grey of Macha streaming with blood, and together they went to the loch-side and saw him headless and bound to the pillar-stone, and the horse came and laid its head on his breast. Conall drove southwards to avenge Cuchulain, and he came on Lewy by the river Liffey, and because Lewy had but one hand Conall tied one of his behind his back, and for half the day they fought, but neither could prevail. Then came Conall's horse, the Dewy-Red, and tore a piece out of Lewy's side, and Conall slew him, and took his head, and returned to Emain Macha. But they made no show of triumph in entering the city, for Cuchulain the Hound of Ulster was no more.

The Recovery of the Tain

The history of the "Tain," or Cattle Raid, of Quelgny was traditionally supposed to have been written by no other than Fergus mac Roy, but for a long time the great lay or saga was lost. It was believed to have been written out in Ogham characters on staves of wood, which a bard who possessed them had taken with him into Italy, whence they never returned.

The recovery of the "Tain" was the subject of a number of legends which Sir S. Ferguson, in his "Lays of the Western Gael," has combined in a poem of so much power, so much insight into the spirit of Gaelic myth, that I venture to reproduce much of it here in telling this singular and beautiful story. It is said that after the loss of the "Tain" Sanchan Torpest, chief bard of Ireland, was once taunted at a feast by the High King Guary on his inability to recite the most famous and splendid of Gaelic poems. This touched the bard to the quick, and he resolved to recover the lost treasure. Far and wide through Erin and through Alba he searched for traces of the lay, but could only recover scattered fragments. He would have conjured up by magic arts the spirit of Fergus to teach it to him, even at the cost of his own life—for such, it seems, would have been the price demanded for the intervention and help of the dead—but the place of Fergus's grave, where the spells must be said, could not be discovered. At last Sanchan sent his son Murgen with his younger brother Eimena to journey to Italy and endeavour to discover there the fate of the staff-book. The brothers set off on their journey.

"Eastward, breadthwise, over Erin straightway travell'd forth the twain,
Till with many days' wayfaring Murgen fainted by Loch Ein:

'Dear my brother, thou art weary : I for present aid am flown :
Thou for my returning tarry here beside this Standing Stone.'

"Shone the sunset red and solemn : Murgen, where he leant, observed
Down the corners of the column letter-strokes of Ogham carved.
''Tis, belike, a burial pillar,' said he, 'and these shallow lines
Hold some warrior's name of valour, could I rightly spell the signs.'

"Letter then by letter tracing, soft he breathed the sound of each ;
Sound and sound then interlacing, lo, the signs took form of speech ;
And with joy and wonder mainly thrilling, part a-thrill with fear,
Murgen read the legend plainly, 'FERGUS SON OF ROY IS HERE.'"

Murgen then, though he knew the penalty, appealed to Fergus to pity a son's distress, and vowed, for the sake of the recovery of the "Tain," to give his life, and abandon his kin and friends and the maiden he loves, so that his father might no more be shamed. But Fergus gave no sign, and Murgen tried another plea :

"Still he stirs not. Love of women thou regard'st not, Fergus, now :
Love of children, instincts human, care for these no more hast thou :
Wider comprehension, deeper insights to the dead belong :—
Since for Love thou wak'st not, Sleeper, yet awake for sake of Song.

"'Thou, the first in rhythmic cadence dressing life's discordant tale,
Wars of chiefs and loves of maidens, gavest the Poem to the Gael ;
Now they've lost their noblest measure, and in dark days hard at hand,
Song shall be the only treasure left them in their native land.'

"Fergus rose. A mist ascended with him, and a flash was seen
As of brazen sandals blended with a mantle's wafture green ;
But so thick the cloud closed o'er him, Eimena, return'd at last,
Found not on the field before him but a mist-heap grey and vast.

"Thrice to pierce the hoar recesses faithful Eimena essay'd ;
Thrice through foggy wildernesses back to open air he stray'd ;
Till a deep voice through the vapours fill'd the twilight far and near
And the Night her starry tapers kindling, stoop'd from heaven to hear.

"Seem'd as though the skiey Shepherd back to earth had cast the fleece
Envying gods of old caught upward from the darkening shrines of Greece;
So the white mists curl'd and glisten'd, so from heaven's expanses bare,
Stars enlarging lean'd and listen'd down the emptied depths of air.

"All night long by mists surrounded Murgen lay in vapoury bars;
All night long the deep voice sounded 'neath the keen, enlarging stars:
But when, on the orient verges, stars grew dim and mists retired,
Rising by the stone of Fergus, Murgen stood a man inspired.

"'Back to Sanchan!—Father, hasten, ere the hour of power be past,
Ask not how obtain'd but listen to the lost lay found at last!'
'Yea, these words have tramp of heroes in them; and the marching rhyme
Rolls the voices of the eras down the echoing steeps of Time.'

"Not till all was thrice related, thrice recital full essay'd,
Sad and shamefaced, worn and faded, Murgen sought the faithful maid.
'Ah, so haggard; ah, so altered; thou in life and love so strong!'
'Dearly purchased,' Murgen falter'd, 'life and love I've sold for song!'

"'Woe is me, the losing bargain! what can song the dead avail?'
'Fame immortal,' murmur'd Murgen, 'long as lay delights the Gael.'
'Fame, alas! the price thou chargest not repays one virgin tear.'
'Yet the proud revenge I've purchased for my sire, I deem not dear.'

"So, again to Gort the splendid, when the drinking boards were spread,
Sanchan, as of old attended, came and sat at table-head.
'Bear the cup to Sanchan Torpest: twin gold goblets, Bard, are thine,
If with voice and string thou harpest, *Tain-Bo-Cuailgne*, line for line.'

"'Yea, with voice and string I'll chant it.' Murgen to his father's knee
Set the harp: no prelude wanted, Sanchan struck the master key,
And, as bursts the brimful river all at once from caves of Cong,
Forth at once, and once for ever, leap'd the torrent of the song.

THE RECOVERY OF THE TAIN

"Floating on a brimful torrent, men go down and banks go by:
Caught adown the lyric current, Guary, captured, ear and eye,
Heard no more the courtiers jeering, saw no more the walls of Gort,
Creeve Roe's [1] meads instead appearing, and Emania's royal fort.

"Vision chasing splendid vision, Sanchan roll'd the rhythmic scene;
They that mock'd in lewd derision now, at gaze, with wondering mien
Sate, and, as the glorying master sway'd the tightening reins of song,
Felt emotion's pulses faster—fancies faster bound along.

"Pity dawn'd on savage faces, when for love of captive Crunn,
Macha, in the ransom-races, girt her gravid loins, to run
'Gainst the fleet Ultonian horses; and, when Deirdra on the road
Headlong dash'd her 'mid the corses, brimming eyelids overflow'd.

"Light of manhood's generous ardour, under brows relaxing shone,
When, mid-ford, on Uladh's border, young Cuchullin stood alone,
Maev and all her hosts withstanding:—'Now, for love of knightly play,
Yield the youth his soul's demanding; let the hosts their marchings stay,

"'Till the death he craves be given; and, upon his burial stone
Champion-praises duly graven, make his name and glory known;
For, in speech-containing token, age to ages never gave
Salutation better spoken, than, "Behold a hero's grave."'

"What, another and another, and he still or combat calls?
Ah, the lot on thee, his brother sworn in arms, Ferdia, falls;
And the hall with wild applauses sobb'd like woman ere they wist,
When the champions in the pauses of the deadly combat kiss'd.

"Now, for love of land and cattle, while Cuchullin in the fords
Stays the march of Connaught's battle, ride and rouse the Northern Lords;
Swift as angry eagles wing them toward the plunder'd eyrie's call,
Thronging from Dun Dealga bring them, bring them from the Red Branch hall!

[1] *Craobh Ruadh*—the Red Branch hostel.

"Heard ye not the tramp of armies? Hark! amid the sudden gloom,
'Twas the stroke of Conall's war-mace sounded through the startled room;
And, while still the hall grew darker, king and courtier chill'd with dread,
Heard the rattling of the war-car of Cuchullin overhead.

"Half in wonder, half in terror, loth to stay and loth to fly,
Seem'd to each beglamour'd hearer shades of kings went thronging by:
But the troubled joy of wonder merged at last in mastering fear,
As they heard through pealing thunder, 'FERGUS SON OF ROY IS HERE!'

"Brazen-sandall'd, vapour-shrouded, moving in an icy blast,
Through the doorway terror-crowded, up the tables Fergus pass'd:—
'Stay thy hand, oh harper, pardon! cease the wild unearthly lay!
Murgen, bear thy sire his guerdon.' Murgen sat, a shape of clay.

"'Bear him on his bier beside me: never more in halls of Gort
Shall a niggard king deride me: slaves, of Sanchan make their sport!
But because the maiden's yearnings needs must also be condoled,
Hers shall be the dear-bought earnings, hers the twin-bright cups of gold.'

"'Cups,' she cried, 'of bitter drinking, fling them far as arm can throw!
Let them in the ocean sinking, out of sight and memory go!
Let the joinings of the rhythm, let the links of sense and sound
Of the *Tain-Bo* perish with them, lost as though they'd ne'er been found!'

"So it comes, the lay, recover'd once at such a deadly cost,
Ere one full recital suffer'd, once again is all but lost:
For, the maiden's malediction still with many a blemish-stain
Clings in coarser garb of fiction round the fragments that remain."

The Phantom Chariot of Cuchulain

Cuchulain, however, makes an impressive reappearance in a much later legend of Christian origin, found in the twelfth-century "Book of the Dun Cow." He was summoned from Hell, we are told, by St. Patrick to prove the truths of Christianity and the horrors of damnation to the pagan monarch, Laery mac Neill, King of Ireland. Laery, with St. Benen, a companion of Patrick, are standing on the Plain of mac Indoc when a blast of icy wind nearly takes them off their feet. It is the wind of Hell, Benen explains, after its opening before Cuchulain. Then a dense mist covers the plain, and anon a huge phantom chariot with galloping horses, a grey and a black, loom up through the mist. Within it are the famous two, Cuchulain and his charioteer, giant figures, armed with all the splendour of the Gaelic warrior.

Cuchulain then talks to Laery, and urges him to "believe in God and in holy Patrick, for it is not a demon that has come to thee, but Cuchulain son of Sualtam." To prove his identity he recounts his famous deeds of arms, and ends by a piteous description of his present state:

> "What I suffered of trouble,
> O Laery, by sea and land—
> Yet more severe was a single night
> When the demon was wrathful!
> Great as was my heroism,
> Hard as was my sword,
> The devil crushed me with one finger
> Into the red charcoal!"

He ends by beseeching Patrick that heaven may be granted to him, and the legend tells that the prayer was granted and that Laery believed.

Death of Conor mac Nessa

Christian ideas have also gathered round the end of Cuchulain's lord, King Conor of Ulster. The manner of his death was as follows: An unjust and cruel attack had been made by him on Mesgedra, King of Leinster, in which that monarch met his death at the hand of Conall of the Victories.[1] Conall took out the brains of the dead king and mingled them with lime to make a sling-stone—such "brain balls," as they were called, being accounted the most deadly of missiles. This ball was laid up in the king's treasure-house at Emain Macha, where the Connacht champion, Ket son of Maga, found it one day when prowling in disguise through Ulster. Ket took it away and kept it always by him. Not long thereafter the Connacht men took a spoil of cattle from Ulster, and the Ulster men, under Conor, overtook them at a river-ford still called Athnurchar (The Ford of the Sling-cast), in Westmeath. A battle was imminent, and many of the ladies of Connacht came to their side of the river to view the famous Ultonian warriors, and especially Conor, the stateliest man of his time. Conor was willing to show himself, and seeing none but women on the other bank he drew near them; but Ket, who was lurking in ambush, now rose and slung the brain-ball at Conor, striking him full in the forehead. Conor fell, and was carried off by his routed followers. When they got him home, still living, to Emain Macha, his physician, Fingen, pronounced that if the ball were extracted from his head he must die; it was accordingly sewn up with golden thread, and the king was bidden to keep himself from horse-riding and from all vehement passion and exertion, and he would do well.

Seven years afterwards Conor saw the sun darken at noonday, and he summoned his Druid to tell him the cause of the portent. The Druid, in a magic trance, tells him of a hill in a distant land on which stand three crosses with a human form nailed to each of them, and one of them is like the Immortals. "Is he a

[1] The story is told in full in the author's "High Deeds of Finn."

malefactor?" then asks Conor. "Nay," says the Druid, but the Son of the living God," and he relates to the king the story of the death of Christ. Conor breaks out in fury, and drawing his sword he hacks at the oak-trees in the sacred grove, crying, "Thus would I deal with his enemies," when with the excitement and exertion the brain-ball bursts from his head, and he falls dead. And thus was the vengeance of Mesgedra fulfilled. With Conor and with Cuchulain the glory ot the Red Branch and the dominance of Ulster passed away. The next, or Ossianic, cycle of Irish legend brings upon the scene different characters, different physical surroundings, and altogether different ideals of life.

Ket and the Boar of mac Datho

The Connacht champion Ket, whose main exploit was the wounding of King Conor at Ardnurchar, figures also in a very dramatic tale entitled "The Carving of mac Datho's Boar." The story runs as follows:

Once upon a time there dwelt in the province of Leinster a wealthy hospitable lord named Mesroda, son of Datho. Two possessions had he; namely, a hound which could outrun every other hound and every wild beast in Erin, and a boar which was the finest and greatest in size that man had ever beheld.

Now the fame of this hound was noised all about the land, and many were the princes and lords who longed to possess it. And it came to pass that Conor King of Ulster and Maev Queen of Connacht sent messengers to mac Datho to ask him to sell them the hound for a price, and both the messengers arrived at the dūn of mac Datho on the same day. Said the Connacht messenger: "We will give thee in exchange for the hound six hundred milch cows, and a chariot with two horses, the best that are to be found in Connacht, and at the end of a year thou shalt have as much again." And the messenger of King Conor said: "We will give no less than Connacht, and the friendship and alliance of Ulster, and that will be better for thee than the friendship of Connacht."

Then Mesroda mac Datho fell silent, and for three days he would not eat or drink, nor could he sleep o' nights, but tossed restlessly on his bed. His wife observed his condition, and said to him: "Thy fast hath been long, Mesroda, though good food is by thee in plenty; and at night thou turnest thy face to the wall, and well I know thou dost not sleep. What is the cause of thy trouble?"

"There is a saying," replied Mac Datho, "'Trust not a thrall with money, nor a woman with a secret.'"

"When should a man talk to a woman," said his wife, "but when something were amiss? What thy mind cannot solve perchance another's may."

Then mac Datho told his wife of the request for his hound both from Ulster and from Connacht at one and the same time. "And whichever of them I deny," he said, "they will harry my cattle and slay my people."

"Then hear my counsel," said the woman. "Give it to both of them, and bid them come and fetch it; and if there be any harrying to be done, let them even harry each other; but in no way mayest thou keep the hound."

Mac Datho followed this wise counsel, and bade both Ulster and Connacht to a great feast on the same day, saying to each of them that they could have the hound afterwards.

So on the appointed day Conor of Ulster, and Maev, and their retinues of princes and mighty men assembled at the dūn of mac Datho. There they found a great feast set forth, and to provide the chief dish mac Datho had killed his famous boar, a beast of enormous size. The question now arose as to who should have the honourable task of carving it, and Bricriu of the Poisoned Tongue characteristically, for the sake of the strife which he loved, suggested that the warriors of Ulster and Connacht should compare their principal deeds of arms, and give the carving of the boar to him who seemed to have done best in the border-fighting which was always going on between the provinces. After much bandying of words and of taunts Ket son of Maga arises and stands over the boar, knife in hand, challenging each of the Ulster lords to match his deeds of valour. One after another they arise, Cuscrid son of Conor, Keltchar, Moonremur, Laery the Triumphant, and others—Cuchulain is not introduced in this story—and in each case Ket has some biting tale to tell of an encounter in which he has come off better than they, and one by one they sit down shamed and silenced. At last a shout of welcome is heard at the door of the hall and the Ulstermen grow jubilant: Conall of the Victories has appeared on the scene. He strides up to the boar, and Ket and he greet each other with chivalrous courtesy:

"And now welcome to thee, O Conall, thou of the iron heart and fiery blood; keen as the glitter of ice, ever-victorious chieftain; hail, mighty son of Finnchoom!" said Ket.

And Conall said: "Hail to thee, Ket, flower of heroes, lord of chariots, a raging sea in battle; a strong, majestic bull; hail, son of Maga!"

"And now," went on Conall, "rise up from the boar and give me place."

"Why so?" replied Ket.

"Dost thou seek a contest from me?" said Conall. "Verily thou shalt have it. By the gods of my nation I swear that since I first took weapons in my hand I have never passed one day that I did not slay a Connacht man, nor one night that I did not make a foray on them, nor have I ever slept but I had the head of a Connacht man under my knee."

"I confess," then said Ket, "that thou art a better man than I, and I yield thee the boar. But if Anluan my brother were here, he would match thee deed for deed, and sorrow and shame it is that he is not."

"Anluan is here," shouted Conall, and with that he drew from his girdle the head of Anluan and dashed it in the face of Ket.

Then all sprang to their feet and a wild shouting and tumult arose, and the swords flew out of themselves, and battle raged in the hall of mac Datho. Soon the hosts burst out through the doors of the dūn and smote and slew each other in the open field, until the Connacht host were put to flight. The hound of mac Datho pursued the chariot of King Ailell of Connacht till the charioteer smote off its head, and so the cause of contention was won by neither party, and mac Datho lost his hound, but saved his lands and life.

The Death of Ket

The death of Ket is told in Keating's "History of Ireland." Returning from a foray in Ulster, he was overtaken by Conall at the place called the Ford of Ket, and they fought long and desperately. At last Ket was slain, but Conall of the Victories was in little better case, and lay bleeding to death when another Connacht champion named Beālcu[1] found him. "Kill me," said Conall to him, "that it be not said I fell at the hand of *one* Connacht man." But Beālcu said: "I will not slay a man at the point of death, but I will bring thee home and heal thee, and when thy strength is come again

[1] Pronounced "Bay-al-koo."

thou shalt fight with me in single combat." Then Beälcu put Conall on a litter and brought him home, and had him tended till his wounds were healed.

The three sons of Beälcu, however, when they saw what the Ulster champion was like in all his might, resolved to assassinate him before the combat should take place. By a stratagem Conall contrived that they slew their own father instead; and then, taking the heads of the three sons, he went back, victoriously as he was wont, to Ulster.

The Death of Maev

The tale of the death of Queen Maev is also preserved by Keating. Fergus mac Roy having been slain by Ailell with a cast of a spear as he bathed in a lake with Maev, and Ailell having been slain by Conall, Maev retired to an island[1] on Loch Ryve, where she was wont to bathe early every morning in a pool near to the landing-place. Forbay son of Conor mac Nessa, having discovered this habit of the queen's, found means one day to go unperceived to the pool and to measure the distance from it to the shore of the mainland. Then he went back to Emania, where he measured out the distance thus obtained, and placing an apple on a pole at one end he shot at it continually with a sling until he grew so good a marksman at that distance that he never missed his aim. Then one day, watching his opportunity by the shores of Loch Ryve, he saw Maev enter the water, and putting a bullet in his sling he shot at her with so good an aim that he smote her in the centre of the forehead and she fell dead.

The great warrior-queen had reigned in Connacht, it was said, for eighty-eight years. She is a signal example

[1] Inis Clothrann, now known as Quaker's Island. The pool no longer exists.

of the kind of women whom the Gaelic bards delighted to portray. Gentleness and modesty were by no means their usual characteristics, but rather a fierce overflowing life. Women-warriors like Skatha and Aifa are frequently met with, and one is reminded of the Gaulish women, with their mighty snow-white arms, so dangerous to provoke, of whom classical writers tell us. The Gaelic bards, who in so many ways anticipated the ideas of chivalric romance, did not do so in setting women in a place apart from men. Women were judged and treated like men, neither as drudges nor as goddesses, and we know that well into historic times they went with men into battle, a practice only ended in the sixth century.

Fergus mac Leda and the Wee Folk

Of the stories of the Ultonian Cycle which do not centre on the figure of Cuchulain, one of the most interesting is that of Fergus mac Leda and the King of the Wee Folk. In this tale Fergus appears as King of Ulster, but as he was contemporary with Conor mac Nessa, and in the Cattle Raid of Quelgny is represented as following him to war, we must conclude that he was really a sub-king, like Cuchulain or Owen of Ferney.

The tale opens in Faylinn, or the Land of the Wee Folk, a race of elves presenting an amusing parody of human institutions on a reduced scale, but endowed (like dwarfish people generally in the literature of primitive races) with magical powers. Iubdan,[1] the King of Faylinn, when flushed with wine at a feast, is bragging of the greatness of his power and the invincibility of his armed forces—have they not the strong man Glower, who with his axe has been known to hew down a thistle at a stroke? But the king's bard,

[1] "Youb'dan."

Eisirt, has heard something of a giant race oversea in a land called Ulster, one man of whom would annihilate a whole battalion of the Wee Folk, and he incautiously allows himself to hint as much to the boastful monarch. He is immediately clapped into prison for his audacity, and only gets free by promising to go immediately to the land of the mighty men, and bring back evidence of the truth of his incredible story.

So off he goes; and one fine day King Fergus and his lords find at the gate of their Dūn a tiny little fellow magnificently clad in the robes of a royal bard, who demands entrance. He is borne in upon the hand of Æda, the king's dwarf and bard, and after charming the court by his wise and witty sayings, and receiving a noble largesse, which he at once distributes among the poets and other court attendants of Ulster, he goes off home, taking with him as a guest the dwarf Æda, before whom the Wee Folk fly as a "Fomorian giant," although, as Eisirt explains, the average man of Ulster can carry him like a child. Iubdan is now convinced, but Eisirt puts him under *geise*, the bond of chivalry which no Irish chieftain can repudiate without being shamed, to go himself, as Eisirt has done, to the palace of Fergus and taste the king's porridge. Iubdan, after he has seen Æda, is much dismayed, but he prepares to go, and bids Bebo, his wife, accompany him. "You did an ill deed," she says, "when you condemned Eisirt to prison; but surely there is no man under the sun that can make thee hear reason."

So off they go, and Iubdan's fairy steed bears them over the sea till they reach Ulster, and by midnight they stand before the king's palace. "Let us taste the porridge as we were bound," says Bebo, "and make off before daybreak." They steal in and find the porridge-pot, to the rim of which Iubdan can only reach by standing on his horse's back. In straining downwards to get at the porridge he overbalances himself and falls in. There in the thick porridge he sticks fast, and there Fergus's scullions find him at the break of day, with the faithful Bebo lamenting. They bear him off to Fergus, who is amazed at finding another wee man, with a woman too, in his palace. He treats them hospitably, but refuses all appeals to let them go. The story now recounts in a spirit of broad humour several Rabelaisian adventures in which Bebo is concerned, and gives a charming poem supposed to have been uttered by Iubdan in the form of advice to Fergus's fire-gillie as to the merits for burning of different kinds of timber. The following are extracts:

"Burn not the sweet apple-tree of drooping branches, of the white blossoms, to whose gracious head each man puts forth his hand."

"Burn not the noble willow, the unfailing ornament of poems; bees drink from its blossoms, all delight in the graceful tent."

"The delicate, airy tree of the Druids, the rowan with its berries, this burn; but avoid the weak tree, burn not the slender hazel."

"The ash-tree of the black buds burn not—timber that speeds the wheel, that yields the rider his switch; the ashen spear is the scale-beam of battle."

At last the Wee Folk come in a great multitude to beg the release of Iubdan. On the king's refusal they visit the country with various plagues, snipping off the ears of corn, letting the calves suck all the cows dry, defiling the wells, and so forth; but Fergus is obdurate. In their quality as earth-gods, *dei terreni*, they promise to make the plains before the palace of Fergus stand thick with corn every year without ploughing or sowing,

King Fergus and the Wee Man

Finn finds the Old Men in the Forest

but all is vain. At last, however, Fergus agrees to ransom Iubdan against the best of his fairy treasures, so Iubdan recounts them—the cauldron that can never be emptied, the harp that plays of itself; and finally he mentions a pair of water-shoes, wearing which a man can go over or under water as freely as on dry land. Fergus accepts the shoes, and Iubdan is released.

The Blemish of Fergus

But it is hard for a mortal to get the better of Fairyland—a touch of hidden malice lurks in magical gifts, and so it proved now. Fergus was never tired of exploring the depths of the lakes and rivers of Ireland; but one day, in Loch Rury, he met with a hideous monster, the *Muirdris*, or river-horse, which inhabited that lake, and from which he barely saved himself by flying to the shore. With the terror of this encounter his face was twisted awry; but since a blemished man could not hold rule in Ireland, his queen and nobles took pains, on some pretext, to banish all mirrors from the palace, and kept the knowledge of his condition from him. One day, however, he smote a bondmaid with a switch, for some negligence, and the maid, indignant, cried out: "It were better for thee, Fergus, to avenge thyself on the river-horse that hath twisted thy face than to do brave deeds on women!" Fergus bade fetch him a mirror, and looked in it. "It is true," he said; "the river-horse of Loch Rury has done this thing."

Death of Fergus

The conclusion may be given in the words of Sir Samuel Ferguson's fine poem on this theme. Fergus donned the magic shoes, took sword in hand, and went to Loch Rury:

> "For a day and night
> Beneath the waves he rested out of sight,
> But all the Ultonians on the bank who stood
> Saw the loch boil and redden with his blood.
> When next at sunrise skies grew also red
> He rose—and in his hand the *Muirdris'* head.
> Gone was the blemish! On his goodly face
> Each trait symmetric had resumed its place:
> And they who saw him marked in all his mien
> A king's composure, ample and serene.
> He smiled; he cast his trophy to the bank,
> Said, 'I, survivor, Ulstermen!' and sank."

This fine tale has been published in full from an Egerton MS., by Mr. Standish Hayes O'Grady, in his "Silva Gadelica." The humorous treatment of the fairy element in the story would mark it as belonging to a late period of Irish legend, but the tragic and noble conclusion unmistakably signs it as belonging to the Ulster bardic literature, and it falls within the same order of ideas, if it were not composed within the same period, as the tales of Cuchulain.

Significance of Irish Place-Names

Before leaving this great cycle of legendary literature let us notice what has already, perhaps, attracted the attention of some readers—the extent to which its chief characters and episodes have been commemorated in the still surviving place-names of the country.[1] This is true of Irish legend in general—it is especially so of the Ultonian Cycle. Faithfully indeed, through many a century of darkness and forgetting, have these names pointed to the hidden treasures of heroic romance

[1] Dr. P. W. Joyce's "Irish Names of Places" is a storehouse of information on this subject.

which the labours of our own day are now restoring to light. The name of the little town of Ardee, as we have seen,[1] commemorates the tragic death of Ferdia at the hand of his "heart companion," the noblest hero of the Gael. The ruins of Dūn Baruch, where Fergus was bidden to the treacherous feast, still look over the waters of Moyle, across which Naisi and Deirdre sailed to their doom. Ardnurchar, the Hill of the Sling-cast, in Westmeath,[2] brings to mind the story of the stately monarch, the crowd of gazing women, and the crouching enemy with the deadly missile which bore the vengeance of Mesgedra. The name of Armagh, or Ard Macha, the Hill of Macha, enshrines the memory of the Fairy Bride and her heroic sacrifice, while the grassy rampart can still be traced where the war-goddess in the earlier legend drew its outline with the pin of her brooch when she founded the royal fortress of Ulster. Many pages might be filled with these instances. Perhaps no modern country has place-names so charged with legendary associations as are those of Ireland. Poetry and myth are there still closely wedded to the very soil of the land—a fact in which there lies ready to hand an agency for education, for inspiration, of the noblest kind, if we only had the insight to see it and the art to make use of it.

[1] P. 211, *note*.

[2] The name is given both to the hill, *ard*, and to the ford, *atha* beneath it.

CHAPTER VI: TALES OF THE OSSIANIC CYCLE

The Fianna of Erin

AS the tales of the Ultonian Cycle cluster round the heroic figure of the Hound of Cullan, so do those of the Ossianic Cycle round that of Finn mac Cumhal,[1] whose son Oisin[2] (or Ossian, as Macpherson called him in the pretended translations from the Gaelic which first introduced him to the English-speaking world) was a poet as well as a warrior, and is the traditional author of most of them. The events of the Ultonian Cycle are supposed to have taken place about the time of the birth of Christ. Those of the Ossianic Cycle fell mostly in the reign of Cormac mac Art, who lived in the third century A.D. During his reign the Fianna of Erin, who are represented as a kind of military Order composed mainly of the members of two clans, Clan Bascna and Clan Morna, and who were supposed to be devoted to the service of the High King and to the repelling of foreign invaders, reached the height of their renown under the captaincy of Finn.

The annalists of ancient Ireland treated the story of Finn and the Fianna, in its main outlines, as sober history. This it can hardly be. Ireland had no foreign invaders during the period when the Fianna are supposed to have flourished, and the tales do not throw a ray of light on the real history of the country; they are far more concerned with a Fairyland populated by supernatural beings, beautiful or terrible, than with any tract of real earth inhabited by real men and women. The modern critical reader of these tales will soon feel that it would be idle to seek for any basis of fact in this glittering

[1] Pronounced "mac Cool." [2] Pronounced "Usheen."

mirage. But the mirage was created by poets and story-tellers of such rare gifts for this kind of literature that it took at once an extraordinary hold on the imagination of the Irish and Scottish Gael.

The Ossianic Cycle

The earliest tales of this cycle now extant are found in manuscripts of the eleventh and twelfth centuries, and were composed probably a couple of centuries earlier. But the cycle lasted in a condition of vital growth for a thousand years, right down to Michael Comyn's "Lay of Oisîn in the Land of Youth," which was composed about 1750, and which ended the long history of Gaelic literature.[1] It has been estimated[2] that if all the tales and poems of the Ossianic Cycle which still remain could be printed they would fill some twenty-five volumes the size of this. Moreover, a very great proportion of this literature, even if there were no manuscripts at all, could during the last and the preceding centuries have been recovered from the lips of what has been absurdly called an "illiterate" peasantry in the Highlands and in the Gaelic-speaking parts of Ireland. It cannot but interest us to study the character of the literature which was capable of exercising such a spell.

Contrasted with the Ultonian Cycle

Let us begin by saying that the reader will find himself in an altogether different atmosphere from that in which the heroes of the Ultonian Cycle live and move. Everything speaks of a later epoch, when life was gentler and softer, when men lived more in settlements and towns,

[1] Subject, of course, to the possibility that the present revival of Gaelic as a spoken tongue may lead to the opening of a new chapter in that history.

[2] See "Ossian and Ossianic Literature," by Alfred Nutt, p. 4.

when the Danaan Folk were more distinctly fairies and less deities, when in literature the elements of wonder and romance predominated, and the iron string of heroism and self-sacrifice was more rarely sounded. There is in the Ossianic literature a conscious delight in wild nature, in scenery, in the song of birds, the music of the chase through the woods, in mysterious and romantic adventure, which speaks unmistakably of a time when the free, open-air life "under the greenwood tree" is looked back on and idealised, but no longer habitually lived, by those who celebrate it. There is also a significant change of *locale*. The Conorian tales were the product of a literary movement having its sources among the bleak hills or on the stern rock-bound coasts of Ulster. In the Ossianic Cycle we find ourselves in the Midlands or South of Ireland. Much of the action takes place amid the soft witchery of the Killarney landscape, and the difference between the two regions is reflected in the ethical temper of the tales.

In the Ultonian Cycle it will have been noticed that however extravagantly the supernatural element may be employed, the final significance of almost every tale, the end to which all the supernatural machinery is worked, is something real and human, something that has to do with the virtues or vices, the passions or the duties or men and women. In the Ossianic Cycle, broadly speaking, this is not so. The nobler vein of literature seems to have been exhausted, and we have now beauty for the sake of beauty, romance for the sake of romance, horror or mystery for the sake of the excitement they arouse. The Ossianic tales are, at their best,

> "Lovely apparitions, sent
> To be a moment's ornament."

They lack that something, found in the noblest art as in

the noblest personalities, which has power "to warn, to comfort, and command."

The Coming of Finn

King Cormac mac Art was certainly a historical character, which is more, perhaps, than we can say of Conor mac Nessa. Whether there is any real personage behind the glorious figure of his great captain, Finn, it is more difficult to say. But for our purpose it is not necessary to go into this question. He was a creation of the Celtic mind in one land and in one stage of its development, and our part here is to show what kind of character the Irish mind liked to idealise and make stories about.

Finn, like most of the Irish heroes, had a partly Danaan ancestry. His mother, Murna of the White Neck, was grand-daughter of Nuada of the Silver Hand, who had wedded that Ethlinn, daughter of Balor the Fomorian, who bore the Sun-god Lugh to Kian. Cumhal son of Trenmōr was Finn's father. He was chief of the Clan Bascna, who were contending with the Clan Morna for the leadership of the Fianna, and was overthrown and slain by these at the battle of Knock.[1]

Among the Clan Morna was a man named Lia, the lord of Luachar in Connacht, who was Treasurer of the Fianna, and who kept the Treasure Bag, a bag made of crane's skin and having in it magic weapons and jewels of great price that had come down from the days of the Danaans. And he became Treasurer to the Clan Morna, and still kept the bag at Rath Luachar.

Murna, after the defeat and death of Cumhal, took refuge in the forests of Slieve Bloom,[2] and there she bore a man-child whom she named Demna. For fear

[1] Now Castleknock, near Dublin.
[2] In the King's County.

that the Clan Morna would find him out and slay him, she gave him to be nurtured in the wildwood by two aged women, and she herself became wife to the King of Kerry. But Demna, when he grew up to be a lad, was called "Finn," or the Fair One, on account of the whiteness of his skin and his golden hair, and by this name he was always known thereafter. His first deed was to slay Lia, who had the Treasure Bag of the Fianna, which he took from him. He then sought out his uncle Crimmal, who, with a few other old men, survivors of the chiefs of Clan Bascna, had escaped the sword at Castleknock, and were living in much penury and affliction in the recesses of the forests of Connacht. These he furnished with a retinue and guard from among a body of youths who followed his fortunes, and gave them the Treasure Bag. He himself went to learn the accomplishments of poetry and science from an ancient sage and Druid named Finegas, who dwelt on the river Boyne. Here, in a pool of this river, under boughs of hazel from which dropped the Nuts of Knowledge on the stream, lived Fintan the Salmon of Knowledge, which whoso ate of him would enjoy all the wisdom of the ages. Finegas had sought many a time to catch this salmon, but failed until Finn had come to be his pupil. Then one day he caught it, and gave it to Finn to cook, bidding him eat none of it himself, but to tell him when it was ready. When the lad brought the salmon, Finegas saw that his countenance was changed. "Hast thou eaten of the salmon?" he asked. "Nay," said Finn, "but when I turned it on the spit my thumb was burnt, and I put it to my mouth." "Take the Salmon of Knowledge and eat it," then said Finegas, "for in thee the prophecy is come true. And now go hence, for I can teach thee no more."

After that Finn became as wise as he was strong and

bold, and it is said that whenever he wished to divine what would befall, or what was happening at a distance, he had but to put his thumb in his mouth and bite it, and the knowledge he wished for would be his.

Finn and the Goblin

At this time Goll son of Morna was the captain of the Fianna of Erin, but Finn, being come to man's estate, wished to take the place of his father Cumhal. So he went to Tara, and during the Great Assembly, when no man might raise his hand against any other in the precincts of Tara, he sat down among the king's warriors and the Fianna. At last the king marked him as a stranger among them, and bade him declare his name and lineage. "I am Finn son of Cumhal," said he, "and I am come to take service with thee, O King, as my father did." The king accepted him gladly, and Finn swore loyal service to him. No long time after that came the period of the year when Tara was troubled by a goblin or demon that came at nightfall and blew fire-balls against the royal city, setting it in flames, and none could do battle with him, for as he came he played on a harp a music so sweet that each man who heard it was lapped in dreams, and forgot all else on earth for the sake of listening to that music. When this was told to Finn he went to the king and said: "Shall I, if I slay the goblin, have my father's place as captain of the Fianna?" "Yea, surely," said the king, and he bound himself to this by an oath.

Now there were among the men-at-arms an old follower of Finn's father, Cumhal, who possessed a magic spear with a head of bronze and rivets of Arabian gold. The head was kept laced up in a leathern case; and it had the property that when the naked blade was laid against the forehead of a man it would fill him with a strength and a battle-fury that would make him invincible in every combat. This spear the man Fiacha gave to Finn, and taught him how to use it, and with it he awaited the coming of the goblin on the ramparts of Tara. As night fell and mists began to gather in the wide plain around the Hill he saw a shadowy form coming swiftly towards him, and heard the notes of the magic harp. But laying the spear to his brow he shook off the spell, and the phantom fled before him to the Fairy Mound of Slieve Fuad, and there Finn overtook and slew him, and bore back his head to Tara.

Then Cormac the King set Finn before the Fianna, and bade them all either swear obedience to him as their captain or seek service elsewhere. And first of all Goll mac Morna swore service, and then all the rest followed, and Finn became Captain of the Fianna of Erin, and ruled them till he died.

Finn's Chief Men: Conan mac Lia

With the coming of Finn the Fianna of Erin came to their glory, and with his life their glory passed away. For he ruled them as no other captain ever did, both strongly and wisely, and never bore a grudge against any, but freely forgave a man all offences save disloyalty to his lord. Thus it is told that Conan, son of the lord of Luachar, him who had the Treasure Bag and whom Finn slew at Rath Luachar, was for seven years an outlaw and marauder, harrying the Fians and killing here a man and there a hound, and firing dwellings, and raiding their cattle. At last they ran him to a corner at Carn Lewy, in Munster, and when he saw that he could escape no more he stole upon Finn as he sat down after a chase, and flung his arms round him from behind, holding him fast and motionless. Finn knew who held him thus, and said : "What wilt thou, Conan ?" Conan said: "To make a covenant of service and fealty with thee, for I may no longer evade thy wrath." So Finn laughed and said : "Be it so, Conan, and if thou prove faithful and valiant I also will keep faith." Conan served him for thirty years, and no man of all the Fianna was keener and hardier in fight.

Conan mac Morna

There was also another Conan, namely, mac Morna, who was big and bald, and unwieldy in manly exercises, but whose tongue was bitter and scurrilous ; no high or brave thing was done that Conan the Bald did not mock and belittle. It is said that when he was stripped he showed down his back and buttocks a black sheep's fleece instead of a man's skin, and this is the way it came about. One day when Conan and certain others of the Fianna were hunting in the forest they came to a stately dūn, white-walled, with coloured thatching on the roof, and they entered it to seek hospitality. But when they were within they found no man, but a great empty hall with pillars of cedar-wood and silken hangings about it, like the hall of a wealthy lord. In the midst there was a table set forth with a sumptuous feast of boar's flesh and venison, and a great vat of yew-wood full of red wine, and cups of gold and silver. So they set themselves gaily to eat and drink, for they were hungry from the chase, and talk and laughter were loud around the board. But one of them ere long started to his feet with a cry of fear and wonder, and they all looked round, and saw before their eyes the tapestried walls changing to rough wooden beams, and the ceiling to foul sooty thatch like that of a herdsman's hut. So they knew they were being entrapped by some enchantment of the Fairy Folk, and all sprang to their feet and made for the doorway, that was no longer high and stately, but was shrinking to the size of a fox earth—all but Conan the Bald, who was gluttonously devouring the good things on the table, and heeded nothing else. Then they shouted to him, and as the last of them went out he strove to rise and follow, but found himself limed to the chair so that he could not stir. So two of the Fianna, seeing his plight, rushed back and seized his arms and tugged with all their might, and as they dragged him away they left the most part of his raiment and his skin sticking to the chair. Then, not knowing what else to do with him in his sore plight, they clapped upon his back the nearest thing they could find, which was the skin of a black sheep that they took from a peasant's flock hard by, and it grew there, and Conan wore it till his death.

Though Conan was a coward and rarely adventured himself in battle with the Fianna, it is told that once a good man fell by his hand. This was on the day of the great battle with the pirate horde on the Hill of Slaughter in Kerry.[1] For Liagan, one of the invaders, stood out before the hosts and challenged the bravest of the Fians to single combat, and the Fians in mockery thrust Conan forth to the fight. When he appeared Liagan laughed, for he had more strength than wit, and he said : "Silly is thy visit, thou bald old man." And as Conan still approached Liagan lifted his hand fiercely, and Conan said : "Truly thou art in more peril from the man behind than from the man in front." Liagan looked round ; and in that instant Conan swept off his head, and then threw his sword and ran for shelter to the ranks of the laughing Fians. But Finn was very wroth because he had won the victory by a trick.

[1] The hill still bears the name, Knockanar.

" Finn heard the notes of the magic harp "

Oisīn and Niam

OSCAR

Dermot O'Dyna

And one of the chiefest of the friends of Finn was Dermot of the Love Spot. He was so fair and noble to look on that no woman could refuse him love, and it was said that he never knew weariness, but his step was as light at the end of the longest day of battle or the chase as it was at the beginning. Between him and Finn there was great love, until the day when Finn, then an old man, was to wed Grania, daughter of Cormac the High King ; but Grania bound Dermot by the sacred ordinances of the Fian chivalry to fly with her on her wedding night, which thing, sorely against his will, he did, and thereby got his death. But Grania went back to Finn, and when the Fianna saw her they laughed through all the camp in bitter mockery, for they would not have given one of the dead man's fingers for twenty such as Grania.

Keelta mac Ronan and Oisín

Another of the chief men that Finn had was Keelta mac Ronan, who was one of his house-stewards, and a strong warrior as well as a golden-tongued reciter of tales and poems. And there was Oisín, the son of Finn, the greatest poet of the Gael, of whom more shall be told hereafter.

Oscar

Oisín had a son, Oscar, who was the fiercest fighter in battle among all the Fians. He slew in his maiden battle three kings, and in his fury he also slew by mischance his own friend and condisciple Linné. His wife was the fair Aideen, who died of grief after Oscar's death in the battle of Gowra, and Oisín buried her on Ben Edar (Howth), and raised over her the great dolmen which is there to this day. Oscar appears in this literature as a type of hard strength, with a heart "like twisted horn sheathed in steel," a character made as purely for war as a sword or spear.

Geena mac Luga

Another good man that Finn had was Geena, the son of Luga; his mother was the warrior-daughter of Finn, and his father was a near kinsman of hers. He was nurtured by a woman that bore the name of Fair Mane, who had brought up many of the Fianna to manhood. When his time to take arms was come he stood before Finn and made his covenant of fealty, and Finn gave him the captaincy of a band. But mac Luga proved slothful and selfish, for ever vaunting himself and his weapon-skill, and never training his men to the chase of deer or boar, and he used to beat his hounds and his serving-men. At last the Fians under him came with their whole company to Finn at Loch Lena, in Killarney, and there they laid their complaint against mac Luga, and said: "Choose now, O Finn, whether you will have us or the son of Luga by himself."

Then Finn sent to mac Luga and questioned him, but mac Luga could say nothing to the point as to why the Fianna would none of him. Then Finn taught him the things befitting a youth of noble birth and a captain of men, and they were these:

Maxims of the Fianna

"Son of Luga, if armed service be thy design, in a great man's household be quiet, be surly in the narrow pass.

"Without a fault of his beat not thy hound; until thou ascertain her guilt, bring not a charge against thy wife.

"In battle meddle not with a buffoon, for, O mac Luga, he is but a fool.

"Censure not any if he be of grave repute; stand not up to take part in a brawl; have naught to do with a madman or a wicked one.

"Two-thirds of thy gentleness be shown to women and to those that creep on the floor (little children) and to poets, and be not violent to the common people.

"Utter not swaggering speech, nor say thou wilt not yield what is right; it is a shameful thing to speak too stiffly unless that it be feasible to carry out thy words.

"So long as thou shalt live, thy lord forsake not; neither for gold nor for other reward in the world abandon one whom thou art pledged to protect.

"To a chief do not abuse his people, for that is no work for a man of gentle blood.

"Be no tale-bearer, nor utterer of falsehoods; be not talkative nor rashly censorious. Stir not up strife against thee, however good a man thou be.

"Be no frequenter of the drinking-house, nor given to carping at the old; meddle not with a man of mean estate.

"Dispense thy meat freely; have no niggard for thy familiar.

"Force not thyself upon a chief, nor give him cause to speak ill of thee.

"Stick to thy gear; hold fast to thy arms till the stern fight with its weapon-glitter be ended.

"Be more apt to give than to deny, and follow after gentleness, O son of Luga."

And the son of Luga, it is written, heeded these counsels, and gave up his bad ways, and he became one of the best of Finn's men.

Character of Finn

Suchlike things also Finn taught to all his followers, and the best of them became like himself in valour and gentleness and generosity. Each of them loved the repute of his comrades more than his own, and each would say that for all noble qualities there was no man in the breadth of the world worthy to be thought of beside Finn.

It was said of him that "he gave away gold as if it were the leaves of the woodland, and silver as if it were the foam of the sea"; and that whatever he had bestowed upon any man, if he fell out with him afterwards, he was never known to bring it against him.

The poet Oisîn once sang of him to St. Patrick:

> "These are the things that were dear to Finn—
> The din of battle, the banquet's glee,
> The bay of his hounds through the rough glen ringing,
> And the blackbird singing in Letter Lee,
>
> "The shingle grinding along the shore
> When they dragged his war-boats down to sea,
> The dawn wind whistling his spears among,
> And the magic song of his minstrels three."

Tests of the Fianna

In the time of Finn no one was ever permitted to be one of the Fianna of Erin unless he could pass through many severe tests of his worthiness. He must be versed in the Twelve Books of Poetry, and must himself be skilled to make verse in the rime and metre of the masters of Gaelic poesy. Then he was buried to his middle in the earth, and must, with a shield and a hazel stick, there defend himself against nine warriors casting spears at him, and if he were wounded he was not accepted. Then his hair was woven into braids, and he was chased through the forest by the Fians. If he were overtaken, or if a braid of his hair were disturbed, or if a dry stick cracked under his foot, he was not accepted. He must be able to leap over a lath level with his brow, and to run at full speed under one level with his knee, and he must be able while running to draw out a thorn from his foot and never slacken speed. He must take no dowry with a wife.

Keelta and St. Patrick

It was said that one of the Fians, namely, Keelta, lived on to a great age, and saw St. Patrick, by whom he was baptized into the faith of the Christ, and to whom he told many tales of Finn and his men, which Patrick's scribe wrote down. And once Patrick asked him how it was that the Fianna became so mighty and so glorious that all Ireland sang of their deeds, as Ireland has done ever since. Keelta answered: "Truth was in our hearts and strength in our arms, and what we said, that we fulfilled."

This was also told of Keelta after he had seen St. Patrick and received the Faith. He chanced to be one day by Leyney, in Connacht, where the Fairy Folk of the Mound of Duma were wont to be sorely harassed and spoiled every year by pirates from oversea. They called Keelta to their aid, and by his counsel and valour the invaders were overcome and driven home; but Keelta was sorely wounded. Then Keelta asked that Owen, the seer of the Fairy Folk, might foretell him how long he had to live, for he was already a very aged man. Owen said: "It will be seventeen years, O Keelta of fair fame, till thou fall by the pool of Tara, and grievous that will be to all the king's household." "Even so did my chief and lord, my guardian and loving protector, Finn, foretell to me," said Keelta. "And now what fee will ye give me for my rescue of you from the worst affliction that ever befell you ?" "A great reward," said the Fairy Folk, "even youth; for by our art we shall change you into a young man again with all the strength and activity of your prime." "Nay, God forbid," said Keelta, "that I should take upon me a shape of sorcery, or any other than that which my Maker, the true and glorious God, hath bestowed upon me." And the Fairy Folk said: "It is the word of a true warrior and hero, and the thing that thou sayest is good." So they healed his wounds, and every bodily evil that he had, and he wished them blessing and victory, and went his way.

The Birth of Oisīn

One day, as Finn and his companions and dogs were returning from the chase to their dūn on the Hill of Allen, a beautiful fawn started up on their path, and the chase swept after her, she taking the way which led to their home. Soon all the pursuers were left far behind save only Finn himself and his two hounds Bran and Skolawn. Now these hounds were of strange breed; for Tyren, sister to Murna, the mother of Finn, had been changed into a hound by the enchantment of a woman of the Fairy Folk, who loved Tyren's husband Ullan; and the two hounds of Finn were the children of Tyren, born to her in that shape. Of all hounds in Ireland they were the best, and Finn loved them much, so that it was said he wept but twice in his life, and once was for the death of Bran.

At last, as the chase went on down a valley-side, Finn saw the fawn stop and lie down, while the two hounds began to play round her, and to lick her face and limbs. So he gave commandment that none should hurt her, and she followed them to the Dūn of Allen, playing with the hounds as she went

The same night Finn awoke and saw standing by his bed the fairest woman his eyes had ever beheld.

"I am Saba, O Finn," she said, "and I was the fawn ye chased to-day. Because I would not give my love to the Druid of the Fairy Folk, who is named the Dark, he put that shape upon me by his sorceries, and I have borne it these three years. But a slave of his, pitying me, once revealed to me that if I could win to thy great Dūn of Allen, O Finn, I should be safe from all enchantments, and my natural shape would come to me again. But I feared to be torn in pieces by thy dogs, or wounded by thy hunters, till at last I let myself be overtaken by thee alone and by Bran and Skolawn, who have the nature of man and would do me no hurt." "Have no fear, maiden," said Finn; "we, the Fianna, are free, and our guest-friends are free; there is none who shall put compulsion on you here."

So Saba dwelt with Finn, and he made her his wife; and so deep was his love for her that neither the battle nor the chase had any delight for him, and for months he never left her side. She also loved him as deeply, and their joy in each other was like that of the Immortals in the Land of Youth. But at last word came to Finn that the warships of the Northmen were in the Bay of Dublin, and he summoned his heroes to the fight; "For," said he to Saba, "the men of Erin give us tribute and hospitality to defend them from the foreigner, and it were shame to take it from them and not to give that to which we, on our side, are pledged." And he called to mind that great saying of Goll mac Morna when they were once sore bestead by a mighty host. "A man," said Goll, "lives after his life, but not after his honour."

Seven days was Finn absent, and he drove the Northmen from the shores of Erin. But on the eighth day he returned, and when he entered his dūn he saw trouble in the eyes of his men, and of their fair women-folk, and Saba was not on the rampart expecting his return. So he bade them tell him what had chanced and they said:

"Whilst thou, our father and lord, wert afar off smiting the foreigner, and Saba looking ever down the pass for thy return, we saw one day as it were the likeness of thee approaching, and Bran and Skolawn at thy heels. And we seemed also to hear the notes of the Fian hunting-call blown on the wind. Then Saba hastened to the great gate, and we could not stay her, so eager was she to rush to the phantom. But when she came near she halted and gave a loud and bitter cry, and the shape of thee smote her with a hazel wand, and lo, there was no woman there any more, but a deer. Then those hounds chased it, and ever as it strove to reach again the gate of the dūn they turned back. We all now seized what arms we could and ran out to drive away the enchanter, but when we reached the place there was nothing to be seen, only still we heard the rushing of flying feet and the baying of dogs, and one thought it came from here, and another from there, till at last the uproar died away and all was still. What we could do, O Finn, we did; Saba is gone."

Finn then struck his hand on his breast, but spoke no word, and he went to his own chamber. No man saw him for the rest of that day, nor for the day after. Then he came forth, and ordered the matters of the Fianna as of old, but for seven years thereafter he went searching for Saba through every remote glen and dark forest and cavern of Ireland, and he would take no hounds with him save Bran and Skolawn. But at last he renounced all hope of finding her again, and went hunting as of old.

)ne day as he was following the chase on Ben Bulban, n Sligo, he heard the musical bay of the dogs change of sudden to a fierce growling and yelping, as though they vere in combat with some beast, and running hastily up ie and his men beheld, under a great tree, a naked boy vith long hair, and around him the hounds struggling o seize him, but Bran and Skolawn fighting with them nd keeping them off. And the lad was tall and shapely, nd as the heroes gathered round he gazed undauntedly n them, never heeding the rout of dogs at his feet. The Fians beat off the dogs and brought the lad home vith them, and Finn was very silent and continually earched the lad's countenance with his eyes. In time he use of speech came to him, and the story that he told vas this :

He had known no father, and no mother save a gentle ind, with whom he lived in a most green and pleasant alley shut in on every side by towering cliffs that could iot be scaled or by deep chasms in the earth. In the ummer he lived on fruits and suchlike, and in the vinter store of provisions was laid for him in a cave. And there came to them sometimes a tall, dark-visaged nan, who spoke to his mother, now tenderly, and now n loud menace, but she always shrank away in fear, and he man departed in anger. At last there came a day vhen the dark man spoke very long with his mother in ll tones of entreaty and of tenderness and of rage, but he would still keep aloof and give no sign save of fear ind abhorrence. Then at length the dark man drew iear and smote her with a hazel wand ; and with that ie turned and went his way, but she this time followed iim, still looking back at her son and piteously com- laining. And he, when he strove to follow, found him- self unable to move a limb ; and crying out with rage ind desolation he fell to the earth, and his senses left him.

When he came to himself he was on the mountain-side on Ben Bulban, where he remained some days, searching for that green and hidden valley, which he never found again. And after a while the dogs found him ; but of the hind his mother and of the Dark Druid there is no man knows the end.

Finn called his name Oisīn (Little Fawn), and he became a warrior of fame, but far more famous for the songs and tales that he made; so that of all things to this day that are told of the Fianna of Erin men are wont to say : "Thus sang the bard Oisīn, son of Finn."

Oisīn and Niam

It happened that on a misty summer morning as Finn and Oisīn with many companions were hunting on the shores of Loch Lena they saw coming towards them a maiden, beautiful exceedingly, riding on a snow-white steed. She wore the garb of a queen ; a crown of gold was on her head, and a dark-brown mantle of silk, set with stars of red gold, fell around her and trailed on the ground. Silver shoes were on her horse's hoofs, and a crest of gold nodded on his head. When she came near she said to Finn : "From very far away I have come, and now at last I have found thee, Finn son of Cumhal."

Then Finn said: "What is thy land and race, maiden, and what dost thou seek from me ?"

"My name," she said, "is Niam of the Golden Hair. I am the daughter of the King of the Land of Youth, and that which has brought me here is the love of thy son Oisīn." Then she turned to Oisīn, and she spoke to him in the voice of one who has never asked anything but it was granted to her.

"Wilt thou go with me, Oisīn, to my father's land ?"

And Oisīn said : "That will I, and to the world's end"; for the fairy spell had so wrought upon his heart that he cared no more for any earthly thing but to have the love of Niam of the Head of Gold.

Then the maiden spoke of the Land Oversea to which she had summoned her lover, and as she spoke a dreamy stillness fell on all things, nor did a horse shake his bit, nor a hound bay, nor the least breath of wind stir in the forest trees till she had made an end. And what she said seemed sweeter and more wonderful as she spoke it than anything they could afterwards remember to have heard, but so far as they could remember it it was this:

"Delightful is the land beyond all dreams,
Fairer than aught thine eyes have ever seen.
There all the year the fruit is on the tree,
And all the year the bloom is on the flower.

"There with wild honey drip the forest trees;
The stores of wine and mead shall never fail.
Nor pain nor sickness knows the dweller there,
Death and decay come near him never more.

"The feast shall cloy not, nor the chase shall tire,
Nor music cease for ever through the hall;
The gold and jewels of the Land of Youth
Outshine all splendours ever dreamed by man.

"Thou shalt have horses of the fairy breed,
Thou shalt have hounds that can outrun the wind;
A hundred chiefs shall follow thee in war,
A hundred maidens sing thee to thy sleep.

"A crown of sovranty thy brow shall wear,
And by thy side a magic blade shall hang,
And thou shalt be lord of all the Land of Youth,
And lord of Niam of the Head of Gold."

As the magic song ended the Fians beheld Oisin mount the fairy steed and hold the maiden in his arms, and ere they could stir or speak she turned her horse's head and shook the ringing bridle, and down the forest glade they fled, as a beam of light flies over the land when clouds drive across the sun; and never did the Fianna behold Oisīn son of Finn on earth again.

Yet what befell him afterwards is known. As his birth was strange, so was his end, for he saw the wonders of the Land of Youth with mortal eyes and lived to tell them with mortal lips.

The Journey to Fairyland

When the white horse with its riders reached the sea it ran lightly over the waves, and soon the green woods and headlands of Erin faded out of sight. And now the sun shone fiercely down, and the riders passed into a golden haze in which Oisīn lost all knowledge of where he was or if sea or dry land were beneath his horse's hoofs. But strange sights sometimes appeared to them in the mist, for towers and palace gateways loomed up and disappeared, and once a hornless doe bounded by them chased by a white hound with one red ear; and again they saw a young maid ride by on a brown steed, bearing a golden apple in her hand, and close behind her followed a young horseman on a white steed, a purple cloak floating at his back and a gold-hilted sword in his hand. And Oisīn would have asked the princess who and what these apparitions were, but Niam bade him ask nothing nor seem to notice any phantom they might see until they were come to the Land of Youth.

Oisīn's Return

The story goes on to tell how Oisīn met with various adventures in the Land of Youth, including the rescue of an imprisoned princess from a Fomorian giant. But at last, after what seemed to him a sojourn of three weeks in the Land of Youth, he was satiated with delights of every kind, and longed to visit his native land again and to see his old comrades. He promised to return when he had done so, and Niam gave him the white fairy steed that had borne him across the sea to Fairyland, but charged him that when he had reached the Land of Erin again he must never alight from its back nor touch the soil of the earthly world with his foot, or the way of return to the Land of Youth would be barred to him for ever. Oisin then set forth, and once more crossed the mystic ocean, finding himself at last on the western shores of Ireland. Here he made at once for the Hill of Allen, where the dūn of Finn was wont to be, but marvelled, as he traversed the woods, that he met no sign of the Fian hunters and at the small size of the folk whom he saw tilling the ground.

At length, coming from the forest path into the great clearing where the Hill of Allen was wont to rise, broad and green, with its rampart enclosing many white-walled dwellings, and the great hall towering high in the midst, he saw but grassy mounds overgrown with rank weeds and whin bushes, and among them pastured a peasant's kine. Then a strange horror fell upon him and he thought some enchantment from the land of Faëry held his eyes and mocked him with false visions. He threw his arms abroad and shouted the names of Finn and Oscar, but none replied, and he thought that perchance the hounds might hear him, so he cried upon Bran and Skolawn and strained his ears if they might catch the faintest rustle or whisper of the world from the sight of which his eyes were holden, but he heard only the sighing of the wind in the whins. Then he rode in terror from that place, setting his face towards the eastern sea, for he meant to traverse Ireland from side to side and end to end in search of some escape from his enchantment.

The Broken Spell

But when he came near to the eastern sea, and was now in the place which is called the Valley of the Thrushes,[1] he saw in a field upon the hillside a crowd of men striving to roll aside a great boulder from their tilled land, and an overseer directing them. Towards them he rode, meaning to ask them concerning Finn and the Fianna. As he came near they all stopped their work to gaze upon him, for to them he appeared like a messenger of the Fairy Folk or an angel from heaven. Taller and mightier he was than the men-folk they knew, with sword-blue eyes and brown, ruddy cheeks; in his mouth, as it were, a shower of pearls, and bright hair clustered beneath the rim of his helmet. And as Oisín looked upon their puny forms, marred by toil and care, and at the stone which they feebly strove to heave from its bed, he was filled with pity, and thought to himself, "Not such were even the churls of Erin when I left them for the Land of Youth" and he stooped from his saddle to help them. He set his hand to the boulder, and with a mighty heave he lifted it from where it lay and set it rolling down the hill. And the men raised a shout of wonder and applause; but their shouting changed in a moment into cries of terror and dismay, and they fled, jostling and overthrowing each other to escape from the place of fear, for a marvel horrible to see had taken place. For Oisín's saddle-girth had burst as he heaved the stone and he fell headlong to the ground. In an instant the white steed had vanished from their eyes like a wreath of mist, and that which rose, feeble and staggering, from the ground was no youthful warrior, but a man stricken with extreme old age, white-bearded and withered, who stretched out

[1] Glanismole, near Dublin.

groping hands and moaned with feeble and bitter cries. And his crimson cloak and yellow silken tunic were now but coarse homespun stuff tied with a hempen girdle, and the gold-hilted sword was a rough oaken staff such as a beggar carries who wanders the roads from farmer's house to house.

When the people saw that the doom that had been wrought was not for them they returned, and found the old man prone on the ground with his face hidden in his arms. So they lifted him up, and asked who he was and what had befallen him. Oisīn gazed round on them with dim eyes, and at last he said: "I was Oisīn the son of Finn, and I pray ye tell me where he dwells, for his dūn on the Hill of Allen is now a desolation, and I have neither seen him nor heard his hunting-horn from the western to the eastern sea." Then the men gazed strangely on each other and on Oisīn, and the overseer asked: "Of what Finn dost thou speak, for there be many of that name in Erin?" Oisīn said: "Surely of Finn mac Cumhal mac Trenmōr, captain of the Fianna of Erin." Then the overseer said: "Thou art daft, old man, and thou hast made us daft to take thee for a youth as we did a while agone. But we at least have now our wits again, and we know that Finn son of Cumhal and all his generation have been dead these three hundred years. At the battle of Gowra fell Oscar, son of Oisīn, and Finn at the battle of Brea, as the historians tell us; and the lays of Oisīn, whose death no man knows the manner of, are sung by our harpers at great men's feasts. But now the Talkenn,[1] Patrick, has come into Ireland, and has preached to us the One God and Christ His Son, by whose might these old days and ways are done away with; and Finn and his Fianna, with their feasting

[1] Talkenn, or "Adze-head," was a name given to St. Patrick by the Irish. Probably it referred to the shape of his tonsure.

and hunting and songs of war and of love, have no such reverence among us as the monks and virgins of Holy Patrick, and the psalms and prayers that go up daily to cleanse us from sin and to save us from the fire of judgment." But Oisīn replied, only half hearing and still less comprehending what was said to him: "If thy God have slain Finn and Oscar, I would say that God is a strong man." Then they all cried out upon him, and some picked up stones, but the overseer bade them let him be until the Talkenn had spoken with him, and till he should order what was to be done.

Oisīn and Patrick

So they brought him to Patrick, who treated him gently and hospitably, and to Patrick he told the story of all that had befallen him. But Patrick bade his scribes write all carefully down, that the memory of the heroes whom Oisīn had known, and of the joyous and free life they had led in the woods and glens and wild places of Erin, should never be forgotten among men.

This remarkable legend is known only in the modern Irish poem written by Michael Comyn about 1750, a poem which may be called the swan-song of Irish literature. Doubtless Comyn worked on earlier traditional material; but though the ancient Ossianic poems tell us of the prolongation of Oisīn's life, so that he could meet St. Patrick and tell him stories of the Fianna, the episodes of Niam's courtship and the sojourn in the Land of Youth are known to us at present only in the poem of Michael Comyn.

The Enchanted Cave

This tale, which I take from S. H. O'Grady's edition in "Silva Gadelica," relates that Finn once made a great hunting in the district of Corann, in Northern Connacht, which was ruled over by one Conaran, a lord of the Danaan Folk. Angered at the intrusion of the Fianna in his hunting-grounds, he sent his three sorcerer-daughters to take vengeance on the mortals.

Finn, it is said, and Conan the Bald, with Finn's two favourite hounds, were watching the hunt from the top of the Hill of Keshcorran and listening to the cries of the beaters and the notes of the horn and the baying of the dogs, when, in moving about on the hill, they came upon the mouth of a great cavern, before which sat three hags of evil and revolting aspect. On three crooked sticks of holly they had twisted left-handwise hanks of yarn, and were spinning with these when Finn and his followers arrived. To view them more closely the warriors drew near, when they found themselves suddenly entangled in strands of the yarn which the hags had spun about the place like the web of a spider, and deadly faintness and trembling came over them, so that they were easily bound fast by the hags and carried into the dark recesses of the cave. Others of the party then arrived, looking for Finn. All suffered the same experience—they lost all their pith and valour at the touch of the bewitched yarn, and were bound and carried into the cave, until the whole party were laid in bonds, with the dogs baying and howling outside.

The witches now seized their sharp, wide-channelled, hard-tempered swords, and were about to fall on the captives and slay them, but first they looked round at the mouth of the cave to see if there was any straggler whom they had not yet laid hold of. At this moment Goll mac Morna, "the raging lion, the torch of onset, the great of soul," came up, and a desperate combat ensued, which ended by Goll cleaving two of the hags in twain, and then subduing and binding the third, whose name was Irnan. She, as he was about to slay her, begged for mercy—"Surely it were better for thee to have the Fianna whole"—and he gave her her life if she would release the prisoners.

Into the cave they went, and one by one the captives were unbound, beginning with the poet Fergus True-lips and the "men of science," and they all sat down on the hill to recover themselves, while Fergus sang a chant of praise in honour of the rescuer, Goll; and Irnan disappeared.

Ere long a monster was seen approaching them, a "gnarled hag" with blazing, bloodshot eyes, a yawning mouth full of ragged fangs, nails like a wild beast's, and armed like a warrior. She laid Finn under *geise* to provide her with single combat from among his men until she should have her fill of it. It was no other than the third sister, Irnan, whom Goll had spared. Finn in vain begged Oisīn, Oscar, Keelta, and the other prime warriors of the Fianna to meet her; they all pleaded inability after the ill-treatment and contumely they had received. At last, as Finn himself was about to do battle with her, Goll said: "O Finn, combat with a crone beseems thee not," and he drew sword for a second battle with this horrible enemy. At last, after a desperate combat, he ran her through her shield and through her heart, so that the blade stuck out at the far side, and she fell dead. The Fianna then sacked the dūn of Conaran, and took possession of all the treasure in it, while Finn bestowed on Goll mac Morna his own daughter, Keva of the White Skin, and, leaving the dūn a heap of glowing embers, they returned to the Hill of Allen.

The Chase of Slievegallion

This fine story, which is given in poetical form, as if narrated by Oisīn, in the Ossianic Society's "Transactions," tells how Cullan the Smith (here represented as

'Patrick bade his scribes write all carefully down"

“ The Fianna raised a pillar stone with her name in Ogham letters ”

a Danaan divinity), who dwelt on or near the mountains of Slievegallion, in Co. Armagh, had two daughters, Ainé and Milucra, each of whom loved Finn mac Cumhal. They were jealous of each other; and on Ainé once happening to say that she would never have a man with grey hair, Milucra saw a means of securing Finn's love entirely for herself. So she assembled her friends among the Danaans round the little grey lake that lies on the top of Slievegallion, and they charged its waters with enchantments.

This introduction, it may be observed, bears strong signs of being a later addition to the original tale, made in a less understanding age or by a less thoughtful class into whose hands the legend had descended. The real meaning of the transformation which it narrates is probably much deeper.

The story goes on to say that not long after this the hounds of Finn, Bran and Skolawn, started a fawn near the Hill of Allen, and ran it northwards till the chase ended on the top of Slievegallion, a mountain which, like Slievenamon[1] in the south, was in ancient Ireland a veritable focus of Danaan magic and legendary lore. Finn followed the hounds alone till the fawn disappeared on the mountain-side. In searching for it Finn at last came on the little lake which lies on the top of the mountain, and saw by its brink a lady of wonderful beauty, who sat there lamenting and weeping. Finn asked her the cause of her grief. She explained that a gold ring which she dearly prized had fallen from her finger into the lake, and she charged Finn by the bonds of *geise* that he should plunge in and find it for her.

Finn did so, and after diving into every recess of the

[1] Pronounced "Sleeve-na-mon'": accent on last syllable. It means the Mountain of the [Fairy] Women.

lake he discovered the ring, and before leaving the water gave it to the lady. She immediately plunged into the lake and disappeared. Finn then surmised that some enchantment was being wrought on him, and ere long he knew what it was, for on stepping forth on dry land he fell down from sheer weakness, and arose again, a tottering and feeble old man, snowy-haired and withered, so that even his faithful hounds did not know him, but ran round the lake searching for their lost master.

Meantime Finn was missed from his palace on the Hill of Allen, and a party soon set out on the track on which he had been seen to chase the deer. They came to the lake-side on Slievegallion, and found there a wretched and palsied old man, whom they questioned, but who could do nothing but beat his breast and moan. At last, beckoning Keelta to come near, the aged man whispered faintly some words into his ear, and lo, it was Finn himself! When the Fianna had ceased from their cries of wonder and lamentation, Finn whispered to Keelta the tale of his enchantment, and told them that the author of it must be the daughter of Cullan the Smith, who dwelt in the Fairy Mound of Slievegallion. The Fianna, bearing Finn on a litter, immediately went to the Mound and began to dig fiercely. For three days and nights they dug at the Fairy Mound, and at last penetrated to its inmost recesses, when a maiden suddenly stood before them holding a drinking-horn of red gold. It was given to Finn. He drank from it, and at once his beauty and form were restored to him, but his hair still remained white as silver. This too would have been restored by another draught, but Finn let it stay as it was, and silver-white his hair remained to the day of his death.

The tale has been made the subject of a very striking

allegorical drama, "The Masque of Finn," by Mr. Standish O'Grady, who, rightly no doubt, interprets the story as symbolising the acquisition of wisdom and understanding through suffering. A leader of men must descend into the lake of tears and know feebleness and despair before his spirit can sway them to great ends.

There is an antique sepulchral monument on the mountain-top which the peasantry of the district still regard—or did in the days before Board schools—as the abode of the "Witch of the Lake"; and a mysterious beaten path, which was never worn by the passage of human feet, and which leads from the rock sepulchre to the lake-side, is ascribed to the going to and fro of this supernatural being.

The "Colloquy of the Ancients"

One of the most interesting and attractive of the relics of Ossianic literature is the "Colloquy of the Ancients," *Agallamh na Senorach*, a long narrative piece dating from about the thirteenth century. It has been published with a translation in O'Grady's "Silva Gadelica." It is not so much a story as a collection of stories skilfully set in a mythical framework. The "Colloquy" opens by presenting us with the figures of Keelta mac Ronan and Oisín son of Finn, each accompanied by eight warriors, all that are left of the great fellowship of the Fianna after the battle of Gowra and the subsequent dispersion of the Order. A vivid picture is given us of the grey old warriors, who had outlived their epoch, meeting for the last time at the dūn of a once famous chieftainess named Camha, and of their melancholy talk over bygone days, till at last a long silence settled on them.

Keelta Meets St. Patrick

Finally Keelta and Oisín resolve to part, Oisín, of whom we hear little more, going to the Fairy Mound, where his Danaan mother (here called Blai) has her dwelling, while Keelta takes his way over the plains of Meath till he comes to Drumderg, where he lights on St. Patrick and his monks. How this is chronologically possible the writer does not trouble himself to explain, and he shows no knowledge of the legend of Oisín in the Land of Youth. "The clerics," says the story, "saw Keelta and his band draw near them, and fear fell on them before the tall men with the huge wolf-hounds that accompanied them, for they were not people of one epoch or of one time with the clergy." Patrick then sprinkles the heroes with holy water, whereat legions of demons who had been hovering over them fly away into the hills and glens, and "the enormous men sat down." Patrick, after inquiring the name of his guest, then says he has a boon to crave of him—he wishes to find a well of pure water with which to baptize the folk of Bregia and of Meath.

The Well of Tradaban

Keelta, who knows every brook and hill and rath and wood in the country, thereon takes Patrick by the hand and leads him away "till," as the writer says, "right in front of them they saw a loch-well, sparkling and translucid. The size and thickness of the cress and of the *fothlacht*, or brooklime, that grew on it was a wonderment to them." Then Keelta began to tell of the fame and qualities of the place, and uttered an exquisite little lyric in praise of it:

"O Well of the Strand of the Two Women, beautiful are thy cresses, luxuriant, branching; since thy produce is neglected on thee thy brooklime is not suffered to grow. Forth from thy banks thy trout are to be seen, thy wild swine in the wilderness; the deer of thy fair hunting crag-land, thy dappled and red-chested fawns! Thy mast all hanging on the branches of the trees; thy fish in estuaries of the rivers; lovely the colours of thy purling streams, O thou that art azure-hued, and again green with reflections of surrounding copse-wood."[1]

St. Patrick and Irish Legend

After the warriors have been entertained Patrick asks: "Was he, Finn mac Cumhal, a good lord with whom ye were?" Keelta praises the generosity of Finn, and goes on to describe in detail the glories of his household, whereon Patrick says:

"Were it not for us an impairing of the devout life, an occasion of neglecting prayer, and of deserting converse with God, we, as we talked with thee, would feel the time pass quickly, warrior!"

Keelta goes on with another tale of the Fianna, and Patrick, now fairly caught in the toils of the enchanter, cries: "Success and benediction attend thee, Keelta! This is to me a lightening of spirit and mind. And now tell us another tale."

So ends the exordium of the "Colloquy." As usual in the openings of Irish tales, nothing could be better contrived; the touch is so light, there is so happy a mingling of pathos, poetry, and humour, and so much dignity in the sketching of the human characters introduced. The rest of the piece consists in the exhibition of a vast amount of topographical and legendary lore by Keelta, attended by the invariable "Success and benediction attend thee!" of Patrick.

They move together, the warrior and the saint, on

[1] Translation by S. H. O'Grady.

Patrick's journey to Tara, and whenever Patrick or some one else in the company sees a hill or a fort or a well he asks Keelta what it is, and Keelta tells its name and a Fian legend to account for it, and so the story wanders on through a maze of legendary lore until they are met by a company from Tara, with the king at its head, who then takes up the *rôle* of questioner. The "Colloquy," as we have it now, breaks off abruptly as the story how the *Lia Fail* was carried off from Ireland is about to be narrated.[1] The interest of the "Colloquy" lies in the tales of Keelta and the lyrics introduced in the course of them. Of the tales there are about a hundred, telling of Fian raids and battles, and love-makings and feastings, but the greater number of them have to do with the intercourse between the Fairy Folk and the Fianna. With these folk the Fianna have constant relations, both of love and of war. Some of the tales are of great elaboration, wrought out in the highest style of which the writer was capable. One of the best is that of the fairy *Brugh*, or mansion of Slievenamon, which Patrick and Keelta chance to pass by, and of which Keelta tells the following history:

The Brugh of Slievenamon

One day as Finn and Keelta and five other champions of the Fianna were hunting at Torach, in the north, they roused a beautiful fawn which fled before them, they holding it in chase all day, till they reached the mountain of Slievenamon towards evening, when the fawn suddenly seemed to vanish underground. A chase like this, in the Ossianic literature, is the common prelude to an adventure in Fairyland. Night now fell rapidly, and with it came heavy snow and storm, and, searching for shelter, the Fianna discovered in the

[1] See p. 105.

wood a great illuminated *Brugh*, or mansion, where they sought admittance. On entering they found themselves in a spacious hall, full of light, with eight-and-twenty warriors and as many fair and yellow-haired maidens, one of the latter seated on a chair of crystal, and making wonderful music on a harp. After the Fian warriors have been entertained with the finest of viands and liquors, it is explained to them that their hosts are Donn, son of Midir the Proud, and his brother, and that they are at war with the rest of the Danaan Folk, and have to do battle with them thrice yearly on the green before the *Brugh*. At first each of the twenty-eight had a thousand warriors under him. Now all are slain except those present, and the survivors have sent out one of their maidens in the shape of a fawn to entice the Fianna to their fairy palace and to gain their aid in the battle that must be delivered to-morrow. We have, in fact, a variant of the well-known theme of the Rescue of Fairyland. Finn and his companions are always ready for a fray, and a desperate battle ensues which lasts from evening till morning, for the fairy host attack at night. The assailants are beaten off, losing over a thousand of their number ; but Oscar, Dermot, and mac Luga are sorely wounded. They are healed by magical herbs ; and more fighting and other adventures follow, until, after a year has passed, Finn compels the enemy to make peace and give hostages, when the Fianna return to earth and rejoin their fellows. No sooner has Keelta finished his tale, standing on the very spot where they had found the fairy palace on the night of snow, than a young warrior is seen approaching them. He is thus described : " A shirt of royal satin was next his skin ; over and outside it a tunic of the same fabric ; and a fringed crimson mantle, confined with a bodkin of gold, upon his breast; in his hand a gold-hilted sword, and a golden helmet on his head." A delight in the colour and material splendour of life is a very marked feature in all this literature. This splendid figure turns out to be Donn mac Midir, one of the eight-and-twenty whom Finn had succoured, and he comes to do homage for himself and his people to St. Patrick, who accepts entertainment from him for the night; for in the "Colloquy" the relations of the Church and of the Fairy World are very cordial.

The Three Young Warriors

Nowhere in Celtic literature does the love of wonder and mystery find such remarkable expression as in the "Colloquy." The writer of this piece was a master of the touch that makes, as it were, the solid framework of things translucent; and shows us, through it, gleams of another world, mingled with ours yet distinct, and having other laws and characteristics. We never get a clue as to what these laws are. The Celt did not, in Ireland at least, systematise the unknown, but let it shine for a moment through the opaqueness of this earth and then withdrew the gleam before we understood what we had seen. Take, for instance, this incident in Keelta's account of the Fianna. Three young warriors come to take service with Finn, accompanied by a gigantic hound. They make their agreement with him, saying what services they can render and what reward they expect, and they make it a condition that they shall camp apart from the rest of the host, and that when night has fallen no man shall come near them or see them.

Finn asks the reason for this prohibition, and it is this: of the three warriors one has to die each night, and the other two must watch him; therefore they would not be disturbed. There is no explanation of this; the writer simply leaves us with the thrill of the mystery upon us.

The Fair Giantess

Again, let us turn to the tale of the Fair Giantess. One day Finn and his warriors, while resting from the chase for their midday meal, saw coming towards them a towering shape. It proved to be a young giant maiden, who gave her name as Vivionn (Bebhionn) daughter of Treon, from the Land of Maidens. The gold rings on her fingers were as thick as an ox's yoke, and her beauty was dazzling. When she took off her gilded helmet, all bejewelled, her fair, curling golden hair broke out in seven score tresses, and Finn cried: "Great gods whom we adore, a huge marvel Cormac and Ethné and the women of the Fianna would esteem it to see Vivionn, the blooming daughter of Treon." The maiden explained that she had been betrothed against her will to a suitor named Æda, son of a neighbouring king; and that hearing from a fisherman, who had been blown to her shores, of the power and nobleness of Finn, she had come to seek his protection. While she was speaking, suddenly the Fianna were aware of another giant form close at hand. It was a young man, smooth-featured and of surpassing beauty, who bore a red shield and a huge spear. Without a word he drew near, and before the wondering Fianna could accost him he thrust his spear through the body of the maiden and passed away. Finn, enraged at this violation of his protection, called on his chiefs to pursue and slay the murderer. Keelta and others chased him to the sea-shore, and followed him into the surf, but he strode out to sea, and was met by a great galley which bore him away to unknown regions. Returning, discomfited, to Finn, they found the girl dying. She distributed her gold and jewels among them, and the Fianna buried her under a great mound, and raised a pillar stone over her with her name in Ogham letters, in the place since called the Ridge of the Dead Woman.

In this tale we have, besides the element of mystery, that of beauty. It is an association of frequent occurrence in this period of Celtic literature; and to this, perhaps, is due the fact that although these tales seem to come from nowhither and to lead nowhither, but move in a dream-world where there is no chase but seems to end in Fairyland and no combat that has any relation to earthly needs or objects, where all realities are apt to dissolve in a magic light and to change their shapes like morning mist, yet they linger in the memory with that haunting charm which has for many centuries kept them alive by the fireside of the Gaelic peasant.

St. Patrick, Oisin, and Keelta

Before we leave the "Colloquy" another interesting point must be mentioned in connexion with it. To the general public probably the best-known things in Ossianic literature—I refer, of course, to the true Gaelic poetry which goes under that name, not to the pseudo-Ossian of Macpherson—are those dialogues in which the pagan and the Christian ideals are contrasted, often in a spirit of humorous exaggeration or of satire. The earliest of these pieces are found in the manuscript called "The Dean of Lismore's Book," in which James Macgregor, Dean of Lismore in Argyllshire, wrote down, some time before the year 1518, all he could remember or discover of traditional Gaelic poetry in his time. It may be observed that up to this period, and, indeed, long after it, Scottish and Irish Gaelic were one language and one literature, the great written monuments of which were in Ireland, though they belonged just as much to the Highland Celt, and the two branches of the Gael had an absolutely common stock of poetic tradition. These Oisin-and-Patrick dialogues are found in abundance both in Ireland and in the Highlands, though, as I have said, "The Dean of Lismore's Book" is their first written record now extant. What relation, then, do these dialogues bear to the Keelta-and-Patrick dialogues with which we make acquaintance in the "Colloquy"? The questions which really came first, where they respectively originated, and what current of thought or sentiment each represented, constitute, as Mr. Alfred Nutt has pointed out, a literary problem of the greatest interest; and one which no critic has yet attempted to solve, or, indeed, until quite lately, even to call attention to. For though these two attempts to represent, in imaginative and artistic form, the contact of paganism with Christianity are nearly identical in machinery and framework, save that one is in verse and the other in prose, yet they differ widely in their point of view.

In the Oisin dialogues [1] there is a great deal of rough humour and of crude theology, resembling those of an English miracle-play rather than any Celtic product that I am acquainted with. St. Patrick in these ballads, as Mr. Nutt remarks, "is a sour and stupid fanatic, harping with wearisome monotony on the damnation of Finn and all his comrades; a hard taskmaster to the poor old blind giant to whom he grudges food, and upon whom he plays shabby tricks in order to terrify him into acceptance of Christianity." Now in the "Colloquy" there is not one word of all this. Keelta embraces Christianity with a wholehearted reverence, and salvation is not denied to the friends and companions of his youth.

[1] Examples of these have been published, with translations, in the "Transactions of the Ossianic Society."

Patrick, indeed, assures Keelta of the salvation of several of them, including Finn himself. One of the Danaan Folk, who has been bard to the Fianna, delighted Patrick with his minstrelsy. Brogan, the scribe whom St. Patrick is employing to write down the Fian legends, says: "If music there is in heaven, why should there not be on earth? Wherefore it is not right to banish minstrelsy." Patrick made answer: "Neither say I any such thing"; and, in fact, the minstrel is promised heaven for his art.

Such are the pleasant relations that prevail in the "Colloquy" between the representatives of the two epochs. Keelta represents all that is courteous, dignified, generous, and valorous in paganism, and Patrick all that is benign and gracious in Christianity; and instead of the two epochs standing over against each other in violent antagonism, and separated by an impassable gulf, all the finest traits in each are seen to harmonise with and to supplement those of the other.

Tales of Dermot

A number of curious legends centre on Dermot O'Dyna, who has been referred to as one of Finn mac Cumhal's most notable followers. He might be described as a kind of Gaelic Adonis, a type of beauty and attraction, the hero of innumerable love tales; and, like Adonis, his death was caused by a wild boar.

The Boar of Ben Bulben

The boar was no common beast. The story of its origin was as follows: Dermot's father, Donn, gave the child to be nurtured by Angus Og in his palace on the Boyne. His mother, who was unfaithful to Donn, bore another child to Roc, the steward of Angus. Donn, one day, when the steward's child ran between his knees to escape from some hounds that were fighting on the floor of the hall, gave him a squeeze with his two knees that killed him on the spot, and he then flung the body among the hounds on the floor. When the steward found his son dead, and discovered (with Finn's aid) the cause of it, he brought a Druid rod and smote the body with it, whereupon, in place of the dead child, there arose a huge boar, without ears or tail; and to it he spake: "I charge you to bring Dermot O'Dyna to his death"; and the boar rushed out from the hall and roamed in the forests of Ben Bulben in Co. Sligo till the time when his destiny should be fulfilled.

But Dermot grew up into a splendid youth, tireless in the chase, undaunted in war, beloved by all his comrades of the Fianna, whom he joined as soon as he was of age to do so.

How Dermot Got the Love Spot

He was called Dermot of the Love Spot, and a curious and beautiful folk-tale recorded by Dr. Douglas Hyde[1] tells how he got this appellation. With three comrades, Goll, Conan, and Oscar, he was hunting one day, and late at night they sought a resting-place. They soon found a hut, in which were an old man, a young girl, a wether sheep, and a cat. Here they asked for hospitality, and it was granted to them. But, as usual in these tales, it was a house of mystery.

When they sat down to dinner the wether got up and mounted on the table. One after another the Fianna strove to throw it off, but it shook them down on the floor. At last Goll succeeded in flinging it off the table, but him too it vanquished in the end, and put them all under its feet. Then the old man bade the cat lead

[1] Taken down from the recital of a peasant in Co. Galway and published at Rennes in Dr. Hyde's "An Sgeuluidhe Gaodhalach," vol. ii. (no translation).

the wether back and fasten it up, and it did so easily. The four champions, overcome with shame, were for leaving the house at once; but the old man explained that they had suffered no discredit—the wether they had been fighting with was the World, and the cat was the power that would destroy the world itself, namely, Death.

At night the four heroes went to rest in a large chamber, and the young maid came to sleep in the same room; and it is said that her beauty made a light on the walls of the room like a candle. One after another the Fianna went over to her couch, but she repelled them all. "I belonged to you once," she said to each, "and I never will again." Last of all Dermot went. "O Dermot," she said, "you, also, I belonged to once, and I never can again, for I am Youth; but come here and I will put a mark on you so that no woman can ever see you without loving you." Then she touched his forehead, and left the Love Spot there; and that drew the love of women to him as long as he lived.

The Chase of the Hard Gilly

The Chase of the Gilla Dacar is another Fian tale in which Dermot plays a leading part. The Fianna, the story goes, were hunting one day on the hills and through the woods of Munster, and as Finn and his captains stood on a hillside listening to the baying of the hounds, and the notes of the Fian hunting-horn from the dark wood below, they saw coming towards them a huge, ugly, misshapen churl dragging along by a halter a great raw-boned mare. He announced himself as wishful to take service with Finn. The name he was called by, he said, was the Gilla Dacar (the Hard Gilly), because he was the hardest servant ever a lord had to get service or obedience from. In spite of this unpromising beginning, Finn, whose principle it was never to refuse any suitor, took him into service; and the Fianna now began to make their uncouth comrade the butt of all sorts of rough jokes, which ended in thirteen of them, including Conan the Bald, all mounting up on the Gilla Dacar's steed. On this the newcomer complained that he was being mocked, and he shambled away in great discontent till he was over the ridge of the hill, when he tucked up his skirts and ran westwards, faster than any March wind, toward the sea-shore in Co. Kerry. Thereupon at once the steed, which had stood still with drooping ears while the thirteen riders in vain belaboured it to make it move, suddenly threw up its head and started off in a furious gallop after its master. The Fianna ran alongside, as well as they could for laughter, while Conan, in terror and rage, reviled them for not rescuing him and his comrades. At last the thing became serious. The Gilla Dacar plunged into the sea, and the mare followed him with her thirteen riders, and one more who managed to cling to her tail just as she left the shore; and all of them soon disappeared towards the fabled region of the West.

Dermot at the Well

Finn and the remaining Fianna now took counsel together as to what should be done, and finally decided to fit out a ship and go in search of their comrades. After many days of voyaging they reached an island guarded by precipitous cliffs. Dermot O'Dyna, as the most agile of the party, was sent to climb them and to discover, if he could, some means of helping up the rest of the party. When he arrived at the top he found himself in a delightful land, full of the song of birds and the humming of bees and the murmur of streams, but with no sign of habitation. Going into a dark forest, he soon came to a well, by which hung a curiously wrought drinking-horn. As he filled it to drink, a low, threatening murmur came from the well, but his thirst was too keen to let him heed it and he drank his fill. In no long time there came through the wood an armed warrior, who violently upbraided him for drinking from his well. The Knight of the Well and Dermot then fought all the afternoon without either of them prevailing over the other, when, as evening drew on, the knight suddenly leaped into the well and disappeared. Next day the same thing happened ; on the third, however, Dermot, as the knight was about to take his leap, flung his arms round him, and both went down together.

The Rescue of Fairyland

Dermot, after a moment of darkness and trance, now found himself in Fairyland. A man of noble appearance roused him and led him away to the castle of a great king, where he was hospitably entertained. It was explained to him that the services of a champion like himself were needed to do combat against a rival monarch of Faëry. It is the same motive which we find in the adventures of Cuchulain with Fand, and which so frequently turns up in Celtic fairy lore. Finn and his companions, finding that Dermot did not return to them, found their way up the cliffs, and, having traversed the forest, entered a great cavern which ultimately led them out to the same land as that in which Dermot had arrived. There too, they are informed, are the fourteen Fianna who had been carried off on the mare of the Hard Gilly. He, of course, was the king who needed their services, and who had taken this method of decoying some thirty of the flower of Irish fighting men to his side. Finn and his men go into the battle with the best of goodwill,

Dermot took the Horn and filled it

“ Half the corn of your country is ground here ”

and scatter the enemy like chaff; Oscar slays the son of the rival king (who is called the King of "Greece"). Finn wins the love of his daughter, Tasha of the White Arms, and the story closes with a delightful mixture of gaiety and mystery. "What reward wilt thou have for thy good services?" asks the fairy king of Finn. "Thou wert once in service with me," replies Finn, "and I mind not that I gave thee any recompense. Let one service stand against the other." "Never shall I agree to that," cries Conan the Bald. "Shall I have nought for being carried off on thy wild mare and haled over-sea?" "What wilt thou have?" asks the fairy king. "None of thy gold or goods," replies Conan, "but mine honour hath suffered, and let mine honour be appeased. Set thirteen of thy fairest womenfolk on the wild mare, O King, and thine own wife clinging to her tail, and let them be transported to Erin in like manner as we were dragged here, and I shall deem the indignity we have suffered fitly atoned for." On this the king smiled and, turning to Finn, said: "O Finn, behold thy men." Finn turned to look at them, but when he looked round again the scene had changed—the fairy king and his host and all the world of Faëry had disappeared, and he found himself with his companions and the fair-armed Tasha standing on the beach of the little bay in Kerry whence the Hard Gilly and the mare had taken the water and carried off his men. And then all started with cheerful hearts for the great standing camp of the Fianna on the Hill of Allen to celebrate the wedding feast of Finn and Tasha.

Effect of Christianity on the Development of Irish Literature

This tale with its fascinating mixture of humour, romance, magic, and love of wild nature, may be taken as a typical specimen of the Fian legends at their best.

As compared with the Conorian legends they show, as I have pointed out, a characteristic lack of any heroic or serious element. That nobler strain died out with the growing predominance of Christianity, which appropriated for definitely religious purposes the more serious and lofty side of the Celtic genius, leaving for secular literature only the elements of wonder and romance. So completely was this carried out that while the Finn legends have survived to this day among the Gaelic-speaking population, and were a subject of literary treatment as long as Gaelic was written at all, the earlier cycle perished almost completely out of the popular remembrance, or survived only in distorted forms; and but for the early manuscripts in which the tales are fortunately enshrined such a work as the "Tain Bo Cuailgné"—the greatest thing undoubtedly which the Celtic genius ever produced in literature—would now be irrecoverably lost.

The Tales of Deirdre and of Grania

Nothing can better illustrate the difference between the two cycles than a comparison of the tale of Deirdre with that with which we have now to deal—the tale of Dermot and Grania. The latter, from one point of view, reads like an echo of the former, so close is the resemblance between them in the outline of the plot. Take the following skeleton story: "A fair maiden is betrothed to a renowned and mighty suitor much older than herself. She turns from him to seek a younger lover, and fixes her attention on one of his followers, a gallant and beautiful youth, whom she persuades, in spite of his reluctance, to fly with her. After evading pursuit they settle down for a while at a distance from the defrauded lover, who bides his time, till at last, under cover of a treacherous reconciliation, he procures the death of his younger rival and retakes possession of the lady." Were a student of Celtic legend asked to listen to the above synopsis, and to say to what Irish tale it referred, he would certainly reply that it must be either the tale of the Pursuit of Dermot and Grania, or that of the Fate of the Sons of Usna; but which of them it was it would be quite impossible for him to tell. Yet in tone and temper the two stories are as wide apart as the poles.

Grania and Dermot

Grania, in the Fian story, is the daughter of Cormac mac Art, High King of Ireland. She is betrothed to Finn mac Cumhal, whom we are to regard at this period as an old and war-worn but still mighty warrior. The famous captains of the Fianna all assemble at Tara for the wedding feast, and as they sit at meat Grania surveys them and asks their names of her father's Druid, Dara. "It is a wonder," she says, "that Finn did not ask me for Oisîn, rather than for himself." "Oisîn would not dare to take thee," says Dara. Grania, after going through all the company, asks: "Who is that man with the spot on his brow, with the sweet voice, with curling dusky hair and ruddy cheek?" "That is Dermot O'Dyna," replies the Druid, "the white-toothed, of the lightsome countenance, in all the world the best lover of women and maidens." Grania now prepares a sleepy draught, which she places in a drinking-cup and passes round by her handmaid to the king, to Finn, and to all the company except the chiefs of the Fianna. When the draught has done its work she goes to Oisîn. "Wilt thou receive courtship from me, Oisîn?" she asks. "That will I not," says Oisîn, "nor from any woman that is betrothed to Finn." Grania, who knew very well what Oisîn's answer would be, now turns to her real mark, Dermot. He at first refuses to have anything to do with her. "I put thee under bonds [*geise*], O Dermot, that thou take me out of Tara to-night." "Evil are these bonds, Grania," says Dermot; "and wherefore hast thou put them on me before all the kings' sons that feast at this table?" Grania then explains that she has loved Dermot ever since she saw him, years ago, from her sunny bower, take part in and win a great hurling match on the green at Tara. Dermot, still very reluctant, pleads the merits of Finn, and urges also that Finn has the keys of the royal fortress, so that they cannot pass out at night. "There is a secret wicket-gate in my bower," says Grania. "I am under *geise* not to pass through any wicket-gate," replies Dermot, still struggling against his destiny. Grania will have none of these subterfuges—any Fian warrior, she has been told, can leap over a palisade with the aid of his spear as a jumping-pole; and she goes oft to make ready for the elopement. Dermot, in great perplexity, appeals to Oisin, Oscar, Keelta, and the others as to what he should do. They all bid him keep his *geise*—the bonds that Grania had laid on him to succour her—and he takes leave of them with tears.

Outside the wicket-gate he again begs Grania to return. "It is certain that I will not go back," says Grania, "nor part from thee till death part us." "Then go forward, O Grania," says Dermot. After they had gone a mile, "I am truly weary, O grandson of Dyna," says Grania. "It is a good time to be weary," says Dermot, making a last effort to rid himself of the entanglement, "and return now to thy household again, for I pledge the word of a true warrior that I will never carry thee nor any other woman to all eternity." "There is no need," replies Grania, and she directs him where to find horses and a chariot, and Dermot, now finally accepting the inevitable, yokes them, and they proceed on their way to the Ford of Luan on the Shannon.[1]

The Pursuit

Next day Finn, burning with rage, sets out with his warriors on their track. He traces out each of their halting-places, and finds the hut of wattles which Dermot has made for their shelter, and the bed of soft rushes, and the remains of the meal they had eaten. And at each place he finds a piece of unbroken bread or uncooked salmon—Dermot's subtle message to Finn that he has respected the rights of his lord and treated Grania as a sister. But this delicacy of Dermot's is not at all to Grania's mind, and she conveys her wishes to him in a manner which is curiously paralleled by an episode in the tale of Tristan and Iseult of Brittany, as told by Heinrich von Freiberg. They are passing through a piece of wet ground when a splash of water strikes Grania. She turns to her companion: "Thou art a mighty warrior, O Dermot, in battle and sieges and forays, yet meseems that this drop of water is bolder than thou." This hint that he was keeping at too respectful a distance was taken by Dermot. The die is now cast, and he will never again meet Finn and his old comrades except at the point of the spear.

The tale now loses much of the originality and charm of its opening scene, and recounts in a somewhat mechanical manner a number of episodes in which Dermot is attacked or besieged by the Fianna, and rescues himself and his lady by miracles of boldness or dexterity, or by aid of the magical devices of his foster-father, Angus Ōg. They are chased all over Ireland, and the dolmens in that country are popularly associated

[1] Now Athlone (*Atha Luain*).

with them, being called in the traditions of the peasantry "Beds of Dermot and Grania."

Grania's character is drawn throughout with great consistency. She is not an heroic woman—hers are not the simple, ardent impulses and unwavering devotion of a Deirdre. The latter is far more primitive. Grania is a curiously modern and what would be called "neurotic" type—wilful, restless, passionate, but full of feminine fascination.

Dermot and Finn Make Peace

After sixteen years of outlawry peace is at last made for Dermot by the mediation of Angus with King Cormac and with Finn. Dermot receives his proper patrimony, the Cantred of O'Dyna, and other lands far away in the West, and Cormac gives another of his daughters to Finn. "Peaceably they abode a long time with each other, and it was said that no man then living was richer in gold and silver, in flocks and herds, than Dermot O'Dyna, nor one that made more preys."[1] Grania bears to Dermot four sons and a daughter.

But Grania is not satisfied until "the two best men that are in Erin, namely, Cormac son of Art and Finn son of Cumhal," have been entertained in her house. "And how do we know," she adds, "but our daughter might then get a fitting husband?" Dermot agrees with some misgiving; the king and Finn accept the invitation, and they and their retinues are feasted for a year at Rath Grania.

[1] How significant is this naïve indication that the making of forays on his neighbours was regarded in Celtic Ireland as the natural and laudable occupation of a country gentleman! Compare Spenser's account of the ideals fostered by the Irish bards of his time, "View of the Present State of Ireland," p. 641 (Globe edition).

The Vengeance of Finn

Then one night, towards the end of the year of feasting, Dermot is awakened from sleep by the baying of a hound. He starts up, "so that Grania caught him and threw her two arms about him and asked him what he had seen." "It is the voice of a hound," says Dermot, "and I marvel to hear it in the night." "Save and protect thee," says Grania; "it is the Danaan Folk that are at work on thee. Lay thee down again." But three times the hound's voice awakens him, and on the morrow he goes forth armed with sword and sling, and followed by his own hound, to see what is afoot.

On the mountain of Ben Bulben in Sligo he comes across Finn with a hunting-party of the Fianna. They are not now hunting, however; they are being hunted; for they have roused up the enchanted boar without ears or tail, the Boar of Ben Bulben, which has slain thirty of them that morning. "And do thou come away," says Finn, knowing well that Dermot will never retreat from a danger; "for thou art under *geise* not to hunt pig." "How is that?" says Dermot, and Finn then tells him the weird story of the death of the steward's son and his revivification in the form of this boar, with its mission of vengeance. "By my word," quoth Dermot, "it is to slay me that thou hast made this hunt, O Finn; and if it be here that I am fated to die, I have no power now to shun it."

The beast then appears on the face of the mountain, and Dermot slips the hound at him, but the hound flies in terror. Dermot then slings a stone which strikes the boar fairly in the middle of his forehead but does not even scratch his skin. The beast is close on him now, and Dermot strikes him with his sword, but the weapon flies in two and not a bristle of the boar is cut.

In the charge of the boar Dermot falls over him, and is carried for a space clinging to his back; but at last the boar shakes him off to the ground, and making "an eager, exceeding mighty spring" upon him, rips out his bowels, while at the same time, with the hilt of the sword still in his hand, Dermot dashes out the brains of the beast, and it falls dead beside him.

Death of Dermot

The implacable Finn then comes up, and stands over Dermot in his agony. "It likes me well to see thee in that plight, O Dermot," he says, "and I would that all the women in Ireland saw thee now; for thy excellent beauty is turned to ugliness and thy choice form to deformity." Dermot reminds Finn of how he once rescued him from deadly peril when attacked during a feast at the house of Derc, and begs him to heal him with a draught of water from his hands, for Finn had the magic gift of restoring any wounded man to health with a draught of well-water drawn in his two hands. "Here is no well," says Finn. "That is not true," says Dermot, "for nine paces from you is the best well of pure water in the world." Finn, at last, on the entreaty of Oscar and the Fianna, and after the recital of many deeds done for his sake by Dermot in old days, goes to the well, but ere he brings the water to Dermot's side he lets it fall through his fingers. A second time he goes, and a second time he lets the water fall, "having thought upon Grania," and Dermot gave a sigh of anguish on seeing it. Oscar then declares that if Finn does not bring the water promptly either he or Finn shall never leave the hill alive, and Finn goes once more to the well, but it is now too late; Dermot is dead before the healing draught can reach his lips. Then Finn takes the hound of Dermot, the chiefs of the Fianna lay their cloaks over the dead man, and they return to Rath Grania. Grania, seeing the hound led by Finn, conjectures what has happened, and swoons upon the rampart of the Rath. Oisín, when she has revived, gives her the hound, against Finn's will, and the Fianna troop away, leaving her to her sorrow. When the people of Grania's household go out to fetch in the body of Dermot they find there Angus Ōg and his company of the People of Dana, who, after raising three bitter and terrible cries, bear away the body on a gilded bier, and Angus declares that though he cannot restore the dead to life, "I will send a soul into him so that he may talk with me each day."

The End of Grania

To a tale like this modern taste demands a romantic and sentimental ending; and such has actually been given to it in the retelling by Dr. P. W. Joyce in his "Old Celtic Romances," as it has to the tale of Deirdre by almost every modern writer who has handled it.[1] But the Celtic story-teller felt differently. The tale of the end of Deirdre is horribly cruel, that of Grania cynical and mocking; neither is in the least sentimental. Grania is at first enraged with Finn, and sends her sons abroad to learn feats of arms, so that they may take vengeance upon him when the time is ripe. But Finn, wily and far-seeing as he is portrayed in this tale, knows how to forestall this danger. When the tragedy on Ben Bulben has begun to grow a little faint in the shallow soul of Grania, he betakes himself to her, and though met at first with scorn and indignation he woos her so sweetly and with such tenderness that at last he brings

[1] Dr. John Todhunter, in his "Three Irish Bardic Tales," has alone, I think, kept the antique ending of the tale of Deirdre.

her to his will, and he bears her back as a bride to the Hill of Allen. When the Fianna see the pair coming towards them in this loving guise they burst into a shout of laughter and derision, "so that Grania bowed her head in shame." "We trow, O Finn," cries Oisín, "that thou wilt keep Grania well from henceforth." So Grania made peace between Finn and her sons, and dwelt with Finn as his wife until he died.

Two Streams of Fian Legends

It will be noticed that in this legend Finn does not appear as a sympathetic character. Our interest is all on the side of Dermot. In this aspect of it the tale is typical of a certain class of Fian stories. Just as there were two rival clans within the Fian organisation—the Clan Bascna and the Clan Morna—who sometimes came to blows for the supremacy, so there are two streams of legends seeming to flow respectively from one or other of these sources, in one of which Finn is glorified, while in the other he is belittled in favour of Goll mac Morna or any other hero with whom he comes into conflict.

End of the Fianna

The story of the end of the Fianna is told in a number of pieces, some prose, some poetry, all of them, however, agreeing in presenting this event as a piece of sober history, without any of the supernatural and mystical atmosphere in which nearly all the Fian legends are steeped.

After the death of Cormac mac Art his son Cairbry came to the High-Kingship of Ireland. He had a fair daughter named *Sgeimh Solais* (Light of Beauty), who was asked in marriage by a son of the King of the Decies. The marriage was arranged, and the Fianna claimed a ransom or tribute of twenty ingots of gold, which, it is said, was customarily paid to them on these occasions.

THE BATTLE OF GOWRA

It would seem that the Fianna had now grown to be a distinct power within the State, and an oppressive one, exacting heavy tributes and burdensome privileges from kings and sub-kings all over Ireland. Cairbry resolved to break them; and he thought he had now a good opportunity to do so. He therefore refused payment of the ransom, and summoned all the provincial kings to help him against the Fianna, the main body of whom immediately went into rebellion for what they deemed their rights. The old feud between Clan Bascna and Clan Morna now broke out afresh, the latter standing by the High King, while Clan Bascna, aided by the King of Munster and his forces, who alone took their side, marched against Cairbry.

The Battle of Gowra

All this sounds very matter-of-fact and probable, but how much real history there may be in it it is very hard to say. The decisive battle of the war which ensued took place at Gowra (Gabhra), the name of which survives in Garristown, Co. Dublin. The rival forces, when drawn up in battle array, knelt and kissed the sacred soil of Erin before they charged. The story of the battle in the poetical versions, one of which is published in the Ossianic Society's "Transactions," and another and finer one in Campbell's "The Fians,"[1] is supposed to be related by Oisīn to St. Patrick. He lays great stress on the feats of his son Oscar:

> "My son urged his course
> Through the battalions of Tara
> Like a hawk through a flock of birds,
> Or a rock descending a mountain-side."

[1] "Waifs and Strays of Celtic Tradition," Argyllshire Series. The tale was taken down in verse, word for word, from the dictation of Roderick mac Fadyen in Tiree, 1868.

The Death of Oscar

The fight was *à outrance*, and the slaughter on both sides tremendous. None but old men and boys, it is said, were left in Erin after that fight. The Fianna were in the end almost entirely exterminated, and Oscar slain. He and the King of Ireland, Cairbry, met in single combat, and each of them slew the other. While Oscar was still breathing, though there was not a palm's breadth on his body without a wound, his father found him:

"I found my own son lying down
On his left elbow, his shield by his side;
His right hand clutched the sword,
The blood poured through his mail.

"Oscar gazed up at me—
Woe to me was that sight!
He stretched out his two arms to me,
Endeavouring to rise to meet me.

"I grasped the hand of my son
And sat down by his left side;
And since I sat by him there,
I have recked nought of the world."

When Finn (in the Scottish version) comes to bewail his grandson, he cries:

"Woe, that it was not I who fell
In the fight of bare sunny Gavra,
And you were east and west
Marching before the Fians, Oscar."

But Oscar replies:

"Were it you that fell
In the fight of bare sunny Gavra,
One sigh, east or west,
Would not be heard for you from Oscar.

"No man ever knew
A heart of flesh was in my breast,
But a heart of the twisted horn
And a sheath of steel over it.

"But the howling of dogs beside me,
And the wail of the old heroes,
And the weeping of the women by turns,
'Tis that vexes my heart."

Oscar dies, after thanking the gods for his father's safety, and Oisin and Keelta raise him on a bier of spears and carry him off under his banner, "The Terrible Sheaf," for burial on the field where he died, and where a great green burial mound is still associated with his name. Finn takes no part in the battle. He is said to have come "in a ship" to view the field afterwards, and he wept over Oscar, a thing he had never done save once before, for his hound, Bran, whom he himself killed by accident. Possibly the reference to the ship is an indication that he had by this time passed away, and came to revisit the earth from the oversea kingdom of Death.

There is in this tale of the Battle of Gowra a melancholy grandeur which gives it a place apart in the Ossianic literature. It is a fitting dirge for a great legendary epoch. Campbell tells us that the Scottish crofters and shepherds were wont to put off their bonnets when they recited it. He adds a strange and thrilling piece of modern folk-lore bearing on it. Two men, it is said, were out at night, probably sheep-stealing or on some other predatory occupation, and telling Fian tales as they went, when they observed two giant and shadowy figures talking to each other across the glen. One of the apparitions said to the other: "Do you see that man down below? I was the second door-post of battle on the day of Gowra, and that man there knows all about it better than myself."

The End of Finn

As to Finn himself, it is strange that in all the extant mass of the Ossianic literature there should be no complete narrative of his death. There are references to it in the poetic legends, and annalists even date it, but the references conflict with each other, and so do the dates. There is no clear light to be obtained on the subject from either annalists or poets. Finn seems to have melted into the magic mist which enwraps so many of his deeds in life. Yet a popular tradition says that he and his great companions, Oscar and Keelta and Oisîn and the rest, never died, but lie, like Kaiser Barbarossa, spell-bound in an enchanted cave where they await the appointed time to reappear in glory and redeem their land from tyranny and wrong.

CHAPTER VII: THE VOYAGE OF MAELDŪN

BESIDES the legends which cluster round great heroic names, and have, or at least pretend to have, the character of history, there are many others, great and small, which tell of adventures lying purely in regions of romance, and out of earthly space and time. As a specimen of these I give here a summary of the "Voyage of Maeldūn," a most curious and brilliant piece of invention, which is found in the manuscript entitled the "Book of the Dun Cow" (about 1100) and other early sources, and edited, with a translation (to which I owe the following extracts), by Dr. Whitley Stokes in the "Revue Celtique" for 1888 and 1889. It is only one of a number of such wonder-voyages found in ancient Irish literature, but it is believed to have been the earliest of them all and model for the rest, and it has had the distinction, in the abridged and modified form given by Joyce in his "Old Celtic Romances," of having furnished the theme for the "Voyage of Maeldune" to Tennyson, who made it into a wonderful creation of rhythm and colour, embodying a kind of allegory of Irish history. It will be noticed at the end that we are in the unusual position of knowing the name of the author of this piece of primitive literature, though he does not claim to have composed, but only to have "put in order," the incidents of the "Voyage." Unfortunately we cannot tell when he lived, but the tale as we have it probably dates from the ninth century. Its atmosphere is entirely Christian, and it has no mythological significance except in so far as it teaches the lesson that the oracular injunctions of wizards should be obeyed. No adventure, or even detail, of importance is omitted in the following summary of the story, which is given thus fully because the reader may take it as representing a large and important section of Irish legendary romance. Apart from the source to which I am indebted, the "Revue Celtique," I know no other faithful reproduction in English of this wonderful tale.

The "Voyage of Maeldūn" begins, as Irish tales often do, by telling us of the conception of its hero.

There was a famous man of the sept of the Owens of Aran, named Ailill Edge-of-Battle, who went with his king on a foray into another territory. They encamped one night near a church and convent of nuns. At midnight Ailill, who was near the church, saw a certain nun come out to strike the bell for nocturns, and caught her by the hand. In ancient Ireland religious persons were not much respected in time of war, and Ailill did not respect her. When they parted, she said to him: "Whence is thy race, and what is thy name?" Said the hero: "Ailill of the Edge-of-Battle is my name, and I am of the Owenacht of Aran, in Thomond."

Not long afterwards Ailill was slain by reavers from Leix, who burned the church of Doocloone over his head.

In due time a son was born to the woman and she called his name Maeldūn. He was taken secretly to her friend, the queen of the territory, and by her Maeldūn was reared. "Beautiful indeed was his form, and it is doubtful if there hath been in flesh any one so beautiful as he. So he grew up till he was a young warrior and fit to use weapons. Great, then, was his brightness and his gaiety and his playfulness. In his play he outwent all his comrades in throwing balls, and in running and leaping and putting stones and racing horses."

One day a proud young warrior who had been

defeated by him taunted him with his lack of knowledge of his kindred and descent. Maeldūn went to his foster-mother, the queen, and said: "I will not eat nor drink till thou tell me who are my mother and my father." "I am thy mother," said the queen, "for none ever loved her son more than I love thee." But Maeldūn insisted on knowing all, and the queen at last took him to his own mother, the nun, who told him: "Thy father was Ailill of the Owens of Aran." Then Maeldūn went to his own kindred, and was well received by them; and with him he took as guests his three beloved foster-brothers, sons of the king and queen who had brought him up.

After a time Maeldūn happened to be among a company of young warriors who were contending at putting the stone in the graveyard of the ruined church of Doocloone. Maeldūn's foot was planted, as he heaved the stone, on a scorched and blackened flagstone; and one who was by, a monk named Briccne,[1] said to him: "It were better for thee to avenge the man who was burnt there than to cast stones over his burnt bones."

"Who was that?" asked Maeldūn.

"Ailill, thy father," they told him.

"Who slew him?" said he.

"Reavers from Leix," they said, "and they destroyed him on this spot."

Then Maeldūn threw down the stone he was about to cast, and put his mantle round him and went home; and he asked the way to Leix. They told him he could only go there by sea.[2]

[1] Here we have evidently a reminiscence of Briccriu of the Poisoned Tongue, the mischief-maker of the Ultonians.

[2] The Arans are three islands at the entrance of Galway Bay. They are a perfect museum of mysterious ruins.

At the advice of a Druid he then built him a boat, or coracle, of skins lapped threefold one over the other; and the wizard also told him that seventeen men only must accompany him, and on what day he must begin the boat and on what day he must put out to sea.

So when his company was ready he put out and hoisted the sail, but had gone only a little way when his three foster-brothers came down to the beach and entreated him to take them. "Get you home," said Maeldūn, "for none but the number I have may go with me." But the three youths would not be separated from Maeldūn, and they flung themselves into the sea. He turned back, lest they should be drowned, and brought them into his boat. All, as we shall see, were punished for this transgression, and Maeldūn condemned to wandering until expiation had been made.

Irish bardic tales excel in their openings. In this case, as usual, the *mise-en-scène* is admirably contrived. The narrative which follows tells how, after seeing his father's slayer on an island, but being unable to land there, Maeldūn and his party are blown out to sea, where they visit a great number of islands and have many strange adventures on them. The tale becomes, in fact, a *cento* of stories and incidents, some not very interesting, while in others, as in the adventure of the Island of the Silver Pillar, or the Island of the Flaming Rampart, or that where the episode of the eagle takes place, the Celtic sense of beauty, romance, and mystery find an expression unsurpassed, perhaps, in literature.

In the following rendering I have omitted the verses given by Joyce at the end of each adventure. They merely recapitulate the prose narrative, and are not found in the earliest manuscript authorities.

THE ISLAND OF THE GREAT BIRDS

The Island of the Slayer

Maeldūn and his crew had rowed all day and half the night when they came to two small bare islands with two forts in them, and a noise was heard from them of armed men quarrelling. "Stand off from me," cried one of them, "for I am a better man than thou. 'Twas I slew Ailill of the Edge-of-Battle and burned the church of Doocloone over him, and no kinsman has avenged his death on me. And *thou* hast never done the like of that."

Then Maeldūn was about to land, and Germān[1] and Diuran the Rhymer cried that God had guided them to the spot where they would be. But a great wind arose suddenly and blew them off into the boundless ocean, and Maeldūn said to his foster-brothers: "Ye have caused this to be, casting yourselves on board in spite of the words of the Druid." And they had no answer, save only to be silent for a little space.

The Island of the Ants

They drifted three days and three nights, not knowing whither to row, when at the dawn of the third day they heard the noise of breakers, and came to an island as soon as the sun was up. Here, ere they could land, they met a swarm of ferocious ants, each the size of a foal, that came down the strand and into the sea to get at them; so they made off quickly, and saw no land for three days more.

The Island of the Great Birds

This was a terraced island, with trees all round it, and great birds sitting on the trees. Maeldūn landed first alone, and carefully searched the island for any

[1] Pronounced "Ghermawn"—the "G" hard.

evil thing, but finding none, the rest followed him, and killed and ate many of the birds, bringing others on board their boat.

The Island of the Fierce Beast

A great sandy island was this, and on it a beast like a horse, but with clawed feet like a hound's. He flew at them to devour them, but they put off in time, and were pelted by the beast with pebbles from the shore as they rowed away.

The Island of the Giant Horses

A great, flat island, which it fell by lot to Germān and Diuran to explore first. They found a vast green racecourse, on which were the marks of horses' hoofs, each as big as the sail of a ship, and the shells of nuts of monstrous size were lying about, and much plunder. So they were afraid, and took ship hastily again, and from the sea they saw a horse-race in progress and heard the shouting of a great multitude cheering on the white horse or the brown, and saw the giant horses running swifter than the wind.[1] So they rowed away with all their might, thinking they had come upon an assembly of demons.

The Island of the Stone Door

A full week passed, and then they found a great, high island with a house standing on the shore. A door with a valve of stone opened into the sea, and through it the sea-waves kept hurling salmon into the house. Maeldūn and his party entered, and found the house

[1] Horse-racing was a particular delight to the ancient Irish, and is mentioned in a ninth-century poem in praise of May as one of the attractions of that month. The name of the month of May given in an ancient Gaulish calendar means "the month of horse-racing."

empty of folk, but a great bed lay ready for the chief to whom it belonged, and a bed for each three of his company, and meat and drink beside each bed. Maeldūn and his party ate and drank their fill, and then sailed off again.

The Island of the Apples

By the time they had come here they had been a long time voyaging, and food had failed them, and they were hungry. This island had precipitous sides from which a wood hung down, and as they passed along the cliffs Maeldūn broke off a twig and held it in his hand. Three days and nights they coasted the cliff and found no entrance to the island, but by that time a cluster of three apples had grown on the end of Maeldūn's rod, and each apple sufficed the crew for forty days.

The Island of the Wondrous Beast

This island had a fence of stone round it, and within the fence a huge beast that raced round and round the island. And anon it went to the top of the island, and then performed a marvellous feat, viz., it turned its body round and round inside its skin, the skin remaining unmoved, while again it would revolve its skin round and round the body. When it saw the party it rushed at them, but they escaped, pelted with stones as they rowed away. One of the stones pierced through Maeldūn's shield and lodged in the keel of the boat.

The Island of the Biting Horses

Here were many great beasts resembling horses, that tore continually pieces of flesh from each other's sides, so that all the island ran with blood. They rowed hastily away, and were now disheartened and full of complaints, for they knew not where they were, nor how to find guidance or aid in their quest.

The Island of the Fiery Swine

With great weariness, hunger, and thirst they arrived at the tenth island, which was full of trees loaded with golden apples. Under the trees went red beasts, like fiery swine, that kicked the trees with their legs, when the apples fell and the beasts consumed them. The beasts came out at morning only, when a multitude of birds left the island, and swam out to sea till nones, when they turned and swam inward again till vespers, and ate the apples all night.

Maeldūn and his comrades landed at night, and felt the soil hot under their feet from the fiery swine in their caverns underground. They collected all the apples they could, which were good both against hunger and thirst, and loaded their boat with them and put to sea once more, refreshed.

The Island of the Little Cat

The apples had failed them when they came hungry and thirsting to the eleventh island. This was, as it were, a tall white tower of chalk reaching up to the clouds, and on the rampart about it were great houses white as snow. They entered the largest of them, and found no man in it, but a small cat playing on four stone pillars which were in the midst of the house, leaping from one to the other. It looked a little on the Irish warriors, but did not cease from its play. On the walls of the houses there were three rows of objects hanging up, one row of brooches of gold and silver, and one of neck-torques of gold and silver, each as big as the hoop of a cask, and one of great swords with gold and silver hilts. Quilts and shining garments lay in the room, and there, also, were a roasted ox and a flitch of bacon and abundance of liquor. "Hath this been left for us?" said Maeldūn to the cat. It looked at him a moment, and then continued its play. So there they ate and drank and slept, and stored up what remained of the food. Next day, as they made to leave the house, the youngest of Maeldūn's foster-brothers took a necklace from the wall, and was bearing it out when the cat suddenly "leaped through him like a fiery arrow," and he fell, a heap of ashes, on the floor. Thereupon Maeldūn, who had forbidden the theft of the jewel, soothed the cat and replaced the necklace, and they strewed the ashes of the dead youth on the sea-shore, and put to sea again.

The Island of the Black and the White Sheep

This had a brazen palisade dividing it in two, and a flock of black sheep on one side and of white sheep on the other. Between them was a big man who tended the flocks, and sometimes he put a white sheep among the black, when it became black at once, or a black sheep among the white, when it immediately turned white.[1] By way of an experiment Maeldūn flung a peeled white wand on the side of the black sheep. It at once turned black, whereat they left the place in terror, and without landing.

The Island of the Giant Cattle

A great and wide island with a herd of huge swine on it. They killed a small pig and roasted it on the spot, as it was too great to carry on board. The island rose up into a very high mountain, and Diuran and Germān went to view the country from the top of it.

[1] The same phenomenon is recorded as being witnessed by Peredur in the Welsh tale of that name in the "Mabinogion."

On their way they met a broad river. To try the depth of the water Germān dipped in the haft of his spear, which at once was consumed as with liquid fire. On the other bank was a huge man guarding what seemed a herd of oxen. He called to them not to disturb the calves, so they went no further and speedily sailed away.

The Island of the Mill

Here they found a great and grim-looking mill, and a giant miller grinding corn in it. "Half the corn of your country," he said, "is ground here. Here comes to be ground all that men begrudge to each other." Heavy and many were the loads they saw going to it, and all that was ground in it was carried away westwards. So they crossed themselves and sailed away.

The Island of the Black Mourners

An island full of black people continually weeping and lamenting. One of the two remaining foster-brothers landed on it, and immediately turned black and fell to weeping like the rest. Two others went to fetch him; the same fate befell them. Four others then went with their heads wrapped in cloths, that they should not look on the land or breathe the air of the place, and they seized two of the lost ones and brought them away perforce, but not the foster-brother. The two rescued ones could not explain their conduct except by saying that they had to do as they saw others doing about them.

The Island of the Four Fences

Four fences of gold, silver, brass, and crystal divided this island into four parts, kings in one, queens in another, warriors in a third, maidens in the fourth.

On landing, a maiden gave them food like cheese, that tasted to each man as he wished it to be, and an intoxicating liquor that put them asleep for three days. When they awoke they were at sea in their boat, and of the island and its inhabitants nothing was to be seen.

The Island of the Glass Bridge

Here we come to one of the most elaborately wrought and picturesque of all the incidents of the voyage. The island they now reached had on it a fortress with a brazen door, and a bridge of glass leading to it. When they sought to cross the bridge it threw them backward.[1] A woman came out of the fortress with a pail in her hand, and lifting from the bridge a slab of glass she let down her pail into the water beneath, and returned to the fortress. They struck on the brazen portcullis before them to gain admittance, but the melody given forth by the smitten metal plunged them in slumber till the morrow morn. Thrice over this happened, the woman each time making an ironical speech about Maeldūn. On the fourth day, however, she came out to them over the bridge, wearing a white mantle with a circlet of gold on her hair, two silver sandals on her rosy feet, and a filmy silken smock next her skin.

"My welcome to thee, O Maeldūn," she said, and she welcomed each man of the crew by his own name. Then she took them into the great house and allotted a couch to the chief, and one for each three of his men. She gave them abundance of food and drink, all out of her one pail, each man finding in it what he most desired. When she had departed they asked Maeldūn if they should woo the maiden for him. "How would

[1] Like the bridge to Skatha's dūn, p. 188.

it hurt you to speak with her?" says Maeldūn. They do so, and she replies: "I know not, nor have ever known, what sin is." Twice over this is repeated. "To-morrow," she says at last, "you shall have your answer." When the morning breaks, however, they find themselves once more at sea, with no sign of the island or fortress or lady.

The Island of the Shouting Birds

They hear from afar a great cry and chanting, as it were a singing of psalms, and rowing for a day and night they come at last to an island full of birds, black, brown, and speckled, all shouting and speaking. They sail away without landing.

The Island of the Anchorite

Here they found a wooded island full of birds, and on it a solitary man, whose only clothing was his hair. They asked him of his country and kin. He tells them that he was a man of Ireland who had put to sea[1] with a sod of his native country under his feet. God had turned the sod into an island, adding a foot's breadth to it and one tree for every year. The birds are his kith and kin, and they all wait there till Doomsday, miraculously nourished by angels. He entertained them for three nights, and then they sailed away.

The Island of the Miraculous Fountain

This island had a golden rampart, and a soft white soil like down. In it they found another anchorite clothed only in his hair. There was a fountain in it

[1] Probably we are to understand that he was an anchorite seeking for an islet on which to dwell in solitude and contemplation. The western islands of Ireland abound in the ruins of huts and oratories built by single monks or little communities.

which yields whey or water on Fridays and Wednesdays, milk on Sundays and feasts of martyrs, and ale and wine on the feasts of Apostles, of Mary, of John the Baptist, and on the high tides of the year.

The Island of the Smithy

As they approached this they heard from afar as it were the clanging of a tremendous smithy, and heard men talking of themselves. "Little boys they seem," said one, "in a little trough yonder." They rowed hastily away, but did not turn their boat, so as not to seem to be flying; but after a while a giant smith came out of the forge holding in his tongs a huge mass of glowing iron, which he cast after them, and all the sea boiled round it, as it fell astern of their boat.

The Sea of Clear Glass

After that they voyaged until they entered a sea that resembled green glass. Such was its purity that the gravel and the sand of the sea were clearly visible through it; and they saw no monsters or beasts therein among the crags, but only the pure gravel and the green sand. For a long space of the day they were voyaging in that sea, and great was its splendour and its beauty.[1]

The Undersea Island

They next found themselves in a sea, thin like mist, that seemed as if it would not support their boat. In the depths they saw roofed fortresses, and a fair land around them. A monstrous beast lodged in a tree there, with droves of cattle about it, and beneath it an armed warrior. In spite of the warrior, the beast ever and

[1] Tennyson has been particularly happy in his description of these undersea islands.

anon stretched down a long neck and seized one of the cattle and devoured it. Much dreading lest they should sink through that mist-like sea, they sailed over it and away.

The Island of the Prophecy

When they arrived here they found the water rising in high cliffs round the island, and, looking down, saw on it a crowd of people, who screamed at them, "It is they, it is they," till they were out of breath. Then came a woman and pelted them from below with large nuts, which they gathered and took with them. As they went they heard the folk crying to each other: "Where are they now?" "They are gone away." "They are not." "It is likely," says the tale, "that there was some one concerning whom the islanders had a prophecy that he would ruin their country and expel them from their land."

The Island of the Spouting Water

Here a great stream spouted out of one side of the island and arched over it like a rainbow, falling on the strand at the further side. And when they thrust their spears into the stream above them they brought out salmon from it as much as they would, and the island was filled with the stench of those they could not carry away.

The Island of the Silvern Column

The next wonder to which they came forms one of the most striking and imaginative episodes of the voyage. It was a great silvern column, four-square, rising from the sea. Each of its four sides was as wide as two oar-strokes of the boat. Not a sod of earth was at its foot, but it rose from the boundless ocean and its summit was lost in the sky. From that summit a huge silver net was flung far away into the sea, and through a mesh of that net they sailed. As they did so Diuran hacked away a piece of the net. "Destroy it not," said Maeldūn, "for what we see is the work of mighty men." Diuran said: "For the praise of God's name I do this, that our tale may be believed, and if I reach Ireland again this piece of silver shall be offered by me on the high altar of Armagh." Two ounces and a half it weighed when it was measured afterwards in Armagh.

"And then they heard a voice from the summit of yonder pillar, mighty, clear, and distinct. But they knew not the tongue it spake, or the words it uttered."

The Island of the Pedestal

The next island stood on a foot, or pedestal, which rose from the sea, and they could find no way of access to it. In the base of the pedestal was a door, closed and locked, which they could not open, so they sailed away, having seen and spoken with no one.

The Island of the Women

Here they found the rampart of a mighty dūn, enclosing a mansion. They landed to look on it, and sat on a hillock near by. Within the dūn they saw seventeen maidens busy at preparing a great bath. In a little while a rider, richly clad, came up swiftly on a racehorse, and lighted down and went inside, one of the girls taking the horse. The rider then went into the bath, when they saw that it was a woman. Shortly after that one of the maidens came out and invited them to enter, saying: "The Queen invites you." They went into the fort and bathed, and then sat down to meat, each man with a maiden over against him, and

Maeldūn opposite to the queen. And Maeldūn was wedded to the queen, and each of the maidens to one of his men, and at nightfall canopied chambers were allotted to each of them. On the morrow morn they made ready to depart, but the queen would not have them go, and said: "Stay here, and old age will never fall on you, but ye shall remain as ye are now for ever and ever, and what ye had last night ye shall have always. And be no longer a-wandering from island to island on the ocean."

She then told Maeldūn that she was the mother of the seventeen girls they had seen, and her husband had been king of the island. He was now dead, and she reigned in his place. Each day she went into the great plain in the interior of the island to judge the folk, and returned to the dūn at night.

So they remained there for three months of winter; but at the end of that time it seemed they had been there three years, and the men wearied of it, and longed to set forth for their own country.

"What shall we find there," said Maeldūn, "that is better than this?"

But still the people murmured and complained, and at last they said: "Great is the love which Maeldūn has for his woman. Let him stay with her alone if he will, but we will go to our own country." But Maeldūn would not be left after them, and at last one day, when the queen was away judging the folk, they went on board their bark and put out to sea. Before they had gone far, however, the queen came riding up with a clew of twine in her hand, and she flung it after them. Maeldūn caught it in his hand, and it clung to his hand so that he could not free himself, and the queen, holding the other end, drew them back to land. And they stayed on the island another three months.

Twice again the same thing happened, and at last the people averred that Maeldūn held the clew on purpose, so great was his love for the woman. So the next time another man caught the clew, but it clung to his hand as before; so Diuran smote off his hand, and it fell with the clew into the sea. "When she saw that she at once began to wail and shriek, so that all the land was one cry, wailing and shrieking." And thus they escaped from the Island of the Women.

The Island of the Red Berries

On this island were trees with great red berries which yielded an intoxicating and slumbrous juice. They mingled it with water to moderate its power, and filled their casks with it, and sailed away.

The Island of the Eagle

A large island, with woods of oak and yew on one side of it, and on the other a plain, whereon were herds of sheep, and a little lake in it; and there also they found a small church and a fort, and an ancient grey cleric, clad only in his hair. Maeldūn asked him who he was.

"I am the fifteenth man of the monks of St. Brennan of Birr," he said. "We went on our pilgrimage into the ocean, and they have all died save me alone." He showed them the tablet (? calendar) of the Holy Brennan, and they prostrated themselves before it, and Maeldūn kissed it. They stayed there for a season, feeding on the sheep of the island.

One day they saw what seemed to be a cloud coming up from the south-west. As it drew near, however, they saw the waving of pinions, and perceived that it was an enormous bird. It came into the island, and, alighting very wearily on a hill near the lake, it began eating the red berries, like grapes, which grew on a huge tree-branch as big as a full-grown oak, that it had brought with it, and the juice and fragments of the berries fell into the lake, reddening all the water. Fearful that it would seize them in its talons and bear them out to sea, they lay hid in the woods and watched it. After a while, however, Maeldūn went out to the foot of the hill, but the bird did him no harm, and then the rest followed cautiously behind their shields, and one of them gathered the berries off the branch which the bird held in its talons, but it did them no evil, and regarded them not at all. And they saw that it was very old, and its plumage dull and decayed.

At the hour of noon two eagles came up from the south-west and alit in front of the great bird, and after resting awhile they set to work picking off the insects that infested its jaws and eyes and ears. This they continued till vespers, when all three ate of the berries again. At last, on the following day, when the great bird had been completely cleansed, it plunged into the lake, and again the two eagles picked and cleansed it. Till the third day the great bird remained preening and shaking its pinions, and its feathers became glossy and abundant, and then, soaring upwards, it flew thrice round the island, and away to the quarter whence it had come, and its flight was now swift and strong; whence it was manifest to them that this had been its renewal from old age to youth, according as the prophet said, *Thy youth is renewed like the eagle's.*[1]

Then Diuran said: "Let us bathe in that lake and renew ourselves where the bird hath been renewed." "Nay," said another, "for the bird hath left his venom in it." But Diuran plunged in and drank of the water. From that time so long as he lived his eyes were strong

[1] Ps. ciii. 5.

and keen, and not a tooth fell from his jaw nor a hair from his head, and he never knew illness or infirmity.

Thereafter they bade farewell to the anchorite, and fared forth on the ocean once more.

The Island of the Laughing Folk

Here they found a great company of men laughing and playing incessantly. They drew lots as to who should enter and explore it, and it fell to Maeldūn's foster-brother. But when he set foot on it he at once began to laugh and play with the others, and could not leave off, nor would he come back to his comrades. So they left him and sailed away.[1]

The Island of the Flaming Rampart

They now came in sight of an island which was not large, and it had about it a rampart of flame that circled round and round it continually. In one part of the rampart there was an opening, and when this opening came opposite to them they saw through it the whole island, and saw those who dwelt therein, even men and women, beautiful, many, and wearing adorned garments, with vessels of gold in their hands. And the festal music which they made came to the ears of the wanderers. For a long time they lingered there, watching this marvel, "and they deemed it delightful to behold."

The Island of the Monk of Tory

Far off among the waves they saw what they took to be a white bird on the water. Drawing near to it they found it to be an aged man clad only in the white hair

[1] This disposes of the last of the foster-brothers, who should not have joined the party.

of his body, and he was throwing himself in prostrations on a broad rock.

"From Torach[1] I have come hither," he said, "and there I was reared. I was cook in the monastery there, and the food of the Church I used to sell for myself, so that I had at last much treasure of raiment and brazen vessels and gold-bound books and all that man desires. Great was my pride and arrogance.

"One day as I dug a grave in which to bury a churl who had been brought on to the island, a voice came from below where a holy man lay buried, and he said: 'Put not the corpse of a sinner on me, a holy, pious person!'"

After a dispute the monk buried the corpse elsewhere, and was promised an eternal reward for doing so. Not long thereafter he put to sea in a boat with all his accumulated treasures, meaning apparently to escape from the island with his plunder. A great wind blew him far out to sea, and when he was out of sight of land the boat stood still in one place. He saw near him a man (angel) sitting on the wave. "Whither goest thou?" said the man. "On a pleasant way, whither I am now looking," said the monk. "It would not be pleasant to thee if thou knewest what is around thee," said the man. "So far as eye can see there is one crowd of demons all gathered around thee, because of thy covetousness and pride, and theft, and other evil deeds. Thy boat hath stopped, nor will it move until thou do my will, and the fires of hell shall get hold of thee."

He came near to the boat, and laid his hand on the arm of the fugitive, who promised to do his will.

"Fling into the sea," he said, "all the wealth that is in thy boat."

[1] Tory Island, off the Donegal coast. There was there a monastery and a church dedicated to St. Columba.

"It is a pity," said the monk, "that it should go to loss."

"It shall in nowise go to loss. There will be one man whom thou wilt profit."

The monk thereupon flung everything into the sea save one little wooden cup, and he cast away oars and rudder. The man gave him a provision of whey and seven cakes, and bade him abide wherever his boat should stop. The wind and waves carried him hither and thither till at last the boat came to rest upon the rock where the wanderers found him. There was nothing there but the bare rock, but remembering what he was bidden he stepped out upon a little ledge over which the waves washed, and the boat immediately left him, and the rock was enlarged for him. There he remained seven years, nourished by otters which brought him salmon out of the sea, and even flaming firewood on which to cook them, and his cup was filled with good liquor every day. "And neither wet nor heat nor cold affects me in this place."

At the noon hour miraculous nourishment was brought for the whole crew, and thereafter the ancient man said to them:

"Ye will all reach your country, and the man that slew thy father, O Maeldûn, ye will find him in a fortress before you. And slay him not, but forgive him; because God hath saved you from manifold great perils, and ye too are men deserving of death."

Then they bade him farewell and went on their accustomed way.

The Island of the Falcon

This is uninhabited save for herds of sheep and oxen. They land on it and eat their fill, and one of them sees there a large falcon. "This falcon," he says, "is like the falcons of Ireland." "Watch it," says Maeldūn, "and see how it will go from us." It flew off to the south-east, and they rowed after it all day till vespers.

The Home-coming

At nightfall they sighted a land like Ireland; and soon came to a small island, where they ran their prow ashore. It was the island where dwelt the man who had slain Ailill.

They went up to the dūn that was on the island, and heard men talking within it as they sat at meat. One man said:

"It would be ill for us if we saw Maeldūn now."

"That Maeldūn has been drowned," said another.

"Maybe it is he who shall waken you from sleep to-night," said a third.

"If he should come now," said a fourth, "what should we do?"

"Not hard to answer that," said the chief of them. "Great welcome should he have if he were to come, for he hath been a long space in great tribulation."

Then Maeldūn smote with the wooden clapper against the door. "Who is there?" asked the door-keeper.

"Maeldūn is here," said he.

They entered the house in peace, and great welcome was made for them, and they were arrayed in new garments. And then they told the story of all the marvels that God had shown them, according to the words of the "sacred poet," who said, *Haec olim meminisse juvabit.*[1]

[1] "One day we shall delight in the remembrance of these things." The quotation is from Vergil, "Æn." i. 203 "Sacred poet" is a translation of the *vates sacer* of Horace.

The Offering of Diuran the Rhymer

The Penance of Rhiannon

THE HOME-COMING

Then Maeldun went to his own home and kindred, and Diuran the Rhymer took with him the piece of silver that he had hewn from the net of the pillar, and laid it on the high altar of Armagh in triumph and exultation at the miracles that God had wrought for them. And they told again the story of all that had befallen them, and all the marvels they had seen by sea and land, and the perils they had endured.

The story ends with the following words:

"Now Aed the Fair [Aed Finn[1]], chief sage of Ireland, arranged this story as it standeth here; and he did so for a delight to the mind, and for the folks of Ireland after him."

[1] This sage and poet has not been identified from any other record. Praise and thanks to him, whoever he may have been.

CHAPTER VIII: MYTHS AND TALES OF THE CYMRY

Bardic Philosophy

THE absence in early Celtic literature of any world-myth, or any philosophic account of the origin and constitution of things, was noticed at the opening of our third chapter. In Gaelic literature there is, as far as I know, nothing which even pretends to represent early Celtic thought on this subject. It is otherwise in Wales. Here there has existed for a considerable time a body of teaching purporting to contain a portion, at any rate, of that ancient Druidic thought which, as Caesar tells us, was communicated only to the initiated, and never written down. This teaching is principally to be found in two volumes entitled "Barddas," a compilation made from materials in his possession by a Welsh bard and scholar named Llewellyn Sion, of Glamorgan, towards the end of the sixteenth century, and edited, with a translation, by J. A. Williams ap Ithel for the Welsh MS. Society. Modern Celtic scholars pour contempt on the pretensions of works like this to enshrine any really antique thought. Thus Mr. Ivor B. John: "All idea of a bardic esoteric doctrine involving pre-Christian mythic philosophy must be utterly discarded." And again: "The nonsense talked upon the subject is largely due to the uncritical invention of pseudo-antiquaries of the sixteenth to seventeenth and eighteenth centuries."[1] Still the bardic Order was certainly at one time in possession of such a doctrine. That Order had a fairly continuous existence in Wales. And though no critical thinker would build with any

[1] "The Mabinogion," pp. 45 and 54.

confidence a theory of pre-Christian doctrine on a document of the sixteenth century, it does not seem wise to scout altogether the possibility that some fragments of antique lore may have lingered even so late as that in bardic tradition.

At any rate, "Barddas" is a work of considerable philosophic interest, and even if it represents nothing but a certain current of Cymric thought in the sixteenth century it is not unworthy of attention by the student of things Celtic. Purely Druidic it does not even profess to be, for Christian personages and episodes from Christian history figure largely in it. But we come occasionally upon a strain of thought which, whatever else it may be, is certainly not Christian, and speaks of an independent philosophic system.

In this system two primary existences are contemplated, God and Cythrawl, who stand respectively for the principle of energy tending towards life, and the principle of destruction tending towards nothingness. Cythrawl is realised in Annwn,[1] which may be rendered, the Abyss, or Chaos. In the beginning there was nothing but God and Annwn. Organised life began by the Word—God pronounced His ineffable Name and the "Manred" was formed. The Manred was the primal substance of the universe. It was conceived as a multitude of minute indivisible particles—atoms, in fact—each being a microcosm, for God is complete in each of them, while at the same time each is a part of God, the Whole. The totality of being as it now exists is represented by three concentric circles. The innermost of them, where life sprang from Annwn, is called "Abred," and is the stage of struggle and evolution—the contest of life with Cythrawl. The next is

[1] Pronounced "Annoon." It was the word used in the early literature for Hades or Fairyland.

the circle of "Gwynfyd," or Purity, in which life is manifested as a pure, rejoicing force, having attained its triumph over evil. The last and outermost circle is called "Ceugant," or Infinity. Here all predicates fail us, and this circle, represented graphically not by a bounding line, but by divergent rays, is inhabited by

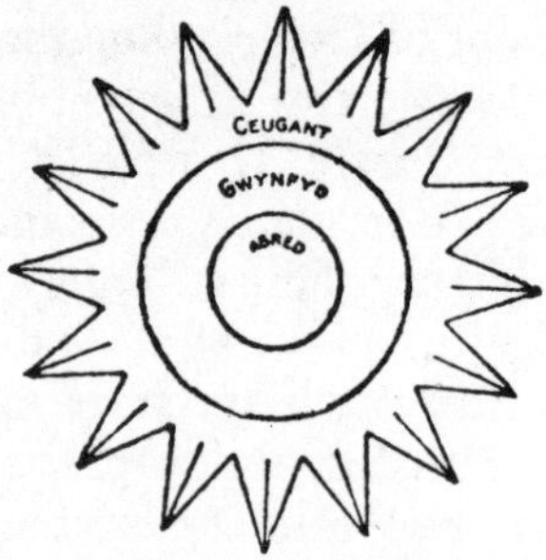

The Circles of Being

God alone. The following extract from "Barddas," in which the alleged bardic teaching is conveyed in catechism form, will serve to show the order of ideas in which the writer's mind moved:

"Q. Whence didst thou proceed?

"A. I came from the Great World, having my beginning in Annwn.

"Q. Where art thou now? and how camest thou to what thou art?

"A. I am in the Little World, whither I came having traversed the circle of Abred, and now I am a Man, at its termination and extreme limits.

"Q. What wert thou before thou didst become a man, in the circle of Abred?

"A. I was in Annwn the least possible that was capable of life and the nearest possible to absolute death; and I came in every form and through every form capable of a body and life to the state of man along the circle of Abred, where my condition was severe and grievous during the age of ages, ever since I was parted in Annwn from the dead, by the gift of God, and His great generosity, and His unlimited and endless love.

"Q. Through how many different forms didst thou come, and what happened unto thee?"

"A. Through every form capable of life, in water, in earth, in air. And there happened unto me every severity, every hardship, every evil, and every suffering, and but little was the goodness or Gwynfyd before I became a man. . . . Gwynfyd cannot be obtained without seeing and knowing everything, but it is not possible to see or to know everything without suffering everything. . . . And there can be no full and perfect love that does not produce those things which are necessary to lead to the knowledge that causes Gwynfyd."

Every being, we are told, shall attain to the circle of Gwynfyd at last.[1]

There is much here that reminds us of Gnostic or Oriental thought. It is certainly very unlike Christian orthodoxy of the sixteenth century. As a product of the Cymric mind of that period the reader may take it for what it is worth, without troubling himself either with antiquarian theories or with their refutations.

Let us now turn to the really ancient work, which is not philosophic, but creative and imaginative, produced by British bards and fabulists of the Middle Ages. But before we go on to set forth what we shall find in this literature we must delay a moment to discuss one thing which we shall not.

[1] "Barddas," vol. i. pp. 224 *sqq*.

The Arthurian Saga

For the majority of modern readers who have not made any special study of the subject, the mention of early British legend will inevitably call up the glories of the Arthurian Saga—they will think of the fabled palace at Caerleon-on-Usk, the Knights of the Round Table riding forth on chivalrous adventure, the Quest of the Grail, the guilty love of Lancelot, flower of knighthood, for the queen, the last great battle by the northern sea, the voyage of Arthur, sorely wounded, but immortal, to the mystic valley of Avalon. But as a matter of fact they will find in the native literature of mediæval Wales little or nothing of all this—no Round Table, no Lancelot, no Grail-Quest, no Isle of Avalon, until the Welsh learned about them from abroad ; and though there was indeed an Arthur in this literature, he is a wholly different being from the Arthur of what we now call the Arthurian Saga.

Nennius

The earliest extant mention of Arthur is to be found in the work of the British historian Nennius, who wrote his "Historia Britonum" about the year 800. He derives his authority from various sources—ancient monuments and writings of Britain and of Ireland (in connexion with the latter country he records the legend of Partholan), Roman annals, and chronicles of saints, especially St. Germanus. He presents a fantastically Romanised and Christianised view of British history, deriving the Britons from a Trojan and Roman ancestry. His account of Arthur, however, is both sober and brief. Arthur, who, according to Nennius, lived in the sixth century, was not a king ; his ancestry was less noble than that of many other British chiefs, who, nevertheless, for his great talents as a military *Imperator*, or *dux bellorum*, chose him for their leader against the Saxons, whom he defeated in twelve battles, the last being at Mount Badon. Arthur's office was doubtless a relic of Roman military organisation, and there is no reason to doubt his historical existence, however impenetrable may be the veil which now obscures his valiant and often triumphant battlings for order and civilisation in that disastrous age.

Geoffrey of Monmouth

Next we have Geoffrey of Monmouth, Bishop of St. Asaph, who wrote his "Historia Regum Britaniæ" in South Wales in the early part of the twelfth century. This work is an audacious attempt to make sober history out of a mass of mythical or legendary matter mainly derived, if we are to believe the author, from an ancient book brought by his uncle Walter, Archdeacon of Oxford, from Brittany. The mention of Brittany in this connexion is, as we shall see, very significant. Geoffrey wrote expressly to commemorate the exploits of Arthur, who now appears as a king, son of Uther Pendragon and of Igerna, wife of Gorlois, Duke of Cornwall, to whom Uther gained access in the shape of her husband through the magic arts of Merlin. He places the beginning of Arthur's reign in the year 505, recounts his wars against the Saxons, and says he ultimately conquered not only all Britain, but Ireland, Norway, Gaul, and Dacia, and successfully resisted a demand for tribute and homage from the Romans. He held his court at Caerleon-on-Usk. While he was away on the Continent carrying on his struggle with Rome his nephew Modred usurped his crown and wedded his wife Guanhumara. Arthur, on this, returned, and after defeating the traitor at Winchester slew him in a last battle in Cornwall, where Arthur himself was sorely wounded (A.D. 542). The queen retired to a convent at Caerleon. Before his death Arthur conferred his kingdom on his kinsman Constantine, and was then carried off mysteriously to "the isle of Avalon" to be cured, and "the rest is silence." Arthur's magic sword "Caliburn" (Welsh *Caladvwlch*; see p. 224, note) is mentioned by Geoffrey and described as having been made in Avalon, a word which seems to imply some kind of fairyland, a Land of the Dead, and may be related to the Norse *Valhall*. It was not until later times that Avalon came to be identified with an actual site in Britain (Glastonbury). In Geoffrey's narrative there is nothing about the Holy Grail, or Lancelot, or the Round Table, and except for the allusion to Avalon the mystical element of the Arthurian saga is absent. Like Nennius, Geoffrey finds a fantastic classical origin for the Britons. His so-called history is perfectly worthless as a record of fact, but it has proved a veritable mine for poets and chroniclers, and has the distinction of having furnished the subject for the earliest English tragic drama, "Gorboduc," as well as for Shakespeare's "King Lear"; and its author may be described as the father—at least on its quasi-historical side—of the Arthurian saga, which he made up partly out of records of the historical *dux bellorum* of Nennius and partly out of poetical amplifications of these records made in Brittany by the descendants of exiles from Wales, many of whom fled there at the very time when Arthur was waging his wars against the heathen Saxons. Geoffrey's book had a wonderful success. It was speedily translated into French by Wace, who wrote "Li Romans de Brut" about 1155, with added details from Breton sources, and translated from Wace's French into Anglo-Saxon by Layamon, who thus anticipated Malory's adaptations of late French prose romances. Except a few scholars who protested unavailingly, no one doubted its strict historical truth, and it had the important effect of giving to early British history a new dignity in the estimation of Continental and of English princes. To sit upon the throne of Arthur was regarded as in itself a glory by Plantagenet monarchs who had not a trace of Arthur's or of any British blood.

The Saga in Brittany: Marie de France

The Breton sources must next be considered. Unfortunately, not a line of ancient Breton literature has come down to us, and for our knowledge of it we must rely on the appearances it makes in the work of French writers. One of the earliest of these is the Anglo-Norman poetess who called herself Marie de France, and who wrote about 1150 and afterwards. She wrote, among other things, a number of "Lais," or tales, which she explicitly and repeatedly tells us were translated or adapted from Breton sources. Sometimes she claims to have rendered a writer's original exactly:

> "Les contes que jo sai verais
> Dunt li Bretun unt fait les lais
> Vos conterai assez briefment;
> Et cief [sauf] di cest coumencement
> Selunc la lettre è l'escriture."

Little is actually said about Arthur in these tales, but the events of them are placed in his time—*en cel tems tint Artus la terre*—and the allusions, which include a mention of the Round Table, evidently imply a general knowledge of the subject among those to whom these Breton "Lais" were addressed. Lancelot is not mentioned, but there is a "Lai" about one Lanval, who is beloved by Arthur's queen, but rejects her because he has a fairy mistress in the "isle d'Avalon." Gawain is mentioned, and an episode is told in the "Lai de Chevrefoil" about Tristan and Iseult, whose maid, "Brangien," is referred to in a way which assumes that the audience knew the part she had played on Iseult's bridal night. In short, we have evidence here of the existence in Brittany of a well-diffused and well-developed body of chivalric legend gathered about the personality of Arthur. The legends are so well known that mere allusions to characters and episodes in them are as well understood as references to Tennyson's "Idylls" would be among us to-day. The "Lais" of Marie de France therefore point strongly to Brittany as the true cradle of the Arthurian saga, on its chivalrous and romantic side. They do not, however, mention the Grail.

Chrestien de Troyes

Lastly, and chiefly, we have the work of the French poet Chrestien de Troyes, who began in 1165 to translate Breton "Lais," like Marie de France, and who practically brought the Arthurian saga into the poetic literature of Europe, and gave it its main outline and character. He wrote a "Tristan" (now lost). He (if not Walter Map) introduced Lancelot of the Lake into the story; he wrote a *Conte del Graal*, in which the Grail legend and Perceval make their first appearance, though he left the story unfinished, and does not tell us what the "Grail" really was.[1] He also wrote a long *conte d'aventure* entitled "Erec," containing the story of Geraint and Enid. These are the earliest poems

[1] Strange as it may seem to us, the character of this object was by no means fixed from the beginning. In the poem of Wolfram von Eschenbach it is a stone endowed with magical properties. The word is derived by the early fabulists from *gréable*, something pleasant to possess and enjoy, and out of which one could have *à son gré*, whatever he chose of good things. The Grail legend will be dealt with later in connexion with the Welsh tale "Peredur."

we possess in which the Arthur of chivalric legend comes prominently forward. What were the sources of Chrestien? No doubt they were largely Breton. Troyes is in Champagne, which had been united to Blois in 1019 by Eudes, Count of Blois, and reunited again after a period of dispossession by Count Theobald de Blois in 1128. Marie, Countess of Champagne, was Chrestien's patroness. And there were close connexions between the ruling princes of Blois and of Brittany. Alain II., a Duke of Brittany, had in the tenth century married a sister of the Count de Blois, and in the first quarter of the thirteenth century Jean I. of Brittany married Blanche de Champagne, while their daughter Alix married Jean de Chastillon, Count of Blois, in 1254. It is highly probable, therefore, that through minstrels who attended their Breton lords at the court of Blois, from the middle of the tenth century onward, a great many Breton "Lais" and legends found their way into French literature during the eleventh, twelfth, and thirteenth centuries. But it is also certain that the Breton legends themselves had been strongly affected by French influences, and that to the *Matière de France*, as it was called by mediæval writers [1]—*i.e.*, the legends of Charlemagne and his Paladins—we owe the Table Round and the chivalric institutions ascribed to Arthur's court at Caerleon-on-Usk.

Bleheris

It must not be forgotten that (as Miss Jessie L. Weston has emphasised in her invaluable studies on the Arthurian saga) Gautier de Denain, the earliest of the continuators or re-workers of Chrestien de Troyes, mentions as his authority for

[1] Distinguished by these from the other great storehouse of poetic legend, the *Matière de Bretagne*—*i.e.*, the Arthurian saga.

stories of Gawain one Bleheris, a poet "born and bred in Wales." This forgotten bard is believed to be identical with *famosus ille fabulator*, *Bledhericus*, mentioned by Giraldus Cambrensis, and with the Bréris quoted by Thomas of Brittany as an authority for the Tristan story.

Conclusion as to the Origin of the Arthurian Saga

In the absence, however, of any information as to when, or exactly what, Bleheris wrote, the opinion must, I think, hold the field that the Arthurian saga, as we have it now, is not of Welsh, nor even of pure Breton origin. The Welsh exiles who colonised part of Brittany about the sixth century must have brought with them many stories of the historical Arthur. They must also have brought legends of the Celtic deity Artaius, a god to whom altars have been found in France. These personages ultimately blended into one, even as in Ireland the Christian St. Brigit blended with the pagan goddess Brigindo.[1] We thus get a mythical figure combining something of the exaltation of a god with a definite habitation on earth and a place in history. An Arthur saga thus arose, which in its Breton (though not its Welsh) form was greatly enriched by material drawn in from the legends of Charlemagne and his peers, while both in Brittany and in Wales it became a centre round which clustered a mass of floating legendary matter relating to various Celtic personages, human and divine. Chrestien de Troyes, working on Breton material, ultimately gave it the form in which it conquered the world, and in which it became in the twelfth and the thirteenth centuries what the Faust legend was in later times, the accepted vehicle for the ideals and aspirations of an epoch.

[1] See p. 103.

The Saga in Wales

From the Continent, and especially from Brittany, the story of Arthur came back into Wales transformed and glorified. The late Dr. Heinrich Zimmer, in one of his luminous studies of the subject, remarks that "In Welsh literature we have definite evidence that the South-Welsh prince, Rhys ap Tewdwr, who had been in Brittany, brought from thence in the year 1070 the knowledge of Arthur's Round Table to Wales, where of course it had been hitherto unknown."[1] And many Breton lords are known to have followed the banner of William the Conqueror into England.[2] The introducers of the saga into Wales found, however, a considerable body of Arthurian matter of a very different character already in existence there. Besides the traditions of the historical Arthur, the *dux bellorum* of Nennius, there was the Celtic deity, Artaius. It is probably a reminiscence of this deity whom we meet with under the name of Arthur in the only genuine Welsh Arthurian story we possess, the story of Kilhwch and Olwen in the "Mabinogion." Much of the Arthurian saga derived from Chrestien and other Continental writers was translated and adapted in Wales as in other European countries, but as a matter of fact it made a later and a lesser impression in Wales than almost anywhere else. It conflicted with existing Welsh traditions, both historical and mythological; it was full of matter entirely foreign to the Welsh spirit, and it remained always in Wales something alien and unassimilated. Into Ireland it never entered at all.

These few introductory remarks do not, of course, profess to contain a discussion of the Arthurian saga —a vast subject with myriad ramifications, historical,

[1] "Cultur der Gegenwart," i. ix.

[2] A list of them is given in Lobineau's "Histoire de Bretagne."

mythological, mystical, and what not—but are merely intended to indicate the relation of that saga to genuine Celtic literature and to explain why we shall hear so little of it in the following accounts of Cymric myths and legends. It was a great spiritual myth which, arising from the composite source above described, overran all the Continent, as its hero was supposed to have done in armed conquest, but it cannot be regarded as a special possession of the Celtic race, nor is it at present extant, except in the form of translation or adaptation, in any Celtic tongue.

Gaelic and Cymric Legend Compared

The myths and legends of the Celtic race which have come down to us in the Welsh language are in some respects of a different character from those which we possess in Gaelic. The Welsh material is nothing like as full as the Gaelic, nor so early. The tales of the "Mabinogion" are mainly drawn from the fourteenth-century manuscript entitled "The Red Book of Hergest." One of them, the romance of Taliesin, came from another source, a manuscript of the seventeenth century. The four oldest tales in the "Mabinogion" are supposed by scholars to have taken their present shape in the tenth or eleventh century, while several Irish tales, like the story of Etain and Midir or the Death of Conary, go back to the seventh or eighth. It will be remembered that the story of the invasion of Partholan was known to Nennius, who wrote about the year 800. As one might therefore expect, the mythological elements in the Welsh romances are usually much more confused and harder to decipher than in the earlier of the Irish tales. The mythic interest has grown less, the story interest greater; the object of the bard is less to hand down a sacred text than to entertain a prince's court. We must remember also that the influence of the Continental romances of chivalry is clearly perceptible in the Welsh tales; and, in fact, comes eventually to govern them completely.

Gaelic and Continental Romance

In many respects the Irish Celt anticipated the ideas of these romances. The lofty courtesy shown to each other by enemies,[1] the fantastic pride which forbade a warrior to take advantage of a wounded adversary,[2] the extreme punctilio with which the duties or observances proper to each man's caste or station were observed[3]—all this tone of thought and feeling which would seem so strange to us if we met an instance of it in classical literature would seem quite familiar and natural in Continental romances of the twelfth and later centuries. Centuries earlier than that it was a marked feature in Gaelic literature. Yet in the Irish romances, whether Ultonian or Ossianic, the element which has since been considered the most essential motive in a romantic tale is almost entirely lacking. This is the element of love, or rather of woman-worship. The Continental fabulist felt that he could do nothing without this motive of action. But the "lady-love" of the English, French, or German knight, whose favour he wore, for whose grace he endured infinite hardship and peril, does not meet us in Gaelic literature. It would have seemed absurd to the Irish Celt to make the plot of a serious story hinge on the kind of passion with which the mediæval Dulcinea inspired her faithful knight. In the two most famous and popular of Gaelic love-tales,

[1] See, *e.g.*, pp. 243 and 218, *note*.

[2] See p. 233, and a similar case in the author's "High Deeds of Finn," p. 82.

[3] See p. 232, and the tale of the recovery of the "Tain," p. 234.

the tale of Deirdre and "The Pursuit of Dermot and Grania," the women are the wooers, and the men are most reluctant to commit what they know to be the folly of yielding to them. Now this romantic, chivalric kind of love, which idealised woman into a goddess, and made the service of his lady a sacred duty to the knight, though it never reached in Wales the height which it did in Continental and English romances, is yet clearly discernible there. We can trace it in "Kilhwch and Olwen," which is comparatively an ancient tale. It is well developed in later stories like "Peredur" and "The Lady of the Fountain." It is a symptom of the extent to which, in comparison with the Irish, Welsh literature had lost its pure Celtic strain and become affected—I do not, of course, say to its loss—by foreign influences.

Gaelic and Cymric Mythology: Nudd

The oldest of the Welsh tales, those called "The Four Branches of the Mabinogi,"[1] are the richest in mythological elements, but these occur in more or less recognisable form throughout nearly all the mediæval tales, and even, after many transmutations, in Malory. We can clearly discern certain mythological figures common to all Celtica. We meet, for instance, a personage called Nudd or Lludd, evidently a solar deity. A temple dating from Roman times, and dedicated to him under the name of Nodens, has been discovered at Lydney, by the Severn. On a bronze plaque found near the spot is a representation of the god. He is encircled by a halo and accompanied by flying spirits and by Tritons. We are reminded of the Danaan deities and their close connexion with the

[1] "Pwyll King of Dyfed," "Bran and Branwen," "Māth Son of Māthonwy," and "Manawyddan Son of Llyr."

sea; and when we find that in Welsh legend an epithet is attached to Nudd, meaning "of the Silver Hand" (though no extant Welsh legend tells the meaning of the epithet), we have no difficulty in identifying this Nudd with Nuada of the Silver Hand, who led the Danaans in the battle of Moytura.[1] Under his name Lludd he is said to have had a temple on the site of St. Paul's in London, the entrance to which, according to Geoffrey of Monmouth, was called in the British tongue *Parth Lludd*, which the Saxons translated *Ludes Geat*, our present Ludgate.

Llyr and Manawyddan

Again, when we find a mythological personage named Llyr, with a son named Manawyddan, playing a prominent part in Welsh legend, we may safely connect them with the Irish Lir and his son Mananan, gods of the sea. Llyr-cester, now Leicester, was a centre of the worship of Llyr.

Llew Llaw Gyffes

Finally, we may point to a character in the "Mabinogi," or tale, entitled "Māth Son of Māthonwy." The name of this character is given as Llew Llaw Gyffes, which the Welsh fabulist interprets as "The Lion of the Sure Hand," and a tale, which we shall recount later on, is told to account for the name. But when we find that this hero exhibits characteristics which point to his being a solar deity, such as an amazingly rapid growth from childhood into manhood, and when we are told, moreover, by Professor Rhys that Gyffes originally meant, not "steady" or "sure," but "long,"[2] it becomes evident that we have here a dim and broken reminiscence of the deity whom the Gaels called Lugh

[1] See p. 107. [2] "Hibbert Lectures," pp. 237–240.

of the Long Arm,[1] *Lugh Lamh Fada*. The misunderstood name survived, and round the misunderstanding legendary matter floating in the popular mind crystallised itself in a new story.

These correspondences might be pursued in much further detail. It is enough here to point to their existence as evidence of the original community of Gaelic and Cymric mythology.[2] We are, in each literature, in the same circle of mythological ideas. In Wales, however, these ideas are harder to discern; the figures and their relationships in the Welsh Olympus are less accurately defined and more fluctuating. It would seem as if a number of different tribes embodied what were fundamentally the same conceptions under different names and wove different legends about them. The bardic literature, as we have it now, bears evidence sometimes of the prominence of one of these tribal cults, sometimes of another. To reduce these varying accounts to unity is altogether impossible. Still, we can do something to afford the reader a clue to the maze.

The Houses of Dōn and of Llyr

Two great divine houses or families are discernible—that of Dōn, a mother-goddess (representing the Gaelic Dana), whose husband is Beli, the Irish Bilé, god of Death, and whose descendants are the Children of Light; and the House of Llyr, the Gaelic Lir, who here represents, not a Danaan deity, but something more like the Irish Fomorians. As in the case of the Irish myth, the

[1] See pp. 88, 109, &c. Lugh, of course, = Lux, Light. The Celtic words *Lamh* and *Llaw* were used indifferently for hand or arm.

[2] Mr. Squire, in his "Mythology of the British Islands," 1905, has brought together in a clear and attractive form the most recent results of studies on this subject.

two families are allied by intermarriage—Penardun, a daughter of Dōn, is wedded to Llyr. Dōn herself has a brother, Māth, whose name signifies wealth or treasure (*cf.* Greek Pluton, *ploutos*), and they descend from a figure indistinctly characterised, called Māthonwy.

The House of Arthur

Into the pantheon of deities represented in the four ancient Mabinogi there came, at a later time, from some other tribal source, another group headed by Arthur, the god Artaius. He takes the place of Gwydion son of Dōn, and the other deities of his circle fall more or less accurately into the places of others of the earlier circle. The accompanying genealogical plans are intended to help the reader to a general view of the relationships and attributes of these personages. It must be borne in mind, however, that these tabular arrangements necessarily involve an appearance of precision and consistency which is not reflected in the fluctuating character of the actual myths taken as a whole. Still, as a sketch-map of a very intricate and obscure region, they may help the reader who enters it for the first time to find his bearings in it, and that is the only purpose they propose to serve.

Gwyn ap Nudd

The deity named Gwyn ap Nudd is said, like Finn in Gaelic legend,[1] to have impressed himself more deeply and lastingly on the Welsh popular imagination than any of the other divinities. A mighty warrior and huntsman, he glories in the crash of breaking spears, and, like Odin, assembles the souls of dead heroes in his shadowy kingdom, for although he belongs

[1] Finn and Gwyn are respectively the Gaelic and Cymric forms of the same name, meaning fair or white.

GODS OF THE HOUSE OF DŌN

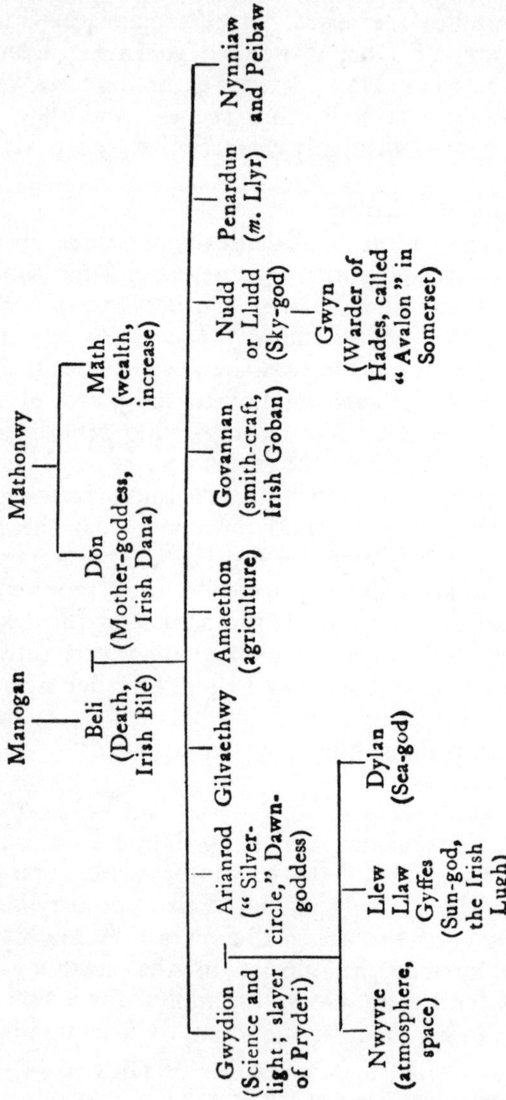
Manogan
Beli (Death, Irish Bilé)
Mathonwy
Dōn (Mother-goddess, Irish Dana)
Math (wealth, increase)
Gwydion (Science and light; slayer of Pryderi)
Arianrod (" Silver-circle," Dawn-goddess)
Gilvaethwy
Amaethon (agriculture)
Govannan (smith-craft, Irish Goban)
Nudd or Lludd (Sky-god)
Penardun (*m.* Llyr)
Nynniaw and Peibaw
Gwyn (Warder of Hades, called " Avalon" in Somerset)
Nwyvre (atmosphere, space)
Llew Llaw Gyffes (Sun-god, the Irish Lugh)
Dylan (Sea-god)

GODS OF THE HOUSE OF LLYR

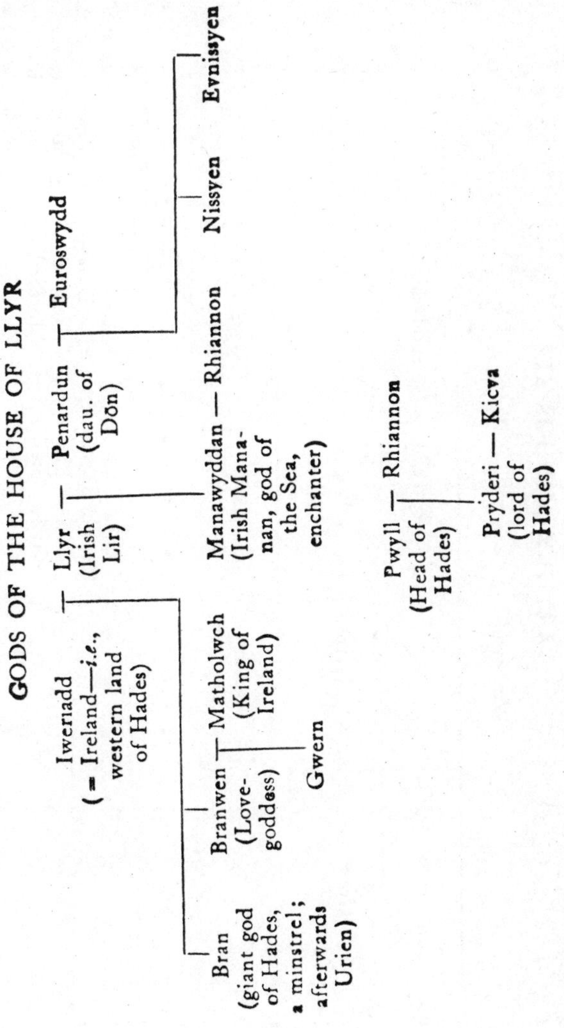

ARTHUR AND HIS KIN

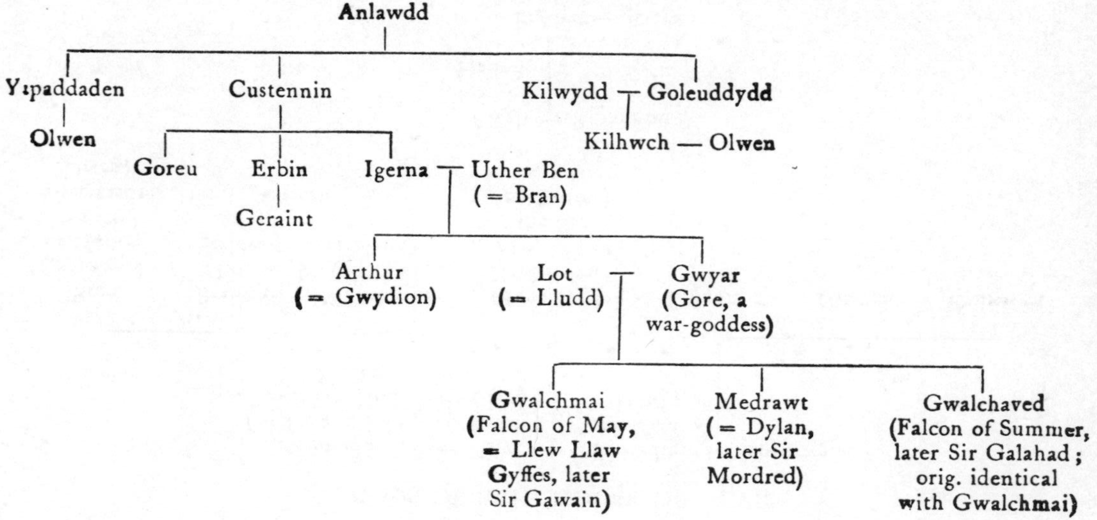

to the kindred of the Light-gods, Hades is his special domain. The combat between him and Gwythur ap Greidawl (Victor, son of Scorcher) for Creudylad, daughter of Lludd, which is to be renewed every May-day till time shall end, represents evidently the contest between winter and summer for the flowery and fertile earth. "Later," writes Mr. Charles Squire, "he came to be considered as King of the *Tylwyth Teg*, the Welsh fairies, and his name as such has hardly yet died out of his last haunt, the romantic vale of Neath. . . . He is the Wild Huntsman of Wales and the West of England, and it is his pack which is sometimes heard at chase in waste places by night."[1] He figures as a god of war and death in a wonderful poem from the "Black Book of Caermarthen," where he is represented as discoursing with a prince named Gwyddneu Garanhir, who had come to ask his protection. I quote a few stanzas: the poem will be found in full in Mr. Squire's excellent volume:

> "I come from battle and conflict
> With a shield in my hand;
> Broken is my helmet by the thrusting of spears.
>
> "Round-hoofed is my horse, the torment of battle,
> Fairy am I called,[2] Gwyn the son of Nudd,
> The lover of Crewrdilad, the daughter of Lludd
>
> . . . .
>
> "I have been in the place where Gwendolen was slain,
> The son of Ceidaw, the pillar of song,
> Where the ravens screamed over blood.
>
> "I have been in the place where Bran was killed,
> The son of Iweridd, of far-extending fame,
> Where the ravens of the battlefield screamed.

[1] "Mythology of the British Islands," p. 225.

[2] The sense appears to be doubtful here, and is variously rendered.

"I have been where Llacheu was slain,
The son of Arthur, extolled in songs,
When the ravens screamed over blood.

"I have been where Mewrig was killed,
The son of Carreian, of honourable fame,
When the ravens screamed over flesh.

"I have been where Gwallawg was killed,
The son of Goholeth, the accomplished,
The resister of Lloegyr,[1] the son of Lleynawg.

"I have been where the soldiers of Britain were slain,
From the east to the north:
I am the escort of the grave.

"I have been where the soldiers of Britain were slain,
From the east to the south:
I am alive, they in death."

Myrddin, or Merlin

A deity named Myrddin holds in Arthur's mythological cycle the place of the Sky- and Sun-god, Nudd. One of the Welsh Triads tells us that Britain, before it was inhabited, was called *Clas Myrddin*, Myrddin's Enclosure. One is reminded of the Irish fashion of calling any favoured spot a "cattle-fold of the sun"—the name is applied by Deirdre to her beloved Scottish home in Glen Etive. Professor Rhys suggests that Myrddin was the deity specially worshipped at Stonehenge, which, according to British tradition as reported by Geoffrey of Monmouth, was erected by "Merlin," the enchanter who represents the form into which Myrddin had dwindled under Christian influences. We are told that the abode of Merlin was a house of glass, or a bush of whitethorn laden with bloom, or a sort of smoke or mist in the air, or "a close neither of iron nor steel nor timber nor of stone, but of the air

[1] Lloegyr = Saxon Britain.

without any other thing, by enchantment so strong that it may never be undone while the world endureth."[1] Finally he descended upon Bardsey Island, "off the extreme westernmost point of Carnarvonshire . . . into it he went with nine attendant bards, taking with him the 'Thirteen Treasures of Britain,' thenceforth lost to men." Professor Rhys points out that a Greek traveller named Demetrius, who is described as having visited Britain in the first century A.D., mentions an island in the west where "Kronos" was supposed to be imprisoned with his attendant deities, and Briareus keeping watch over him as he slept, "for sleep was the bond forged for him." Doubtless we have here a version, Hellenised as was the wont of classical writers on barbaric myths, of a British story of the descent of the Sun-god into the western sea, and his imprisonment there by the powers of darkness, with the possessions and magical potencies belonging to Light and Life.[2]

Nynniaw and Peibaw

The two personages called Nynniaw and Peibaw who figure in the genealogical table play a very slight part in Cymric mythology, but one story in which they appear is interesting in itself and has an excellent moral. They are represented[3] as two brothers, Kings of Britain, who were walking together one starlight night. "See what a fine far-spreading field I have," said Nynniaw. "Where is it?" asked Peibaw. "There aloft and as far as you can see," said Nynniaw, pointing to the sky. "But look at all my cattle grazing in your field," said Peibaw.

[1] Rhys, "Hibbert Lectures," quoting from the ancient saga of Merlin published by the English Text Society, p. 693.

[2] "Mythology of the British Islands," pp. 325, 326; and Rhys, "Hibbert Lectures," p. 155 *sqq*.

[3] In the "Iolo MSS.," collected by Edward Williams.

"Where are they?" said Nynniaw. "All the golden stars," said Peibaw, "with the moon for their shepherd." "They shall not graze on my field," cried Nynniaw. "I say they shall," returned Peibaw. "They shall not." "They shall." And so they went on: first they quarrelled with each other, and then went to war, and armies were destroyed and lands laid waste, till at last the two brothers were turned into oxen as a punishment for their stupidity and quarrelsomeness.

The "Mabinogion"

We now come to the work in which the chief treasures of Cymric myth and legend were collected by Lady Charlotte Guest sixty years ago, and given to the world in a translation which is one of the masterpieces of English literature. The title of this work, the "Mabinogion," is the plural form of the word *Mabinogi*, which means a story belonging to the equipment of an apprentice-bard, such a story as every bard had necessarily to learn as part of his training, whatever more he might afterwards add to his *rèpertoire*. Strictly speaking, the *Mabinogi* in the volume are only the four tales given first in Mr. Alfred Nutt's edition, which were entitled the "Four Branches of the Mabinogi," and which form a connected whole. They are among the oldest relics of Welsh mythological saga.

Pwyll, Head of Hades

The first of them is the story of Pwyll, Prince of Dyfed, and relates how that prince got his title of *Pen Annwn*, or "Head of Hades"—Annwn being the term under which we identify in Welsh literature the Celtic Land of the Dead, or Fairyland. It is a story with a mythological basis, but breathing the purest spirit of chivalric honour and nobility.

PWYLL, HEAD OF HADES

Pwyll, it is said, was hunting one day in the woods of Glyn Cuch when he saw a pack of hounds, not his own, running down a stag. These hounds were snow-white in colour, with red ears. If Pwyll had had any experience in these matters he would have known at once what kind of hunt was up, for these are the colours of Faëry—the red-haired man, the red-eared hound are always associated with magic.[1] Pwyll, however, drove off the strange hounds, and was setting his own on the quarry when a horseman of noble appearance came up and reproached him for his discourtesy. Pwyll offered to make amends, and the story now develops into the familiar theme of the Rescue of Fairyland. The stranger's name is Arawn, a king in Annwn. He is being harried and dispossessed by a rival, Havgan, and he seeks the aid of Pwyll, whom he begs to meet Havgan in single combat a year hence. Meanwhile he will put his own shape on Pwyll, who is to rule in his kingdom till the eventful day, while Arawn will go in Pwyll's shape to govern Dyfed. He instructs Pwyll how to deal with the foe. Havgan must be laid low with a single stroke—if another is given to him he immediately revives again as strong as ever.

Pwyll agreed to follow up the adventure, and accordingly went in Arawn's shape to the kingdom of Annwn. Here he was placed in an unforeseen difficulty. The beautiful wife of Arawn greeted him as her husband. But when the time came for them to retire to rest he set his face to the wall and said no word to her, nor touched her at all until the morning broke. Then they rose up, and Pwyll went to the hunt, and ruled his kingdom, and did all things as if he were monarch of the land. And whatever affection he showed to the queen

[1] See, *e.g.*, pp. 111, 272.

in public during the day, he passed every night even as this first.

At last the day of battle came, and, like the chieftains in Gaelic story, Pwyll and Havgan met each other in the midst of a river-ford. They fought, and at the first clash Havgan was hurled a spear's length over the crupper of his horse and fell mortally wounded.[1] "For the love of heaven," said he, "slay me and complete thy work." "I may yet repent that," said Pwyll. "Slay thee who may, I will not." Then Havgan knew that his end was come, and bade his nobles bear him off; and Pwyll with all his army overran the two kingdoms of Annwn, and made himself master of all the land, and took homage from its princes and lords.

Then he rode off alone to keep his tryst in Glyn Cuch with Arawn as they had appointed. Arawn thanked him for all he had done, and added: "When thou comest thyself to thine own dominions thou wilt see what I have done for thee." They exchanged shapes once more, and each rode in his own likeness to take possession of his own land.

At the court of Annwn the day was spent in joy and feasting, though none but Arawn himself knew that anything unusual had taken place. When night came Arawn kissed and caressed his wife as of old, and she pondered much as to what might be the cause of his change towards her, and of his previous change a year and a day before. And as she was thinking over these things Arawn spoke to her twice or thrice, but got no answer. He then asked her why she was silent. "I tell thee," she said, "that for a year I have not spoken so much in this

[1] We see here that we have got far from primitive Celtic legend. The heroes fight like mediæval knights on horseback, tilting at each other with spears, not in chariots or on foot, and not with the strange weapons which figure in Gaelic battle-tales.

place." "Did not we speak continually?" he said. "Nay," said she, "but for a year back there has been neither converse nor tenderness between us." "Good heaven!" thought Arawn, "a man as faithful and firm in his friendship as any have I found for a friend." Then he told his queen what had passed. "Thou hast indeed laid hold of a faithful friend," she said.

And Pwyll when he came back to his own land called his lords together and asked them how they thought he had sped in his kingship during the past year. "Lord," said they, "thy wisdom was never so great, and thou wast never so kind and free in bestowing thy gifts, and thy justice was never more worthily seen than in this year." Pwyll then told them the story of his adventure. "Verily, lord," said they, "render thanks unto heaven that thou hast such a fellowship, and withhold not from us the rule which we have enjoyed for this year past." "I take heaven to witness that I will not withhold it," said Pwyll.

So the two kings made strong the friendship that was between them, and sent each other rich gifts of horses and hounds and jewels; and in memory of the adventure Pwyll bore thenceforward the title of "Lord of Annwn."

The Wedding of Pwyll and Rhiannon

Near to the castle of Narberth, where Pwyll had his court, there was a mound called the Mound of Arberth, of which it was believed that whoever sat upon it would have a strange adventure: either he would receive blows and wounds or he would see a wonder. One day when all his lords were assembled at Narberth for a feast Pwyll declared that he would sit on the mound and see what would befall.

He did so, and after a little while saw approaching

him along the road that led to the mound a lady clad in garments that shone like gold, and sitting on a pure white horse. "Is there any among you," said Pwyll to his men, "who knows that lady?" "There is not," said they. "Then go to meet her and learn who she is." But as they rode towards the lady she moved away from them, and however fast they rode she still kept an even distance between her and them, yet never seemed to exceed the quiet pace with which she had first approached.

Several times did Pwyll seek to have the lady overtaken and questioned, but all was in vain—none could draw near to her.

Next day Pwyll ascended the mound again, and once more the fair lady on her white steed drew near. This time Pwyll himself pursued her, but she flitted away before him as she had done before his servants, till at last he cried: "O maiden, for the sake of him thou best lovest, stay for me." "I will stay gladly," said she, "and it were better for thy horse had thou asked it long since."

Pwyll then questioned her as to the cause of her coming, and she said: "I am Rhiannon, the daughter of Hevydd Hēn,[1] and they sought to give me to a husband against my will. But no husband would I have, and that because of my love for thee; neither will I yet have one if thou reject me." "By heaven!" said Pwyll, "if I might choose among all the ladies and damsels of the world, thee would I choose."

They then agree that in a twelvemonth from that day Pwyll is to come and claim her at the palace of Hevydd Hēn.

Pwyll kept his tryst, with a following of a hundred

[1] Hēn, "the Ancient"; an epithet generally implying a hoary antiquity associated with mythological tradition.

knights, and found a splendid feast prepared for him, and he sat by his lady, with her father on the other side. As they feasted and talked there entered a tall, auburn-haired youth of royal bearing, clad in satin, who saluted Pwyll and his knights. Pwyll invited him to sit down. "Nay, I am a suitor to thee," said the youth; "to crave a boon am I come." "Whatever thou wilt thou shalt have," said Pwyll unsuspiciously, "if it be in my power." "Ah," cried Rhiannon, "wherefore didst thou give that answer?" "Hath he not given it before all these nobles?" said the youth; "and now the boon I crave is to have thy bride Rhiannon, and the feast and the banquet that are in this place." Pwyll was silent. "Be silent as long as thou wilt," said Rhiannon. "Never did man make worse use of his wits than thou hast done." She tells him that the auburn-haired young man is Gwawl, son of Clud, and is the suitor to escape from whom she had fled to Pwyll.

Pwyll is bound in honour by his word, and Rhiannon explains that the banquet cannot be given to Gwawl, for it is not in Pwyll's power, but that she herself will be his bride in a twelvemonth; Gwawl is to come and claim her then, and a new bridal feast will be prepared for him. Meantime she concerts a plan with Pwyll, and gives him a certain magical bag, which he is to make use of when the time shall come.

A year passed away, Gwawl appeared according to the compact, and a great feast was again set forth, in which he, and not Pwyll, had the place of honour. As the company were making merry, however, a beggar clad in rags and shod with clumsy old shoes came into the hall, carrying a bag, as beggars are wont to do. He humbly craved a boon of Gwawl. It was merely that the full of his bag of food might be given him from the banquet. Gwawl cheerfully consented, and an attendant went to fill the bag. But however much they put into it it never got fuller—by degrees all the good things on the tables had gone in; and at last Gwawl cried: "My soul, will thy bag never be full?" "It will not, I declare to heaven," answered Pwyll —for he, of course, was the disguised beggar man— "unless some man wealthy in lands and treasure shall get into the bag and stamp it down with his feet, and declare, 'Enough has been put herein.'" Rhiannon urged Gwawl to check the voracity of the bag. He put his two feet into it; Pwyll immediately drew up the sides of the bag over Gwawl's head and tied it up. Then he blew his horn, and the knights he had with him, who were concealed outside, rushed in, and captured and bound the followers of Gwawl. "What is in the bag?" they cried, and others answered, "A badger," and so they played the game of "Badger in the Bag," striking it and kicking it about the hall.

At last a voice was heard from it. "Lord," cried Gwawl, "if thou wouldst but hear me, I merit not to be slain in a bag." "He speaks truth," said Hevydd Hen.

So an agreement was come to that Gwawl should provide means for Pwyll to satisfy all the suitors and minstrels who should come to the wedding, and abandon Rhiannon, and never seek to have revenge for what had been done to him. This was confirmed by sureties, and Gwawl and his men were released and went to their own territory. And Pwyll wedded Rhiannon, and dispensed gifts royally to all and sundry; and at last the pair, when the feasting was done, journeyed down to the palace of Narberth in Dyfed, where Rhiannon gave rich gifts, a bracelet and a ring or a precious stone to all the lords and ladies of her new country, and they ruled the land in peace both that year and the next. But the reader will find that we have not yet done with Gwawl.

The Penance of Rhiannon

Now Pwyll was still without an heir to the throne, and his nobles urged him to take another wife. "Grant us a year longer," said he, "and if there be no heir after that it shall be as you wish." Before the year's end a son was born to them in Narberth. But although six women sat up to watch the mother and the infant, it happened towards the morning that they all fell asleep, and Rhiannon also slept, and when the women awoke, behold, the boy was gone! "We shall be burnt for this," said the women, and in their terror they concocted a horrible plot: they killed a cub of a staghound that had just been littered, and laid the bones by Rhiannon, and smeared her face and hands with blood as she slept, and when she woke and asked for her child they said she had devoured it in the night, and had overcome them with furious strength when they would have prevented her—and for all she could say or do the six women persisted in this story.

When the story was told to Pwyll he would not put away Rhiannon, as his nobles now again begged him to do, but a penance was imposed on her—namely, that she was to sit every day by the horse-block at the gate of the castle and tell the tale to every stranger who came, and offer to carry them on her back into the castle. And this she did for part of a year.

The Finding of Pryderi[1]

Now at this time there lived a man named Teirnyon of Gwent Is Coed, who had the most beautiful mare in

[1] Pronounced "Pry-dair'y."

the world, but there was this misfortune attending her, that although she foaled on the night of every first of May, none ever knew what became of the colts. At last Teirnyon resolved to get at the truth of the matter, and the next night on which the mare should foal he armed himself and watched in the stable. So the mare foaled, and the colt stood up, and Teirnyon was admiring its size and beauty when a great noise was heard outside, and a long, clawed arm came through the window of the stable and laid hold of the colt. Teirnyon immediately smote at the arm with his sword, and severed it at the elbow, so that it fell inside with the colt, and a great wailing and tumult was heard outside. He rushed out, leaving the door open behind him, but could see nothing because of the darkness of the night, and he followed the noise a little way. Then he came back, and behold, at the door he found an infant in swaddling-clothes and wrapped in a mantle of satin. He took up the child and brought it to where his wife lay sleeping. She had no children, and she loved the child when she saw it, and next day pretended to her women that she had borne it as her own. And they called its name Gwri of the Golden Hair, for its hair was yellow as gold; and it grew so mightily that in two years it was as big and strong as a child of six; and ere long the colt that had been foaled on the same night was broken in and given him to ride.

While these things were going on Teirnyon heard the tale of Rhiannon and her punishment. And as the lad grew up he scanned his face closely and saw that he had the features of Pwyll Prince of Dyfed. This he told to his wife, and they agreed that the child shonld be taken to Narberth, and Rhiannon released from her penance.

As they drew near to the castle, Teirnyon and two knights and the child riding on his colt, there was

Rhiannon sitting by the horse-block. "Chieftains," said she, "go not further thus ; I will bear every one of you into the palace, and this is my penance for slaying my own son and devouring him." But they would not be carried, and went in. Pwyll rejoiced to see Teirnyon, and made a feast for him. Afterwards Teirnyon declared to Pwyll and Rhiannon the adventure of the man and the colt, and how they had found the boy. "And behold, here is thy son, lady," said Teirnyon, "and whoever told that lie concerning thee has done wrong." All who sat at table recognised the lad at once as the child of Pwyll, and Rhiannon cried : "I declare to heaven that if this be true there is an end to my trouble." And a chief named Pendaran said : "Well hast thou named thy son Pryderi [trouble], and well becomes him the name of Pryderi son of Pwyll, Lord of Annwn." It was agreed that his name should be Pryderi, and so he was called thenceforth.

Teirnyon rode home, overwhelmed with thanks and love and gladness ; and Pwyll offered him rich gifts of horses and jewels and dogs, but he would take none of them. And Pryderi was trained up, as befitted a king's son, in all noble ways and accomplishments, and when his father Pwyll died he reigned in his stead over the Seven Cantrevs of Dyfed. And he added to them many other fair dominions, and at last he took to wife Kicva, daughter of Gwynn Gohoyw, who came of the lineage of Prince Casnar of Britain.

The Tale of Bran and Branwen

Bendigeid Vran, or "Bran the Blessed," by which latter name we shall designate him here, when he had been made King of the Isle of the Mighty (Britain), was one time in his court at Harlech. And he had with him his brother Manawyddan son of Llyr, and his sister Branwen, and the two sons, Nissyen and Evnissyen, that Penardun his mother bore to Eurosswyd. Now Nissyen was a youth of gentle nature, and would make peace among his kindred and cause them to be friends when their wrath was at its highest; but Evnissyen loved nothing so much as to turn peace into contention and strife.

One afternoon, as Bran son of Llyr sat on the rock of Harlech looking out to sea, he beheld thirteen ships coming rapidly from Ireland before a fair wind. They were gaily furnished, bright flags flying from the masts, and on the foremost ship, when they came near, a man could be seen holding up a shield with the point upwards in sign of peace.[1]

When the strangers landed they saluted Bran and explained their business. Matholwch,[2] King of Ireland, was with them; his were the ships, and he had come to ask for the hand in marriage of Bran's sister, Branwen, so that Ireland and Britain might be leagued together and both become more powerful. "Now Branwen was one of the three chief ladies of the island, and she was the fairest damsel in the world."

The Irish were hospitably entertained, and after taking counsel with his lords Bran agreed to give his sister to Matholwch. The place of the wedding was fixed at Aberffraw, and the company assembled for the feast in tents because no house could hold the giant form of Bran. They caroused and made merry in peace and amity, and Branwen became the bride of the Irish king.

Next day Evnissyen came by chance to where the

[1] Evidently this was the triangular Norman shield, not the round or oval Celtic one. It has already been noticed that in these Welsh tales the knights when they fight tilt at each other with spears.

[2] The reader may pronounce this "Matholaw."

horses of Matholwch were ranged, and he asked whose they were. "They are the horses of Matholwch, who is married to thy sister." "And is it thus," said he, "they have done with a maiden such as she, and, moreover, my sister, bestowing her without my consent? They could offer me no greater insult." Thereupon he rushed among the horses and cut off their lips at the teeth, and their ears to their heads, and their tails close to the body, and where he could seize the eyelids he cut them off to the bone.

When Matholwch heard what had been done he was both angered and bewildered, and bade his people put to sea. Bran sent messengers to learn what had happened, and when he had been informed he sent Manawyddan and two others to make atonement. Matholwch should have sound horses for every one that was injured, and in addition a staff of silver as large and as tall as himself, and a plate of gold the size of his face. "And let him come and meet me," he added, "and we will make peace in any way he may desire." But as for Evnissyen, he was the son of Bran's mother, and therefore Bran could not put him to death as he deserved.

The Magic Cauldron

Matholwch accepted these terms, but not very cheerfully, and Bran now offered another treasure, namely, a magic cauldron which had the property that if a slain man were cast into it he would come forth well and sound, only he would not be able to speak. Matholwch and Bran then talked about the cauldron, which originally, it seems, came from Ireland. There was a lake in that country near to a mound (doubtless a fairy mound) which was called the Lake of the Cauldron. Here Matholwch had once met a tall and ill-looking fellow with a wife bigger than himself, and the cauldron strapped on his back. They took service with Matholwch. At the end of a period of six weeks the wife gave birth to a son, who was a warrior fully armed. We are apparently to understand that this happened every six weeks, for by the end of the year the strange pair, who seem to be a war-god and goddess, had several children, whose continual bickering and the outrages they committed throughout the land made them hated. At last, to get rid of them, Matholwch had a house of iron made, and enticed them into it. He then barred the door and heaped coals about the chamber, and blew them into a white heat, hoping to roast the whole family to death. As soon, however, as the iron walls had grown white-hot and soft the man and his wife burst through them and got away, but the children remained behind and were destroyed. Bran then took up the story. The man, who was called Llassar Llaesgyvnewid, and his wife Kymideu Kymeinvoll, come across to Britain, where Bran took them in, and in return for his kindness they gave him the cauldron. And since then they had filled the land with their descendants, who prospered everywhere and dwelt in strong fortified burgs and had the best weapons that ever were seen.

So Matholwch received the cauldron along with his bride, and sailed back to Ireland, where Branwen entertained the lords and ladies of the land, and gave to each, as he or she took leave, "either a clasp or a ring or a royal jewel to keep, such as it was honourable to be seen departing with." And when the year was out Branwen bore a son to Matholwch, whose name was called Gwern.

The Punishment of Branwen

There occurs now an unintelligible place in the story. In the second year, it appears, and not till then, the men of Ireland grew indignant over the insult to their king committed by Evnissyen, and took revenge for it by having Branwen degraded to the position of a cook, and they caused the butcher every day to give her a blow on the ears. They also forbade all ships and ferry-boats to cross to Cambria, and any who came thence into Ireland were imprisoned so that news of Branwen's ill-treatment might not come to the ears of Bran. But Branwen reared up a young starling in a corner of her kneading-trough, and one day she tied a letter under its wing and taught it what to do. It flew away towards Britain, and finding Bran at Caer Seiont in Arvon, it lit on his shoulder, ruffling its feathers, and the letter was found and read. Bran immediately prepared a great hosting for Ireland, and sailed thither with a fleet of ships, leaving his land of Britain under his son Caradawc and six other chiefs.

The Invasion of Bran

Soon there came messengers to Matholwch telling him of a wondrous sight they had seen; a wood was growing on the sea, and beside the wood a mountain with a high ridge in the middle of it, and two lakes, one at each side. And wood and mountain moved towards the shore of Ireland. Branwen is called up to explain, if she could, what this meant. She tells them the wood is the masts and yards of the fleet of Britain, and the mountain is Bran, her brother, coming into shoal water, "for no ship can contain him"; the ridge is his nose, the lakes his two eyes.[1]

The King of Ireland and his lords at once took counsel together how they might meet this danger; and the plan they agreed upon was as follows: A huge

[1] Compare the description of Mac Cecht in the tale of the Hostel of De Derga, p. 173.

hall should be built, big enough to hold Bran—this, it was hoped, would placate him—there should be a great feast made there for himself and his men, and Matholwch should give over the kingdom of Ireland to him and do homage. All this was done by Branwen's advice. But the Irish added a crafty device of their own. From two brackets on each of the hundred pillars in the hall should be hung two leather bags, with an armed warrior in each of them ready to fall upon the guests when the moment should arrive.

The Meal-bags

Evnissyen, however, wandered into the hall before the rest of the host, and scanning the arrangements "with fierce and savage looks," he saw the bags which hung from the pillars. "What is in this bag?" said he to one of the Irish. "Meal, good soul," said the Irishman. Evnissyen laid his hand on the bag, and felt about with his fingers till he came to the head of the man within it. Then "he squeezed the head till he felt his fingers meet together in the brain through the bone." He went to the next bag, and asked the same question. "Meal," said the Irish attendant, but Evnissyen crushed this warrior's head also, and thus he did with all the two hundred bags, even in the case of one warrior whose head was covered with an iron helm.

Then the feasting began, and peace and concord reigned, and Matholwch laid down the sovranty of Ireland, which was conferred on the boy Gwern. And they all fondled and caressed the fair child till he came to Evnissyen, who suddenly seized him and flung him into the blazing fire on the hearth. Branwen would have leaped after him, but Bran held her back. Then there was arming apace, and tumult and shouting,

" Evnissyen laid his hand on the bag "

" I will not let it go "

and the Irish and British hosts closed in battle and fought until the fall of night.

Death of Evnissyen

But at night the Irish heated the magic cauldron and threw into it the bodies of their dead, who came out next day as good as ever, but dumb. When Evnissyen saw this he was smitten with remorse for having brought the men of Britain into such a strait: "Evil betide me if I find not a deliverance therefrom." So he hid himself among the Irish dead, and was flung into the cauldron with the rest at the end of the second day, when he stretched himself out so that he rent the cauldron into four pieces, and his own heart burst with the effort, and he died.

The Wonderful Head

In the end, all the Irishmen were slain, and all but seven of the British besides Bran, who was wounded in the foot with a poisoned arrow. Among the seven were Pryderi and Manawyddan. Bran then commanded them to cut off his head. "And take it with you," he said, "to London, and there bury it in the White Mount[1] looking towards France, and no foreigner shall invade the land while it is there. On the way the Head will talk to you, and be as pleasant company as ever in life. In Harlech ye will be feasting seven years and the birds of Rhiannon will sing to you. And at Gwales in Penvro ye will be feasting fourscore years, and the Head will talk to you and be uncorrupted till ye open the door looking towards Cornwall. After that ye may no longer tarry, but set forth to London and bury the Head."

Then the seven cut off the head of Bran and went

[1] Where the Tower of London now stands.

forth, and Branwen with them, to do his bidding. But when Branwen came to land at Aber Alaw she cried, "Woe is me that I was ever born; two islands have been destroyed because of me." And she uttered a loud groan, and her heart broke. They made her a four-sided grave on the banks of the Alaw, and the place was called *Ynys Branwen* to this day.[1]

The seven found that in the absence of Bran, Caswallan son of Beli had conquered Britain and slain the six captains of Caradawc. By magic art he had thrown on Caradawc the Veil of Illusion, and Caradawc saw only the sword which slew and slew, but not him who wielded it, and his heart broke for grief at the sight.

They then went to Harlech and remained there seven years listening to the singing of the birds of Rhiannon —"all the songs they had ever heard were unpleasant compared thereto." Then they went to Gwales in Penvro and found a fair and spacious hall overlooking the ocean. When they entered it they forgot all the sorrow of the past and all that had befallen them, and remained there fourscore years in joy and mirth, the wondrous Head talking to them as if it were alive. And bards call this "the Entertaining of the Noble Head." Three doors were in the hall, and one of them which looked to Cornwall and to Aber Henvelyn was closed, but the other two were open. At the end of the time, Heilyn son of Gwyn said, "Evil betide me if I do not open the door to see if what was said is true." And he opened it, and at once remembrance and sorrow fell upon them, and they set forth at once for London and buried the Head in the White Mount, where it remained

[1] These stories, in Ireland and in Wales, always attach themselves to actual burial-places. In 1813 a funeral urn containing ashes and half-burnt bones was found in the spot traditionally supposed to be Branwen's sepulchre.

until Arthur dug it up, for he would not have the land defended but by the strong arm. And this was "the Third Fatal Disclosure" in Britain.

So ends this wild tale, which is evidently full of mythological elements, the key to which has long been lost. The touches of Northern ferocity which occur in it have made some critics suspect the influence of Norse or Icelandic literature in giving it its present form. The character of Evnissyen would certainly lend countenance to this conjecture. The typical mischief-maker of course occurs in purely Celtic sagas, but not commonly in combination with the heroic strain shown in Evnissyen's end, nor does the Irish "poison-tongue" ascend to anything like the same height of daimonic malignity.

The Tale of Pryderi and Manawyddan

After the events of the previous tales Pryderi and Manawyddan retired to the dominions of the former, and Manawyddan took to wife Rhiannon, the mother of his friend. There they lived happily and prosperously till one day, while they were at the Gorsedd, or Mound, near Narberth, a peal of thunder was heard and a thick mist fell so that nothing could be seen all round. When the mist cleared away, behold, the land was bare before them—neither houses nor people nor cattle nor crops were to be seen, but all was desert and uninhabited. The palace of Narberth was still standing, but it was empty and desolate—none remained except Pryderi and Manawyddan and their wives, Kicva and Rhiannon.

Two years they lived on the provisions they had, and on the prey they killed, and on wild honey ; and then they began to be weary. "Let us go into Lloegyr,"[1]

[1] Saxon Britain.

then said Manawyddan, "and seek out some craft to support ourselves." So they went to Hereford and settled there, and Manawyddan and Pryderi began to make saddles and housings, and Manawyddan decorated them with blue enamel as he had learned from a great craftsman, Llasar Llaesgywydd. After a time, however, the other saddlers of Hereford, finding that no man would purchase any but the work of Manawyddan, conspired to kill them. And Pryderi would have fought with them, but Manawyddan held it better to withdraw elsewhere, and so they did.

They settled then in another city, where they made shields such as never were seen, and here, too, in the end, the rival craftsmen drove them out. And this happened also in another town where they made shoes; and at last they resolved to go back to Dyfed. Then they gathered their dogs about them and lived by hunting as before.

One day they started a wild white boar, and chased him in vain until he led them up to a vast and lofty castle, all newly built in a place where they had never seen a building before. The boar ran into the castle, the dogs followed him, and Pryderi, against the counsel of Manawyddan, who knew there was magic afoot, went in to seek for the dogs.

He found in the centre of the court a marble fountain beside which stood a golden bowl on a marble slab, and being struck by the rich workmanship of the bowl, he laid hold of it to examine it, when he could neither withdraw his hand nor utter a single sound, but he remained there, transfixed and dumb, beside the fountain.

Manawyddan went back to Narberth and told the story to Rhiannon. "An evil companion hast thou been," said she, "and a good companion hast thou lost."

Next day she went herself to explore the castle. She found Pryderi still clinging to the bowl and unable to speak. She also, then, laid hold of the bowl, when the same fate befell her, and immediately afterwards came a peal of thunder, and a heavy mist fell, and when it cleared off the castle had vanished with all that it contained, including the two spell-bound wanderers.

Manawyddan then went back to Narberth, where only Kicva, Pryderi's wife, now remained. And when she saw none but herself and Manawyddan in the place, "she sorrowed so that she cared not whether she lived or died." When Manawyddan saw this he said to her, "Thou art in the wrong if through fear of me thou grievest thus. I declare to thee were I in the dawn of youth I would keep my faith unto Pryderi, and unto thee also will I keep it." "Heaven reward thee," she said, "and that is what I deemed of thee." And thereupon she took courage and was glad.

Kicva and Manawyddan then again tried to support themselves by shoemaking in Lloegyr, but the same hostility drove them back to Dyfed. This time, however, Manawyddan took back with him a load of wheat, and he sowed it, and he prepared three crofts for a wheat crop. Thus the time passed till the fields were ripe. And he looked at one of the crofts and said, "I will reap this to-morrow." But on the morrow when he went out in the grey dawn he found nothing there but bare straw—every ear had been cut off from the stalk and carried away.

Next day it was the same with the second croft. But on the following night he armed himself and sat up to watch the third croft to see who was plundering him. At midnight, as he watched, he heard a loud noise, and behold, a mighty host of mice came pouring into the croft, and they climbed up each on a stalk and nibbled off the ears and made away with them. He chased them in anger, but they fled far faster than he could run, all save one which was slower in its movements, and this he barely managed to overtake, and he bound it into his glove and took it home to Narberth, and told Kicva what had happened. "To-morrow," he said, "I will hang the robber I have caught," but Kicva thought it beneath his dignity to take vengeance on a mouse.

Next day he went up to the Mound of Narberth and set up two forks for a gallows on the highest part of the hill. As he was doing this a poor scholar came towards him, and he was the first person Manawyddan had seen in Dyfed, except his own companions, since the enchantment began.

The scholar asked him what he was about and begged him to let go the mouse—"Ill doth it become a man of thy rank to touch such a reptile as this." "I will not let it go, by Heaven," said Manawyddan, and by that he abode, although the scholar offered him a pound of money to let it go free. "I care not," said the scholar, "except that I would not see a man of rank touching such a reptile," and with that he went his way.

As Manawyddan was placing the cross-beam on the two forks of his gallows, a priest came towards him riding on a horse with trappings, and the same conversation ensued. The priest offered three pounds for the mouse's life, but Manawyddan refused to take any price for it. "Willingly, lord, do thy good pleasure," said the priest, and he, too, went his way.

Then Manawyddan put a noose about the mouse's neck and was about to draw it up when he saw coming towards him a bishop with a great retinue of sumpter-horses and attendants. And he stayed his work and asked the bishop's blessing. "Heaven's blessing be unto thee," said the bishop; "what work art thou upon?" "Hanging a thief," replied Manawyddan. The bishop offered seven pounds "rather than see a man of thy rank destroying so vile a reptile." Manawyddan refused. Four-and-twenty pounds was then offered, and then as much again, then all the bishop's horses and baggage—all in vain. "Since for this thou wilt not," said the bishop, "do it at whatever price thou wilt." "I will do so," said Manawyddan; "I will that Rhiannon and Pryderi be free." "That thou shalt have," said the (pretended) bishop. Then Manawyddan demands that the enchantment and illusion be taken off for ever from the seven Cantrevs of Dyfed, and finally insists that the bishop shall tell him who the mouse is and why the enchantment was laid on the country. "I am Llwyd son of Kilcoed," replies the enchanter, "and the mouse is my wife; but that she is pregnant thou hadst never overtaken her." He goes on with an explanation which takes us back to the first *Mabinogi* of the Wedding of Rhiannon. The charm was cast on the land to avenge the ill that was done Llwyd's friend, Gwawl son of Clud, with whom Pryderi's father and his knights had played "Badger in the Bag" at the court of Hevydd Hēn. The mice were the lords and ladies of Llwyd's court.

The enchanter is then made to promise that no further vengeance shall be taken on Pryderi, Rhiannon, or Manawyddan, and the two spell-bound captives having been restored, the mouse is released. "Then Llwyd struck her with a magic wand, and she was changed into a young woman, the fairest ever seen." And on looking round Manawyddan saw all the land tilled and peopled as in its best state, and full of herds and dwellings. "What bondage," he asks, "has there been upon Pryderi and Rhiannon?" "Pryderi has had the knockers of the gate of my palace about his neck, and Rhiannon has had the collars of the asses after they have been carrying hay about her neck." And such had been their bondage.

The Tale of Math Son of Māthonwy

The previous tale was one of magic and illusion in which the mythological element is but faint. In that which we have now to consider we are, however, in a distinctly mythological region. The central motive of the tale shows us the Powers of Light contending with those of the Under-world for the prized possessions of the latter, in this case a herd of magic swine. We are introduced in the beginning of the story to the deity, Māth, of whom the bard tells us that he was unable to exist unless his feet lay in the lap of a maiden, except when the land was disturbed by war.[1] Māth is represented as lord of Gwynedd, while Pryderi rules over the one-and-twenty cantrevs of the south. With Māth were his nephews Gwydion and Gilvaethwy sons of Dōn, who went the circuit of the land in his stead, while Māth lay with his feet in the lap of the fairest maiden of the land and time, Goewin daughter of Pebin of Dōl Pebin in Arvon.

Gwydion and the Swine of Pryderi

Gilvaethwy fell sick of love for Goewin, and confided the secret to his brother Gwydion, who undertook to help him to his desire. So he went to Māth one day, and asked his leave to go to Pryderi and beg from him the gift, for Māth, of a herd of swine which had been bestowed on him by Arawn King of Annwn. "They are beasts," he said, "such as never were known in

[1] This is a distorted reminiscence of the practice which seems to have obtained in the courts of Welsh princes, that a high officer should hold the king's feet in his lap while he sat at meat.

this island before . . . their flesh is better than the flesh of oxen." Math bade him go, and he and Gilvaethwy started with ten companions for Dyfed. They came to Pryderi's palace in the guise of bards, and Gwydion, after being entertained at a feast, was asked to tell a tale to the court. After delighting every one with his discourse he begged for a gift of the swine. But Pryderi was under a compact with his people neither to sell nor give them until they had produced double their number in the land. "Thou mayest exchange them, though," said Gwydion, and thereupon he made by magic arts an illusion of twelve horses magnificently caparisoned, and twelve hounds, and gave them to Pryderi and made off with the swine as fast as possible, "for," said he to his companions, "the illusion will not last but from one hour to the same to-morrow."

The intended result came to pass—Pryderi invaded the land to recover his swine, Math went to meet him in arms, and Gilvaethwy seized his opportunity and made Goewin his wife, although she was unwilling.

Death of Pryderi

The war was decided by a single combat between Gwydion and Pryderi. "And by force of strength and fierceness, and by the magic and charms of Gwydion, Pryderi was slain. And at Maen Tyriawc, above Melenryd, was he buried, and there is his grave."

The Penance of Gwydion and Gilvaethwy

When Math came back he found what Gilvaethwy had done, and he took Goewin to be his queen, but Gwydion and Gilvaethwy went into outlawry, and dwelt on the borders of the land. At last they came and submitted themselves for punishment to Math. "Ye cannot compensate me my shame, setting aside the death of Pryderi," he said, "but since ye come hither to be at my will, I shall begin your punishment forthwith." So he turned them both into deer, and bade them come hither again in a twelvemonth.

They came at the appointed time, bringing with them a young fawn. And the fawn was brought into human shape and baptized, and Gwydion and Gilvaethwy were changed into two wild swine. At the next year's end they came back with a young one who was treated as the fawn before him, and the brothers were made into wolves. Another year passed; they came back again with a young wolf as before, and this time their penance was deemed complete, and their human nature was restored to them, and Math gave orders to have them washed and anointed, and nobly clad as was befitting.

The Children of Arianrod: Dylan

The question then arose of appointing another virgin foot-holder, and Gwydion suggests his sister, Arianrod. She attends for the purpose, and Math asks her if she is a virgin. "I know not, lord, other than that I am," she says. But she failed in a magical test imposed by Math, and gave birth to two sons. One of these was named Dylan, "Son of the Wave," evidently a Cymric sea-deity. So soon as he was baptized "he plunged into the sea and swam as well as the best fish that was therein. . . . Beneath him no wave ever broke." A wild sea-poetry hangs about his name in Welsh legend. On his death, which took place, it is said, at the hand of his uncle Govannon, all the waves of Britain and Ireland wept for him. The roar of the incoming tide at the mouth of the river Conway is still called the "death-groan of Dylan."

Llew Llaw Gyffes

The other infant was seized by Gwydion and brought up under his protection. Like other solar heroes, he grew very rapidly ; when he was four he was as big as if he were eight, and the comeliest youth that ever was seen. One day Gwydion took him to visit his mother Arianrod. She hated the children who had exposed her false pretensions, and upbraided Gwydion for bringing the boy into her sight. "What is his name ?" she asked. "Verily," said Gwydion, "he has not yet a name." "Then I lay this destiny upon him," said Arianrod, "that he shall never have a name till one is given him by me." On this Gwydion went forth in wrath, and remained in his castle of Caer Dathyl that night.

Though the fact does not appear in this tale, it must be remembered that Gwydion is, in the older mythology, the father of Arianrod's children.

How Llew Got his Name

He was resolved to have a name for his son. Next day he went to the strand below Caer Arianrod, bringing the boy with him. Here he sat down by the beach, and in his character of a master of magic he made himself look like a shoemaker, and the boy like an apprentice, and he began to make shoes out of sedges and seaweed, to which he gave the semblance of Cordovan leather. Word was brought to Arianrod of the wonderful shoes that were being made by a strange cobbler, and she sent her measure for a pair. Gwydion made them too large. She sent it again, and he made them too small. Then she came herself to be fitted. While this was going on, a wren came and lit on the boat's mast, and the boy, taking up a bow, shot an arrow that transfixed the leg between the sinew and the bone. Arianrod admired the brilliant shot. "Verily," she said, "with a steady hand (*llaw gyffes*) did the lion (*llew*) hit it." "No thanks to thee," cried Gwydion, "now he has got a name. Llew Llaw Gyffes shall he be called henceforward."

We have seen that the name really means the same thing as the Gaelic Lugh Lamfada, Lugh (Light) of the Long Arm; so that we have here an instance of a legend growing up round a misunderstood name inherited from a half-forgotten mythology.

How Llew Took Arms

The shoes went back immediately to sedges and seaweed again, and Arianrod, angry at being tricked, laid a new curse on the boy. "He shall never bear arms till I invest him with them." But Gwydion, going to Caer Arianrod with the boy in the semblance of two bards, makes by magic art the illusion of a foray of armed men round the castle. Arianrod gives them weapons to help in the defence, and thus again finds herself tricked by the superior craft of Gwydion.

The Flower-Wife of Llew

Next she said, "He shall never have a wife of the race that now inhabits this earth." This raised a difficulty beyond the powers of even Gwydion, and he went to Math, the supreme master of magic. "Well," said Math, "we will seek, I and thou, to form a wife for him out of flowers." "So they took the blossoms of the oak, and the blossoms of the broom, and the blossoms of the meadow-sweet, and produced from them a maiden, the fairest and most graceful that man ever saw. And they baptized her, and gave her the name of Blodeuwedd, or Flower-face." They wedded her to Llew, and gave them the cantrev of Dinodig to reign over, and there Llew and his bride dwelt for a season, happy, and beloved by all.

Betrayal of Llew

But Blodeuwedd was not worthy of her beautiful name and origin. One day when Llew was away on a visit with Māth, a lord named Gronw Pebyr came a-hunting by the palace of Llew, and Blodeuwedd loved him from the moment she looked upon him. That night they slept together, and the next, and the next, and then they planned how to be rid of Llew for ever. But Llew, like the Gothic solar hero Siegfried, is invulnerable except under special circumstances, and Blodeuwedd has to learn from him how he may be slain. This she does under pretence of care for his welfare. The problem is a hard one. Llew can only be killed by a spear which has been a year in making, and has only been worked on during the Sacrifice of the Host on Sundays. Furthermore, he cannot be slain within a house or without, on horseback or on foot. The only way, in fact, is that he should stand with one foot on a dead buck and the other in a cauldron, which is to be used for a bath and thatched with a roof—if he is wounded while in this position with a spear made as directed the wound may be fatal, not otherwise. After a year, during which Gronw wrought at the spear, Blodeuwedd begged Llew to show her more fully what she must guard against, and he took up the required position to please her. Gronw, lurking in a wood hard by, hurled the deadly spear, and the head, which was poisoned, sank into Llew's body, but the shaft broke off. Then Llew changed into an eagle, and with a loud scream he soared up into the air and was no more seen, and Gronw took his castle and lands and added them to his own.

These tidings at last reached Gwydion and Math, and Gwydion set out to find Llew. He came to the house of a vassal of his, from whom he learned that a sow that he had disappeared every day and could not be traced, but it came home duly each night. Gwydion followed the sow, and it went far away to the brook since called Nant y Llew, where it stopped under a tree and began feeding. Gwydion looked to see what it ate, and found that it fed on putrid flesh that dropped from an eagle sitting aloft on the tree, and it seemed to him that the eagle was Llew. Gwydion sang to it, and brought it gradually down the tree till it came to his knee, when he struck it with his magic wand and restored it to the shape of Llew, but worn to skin and bone—" no one ever saw a more piteous sight."

The Healing of Llew

When Llew was healed, he and Gwydion took vengeance on their foes. Blodeuwedd was changed into an owl and bidden to shun the light of day, and Gronw was slain by a cast of the spear of Llew that passed through a slab of stone to reach him, and the slab with the hole through it made by the spear of Llew remains by the bank of the river Cynvael in Ardudwy to this day. And Llew took possession, for the second time, of his lands, and ruled them prosperously all his days.

The four preceding tales are called the Four Branches of the Mabinogi, and of the collection called the " Mabinogion " they form the most ancient and important part.

The Dream of Maxen Wledig

Following the order of the tales in the "Mabinogion," as presented in Mr. Nutt's edition, we come next to one which is a pure work of invention, with no mythical or legendary element at all. It recounts how Maxen Wledig, Emperor of Rome, had a vivid dream, in which he was led into a strange country, where he saw a king in an ivory chair carving chessmen with a steel file from a rod of gold. By him, on a golden throne, was the fairest of maidens he had ever beheld. Waking, he found himself in love with the dream-maiden, and sent messengers far and wide to discover, if they could, the country and people that had appeared to him. They were found in Britain. Thither went Maxen, and wooed and wedded the maiden. In his absence a usurper laid hold of his empire in Rome, but with the aid of his British friends he reconquered his dominions, and many of them settled there with him, while others went home to Britain. The latter took with them foreign wives, but, it is said, cut out their tongues, lest they should corrupt the speech of the Britons. Thus early and thus powerful was the devotion to their tongue of the Cymry, of whom the mythical bard Taliesin prophesied:

> "Their God they will praise,
> Their speech they will keep,
> Their land they will lose,
> Except wild Walia."

The Story of Lludd and Llevelys

This tale is associated with the former one in the section entitled Romantic British History. It tells how Lludd son of Beli, and his brother Llevelys, ruled respectively over Britain and France, and how Lludd sought his brother's aid to stay the three plagues that were harassing the land. These three plagues were, first, the presence of a demoniac race called the Coranians; secondly, a fearful scream that was heard in every home in Britain on every May-eve, and scared the people out of their senses; thirdly, the unaccountable disappearance of all provisions in the king's court every night, so that nothing that was not consumed by the household could be found the next morning. Lludd and Llevelys talked over these matters through a brazen tube, for the Coranians could hear everything that was said if once the winds got hold of it—a property also attributed to Math, son of Mathonwy. Llevelys destroyed the Coranians by giving to Lludd a quantity of poisonous insects which were to be bruised up and scattered over the people at an assembly. These insects would slay the Coranians, but the people of Britain would be immune to them. The scream Llevelys explained as proceeding from two dragons, which fought each other once a year. They were to be slain by being intoxicated with mead, which was to be placed in a pit dug in the very centre of Britain, which was found on measurement to be at Oxford. The provisions, said Llevelys, were taken away by a giant wizard, for whom Lludd watched as directed, and overcame him in combat, and made him his faithful vassal thenceforward. Thus Lludd and Llevelys freed the island from its three plagues.

Tales of Arthur

We next come to five Arthurian tales, one of which, the tale of Kilhwch and Olwen, is the only native Arthurian legend which has come down to us in Welsh literature. The rest, as we have seen, are more or less reflections from the Arthurian literature as developed by foreign hands on the Continent.

Kilhwch and Olwen

Kilhwch was son to Kilydd and his wife Goleuddydd, and is said to have been cousin to Arthur. His mother having died, Kilydd took another wife, and she, jealous of her stepson, laid on him a quest which promised to be long and dangerous. "I declare," she said, "that it is thy destiny"—the Gael would have said *geis*—"not to be suited with a wife till thou obtain Olwen daughter of Yspaddaden Penkawr."[1] And Kilhwch reddened at the name, and "love of the maiden diffused itself through all his frame." By his father's advice he set out to Arthur's Court to learn how and where he might find and woo her.

A brilliant passage then describes the youth in the flower of his beauty, on a noble steed caparisoned with gold, and accompanied by two brindled white-breasted greyhounds with collars of rubies, setting forth on his journey to King Arthur. "And the blade of grass bent not beneath him, so light was his courser's tread."

Kilhwch at Arthur's Court

After some difficulties with the Porter and with Arthur's seneschal, Kai, who did not wish to admit the lad while the company were sitting at meat, Kilhwch was brought into the presence of the King, and declared his name and his desire. "I seek this boon," he said, "from thee and likewise at the hands of thy warriors," and he then enumerates an immense list full of mythological personages and details—Bedwyr, Gwyn ap Nudd, Kai, Manawyddan,[2] Geraint, and many others, including "Morvran son of Tegid, whom no one struck at in the battle of Camlan by reason of his ugliness; all thought he was a devil," and "Sandde Bryd Angel, whom no one touched with a spear in the battle of Camlan because of his beauty; all thought he was a ministering angel."

[1] "Hawthorn, King of the Giants."

[2] The gods of the family of Dōn are thus conceived as servitors to Arthur, who in this story is evidently the god Artaius.

The list extends to many scores of names and includes many women, as, for instance, "Creiddylad the daughter of Lludd of the Silver Hand—she was the most splendid maiden in the three Islands of the Mighty, and for her Gwythyr the son of Greidawl and Gwyn the son of Nudd fight every first of May till doom," and the two Iseults and Arthur's Queen, Gwenhwyvar. "All these did Kilydd's son Kilhwch adjure to obtain his boon."

Arthur, however, had never heard of Olwen nor of her kindred. He promised to seek for her, but at the end of a year no tidings of her could be found, and Kilhwch declared that he would depart and leave Arthur shamed. Kai and Bedwyr, with the guide Kynddelig, are at last bidden to go forth on the quest.

Servitors of Arthur

These personages are very different from those who are called by the same names in Malory or Tennyson. Kai, it is said, could go nine days under water. He could render himself at will as tall as a forest tree. So hot was his physical constitution that nothing he bore in his hand could get wetted in the heaviest rain. "Very subtle was Kai." As for Bedwyr—the later Sir Bedivere—we are told that none equalled him in swiftness, and that, though one-armed, he was a match for any three warriors on the field of battle; his lance made a wound equal to those of nine. Besides these three there went also on the quest Gwrhyr, who knew all tongues, and Gwalchmai son of Arthur's sister Gwyar, and Menw, who could make the party invisible by magic spells.

Custennin

The party journeyed till at last they came to a great castle before which was a flock of sheep kept by a shepherd who had by him a mastiff big as a horse. The breath of this shepherd, we are told, could burn up a tree. "He let no occasion pass without doing some hurt or harm." However, he received the party well, told them that he was Custennin, brother of Yspaddaden whose castle stood before them, and brought them home to his wife. The wife turned out to be a sister of Kilhwch's mother Goleuddydd, and she was rejoiced at seeing her nephew, but sorrowful at the thought that he had come in search of Olwen, "for none ever returned from that quest alive." Custennin and his family, it appears, have suffered much at the hands of Yspaddaden—all their sons but one being slain, because Yspaddaden envied his brother his share of their patrimony. So they associated themselves with the heroes in their quest.

Olwen of the White Track

Next day Olwen came down to the herdsman's house as usual, for she was wont to wash her hair there every Saturday, and each time she did so she left all her rings in the vessel and never sent for them again. She is described in one of those pictorial passages in which the Celtic passion for beauty has found such exquisite utterance.

"The maiden was clothed in a robe of flame-coloured silk, and about her neck was a collar of ruddy gold on which were precious emeralds and rubies. More yellow was her head than the flower of the broom, and her skin was whiter than the foam of the wave, and fairer were her hands and her fingers than the blossoms of the wood-anemone amidst the spray of the meadow fountain. The eye of the trained hawk, the glance of the three-mewed falcon, was not brighter than hers.

Her bosom was more snowy than the breast of the white swan, her cheek was redder than the reddest roses. Whoso beheld her was filled with her love. Four white trefoils sprang up wherever she trod. And therefore was she called Olwen."[1]

Kilhwch and she conversed together and loved each other, and she bade him go and ask her of her father and deny him nothing that he might demand. She had pledged her faith not to wed without his will, for his life would only last till the time of her espousals.

Yspaddaden

Next day the party went to the castle and saw Yspaddaden. He put them off with various excuses, and as they left flung after them a poisoned dart. Bedwyr caught it and flung it back, wounding him in the knee, and Yspaddaden cursed him in language of extraordinary vigour; the words seem to crackle and spit like flame. Thrice over this happened, and at last Yspaddaden declared what must be done to win Olwen.

The Tasks of Kilhwch

A long series of tasks follows. A vast hill is to be ploughed, sown, and reaped in one day; only Amathaon son of Dōn can do it, and he will not. Govannon, the smith, is to rid the ploughshare at each headland, and he will not do it. The two dun oxen of Gwlwlyd are to draw the plough, and he will not lend them. Honey nine times sweeter than that of the bee must be got to make bragget for the wedding feast. A magic cauldron, a magic basket out of which comes any meat that a man desires, a magic horn, the sword of Gwrnach the Giant

[1] "She of the White Track." Compare the description of Etain, pp. 157, 158.

—all these must be won; and many other secret and difficult things, some forty in all, before Kilhwch can call Olwen his own. The most difficult quest is that of obtaining the comb and scissors that are between the two ears of Twrch Trwyth, a king transformed into a monstrous boar. To hunt the boar a number of other quests must be accomplished—the whelp of Greid son of Eri is to be won, and a certain leash to hold him, and a certain collar for the leash, and a chain for the collar, and Mabon son of Modron for the huntsman and the horse of Gweddw to carry Mabon, and Gwyn son of Nudd to help, "whom God placed over the brood of devils in Annwn . . . he will never be spared them," and so forth to an extent which makes the famous *eric* of the sons of Turenn seem trifling by comparison. "Difficulties shalt thou meet with, and nights without sleep, in seeking this [bride price], and if thou obtain it not, neither shalt thou have my daughter." Kilhwch has one answer for every demand: "It will be easy for me to accomplish this, although thou mayest think that it will not be easy. And I shall gain thy daughter and thou shalt lose thy life."

So they depart on their way to fulfil the tasks, and on their way home they fall in with Gwrnach the Giant, whose sword Kai, pretending to be a sword-polisher, obtains by a stratagem. On reaching Arthur's Court again, and telling the King what they have to do, he promises his aid. First of the marvels they accomplished was the discovery and liberation of Mabon son of Modron, "who was taken from his mother when three nights old, and it is not known where he is now, nor whether he is living or dead." Gwrhyr inquires of him from the Ousel of Cilgwri, who is so old that a smith's anvil on which he was wont to peck has been worn to the size of a nut, yet he has never heard of

Mabon. But he takes them to a beast older still, the Stag of Redynvre, and so on to the Owl of Cwm Cawlwyd, and the Eagle of Gwern Abwy, and the Salmon of Llyn Llyw, the oldest of living things, and at last they find Mabon imprisoned in the stone dungeon of Gloucester, and with Arthur's help they release him, and so the second task is fulfilled. In one way or another, by stratagem, or valour, or magic art, every achievement is accomplished, including the last and most perilous one, that of obtaining "the blood of the black witch Orddu, daughter of the white witch Orwen, of Penn Nart Govid on the confines of Hell." The combat here is very like that of Finn in the cave of Keshcorran, but Arthur at last cleaves the hag in twain, and Kaw of North Britain takes her blood.

So then they set forth for the castle of Yspaddaden again, and he acknowledges defeat. Goreu son of Custennin cuts off his head, and that night Olwen became the happy bride of Kilhwch, and the hosts of Arthur dispersed, every man to his own land.

The Dream of Rhonabwy

Rhonabwy was a man-at-arms under Madawc son of Maredudd, whose brother Iorwerth rose in rebellion against him ; and Rhonabwy went with the troops of Madawc to put him down. Going with a few companions into a mean hut to rest for the night, he lies down to sleep on a yellow calf-skin by the fire, while his friends lie on filthy couches of straw and twigs. On the calf-skin he has a wonderful dream. He sees before him the court and camp of Arthur—here the *quasi*-historical king, neither the legendary deity of the former tale nor the Arthur of the French chivalrous romances—as he moves towards Mount Badon for his great battle with the heathen. A character named Iddawc is his guide to the King, who smiles at Rhonabwy and his friends, and asks: "Where, Iddawc, didst thou find these little men?" "I found them, lord, up yonder on the road." "It pitieth me," said Arthur, "that men of such stature as these should have the island in their keeping, after the men that guarded it of yore." Rhonabwy has his attention directed to a stone in the King's ring. "It is one of the properties of that stone to enable thee to remember that which thou seest here to-night, and hadst thou not seen the stone, thou wouldst never have been able to remember aught thereof."

The different heroes and companions that compose Arthur's army are minutely described, with all the brilliant colour and delicate detail so beloved by the Celtic fabulist. The chief incident narrated is a game of chess that takes place between Arthur and the knight Owain son of Urien. While the game goes on, first the knights of Arthur harry and disturb the Ravens of Owain, but Arthur, when Owain complains, only says: "Play thy game." Afterwards the Ravens have the better of it, and it is Owain's turn to bid Arthur attend to his game. Then Arthur took the golden chessmen and crushed them to dust in his hand, and besought Owain to quiet his Ravens, which was done, and peace reigned again. Rhonabwy, it is said, slept three days and nights on the calf-skin before awaking from his wondrous dream. An epilogue declares that no bard is expected to know this tale by heart and without a book, "because of the various colours that were upon the horses, and the many wondrous colours of the arms and of the panoply, and of the precious scarfs, and of the virtue-bearing stones." The "Dream of Rhonabwy" is rather a gorgeous vision of the past than a story in the ordinary sense of the word.

The Lady of the Fountain

We have here a Welsh reproduction of the *Conte* entitled "Le Chevalier au lion" of Chrestien de Troyes. The principal personage in the tale is Owain son of Urien, who appears in a character as foreign to the spirit of Celtic legend as it was familiar on the Continent, that of knight-errant.

The Adventure of Kymon

We are told in the introduction that Kymon, a knight of Arthur's Court, had a strange and unfortunate adventure. Riding forth in search of some deed of chivalry to do, he came to a splendid castle, where he was hospitably received by four-and-twenty damsels, of whom "the least lovely was more lovely than Gwenhwyvar, the wife of Arthur, when she has appeared loveliest at the Offering on the Day of the Nativity, or at the feast of Easter." With them was a noble lord, who, after Kymon had eaten, asked of his business. Kymon explained that he was seeking for his match in combat. The lord of the castle smiled, and bade him proceed as follows: He should take the road up the valley and through a forest till he came to a glade with a mound in the midst of it. On the mound he would see a black man of huge stature with one foot and one eye, bearing a mighty iron club. He was wood-ward of that forest, and would have thousands of wild animals, stags, serpents, and what not, feeding around him. He would show Kymon what he was in quest of.

Kymon followed the instructions, and the black man directed him to where he should find a fountain under a great tree; by the side of it would be a silver bowl on a slab of marble. Kymon was to take the bowl and throw a bowlful of water on the slab, when a terrific storm of hail and thunder would follow—then there would break forth an enchanting music of singing birds —then would appear a knight in black armour riding on a coal-black horse, with a black pennon upon his lance. "And if thou dost not find trouble in that adventure, thou needst not seek it during the rest of thy life."

The Character of Welsh Romance

Here let us pause for a moment to point out how clearly we are in the region of mediæval romance, and how far from that of Celtic mythology. Perhaps the Celtic "Land of Youth" may have remotely suggested those regions of beauty and mystery into which the Arthurian knight rides in quest of adventure. But the scenery, the motives, the incidents, are altogether different. And how beautiful they are—how steeped in the magic light of romance! The colours live and glow, the forest murmurs in our ears, the breath of that springtime of our modern world is about us, as we follow the lonely rider down the grassy track into an unknown world of peril and delight. While in some respects the Continental tales are greater than the Welsh, more thoughtful, more profound, they do not approach them in the exquisite artistry with which the exterior aspect of things is rendered, the atmosphere of enchantment maintained, and the reader led, with ever-quickening interest, from point to point in the development of the tale. Nor are these Welsh tales a whit behind in the noble and chivalrous spirit which breathes through them. A finer school of character and of manners could hardly be found in literature. How strange that for many centuries this treasure beyond all price should have lain unnoticed in our midst! And how deep must be our gratitude to the nameless bards whose thought created it, and to the nobly inspired hand which first made it a possession for all the English-speaking world!

Defeat of Kymon

But to resume our story. Kymon did as he was bidden, the Black Knight appeared, silently they set lance in rest and charged. Kymon was flung to earth, while his enemy, not bestowing one glance upon him, passed the shaft of his lance through the rein of Kymon's horse and rode off with it in the direction whence he had come. Kymon went back afoot to the castle, where none asked him how he had sped, but they gave him a new horse, "a dark bay palfrey with nostrils as red as scarlet," on which he rode home to Caerleon.

Owain and the Black Knight

Owain was, of course, fired by the tale of Kymon, and next morning at the dawn of day he rode forth to seek for the same adventure. All passed as it had done in Kymon's case, but Owain wounded the Black Knight so sorely that he turned his horse and fled, Owain pursuing him hotly. They came to a "vast and resplendent castle." Across the drawbridge they rode, the outer portcullis of which fell as the Black Knight passed it. But so close at his heels was Owain that the portcullis fell behind him, cutting his horse in two behind the saddle, and he himself remained imprisoned between the outer gate of the drawbridge and the inner. While he was in this predicament a maiden came to him and gave him a ring. When he wore it with the stone reversed and clenched in his hand he would become invisible, and when the servants of the lord of the castle came for him he was to elude them and follow her.

This she did knowing apparently who he was, "for as a friend thou art the most sincere, and as a lover the most devoted."

Owain did as he was bidden, and the maiden concealed him. In that night a great lamentation was heard in the castle—its lord had died of the wound which Owain had given him. Soon afterwards Owain got sight of the mistress of the castle, and love of her took entire possession of him. Luned, the maiden who had rescued him, wooed her for him, and he became her husband, and lord of the Castle of the Fountain and all the dominions of the Black Knight. And he then defended the fountain with lance and sword as his forerunner had done, and made his defeated antagonists ransom themselves for great sums, which he bestowed among his barons and knights. Thus he abode for three years.

The Search for Owain

After this time Arthur, with his nephew Gwalchmai and with Kymon for guide, rode forth at the head of a host to search for tidings of Owain. They came to the fountain, and here they met Owain, neither knowing the other as their helms were down. And first Kai was overthrown, and then Gwalchmai and Owain fought, and after a while Gwalchmai was unhelmed. Owain said, "My lord Gwalchmai, I did not know thee; take my sword and my arms." Said Gwalchmai, "Thou, Owain, art the victor; take thou my sword." Arthur ended the contention in courtesy by taking the swords of both, and then they all rode to the Castle of the Fountain, where Owain entertained them with great joy. And he went back with Arthur to Caerleon, promising to his countess that he would remain there but three months and then return.

Owain Forgets his Lady

But at the Court of Arthur he forgot his love and his duty, and remained there three years. At the end of that time a noble lady came riding upon a horse caparisoned with gold, and she sought out Owain and took the ring from his hand. "Thus," she said, "shall be treated the deceiver, the traitor, the faithless, the disgraced, and the beardless." Then she turned her horse's head and departed. And Owain, overwhelmed with shame and remorse, fled from the sight of men and lived in a desolate country with wild beasts till his body wasted and his hair grew long and his clothing rotted away.

Owain and the Lion

In this guise, when near to death from exposure and want, he was taken in by a certain widowed countess and her maidens, and restored to strength by magic balsams; and although they besought him to remain with them, he rode forth again, seeking for lonely and desert lands. Here he found a lion in battle with a great serpent. Owain slew the serpent, and the lion followed him and played about him as if it had been a greyhound that he had reared. And it fed him by catching deer, part of which Owain cooked for himself, giving the rest to his lion to devour; and the beast kept watch over him by night.

Release of Luned

Owain next finds an imprisoned damsel, whose sighs he hears, though he cannot see her nor she him. Being questioned, she told him that her name was Luned—she was the handmaid of a countess whose husband had left her, "and he was the friend I loved best in the world." Two of the pages of the countess had traduced him, and because she defended him she was condemned to be burned if before a year was out he (namely, Owain son of Urien) had not appeared to deliver her. And the year would end to-morrow. On the next day Owain met the two youths leading Luned to execution and did battle with them. With the help of the lion he overcame them, rescued Luned, and returned to the Castle of the Fountain, where he was reconciled with his love. And he took her with him to Arthur's Court, and she was his wife there as long as she lived. Lastly comes an adventure in which, still aided by the lion, he vanquishes a black giant and releases four-and-twenty noble ladies, and the giant vows to give up his evil ways and keep a hospice for wayfarers as long as he should live.

"And thenceforth Owain dwelt at Arthur's Court, greatly beloved, as the head of his household, until he went away with his followers; and these were the army of three hundred ravens which Kenverchyn[1] had left him. And wherever Owain went with these he was victorious. And this is the tale of the Lady of the Fountain."

The Tale of Enid and Geraint

In this tale, which appears to be based on the "Erec" of Chrestien de Troyes, the main interest is neither mythological nor adventurous, but sentimental. How Geraint found and wooed his love as the daughter of a great lord fallen on evil days; how he jousted for her with Edeyrn, son of Nudd—a Cymric deity transformed into the "Knight of the Sparrowhawk"; how, lapped in love of her, he grew careless of his fame and his duty; how he misunderstood the words she

[1] There is no other mention of this Kenverchyn or of how Owain got his raven-army, also referred to in "The Dream of Rhonabwy." We have here evidently a piece of antique mythology embedded in a more modern fabric.

murmured over him as she deemed him sleeping, and doubted her faith; how despitefully he treated her; and in how many a bitter test she proved her love and loyalty—all these things have been made so familiar to English readers in Tennyson's "Enid" that they need not detain us here. Tennyson, in this instance, has followed his original very closely.

Legends of the Grail: The Tale of Peredur

The Tale of Peredur is one of great interest and significance in connexion with the origin of the Grail legend. Peredur corresponds to the Perceval of Chrestien de Troyes, to whom we owe the earliest extant poem on the Grail; but that writer left his Grail story unfinished, and we never learn from him what exactly the Grail was or what gave it its importance. When we turn for light to "Peredur," which undoubtedly represents a more ancient form of the legend, we find ourselves baffled. For "Peredur" may be described as the Grail story without the Grail.[1] The strange personages, objects, and incidents which form the usual setting for the entry upon the scene of this mystic treasure are all here; we breath the very atmosphere of the Grail Castle; but of the Grail itself there is no word. The story is concerned simply with the vengeance taken by the hero for the slaying of a kinsman, and for this end only are the mysteries of the Castle of Wonders displayed to him.

We learn at the opening of the tale that Peredur was in the significant position of being a seventh son. To be a seventh son was, in this world of mystical romance,

[1] Like the Breton Tale of "Peronnik the Fool," translated in "Le Foyer Bréton," by Emile Souvestre. The syllable *Per* which occurs in all forms of the hero's name means in Welsh and Cornish a bowl or vessel (Irish *coire*—see p. 35, note). No satisfactory derivation has in any case been found of the latter part of the name.

equivalent to being marked out by destiny for fortunes high and strange. His father, Evrawc, an earl of the North, and his six brothers had fallen in fight. Peredur's mother, therefore, fearing a similar fate for her youngest child, brought him up in a forest, keeping from him all knowledge of chivalry or warfare and of such things as war-horses or weapons. Here he grew up a simple rustic in manner and in knowledge, but of an amazing bodily strength and activity.

He Goes Forth in Quest of Adventure

One day he saw three knights on the borders of the forest. They were all of Arthur's Court—Gwalchmai, Geneir, and Owain. Entranced by the sight, he asked his mother what these beings were. "They are angels, my son," said she. "By my faith," said Peredur, "I will go and become an angel with them." He goes to meet them, and soon learns what they are. Owain courteously explains to him the use of a saddle, a shield, a sword, all the accoutrements of warfare; and Peredur that evening picked out a bony piebald draught-horse, and dressed him up in a saddle and trappings made of twigs, and imitated from those he had seen. Seeing that he was bent on going forth to deeds of chivalry, his mother gave him her blessing and sundry instructions, and bade him seek the Court of Arthur; "there there are the best, and the boldest, and the most beautiful of men."

His First Feat of Arms

Peredur mounted his Rosinante, took for weapons a handful of sharp-pointed stakes, and rode forth to Arthur's Court. Here the steward, Kai, rudely repulsed him for his rustic appearance, but a dwarf and dwarfess, who had been a year at the Court without speaking one word to any one there, cried: "Goodly Peredur, son of Evrawc; the welcome of Heaven be unto thee, flower of knights and light of chivalry." Kai chastised the dwarfs for breaking silence by lauding such a fellow as Peredur, and when the latter demanded to be brought to Arthur, bade him first go and overcome a stranger knight who had just challenged the whole Court by throwing a goblet of wine into the face of Gwenhwyvar, and whom all shrank from meeting. Peredur went out promptly to where the ruffian knight was swaggering up and down, awaiting an opponent, and in the combat that ensued pierced his skull with one of his sharp stakes and slew him. Owain then came out and found Peredur dragging his fallen enemy about. "What art thou doing there?" said Owain. "This iron coat," said Peredur, "will never come off from him; not by my efforts at any rate." So Owain showed him how to unfasten the armour, and Peredur took it, and the knight's weapons and horse, and rode forth to seek what further adventures might befall.

Here we have the character of *der reine Thor*, the valiant and pure-hearted simpleton, clearly and vividly drawn.

Peredur on leaving Arthur's Court had many encounters in which he triumphed with ease, sending the beaten knights to Caerleon-on-Usk with the message that he had overthrown them for the honour of Arthur and in his service, but that he, Peredur, would never come to the Court again till he had avenged the insult to the dwarfs upon Kai, who was accordingly reproved by Arthur and was greatly grieved thereat.

The Castle of Wonders

We now come into what the reader will immediately recognise as the atmosphere of the Grail legend. Peredur came to a castle beside a lake, where he found a venerable man with attendants about him who were fishing in the lake. As Peredur approached, the aged man rose and went into the castle, and Peredur saw that he was lame. Peredur entered, and was hospitably received in a great hall. The aged man asked him, when they had done their meal, if he knew how to fight with the sword, and promised to teach him all knightly accomplishments, and "the manners and customs of different countries, and courtesy and gentleness and noble bearing." And he added: "I am thy uncle, thy mother's brother." Finally, he bade him ride forth, and remember, whatever he saw that might cause him wonder, not to ask the meaning of it if no one had the courtesy to inform him. This is the test of obedience and self-restraint on which the rest of the adventure turns.

On next riding forth, Peredur came to a vast desert wood, beyond which he found a great castle, the Castle of Wonders. He entered it by the open door, and found a stately, hoary-headed man sitting in a great hall with many pages about him, who received Peredur honourably. At meat Peredur sat beside the lord of the castle, who asked him, when they had done, if he could fight with a sword. "Were I to receive instruction," said Peredur, "I think I could." The lord then gave Peredur a sword, and bade him strike at a great iron staple that was in the floor. Peredur did so, and cut the staple in two, but the sword also flew into two parts. "Place the two parts together," said the lord. Peredur did so, and they became one again, both sword and staple. A second time this was done with the same result. The third time neither sword nor staple would reunite.

"Thou hast arrived," said the lord, "at two-thirds of thy strength." He then declared that he also was

Peredur's uncle, and brother to the fisher-lord with whom Peredur had lodged on the previous night. As they discoursed, two youths entered the hall bearing a spear of mighty size, from the point of which three streams of blood dropped upon the ground, and all the company when they saw this began wailing and lamenting with a great outcry, but the lord took no notice and did not break off his discourse with Peredur. Next there came in two maidens carrying between them a large salver, on which, amid a profusion of blood, lay a man's head. Thereupon the wailing and lamenting began even more loudly than before. But at last they fell silent, and Peredur was led off to his chamber. Mindful of the injunction of the fisher-lord, he had shown no surprise at what he saw, nor had he asked the meaning of it. He then rode forth again in quest of other adventures, which he had in bewildering abundance, and which have no particular relation to the main theme. The mystery of the castle is not revealed till the last pages of the story. The head in the silver dish was that of a cousin of Peredur's. The lance was the weapon with which he was slain, and with which also the uncle of Peredur, the fisher-lord, had been lamed. Peredur had been shown these things to incite him to avenge the wrong, and to prove his fitness for the task. The "nine sorceresses of Gloucester" are said to have been those who worked these evils on the relatives of Peredur. On learning these matters Peredur, with the help of Arthur, attacked the sorceresses, who were slain every one, and the vengeance was accomplished.

The Conte del Graal

The tale of Chrestien de Troyes called the "Conte del Graal" or "Perceval le Gallois" launched the story in European literature. It was written about the year

" The wailing and lamenting began even more loudly than before "

1180. It agrees in the introductory portion with "Peredur," the hero being here called Perceval. He is trained in knightly accomplishments by an aged knight named Gonemans, who warns him against talking overmuch and asking questions. When he comes to the Castle of Wonders the objects brought into the hall are a blood-dripping lance, a "graal" accompanied by two double-branched candlesticks, the light of which is put out by the shining of the graal, a silver plate and sword, the last of which is given to Perceval. The bleeding head of the Welsh story does not appear, nor are we told what the graal was. Next day when Perceval rode forth he met a maiden who upbraided him fiercely for not having asked the meaning of what he saw—had he done so the lame king (who is here identical with the lord of the Castle of Wonders) would have been made whole again. Perceval's sin in quitting his mother against her wish was the reason why he was withholden from asking the question which would have broken the spell. This is a very crude piece of invention, for it was manifestly Peredur's destiny to take arms and achieve the adventure of the Grail, and he committed no sin in doing so. Later on in the story Perceval is met by a damsel of hideous appearance, who curses him for his omission to ask concerning the lance and the other wonders—had he done so the king would have been restored and would have ruled his land in peace, but now maidens will be put to shame, knights will be slain, widows and orphans will be made.

This conception of the question episode seems to me radically different from that which was adopted in the Welsh version. It is characteristic of Peredur that he always does as he is told by proper authority. The question was a test of obedience and self-restraint, and he succeeded in the ordeal. In fairy literature one is often punished for curiosity, but never for discretion and reserve. The Welsh tale here preserves, I think, the original form of the story. But the French writers mistook the omission to ask questions for a failure on the part of the hero, and invented a shallow and incongruous theory of the episode and its consequences. Strange to say, however, the French view found its way into later versions of the Welsh tale, and such a version is that which we have in the "Mabinogion." Peredur, towards the end of the story, meets with a hideous damsel, the terrors of whose aspect are vividly described, and who rebukes him violently for not having asked the meaning of the marvels at the castle: "Hadst thou done so the king would have been restored to health, and his dominions to peace. Whereas from henceforth he will have to endure battles and conflicts, and his knights will perish, and wives will be widowed, and maidens will be left portionless, and all this is because of thee." I regard this loathly damsel as an obvious interpolation in the Welsh tale. She came into it straight out of the pages of Chrestien. That she did not originally belong to the story of Peredur seems evident from the fact that in this tale the lame lord who bids Peredur refrain from asking questions is, according to the damsel, the very person who would have benefited by his doing so. As a matter of fact, Peredur never does ask the question, and it plays no part in the conclusion of the story.

Chrestien's unfinished tale tells us some further adventures of Perceval and of his friend and fellow-knight, Gauvain, but never explains the significance of the mysterious objects seen at the castle. His continuators, of whom Gautier was the first, tell us that the Graal was the Cup of the Last Supper and the lance that which had pierced the side of Christ at the Crucifixion ; and that Peredur ultimately makes his way back to the castle, asks the necessary question, and succeeds his uncle as lord of the castle and guardian of its treasures.

Wolfram von Eschenbach

In the story as given by Wolfram von Eschenbach, who wrote about the year 1200—some twenty years later than Chrestien de Troyes, with whose work he was acquainted—we meet with a new and unique conception of the Grail. He says of the knights of the Grail Castle :

> " Si lebent von einem steine
> Des geslähte ist vîl reine . . .
> Es heizet *lapsit* [*lapis*] *exillîs*,
> Der stein ist ouch genannt der Grâl." [1]

It was originally brought down from heaven by a flight of angels and deposited in Anjou, as the worthiest region for its reception. Its power is sustained by a dove which every Good Friday comes from heaven and lays on the Grail a consecrated Host. It is preserved in the Castle of Munsalväsche [Montsalvat] and guarded by four hundred knights, who are all, except their king, vowed to virginity. The king may marry, and is indeed, in order to maintain the succession, commanded to do so by the Grail, which conveys its messages to mankind by writing which appears upon it and which fades away when deciphered. In the time of Parzival the king is Anfortas. He cannot die in presence of the Grail, but he suffers from a wound which, because he received it in the cause of worldly pride and in

1 "They are nourished by a stone of most noble nature . . . it is called *lapsit exillîs* ; the stone is also called the Grail." The term *lapsit exillîs* appears to be a corruption for *lapis ex celis*, " the stone from heaven."

seeking after illicit love, the influence of the Grail cannot heal until the destined deliverer shall break the spell. This Parzival should have done by asking the question, "What aileth thee, uncle?" The French version makes Perceval fail in curiosity—Wolfram conceives the failure as one in sympathy. He fails, at any rate, and next morning finds the castle empty and his horse standing ready for him at the gate; as he departs he is mocked by servitors who appear at the windows of the towers. After many adventures, which are quite unlike those either in Chrestien's "Conte del Graal" or in "Peredur," Parzival, who has wedded the maiden Condwiramur, finds his way back to the Grail Castle—which no one can reach except those destined and chosen to do so by the Grail itself—breaks the spell, and rules over the Grail dominions, his son Loherangrain becoming the Knight of the Swan, who goes abroad righting wrongs, and who, like all the Grail knights, is forbidden to reveal his name and origin to the outside world. Wolfram tells us that he had the substance of the tale from the Provençal poet Kyot or Guiot—"Kyot, der meister wol bekannt"—who in his turn—but this probably is a mere piece of romantic invention—professed to have found it in an Arabic book in Toledo, written by a heathen named Flegetanis.

The Continuators of Chrestien

What exactly may have been the material before Chrestien de Troyes we cannot tell, but his various co-workers and continuators, notably Manessier, all dwell on the Christian character of the objects shown to Perceval in the castle, and the question arises, How did they come to acquire this character? The Welsh story, certainly the most archaic form of the legend, shows that they did not have it from the beginning. An indication in one of the French continuations to Chrestien's "Conte" may serve to put us on the track. Gautier, the author of this continuation, tells us of an attempt on the part of Gauvain [Sir Gawain] to achieve the adventure of the Grail. He partially succeeds, and this half-success has the effect of restoring the lands about the castle, which were desert and untilled, to blooming fertility. The Grail therefore, besides its other characters, had a talismanic power in promoting increase, wealth, and rejuvenation.

The Grail a Talisman of Abundance

The character of a cornucopia, a symbol and agent of abundance and vitality, clings closely to the Grail in all versions of the legend. Even in the loftiest and most spiritual of these, the "Parzival" of Wolfram von Eschenbach, this quality is very strongly marked. A sick or wounded man who looked on it could not die within the week, nor could its servitors grow old: "though one looked on it for two hundred years, his hair would never turn grey." The Grail knights lived from it, apparently by its turning into all manner of food and drink the bread which was presented to it by pages. Each man had of it food according to his pleasure, *à son gré*—from this word *gré*, *gréable*, the name Gral, which originated in the French versions, was supposed to be derived.[1] It was the satisfaction of all desires. In Wolfram's poem the Grail, though connected with the Eucharist, was, as we have seen, a stone, not a cup. It thus appears as a relic of ancient stone-worship. It is remarkable that a similar Stone of Abundance occurs also in the Welsh "Peredur," though not as one of the mysteries of the castle. It

[1] The true derivation is from the Low Latin *cratella*, a small vessel or chalice.

was guarded by a black serpent, which Peredur slew, and he gave the stone to his friend Etlyn.

The Celtic Cauldron of Abundance

Now the reader has by this time become well acquainted with an object having the character of a talisman of abundance and rejuvenation in Celtic myth. As the Cauldron of the Dagda it came into Ireland with the Danaans from their mysterious fairy-land. In Welsh legend Bran the Blessed got it from Ireland, whither it returned again as part of Branwen's dowry. In a strange and mystic poem by Taliesin it is represented as part of the spoils of Hades, or Annwn, brought thence by Arthur, in a tragic adventure not otherwise recorded. It is described by Taliesin as lodged in Caer Pedryvan, the Four-square Castle of Pwyll; the fire that heated it was fanned by the breath of nine maidens, its edge was rimmed with pearls, and it would not cook the food of a coward or man forsworn:[1]

> "Am I not a candidate for fame, to be heard in song
> In Caer Pedryvan, four times revolving?
> The first word from the cauldron, when was it spoken?
> By the breath of nine maidens it was gently warmed.
> Is it not the cauldron of the chief of Annwn? What is its fashion?
> A rim of pearls is round its edge.
> It will not cook the food of a coward or one forsworn.
> A sword flashing bright will be raised to him,
> And left in the hand of Lleminawg.

[1] A similar selective action is ascribed to the Grail by Wolfram. It can only be lifted by a pure maiden when carried into the hall, and a heathen cannot see it or be benefited by it. The same idea is also strongly marked in the story narrating the early history of the Grail by Robert de Borron, about 1210: the impure and sinful cannot benefit by it. Borron, however, does not touch upon the Perceval or "quest" portion of the story at all.

And before the door of the gate of Uffern[1] the lamp was burning.
When we went with Arthur—a splendid labour—
Except seven, none returned from Caer Vedwyd.[2]

More remotely still the cauldron represents the Sun, which appears in the earliest Aryo-Indian myths as a golden vessel which pours forth light and heat and fertility. The lance is the lightning-weapon of the Thunder God, Indra, appearing in Norse mythology as the hammer of Thor. The quest for these objects represents the ideas of the restoration by some divine champion of the wholesome order of the seasons, disturbed by some temporary derangement such as those which to this day bring famine and desolation to India.

Now in the Welsh "Peredur" we have clearly an outline of the original Celtic tale, but the Grail does not appear in it. We may conjecture, however, from Gautier's continuation of Chrestien's poem that a talisman of abundance figured in early Continental, probably Breton, versions of the legend. In one version at least—that on which Wolfram based his "Parzival"—this talisman was a stone. But usually it would have been, not a stone, but a cauldron or vessel of some kind endowed with the usual attributes of the magic cauldron of Celtic myth. This vessel was associated with a blood-dripping lance. Here were the suggestive elements from which some unknown singer, in a flash of inspiration, transformed the ancient tale of vengeance and redemption into the mystical romance which at once took possession of the heart and soul of Christendom. The magic cauldron became the cup of the Eucharist, the lance was invested with a more tremendous guilt than that of the death of Peredur's

[1] Hades.

[2] Caer Vedwyd means the Castle of Revelry. I follow the version of this poem given by Squire in his "Mythology of the British Islands," where it may be read in full.

kinsman.[1] Celtic poetry, German mysticism, Christian chivalry, and ideas of magic which still cling to the rude stone monuments of Western Europe—all these combined to make the story of the Grail, and to endow it with the strange attraction which has led to its re-creation by artist after artist for seven hundred years. And who, even now, can say that its course is run at last, and the towers of Montsalvat dissolved into the mist from which they sprang?

The Tale of Taliesin

Alone of the tales in the collection called by Lady Charlotte Guest the "Mabinogion," the story of the birth and adventures of the mythical bard Taliesin, the Amergin of Cymric legend, is not found in the fourteenth-century manuscript entitled "The Red Book of Hergest." It is taken from a manuscript of the late sixteenth or seventeenth century, and never appears to have enjoyed much popularity in Wales. Much of the very obscure poetry attributed to Taliesin is to be found in it, and this is much older than the prose. The object of the tale, indeed, as Mr. Nutt has pointed out in his edition of the "Mabinogion," is rather to provide a sort of framework for stringing together scattered pieces of verse supposed to be the work of Taliesin than to tell a connected story about him and his doings.

The story of the birth of the hero is the most interesting thing in the tale. There lived, it was said, "in the time of Arthur of the Round Table,"[2] a man named

[1] The combination of objects at the Grail Castle is very significant. They were a sword, a spear, and a vessel, or, in some versions, a stone. These are the magical treasures brought by the Danaans into Ireland—a sword, a spear, a cauldron, and a stone. See pp. 105, 106.

[2] The Round Table finds no mention in Cymric legend earlier than the fifteenth century.

Tegid Voel of Penllyn, whose wife was named Ceridwen. They have a son named Avagddu, who was the most ill-favoured man in the world. To compensate for his lack of beauty, his mother resolved to make him a sage. So, according to the art of the books of Feryllt,[1] she had recourse to the great Celtic source of magical influence—a cauldron. She began to boil a "cauldron of inspiration and science for her son, that his reception might be honourable because of his knowledge of the mysteries of the future state of the world." The cauldron might not cease to boil for a year and a day, and only in three drops of it were to be found the magical grace of the brew.

She put Gwion Bach the son of Gwreang of Llanfair to stir the cauldron, and a blind man named Morda to keep the fire going, and she made incantations over it and put in magical herbs from time to time as Feryllt's book directed. But one day towards the end of the year three drops of the magic liquor flew out of the cauldron and lighted on the finger of Gwion. Like Finn mac Cumhal on a similar occasion, he put his finger in his mouth, and immediately became gifted with supernatural insight. He saw that he had got what was intended for Avagddu, and he saw also that Ceridwen would destroy him for it if she could. So he fled to his own land, and the cauldron, deprived of the sacred drops, now contained nothing but poison, the power of which burst the vessel, and the liquor ran into a stream hard by and poisoned the horses of Gwyddno Garanhir which drank of the water. Whence the stream is called the Poison of the Horses of Gwyddno from that time forth.

Ceridwen now came on the scene and saw that her year's labour was lost. In her rage she smote Morda

[1] Vergil, in his mediæval character of magician.

with a billet of firewood and struck out his eye, and she then pursued after Gwion Bach. He saw her and changed himself into a hare. She became a greyhound. He leaped into a river and became a fish, and she chased him as an otter. He became a bird and she a hawk. Then he turned himself into a grain of wheat and dropped among the other grains on a threshing-floor, and she became a black hen and swallowed him. Nine months afterwards she bore him as an infant; and she would have killed him, but could not on account of his beauty, "so she wrapped him in a leathern bag, and cast him into the sea to the mercy of God."

The Luck of Elphin

Now Gwyddno, of the poisoned horses, had a salmon weir on the strand between Dyvi and Aberystwyth. And his son Elphin, a needy and luckless lad, one day fished out the leathern bag as it stuck on the weir. They opened it, and found the infant within. "Behold a radiant brow!"[1] said Gwyddno. "Taliesin be he called," said Elphin. And they brought the child home very carefully and reared it as their own. And this was Taliesin, prime bard of the Cymry; and the first of the poems he made was a lay of praise to Elphin and promise of good fortune for the future. And this was fulfilled, for Elphin grew in riches and honour day after day, and in love and favour with King Arthur.

But one day as men praised King Arthur and all his belongings above measure, Elphin boasted that he had a wife as virtuous as any at Arthur's Court and a bard more skilful than any of the King's; and they flung him into prison until they should see if he could make good his boast. And as he lay there with a silver chain

[1] Taliesin.

about his feet, a graceless fellow named Rhun was sent to court the wife of Elphin and to bring back proofs of her folly; and it was said that neither maid nor matron with whom Rhun conversed but was evil-spoken of.

Taliesin then bade his mistress conceal herself, and she gave her raiment and jewels to one of the kitchen-maids, who received Rhun as if she were mistress of the household. And after supper Rhun plied the maid with drink, and she became intoxicated and fell in a deep sleep; whereupon Rhun cut off one of her fingers, on which was the signet-ring of Elphin that he had sent his wife a little while before. Rhun brought the finger and the ring on it to Arthur's Court.

Next day Elphin was fetched out of prison and shown the finger and the ring. Whereupon he said: "With thy leave, mighty king, I cannot deny the ring, but the finger it is on was never my wife's. For this is the little finger, and the ring fits tightly on it, but my wife could barely keep it on her thumb. And my wife, moreover, is wont to pare her nails every Saturday night, but this nail hath not been pared for a month. And thirdly, the hand to which this finger belonged was kneading rye-dough within three days past, but my wife has never kneaded rye-dough since my wife she has been."

Then the King was angry because his test had failed, and he ordered Elphin back to prison till he could prove what he had affirmed about his bard.

Taliesin, Prime Bard of Britain

Then Taliesin went to court, and one high day when the King's bards and minstrels should sing and play before him, Taliesin, as they passed him sitting quietly in a corner, pouted his lips and played "Blerwm, blerwm" with his finger on his mouth. And when the bards came to perform before the King, lo! a spell was on them, and they could do nothing but bow before him and play "Blerwm, blerwm" with their fingers on their lips. And the chief of them, Heinin, said: "O king, we be not drunken with wine, but are dumb through the influence of the spirit that sits in yon corner under the form of a child." Then Taliesin was brought forth, and they asked him who he was and whence he came. And he sang as follows:

"Primary chief bard am I to Elphin,
And my original country is the region of the summer stars;
Idno and Heinin called me Merddin,
At length every being will call me Taliesin.

"I was with my Lord in the highest sphere,
On the fall of Lucifer into the depth of hell;
I have borne a banner before Alexander;
I know the names of the stars from north to south.

"I was in Canaan when Absalom was slain,
I was in the court of Dōn before the birth of Gwydion.
I was at the place of the crucifixion of the merciful Son of God;
I have been three periods in the prison of Arianrod.

"I have been in Asia with Noah in the ark,
I have seen the destruction of Sodom and Gomorrah.
I have been in India when Roma was built.
I am now come here to the remnant of Troia.[1]

"I have been with my Lord in the ass's manger,
I strengthened Moses through the waters of Jordan;
I have been in the firmament with Mary Magdalene;
I have obtained the Muse from the cauldron of Ceridwen.

"I shall be until the day of doom on the face of the earth;
And it is not known whether my body is flesh or fish.

[1] Alluding to the imaginary Trojan ancestry of the Britons.

"Then was I for nine months
In the womb of the witch Ceridwen;
I was originally little Gwion,
And at length I am Taliesin."[1]

While Taliesin sang a great storm of wind arose, and the castle shook with the force of it. Then the King bade Elphin be brought in before him, and when he came, at the music of Taliesin's voice and harp the chains fell open of themselves and he was free. And many other poems concerning secret things of the past and future did Taliesin sing before the King and his lords, and he foretold the coming of the Saxon into the land, and his oppression of the Cymry, and foretold also his passing away when the day of his destiny should come.

Conclusion

Here we end this long survey of the legendary literature of the Celt. The material is very abundant, and it is, of course, not practicable in a volume of this size to do more than trace the main current of the development of the legendary literature down to the time when the mythical and legendary element entirely faded out and free literary invention took its place. The reader of these pages will, however, it is hoped, have gained a general conception of the subject which will enable him to understand the significance of such tales as we have not been able to touch on here, and to fit them into their proper places in one or other of the great cycles of Celtic legend. It will be noticed that we have not entered upon the vast region of Celtic

[1] I have somewhat abridged this curious poem. The connexion with ideas of transmigration, as in the legend of Tuan mac Carell (see pp. 97–101), is obvious. Tuan's last stage, it may be recalled, was a fish, and Taliesin was taken in a salmon-weir.

folk-lore. Folk-lore has not been regarded as falling within the scope of the present work. Folk-lore may sometimes represent degraded mythology, and sometimes mythology in the making. In either case, it is its special characteristic that it belongs to and issues from a class whose daily life lies close to the earth, toilers in the field and in the forest, who render with simple directness, in tales or charms, their impressions of natural or supernatural forces with which their own lives are environed. Mythology, in the proper sense of the word, appears only where the intellect and the imagination have reached a point of development above that which is ordinarily possible to the peasant mind—when men have begun to co-ordinate their scattered impressions and have felt the impulse to shape them into poetic creations embodying universal ideas. It is not, of course, pretended that a hard-and-fast line can always be drawn between mythology and folk-lore; still, the distinction seems to me a valid one, and I have tried to observe it in these pages.

After the two historical chapters with which our study has begun, the object of the book has been literary rather than scientific. I have, however, endeavoured to give, as the opportunity arose, such results of recent critical work on the relics of Celtic myth and legend as may at least serve to indicate to the reader the nature of the critical problems connected therewith. I hope that this may have added somewhat to the value of the work for students, while not impairing its interest for the general reader. Furthermore, I may claim that the book is in this sense scientific, that as far as possible it avoids any adaptation of its material for the popular taste. Such adaptation, when done for an avowed artistic purpose, is of course entirely legitimate; if it were not, we should have to condemn half the great poetry of the world. But here the object has been to present the myths and legends of the Celt as they actually are. Crudities have not been refined away, things painful or monstrous have not been suppressed, except in some few instances, where it has been necessary to bear in mind that this volume appeals to a wider audience than that of scientific students alone. The reader may, I think, rely upon it that he has here a substantially fair and not over-idealised account of the Celtic outlook upon life and the world at a time when the Celt still had a free, independent, natural life, working out his conceptions in the Celtic tongue, and taking no more from foreign sources than he could assimilate and make his own. The legendary literature thus presented is the oldest non-classical literature of Europe. This alone is sufficient, I think, to give it a strong claim on our attention. As to what other claims it may have, many pages might be filled with quotations from the discerning praises given to it by critics not of Celtic nationality, from Matthew Arnold downwards. But here let it speak for itself. It will tell us, I believe, that, as Maeldūn said of one of the marvels he met with in his voyage into Fairyland: "What we see here was a work of mighty men."

GLOSSARY AND INDEX

THE PRONUNCIATION OF CELTIC NAMES

To render these names accurately without the living voice is impossible. But with the phonetic renderings given, where required, in the following index, and with attention to the following general rules, the reader will get as near to the correct pronunciation as it is at all necessary for him to do.

I. Gaelic

Vowels are pronounced as in French or German; thus *i* (long) is like *ee*, *e* (long) like *a* in "date," *u* (long) like *oo*. A stroke over a letter signifies length; thus dūn is pronounced "doon" (not "dewn").

ch is a guttural, as in the word "loch." It is never pronounced with a *t* sound, as in English "chip."

c is always like *k*.

gh is silent, as in English.

II. Cymric

w, when a consonant, is pronounced as in English; when a vowel, like *oo*.

y, when long, is like *ee*; when short, like *u* in "but."

ch and *c* as in Gaelic.

dd is like *th* in "breathe."

f is like *v*; *ff* like English *f*.

The sound of *ll* is perhaps better not attempted by the English reader. It is a thickened *l*, something between *cl* and *th*.

Vowels as in Gaelic, but note that there are strictly no diphthongs in Welsh; in combinations of vowels each is given its own sound.

A

ABRED. The innermost of three concentric circles representing the totality of being in the Cymric cosmogony—the stage of struggle and evolution, 333

ABUNDANCE. See Stone of Abundance

ÆDA (ay'da). 1. Dwarf of King Fergus mac Leda, 247. 2. Royal suitor for Vivionn's hand; Vivionn slain by, 287

ÆD'UANS. Familiar with plating of copper and tin, 44

ÆGIRA. Custom of the priestess of Earth at, in Achæa, ere prophesying, 167

ÆSUN. Umbrian deity, 86

ÆSUS. Deity mentioned by Lucan, 86

AED THE FAIR (AED FINN) (aid). Chief sage of Ireland; author of "Voyage of Maeldūn," 331

AEI (ay'ee), PLAIN OF, where Brown Bull of Quelgny meets and slays Bull of Ailell, 225

AFRICAN ORIGIN. Primitive population of Great Britain and Ireland, evidence of language suggests, 78

AGE, IRON. The ship a well-recognised form of sepulchral enclosure in cemeteries of the, 76

AG'NOMAN. Nemed's father, 98

AIDEEN. Wife of Oscar, 261; dies of grief after Oscar's death, 261; buried on Ben Edar (Howth), 261, 262

AIFA (eefa). Princess of Land of Shadows; war made upon, by Skatha, 189; Cuchulain overcomes by a trick, 190;

life spared conditionally by Cuchulain, 190; bears a son named Connla, 190

AILBACH (el-yach). Fortress in Co. Donegal, where Ith hears MacCuill and his brothers are arranging the division of the land, 132

AILILL (el'yill), or AILELL. 1. Son of Laery, treacherously slain by his uncle Covac, 152. 2. Brother of Eochy; his desperate love for Etain, 158–160. 3. King of Connacht, 122; Angus Ōg seeks aid of, 122; Fergus seeks aid of, 202; assists in foray against province of Ulster, 203–251; White-horned Bull of, slain by Brown Bull of Quelgny, 225; makes seven years' peace with Ulster, 225; hound of mac Datho pursues chariot of, 244; slain by Conall, 245

AILILL EDGE-OF-BATTLE. Of the sept of the Owens of Aran; father of Maeldūn, slain by reavers from Leix, 310

AILILL OLUM (el-yill olum). King of Munster; ravishes Ainé and is slain by her, 127

AINÉ. A love-goddess, daughter of the Danaan Owel; Ailill Olum and Fitzgerald her lovers, 127; mother of Earl Gerald, 128; still worshipped on Midsummer Eve, 128; appears on a St. John's Night, among girls on the Hill, 128

AINLÉ. Brother of Naisi, 198

ALEXANDER THE GREAT. Countermove of Hellas against the East under, 22; compact with Celts referred to by Ptolemy Soter, 23

ALLEN, MR. ROMILLY. On Celtic art, 29, 30

ALLEN, HILL OF. In Kildare; Finn's chief fortress, 266, 273

AMA'SIS I. Human sacrifices abolished by, 86

AMATHA'ON. Son of Dōn; and the ploughing task, 390

AMER'GIN. Milesian poet, son of Miled, husband of Skena, 133; his strange lay, sung when his foot first touched Irish soil, 134; his judgment, delivered as between the Danaans and Milesians, 135; chants incantation to land of Erin, 136; the Druid, gives judgment as to claims to sovranty of Eremon and Eber, 148; Ollav Fōla compared with, 150

AMMIA'NUS MARCELLIN'US. Gauls described by, 42

AMOR'GIN. Father of Conall of the Victories, 177

AMYN'TAS II. King of Macedon, defeated and exiled, 23

ANGLO-SAXON. Wace's French translation of "Historia Regum Britaniæ" translated by Layamon into, 338

ANGUS. A Danaan deity, 143. See Angus Ōg

ANGUS ŌG (ANGUS THE YOUNG). Son of the Dagda, Irish god of love, 121, 123; wooes and wins Caer, 121–123; Dermot of the Love-spot bred up with, 123; Dermot of the Love-spot revived by, 123; father of Maga, 181; Dermot and Grania rescued by magical devices of, 299; Dermot's body borne away by, 303

ANKH, THE. Found on Megalithic carvings, 77, 78; the symbol of vitality or resurrection, 78

AN'LUAN. Son of Maga; rallies to Maev's foray against Ulster, 204; Conall produces the head of, to Ket, 244

ANNWN (annoon). Corresponds with Abyss, or Chaos; the principle of destruction in Cymric cosmogony, 333

ANSWERER, THE. Mananan's magical sword, 125

AOIFE (eefa). Lir's second wife; her jealousy of her step-children, 139, 140; her punishment by Bōv the Red, 140

AONBARR (ain-barr). Mananan's magical steed, 125

GLOSSARY AND INDEX

Apollo. Celtic equivalent, Lugh. Magical services in honour of, described by Hecatæus, 58; regarded by Gauls as deity of medicine, 87, 88

Aquitan'i. One of three peoples inhabiting Gaul when Cæsar's conquest began, 58

Arabia. Dolmens found in, 53

Arawn. A king in Annwn; appeals to Pwyll for help against Havgan, 357; exchanges kingdoms for a year with Pwyll, 357–359

Ard Macha (Armagh). Emain Macha now represented by grassy ramparts of a hill-fortress close to, 150; significance, 251

Ard Righ (ard ree) (*i.e.*, High King). Dermot MacKerval, of Ireland, 47

Ardan. Brother of Naisi, 198

Ardcullin. Cuchulain places withe round pillar-stone of, 207

Ardeb. Significance, 251

Ari'anrod. Sister of Gwydion; proposed as virgin foot-holder to Māth; Dylan and Llew sons of, 380, 381

Aristotle. Celts and, 17

Armagh. Invisible dwelling of Lir on Slieve Fuad in County, 125

Arnold, Matthew. Reference to, in connexion with Celtic legendary literature, 419

Arr'ian. Celtic characteristics, evidence of, regarding, 36

Artaius. A god in Celtic mythology who occupies the place of Gwydion, 349

Arthur. Chosen leader against Saxons, whom he finally defeated in battle of Mount Badon, 337; Geoffrey of Monmouth's "Historia Regum Britaniæ" commemorates exploits of, 337; son of Uther Pendragon and Igerna, 337; Modred, his nephew, usurps crown of, 337; Guanhumara, wife of, retires to convent, 337, 338; genealogy set forth, 352; tales of, in Welsh literature, 386; Kilhwch at court of, 387, 388; the "Dream of Rhonabwy" and, 392, 393; Owain, son of Urien, plays chess with, 393; adventure of Kymon, knight of court of, 394–396; Gwenhwyvar, wife of, 394; Owain at court of, 396 397, 399; Peredur at court of, 401, 402

Arthurian Saga. Mention of early British legend suggests, 336; the saga in Brittany and Marie de France, 339 340, Miss Jessie L. Weston's article on, in the "Encyc. Britann.," 341; Chrestien de Troyes influential in bringing into the poetic literature of Europe the, 340, 341; various sources of, discussed, 342; the saga in Wales, 343, 344; never entered Ireland, 343; why so little is heard of, in accounts of Cymric myths, 344

Asa. Scandinavian deity, 86

Asal. Of the Golden Pillars King, 115

Asura-masda. Persian deity, 86

Athnurchar (ath-nur'char), or **Ardnurchar** (The Ford of the Sling-cast). The river-ford where Ket slings Conall's "brain ball" at Conor mac Nessa, 240; significance, 251

Atlantic, The. Aoife's cruelty to her step-children on waters of, 140, 141

Austria. Discovery of pre-Roman necropolis in, 28; relics found in, developed into the La Tène culture, 29

Avagddu (avagdhoo). Son of Tegid Voel, 413; deprived of gift of supernatural insight, 413

A'valon. Land of the Dead; bears relation with Norse *Valhall*, 338; its later identification with Glastonbury, 338

Avon Dia. Duel between Cuchulain and Ferdia causes waters of, to hold back, 121

GLOSSARY AND INDEX

B

GLOSSARY AND INDEX

Spain from, 21; Greeks break monopoly of trade of, with Britain and Spain, 22

CAS'CORACH. Son of a minstrel of the Danaan Folk; and St. Patrick, 119

CASTLE OF WONDERS. Peredur at, 405, 406

CAS'WALLAN. Son of Beli; conquers Britain during Bran's absence, 372

CATHBAD. Druid; wedded to Maga, wife of Ross the Red, 181; his spell of divination overheard by Cuchulain, 185; draws Deirdre's horoscope, 197; casts evil spells over Naisi and Deirdre, 200

CATHOLIC CHURCH. Mediæval interdicts of, 46

CATO, M. PORCIUS. Observances of, regarding Gauls, 37

CAULDRON OF ABUNDANCE. See equivalent, Stone of Abundance; also see Grail

CELTÆ. One of three peoples inhabiting Gaul when Cæsar's conquest began, 58

CELTCHAR (kelt-yar). Son of Hornskin; under debility curse, 205

CELTDOM. The Golden Age of, in Continental Europe, 21

CELTIC. Power, diffusion of, in Mid-Europe, 26; place-names in Europe, 27; art-work relics, story told by, 28; Germanic words, Celtic element in, 32; empire, downfall of, 34; weak policy of peoples, 44; religion, the, 46, 47; High Kings, traditional burial-places of, 69; doctrine of immortality, origin of so-called "Celtic," 75, 76; ideas of immortality, 78–87; deities, names and attributes of, 86–88; conception of death, the, 89; culture, five factors in ancient, 89, 90; the present-day populations, 91, 92; cosmogony, the, 94, 95; things, "Barddas" a work not unworthy the student of, 333

CELTICA. Never inhabited by a single pure and homogeneous race, 18; Greek type of civilisation preserved by, 22; art of enamelling originated in, 30; the Druids formed the sovran power in, 46; Brigit (Dana) most widely worshipped goddess in, 126

CELTS. Term first found in Hecatæus; equivalent, Hyperboreans, 17; Herodotus and dwelling-place of, 17; Aristotle and, 17; Hellanicus of Lesbos and, 17; Ephorus and, 17; Plato and, 17; their attack on Rome, a landmark of ancient history, 18; described by Dr. T. Rice Holmes, 18, 19; dominion of, over Mid-Europe, Gaul, Spain, and the British Isles, 20; their place among these races, 20; Giraldus Cambrensis and, 21; Spain conquered from the Carthaginians by, 21; Northern Italy conquered from the Etruscans by, 21; Vergil and, 21; conquer the Illyrians, 21; alliance with the Greeks, 22; conquests of, in valleys of Danube and Po, 23; Alexander makes compact with, 23; national oath of, 24; welded into unity by Ambicatus, 25; defeat Romans, 26; Germanic peoples and, 26, 33; decorative motives derived from Greek art, 29; art of enamelling learnt by classical nations from, 30; burial rites practised by, 33; character, elements comprising, 36; Strabo's description of, 39; love of splendour and methods of warfare, 40; Polybius' description of warriors in battle of Clastidium, 41; their influence on European literature and philosophy, 49, 50; the Religion of the, 51–93; ranges of the Balkans and Carpathians earliest home of mountain, 57; musical services of, described by Hecatæus, 58; Switzerland, Burgundy, the Palatinate, Northern France, parts of Britain, &c., occupied by mountain, 58; origin of doctrine of immortality, 75; idea of immortality and doctrine of transmigration, 80, 81; the present-day, 91, 92; no non-Christian conception of origin of things, 94; victories at the Allia and at Delphi attributed to Brenos (Brian), 126; true worship of, paid to elemental forces represented by actual natural phenomena, 147

CENCHOS. Otherwise The Footless; related to Vitra, the God of Evil in Vedantic mythology, 97

CER'IDWEN. Wife of Tegid, 413; sets Gwion Bach and Morda to attend to the magic cauldron, 413

CEUGANT (Infinity). The outermost of three concentric circles representing the totality of being in the Cymric cosmogony, inhabited by God alone, 334

CHAILLU, DU. His "Viking Age," 72

CHAMPION OF IRELAND. Test at feast of Briccriu, to decide who is the, 195, 196; Cuchulain proclaimed such by demon The Terrible, 196

CHARLEMAGNE. Tree- and stone-worship denounced by, 66

CHILDREN OF LIR. Reference to, 121

CHRESTIEN DE TROYES. French poet, influential in bringing the Arthurian saga into the poetic literature of Europe, 340, 341; Gautier de Denain the earliest continuator of, 341; variation of his "Le Chevalier au lion" seen in "The Lady of the Fountain," 394-399; the "Tale of Enid and Geraint" based on "Erec" of, 399; Peredur corresponds to the Perceval of, 400; his "Conte del Graal," or "Perceval le Gallois," 404; Manessier a continuator of, 408

CHRISTIAN. Symbolism, the hand as emblem of power in, 65; faith, heard of by King Cormac ere preached in Ireland by St. Patrick, 69; influences in Ireland, and the Milesian myth, 138; ideas, gathered around Cuchulain and his lord King Conor of Ulster, 239, 240; pagan ideals contrasted with, in Oisin dialogues, 288; Myrddin dwindles under influences, 354

CHRISTIANITY. Reference to conversion of Ireland to, 83; People of Dana in their overthrow, and attitude of, 138; Cuchulain summoned from Hell by St. Patrick to prove truths of, to High King Laery, 239; effect of on Irish literature, 295, 296

CHRY'SOSTOM, DION. Testimony of, to power of the Druids, 83

CLAN BASCNA. One of the divisions of the Fianna of Erin, 252; Cumhal, father of Finn, chief of, 255; Cairbry causes feud between Clan Morna and, 305-308

CLAN CALATIN. Sent by men of Erin against Cuchulain, 215; Fiacha, son of Firaba, cuts off the eight-and-twenty hands of, 216; Cuchulain slays, 216; the widow of, gives birth to six children whom Maev has instructed in magic and then looses against Cuchulain, 228-233; cause Cuchulain to break his *geise*, 231

CLAN MORNA. One of the divisions of the Fianna of Erin, 252; Lia becomes treasurer to, 255; Cairbry causes feud between Clan Bascna and, 305-308

CLASTID'IUM. Battle of, Polybius' description of behaviour of the Gæsati in, 41

CLEENA. A Danaan maiden once living in Mananan's country; the story of, 127

GLOSSARY AND INDEX

D

GLOSSARY AND INDEX

F

FUAMNACH (foo'am-nach). Wife of Midir the Proud, 156; her jealousy of a second bride, Etain, 156; transforms Etain into a butterfly by magic art, 156–158; Midir tells of her death, 160

G

GAE BOLG. The thrust of, taught by Skatha to Cuchulain, 188, 189; Cuchulain slays his son Connla by, 192; Cuchulain slays Loch by, 213; Cuchulain slays Ferdia by, 220

GAELIC. Cymric language and, 35; effect of legends of, on Continental poets, 50; bards' ideas of chivalric romance anticipated by, 246; Cymric legend and, compared, 344–419; Continental romance and, 345

GAELS. Sacrifices of children by, to idol Crom Cruach, 85

GÆSAT'I. Celtic warriors, in battle of Clastidium, 41

GALATIA. Celtic state of, St. Jerome's attestation *re*, 34

GAL'IOIN. See Firbolgs, 103

GALLES, M. RENÉ. Tumulus of Mané-er-H'oeck described by, 63

GARACH. Mac Roth views Ulster men on Plain of, 223; the battle of, 223–225

GAUL-S. Under Roman yoke, 35; Cæsar's account of, 37; described by Diodorus Siculus, 41, 42; described by Ammianus Marcellinus, 42; Dr. Rice Holmes describes, 43; commerce on Mediterranean, Bay of Biscay, &c., of, 44; religious beliefs and rites described by Julius Cæsar, 51, 52; human sacrifices in, 84; votive inscriptions to Æsus, Teutates, and Taranus, found in, 86, 87; Dis, or Pluto, a most notable god of, 88; dead carried from, to Britain, 131; Maon taken to, 153

"GAULOIS, LA RELIGION DES." Reference to, 55, 83

GAUVAIN (SIR GAWAIN). Fellow-knight with Perceval, 406

GAVR'INIS. Chiromancy at, 64

GEENA MAC LUGA. Son of Luga, one of Finn's men, 262; Finn teaches the maxims of the Fianna to, 262, 263

GEIS-E (singular, gaysh; plural, gaysha). The law of the, 164; meaning of this Irish word explained, 164; instances: Dermot of the Love Spot, Conary Mōr, and Fergus mac Roy, 165; Grania puts Dermot under, 298

GELON. Defeat of Hamilcar by, at Himera, 22

GENEALOGY. Of Conary Mōr, from Eochy, 164; of Conor mac Nessa, from Ross the Red, 181; of Cuchulain and Conall of the Victories, from Druid Cathbad, 181; of Dōn, 350; of Llyr, 351; of Arthur, 352

GENEIR. Knight of Arthur's court, 401

GEOFFREY OF MONMOUTH. Bishop of St. Asaph; his "Historia Regum Britaniæ" written to commemorate Arthur's exploits, 337

GERAINT. The tale of Enid and, 399, 400

GERALD, EARL. Son of goddess Ainé, 128

GERMAN (ghermawn — *g* hard). Diuran and, companions of Maeldūn on his wonderful voyage, 313

GERMANIC WORDS. Many important, traceable to Celtic origin, 32

GERMANS. Menace to classical civilisation of, under names of Cimbri and Teutones, 31; de Jubainville's explanation regarding, as a subject people, 31; overthrow of Celtic supremacy by, 33; burial rites practised by, 33; chastity of, 41

GERMANY. Place-names of, Celtic element in, 27

GLOSSARY AND INDEX

GILLA DACAR (THE HARD GILLY). Story of, 292–295

GILVAETH'WY. Son of Dōn; nephew of Māth, 378; his love for Goewin, and its sequel, 378–380

GIRALDUS CAMBRENSIS. Testimony to the fairness of the Irish Celt, 21. See Bleheris

GLEN ETIVE. Dwelling-place of Naisi and Deirdre, 198

GLOUCESTER. Mabon released from prison in, 392; the "nine sorceresses" of, 404

GLOWER. The strong man of the Wee Folk, 246

GLYN CUCH. Pwyll's hunt in woods of, 357

GOBAN THE SMITH. Brother of Kian and Sawan; corresponds to Wayland Smith in Germanic legend, 110, 117; Ollav Fōla compared with, 150

GOD. Cythrawl and, two primary existences in the Cymric cosmogony, standing for principles of life and destruction, 333–335; the ineffable Name of, pronounced, and the "Manred" formed, 333

GODS. Megalithic People's conception of their, 86, 87; of Aryan Celts, equated by Cæsar with Mercury, Apollo, Mars, &c., 86; triad of, Æsus, Teutates, and Taranus, mentioned by Lucan, 86; Lugh, or Lugus, the god of Light, 88

GOEWIN (go-ay'win). Daughter of Pebin; Gilvaethwy's love for, and its sequel, 378–380

GOLASECCA. A great settlement of the Lowland Celts, in Cisalpine Gaul, 56

GOLEUDDYDD. Wife of Kilydd; mother of Kilhwch, 386, 387

GOLL MAC MORNA. Son of Morna, captain of the Fianna of Erin, 257; swears service to Finn, 258; Finn recalls the great saying of, 267; rescues Finn from the enchanted cave, 277, 278; Keva of the White Skin given as wife to, 278; adventure with the wether, 291, 292

GONEMANS. Knight who trains Perceval (Peredur), 405

GORBODUC. "Historia Regum Britaniæ" furnished subject for, 337, 338

GOR'IAS, THE CITY OF (see Dana), 105, 106

GOWRA (GABHRA). References to Oscar's death at, 261–275; battle of, between Clan Bascna and Clan Morna, 305–309; Oscar's death at, 305–308; King of Ireland's death at, 306

GRAIL. Legends of the, 400; the tale of Peredur and the, 400; Chrestien de Troyes' story of, 404; identical with the Cup of the Last Supper, 406; Wolfram von Eschenbach's conception of the story of the, 407; preserved in Castle of Munsalväsche, 407; the, a talisman of abundance, 409; false derivation of the word, from *gréable*, 409; true derivation, 409, *note*; combination of Celtic poetry, German mysticism, Christian chivalry, and ancient sun-myths contained in, 411, 412

GRANIA. Loved by Dermot of the Love Spot, 123; elopes with Dermot, 261; tales of Deirdre and, compared, 296–304; borne to Hill of Allen as Finn's bride, 304

GREAT BRITAIN. Western extremity of, is Land of the Dead, 131

GREECE. Dolmens found in, 53; oppression in, of the Firbolgs, 102, 103

GREEK-S. Celts and, 17; wars in alliance with Celts, 22; break monopoly of Carthaginian trade with Britain and Spain, 22; secure overland route across France to Britain, 22; type of civilisation, Celtica preserved, 22

GREY OF MACHA. Cuchulain's horse, ridden by Sualtam to

H

GLOSSARY AND INDEX

J

GLOSSARY AND INDEX

GLOSSARY AND INDEX

S

stone of Pergamos and Second Punic War, 66; the Grail a relic of ancient, 409

STONEHENGE. Dressed stones used in megalithic monument at, 54; Professor Rhys' suggestion that Myrddin was worshipped at, 354; Geoffrey of Monmouth and, 354

STRABO. Characteristics of Celts, told by, 39, 46

STRAITS OF MOYLE (between Ireland and Scotland). Aoife's cruelty to her step-children on the, 140

STRAND OF THE FOOTPRINTS. How name derived, 191

SUALTAM (soo'al-tam). Father of Cuchulain (see Lugh), 206; his attempts to arouse Ulster, 221; his death, 222

SWEDEN. The ship symbol on rock-sculptures of, 72, 73

SWITZERLAND. Place-names of, Celtic element in, 27; lake-dwellings in, 56

T

"TAIN BO CUAILGNÉ" (thawn bo quel'gny). Significance, 203; tale of, all written out by Finn mac Gorman, Bishop of Kildare, in 1150, 225; the recovery of, 234; reputed author, Fergus mac Roy, 234; Sir S. Ferguson treats of recovery of, in "Lays of the Western Gael," 234; Sanchan Torpest, taunted by High King Guary, resolves to find the lost, 234–236; early Celtic MSS. and, 296

TALIESIN (tal-i-es'in). A mythical bard; his prophecy regarding the devotion of the Cymry to their tongue, 385; the tale of, 412–417; found by Elphin, son of Gwyddno, 414; made prime bard of Britain, 415–417

TALKENN. (Adze-head). Name given by the Irish to St. Patrick, 275

TALTIU, or TELTA. Daughter of the King of the "Great Plain" (the Land of the Dead), wedded by Eochy mac Erc, 103

TARA. Seat of the High Kings of Ireland; the cursing of, 47, 48–49; Stone of Scone sent to Scotland from, 105; Lugh accuses sons of Turenn at, of his father's murder, 115; appearance of Midir the Proud to Eochy on Hill of, 124, 161; Milesian host at, 135; institution of triennial Festival at, 149–150; bull-feast at, to decide by divination who should be king in Eterskel's stead, 167, 168; Conary commanded to go to, by Nemglan, 168; proclaimed King of Erin at, 168; pointed out to Cuchulain, 193; Cuchulain's head and hand buried at, 233; Finn at, 257, 258

TAR'ANUS (? Thor). Deity mentioned by Lucan, 86, 87

TEGID VOEL. A man of Penllyn, husband of Ceridwen, father of Avagddu, 413

TEIRNYON (ter'ny-on). A man of Gwent Is Coed; finds Pryderi, 364; restores Pryderi, 365

TELLTOWN (TELTIN). Palace at, of Telta, Eochy mac Erc's wife, 103; great battle at, between Danaans and Milesians, 136; Conall of the Victories makes his way to, after Conary's death, 176; pointed out to Cuchulain, 193

TENNYSON, LORD. Reference to source of his "Voyage of Maeldune," 309; Cymric myths and, 388; reference to his "Enid," 400

TEUTAT'ES. Deity mentioned by Lucan, 86

TEUTONIC. Loyalty of races, 45, 46

TEZCATLIPOCA. Sun-god; festival of, in Mexico, 77

THE TERRIBLE. A demon who by strange test decides the Championship of Ireland, 196

THOMAS OF BRITTANY. See Bleheris

TIBERIUS, EMPEROR. Druids, prophets, and medicine-men suppressed by, 62

TIBRNA (Teer'na). Abbot of Clonmacnois, eleventh-century historian, 150

TIBRNMAS (teern'mas). Fifth Irish king who succeeded Eremon, 148; idol Crom Cruach and, 148, 149; his death, 149

TONN CLIODHNA (thown cleena). Otherwise "Wave of Cleena." One of the most notable landmarks of Ireland, 127

TOR MÕR. Precipitous headland in Tory Island; Ethlinn imprisoned by Balor in tower built on, 110

TORY ISLAND. Stronghold of Fomorian power, 101; invaded by Nemedians, 101

TRADABAN', THE WELL OF. Keelta's praises of, 282, 283

TRANSMIGRATION. The doctrine of, allegation that Celtic idea of immortality embodied Oriental conception of, 80; doctrine of, not held by Celts in same way as by Pythagoras and the Orientals, 81; Welsh Taliessin who became an eagle, 100. See Tuan mac Carell

TRENDORN. Conor's servant, 199; spies on Deirdre, 200; is blinded in one eye by Naisi, 200; declares Deirdre's beauty to Conor, 200

TREON (tray'on). Father of Vivionn, 287

TRISTAN AND ISEULT. Tale of Dermot and Grania paralleled in story as told by Heinrich von Freiberg, 299

TROYES. See Chrestien de Troyes

TUAN MAC CARELL. The legend of, recorded in MS. "Book of the Dun Cow," 97; king of all deer in Ireland, 99; name of "gods" given to the People of Dana by, 104

TUATHA DE DANANN (thoo'a-haw day danawn'). Literal meaning, "the folk of the god whose mother is Dana," 103

TUMULI. See Dolmens, 53

TURENN. The quest of the Sons of, 113–116; reference to Lugh in the quest of the Sons of, 123

TWRCH TRWYTH (toorch troo'-with). A king in shape of a monstrous boar, 391

TYLER. Reference of, in his "Primitive Culture," to festival of Sun-god, Tezcatlipoca, 77

TYLWYTH TEG. Welsh fairies; Gwyn ap Nudd, King of the, 353

TYREN. Sister to Murna, 266; Ullan, husband of, 266; changed by a woman of the Fairy Folk into a hound, 266

U

UGAINY THE GREAT (oo'gany). Ruler of Ireland, &c., husband of Kesair, father of Laery and Covac, 152

ULSTER. Kingdom of, founded in reign of Kimbay, 150; Dithorba's five sons expelled from, 151; Dectera's gift of Cuchulain to, 182; Conor, King of, 180, 190, 191; Felim, son of Dall, a lord of, 196; Maev's war against province of, to secure Brown Bull of Quelgny, 202–251; under the Debility curse, 205; passes of, guarded by Cuchulain of Murthemney, 206; aroused by Sualtam, 221, 222; Macha's curse lifted from men of, 222; Ailell and Maev make a seven years peace with, 225; curse of Macha again on the men of, 229; Wee Folk swarm into 248, 249

ULTONIAN-S. Great fair of, visited by Crundchu, 178; his boast of Macha's swiftness, 179; the debility of, caused by Macha's curse, 179, 180; the debility of, descends